Lecture Notes in Computer Science 15917

Founding Editors

Gerhard Goos
Juris Hartmanis

AF173863

The series Lecture Notes in Computer Science (LNCS), including its subseries Lecture Notes in Artificial Intelligence (LNAI) and Lecture Notes in Bioinformatics (LNBI), has established itself as a medium for the publication of new developments in computer science and information technology research, teaching, and education.

LNCS enjoys close cooperation with the computer science R & D community, the series counts many renowned academics among its volume editors and paper authors, and collaborates with prestigious societies. Its mission is to serve this international community by providing an invaluable service, mainly focused on the publication of conference and workshop proceedings and postproceedings. LNCS commenced publication in 1973.

Sharib Ali · David C. Hogg · Michelle Peckham

Editors

Medical Image Understanding and Analysis

29th Annual Conference, MIUA 2025
Leeds, UK, July 15–17, 2025
Proceedings, Part II

 Springer

Editors
Sharib Ali 🆔
University of Leeds
Leeds, UK

David C. Hogg 🆔
University of Leeds
Leeds, UK

Michelle Peckham 🆔
University of Leeds
Leeds, UK

ISSN 0302-9743   ISSN 1611-3349 (electronic)
Lecture Notes in Computer Science
ISBN 978-3-031-98690-1   ISBN 978-3-031-98691-8 (eBook)
https://doi.org/10.1007/978-3-031-98691-8

This Springer imprint is published by the registered company Springer Nature Switzerland AG
The registered company address is: Gewerbestrasse 11, 6330 Cham, Switzerland

If disposing of this product, please recycle the paper.

Preface

The 29th Conference on Medical Image Understanding and Analysis (MIUA 2025) was held at the University of Leeds, UK, during July 15–17, 2025. The MIUA 2025 proceedings feature presentations from the authors of all accepted papers. MIUA is a UK-based international conference for the communication of image processing and analysis research and its application to medical and biomedical imaging and analysis. This year's edition was co-chaired by Sharib Ali (Lecturer/researcher in Medical and Biomedical Image Analysis, University of Leeds), David Hogg (Professor of Artificial Intelligence, University of Leeds), and Michelle Peckham (Professor of Cell Biology, University of Leeds). The conference was organized with sponsorship received from Frontiers in Medical Technology (Gold), AI-Medical (Silver) and Springer (Best Paper Award). The conference proceedings were published in partnership with Springer. The diverse range of topics covered in these proceedings reflects the growth in the development and application of medical and biomedical imaging including surgical data science. The conference proceedings feature the most recent work in the fields of (1) Image synthesis and generative AI; (2) Image-guided diagnosis; (3) Image-guided intervention; (4) Medical image segmentation; (5) Retinal and vascular image analysis; and (6) Frontiers in Computational Pathology.

The number of submissions to MIUA 2025 continued the growth trend that begun with MIUA 2024. In total, 99 submissions were submitted to the Conference Management Toolkit (CMT), and after an initial quality check, the papers were sent out for the peer-review process completed by the Program Committee and 134 volunteer reviewers. To keep the quality of the reviews consistent with the previous editions of MIUA, the majority of the reviewers were invited from (i) a pool of previous MIUA conference reviewers, (ii) a call for reviewers form, and (iii) authors and co-authors of papers presented at the past and current MIUA conferences. All submissions were subject to double-blind review by at least two reviewers and meta-reviewed by at least one of the Program Committee members. Based on their recommendations, 54 papers were among early accept papers, 25 papers were among early rejected and 20 papers proceeded into the rebuttal stage. The final outcome of the review decisions results in a total of 67 full paper accepted (68%). Out of these, 45 papers had an oral presentation (67%) and 22 papers were presented as posters (33%). These papers comprise three volumes of Lecture Notes in Computer Science (LNCS) proceedings.

Submissions were received from authors at different institutes from 23 countries, including Australia (6), Austria (3), Denmark (3), Finland (1), Germany (5), India (10), Republic of Ireland (2), Mexico (4), Nepal (2), Netherlands (1), Norway (2), Pakistan (2), Poland (1), Portugal (1), Russia (1), Singapore (1), Spain (4), Switzerland (1), T˙urkiye (2), the UK (36), the UAE (2), and the USA (5). We thank all members of the MIUA 2025 Organizing, Steering, Program, Publicity, Social Media, Special Session, Sponsorship, and Doctoral Community Committees. In particular, we sincerely thank all who contributed greatly to the success of MIUA 2025: the authors for submitting their work, the reviewers for insightful comments improving the quality of the proceedings, the sponsors for financial support, and all participants in this year's in-person MIUA conference.

We thank our keynote speakers Andrew King (School of Biomedical Engineering and Imaging Sciences, King's College London) and Susan Astley Theodossiadis (University of Manchester) for sharing their success, knowledge, and experiences. The conference also hosted a panel discussion on "Transforming Medical Imaging with AI: Challenges, Data & Infrastructure, Advancing Research, and Translating Innovations", chaired by Susan Astley Theodossiadis and Bogdan Matuszewski. Our thanks to the session chairs and all the other people who made this event possible.

July 2025

Sharib Ali
David C. Hogg
Michelle Peckham

Organization

General Chairs

Sharib Ali   University of Leeds, UK
David C. Hogg   University of Leeds, UK
Michelle Peckham   University of Leeds, UK

Program Chairs

Nashid Alam   Aberystwyth University, UK
Binod Bhattarai   University of Aberdeen, UK
Luisa Cutillo   University of Leeds, UK
Ping Lu   University of Leeds, UK
Bartlomiej Papiez   University of Oxford, UK
Arash Rabbani   University of Leeds, UK
Nishant Ravikumar   University of Leeds, UK
Duygu Sarikaya   University of Leeds, UK

Special Session Chairs

Derek Magee   University of Leeds, UK
Anh Nguyen   University of Liverpool, UK
Pietro Valdastri   University of Leeds, UK

Sponsor and Publicity Chairs

Owen A. Johnson   University of Leeds, UK
Gilberto Ochoa-Ruiz   Monterrey Institute of Technology and Higher
                          Education, Mexico
Mohammad Yaqub   Mohamed bin Zayed University of Artificial
                          Intelligence, UAE

Doctoral Community

Pedro Chavarrias   University of Leeds, UK
Edward Ellis   University of Leeds, UK
Francisco Lopez-Tiro   Monterrey Institute of Technology and Higher
                                   Education, Mexico
Raneem Toman   University of Leeds, UK

Proceeding Chairs

Toni Lassila   University of Leeds, UK
Christian Mata   Polytechnic University of Catalonia, Spain

Local Organising Committee

Pedro Chavarrias   University of Leeds, UK
Alison Whiteley   University of Leeds, UK

Reviewers

Abdul Karim Abbas   William Cancino
Bashayer Abdallah   Jacob Carse
Asfak Ali   Volodymyr Chapman
Mansoor Ali   Nilanjan Chattopadhyay
Mohsin Ali   Veronika Cheplygina
Omar Al-Kadi   Wing Keung Cheung
Anissa Alloula   Omar Choudhry
Ahmed Alshenoudy   Allison Clement
Mohammed Yusuf Ansari   Rhys Compton
Connor Atkins   Timothy Cootes
Akoramurthy Balasubramaniam   Fredrik Dahl
Shashvat Bargale   Theo Dapamede
Subrata Bhattacharjee   Noémie Debroux
Binod Bhattarai   Rocio del Amor
Zhiyan Bo   Nanyu Dong
James Borgars   Daniel Dorda

Ant Duru
Mohamed Elawady
Di Fan
Xinqi Fan
Umar Farooq
Jamil Fayyad
Jiling Feng
Mona Furukawa
Carles Garcia Cabrera
Guillaume Garret
Elham Ghelichkhan
Sushobhan Ghosh
Deep Gupta
Gourav Gupta
Gousia Habib
Palak Handa
Mohammad Mehedi Hassain
Mansoor Hayat
Angie Hernandez
Rahmat Heroza
Mohammad Mithun Hossain
Raza Imam
Mostafa Jahanifar
Bushra Jalil
Syed Javed
Muhammad Jawaid
Xi Jia
Benjamin Jin
Robert John
Dmitrii Kaplun
Tushar Kataria
Benjamin Keel
Ayse Keles
Charan Kodi
Adrian Krenzer
Lalit Kumar
Marie-Ange Lebre
Duway Lesmes Leon
Zhibin Liao
Derek Magee
Anish Mahishi
Stephen J. McKenna
Oliver Mills
Nandini Modi
Carmel Moran

Souradeep Mukhopadhyay
Muhammad Amin Nadim
Sabrina Nefoussi
Fnu Neha
Mark Nixon
Varun Ojha
Pedro Osorio
Alessandro Perelli
Michalis Pistos
Sandesh Pokhrel
Nakul Poudel
Pranav Poudel
Payel Pramanik
Muhammad Qadir
Mohammad Areeb Qazi
Lavdie Rada
Aimon Rahman
Mohammad Masudur Rahman
Kashif Rajpoot
Shan Raza
Zia Rehman
Samuel D. Relton
Dewinda Rumala
Bertram Sabrowsky-Hirsch
Shaheer Ullah Saeed
Nematollah Saeidi
Johannes Schuiki
Mehwish Shaikh
Mohd Faraz Shaikh
Fahad Shamshad
Bheeshm Sharma
Tahira Shehzadi
MohammadJavad Shokri
Zuzanna Skórniewska
Ikboljon Sobirov
Yang Sun
Arvapalli Susmitha
Maciej Szymkowski
Aashay Tinaikar
Raneem Toman
Emanuele Trucco
María del C. Valdés Hernández
Maria Vasconcelos
Irina Voiculescu
Juan Wachs

Muhammad Wahab
Patryk Wasniewski
Fuping Wu
Hao Wu
Ye Wu
Varduhi Yeghiazaryan

Pak Hei Yeung
Louai Zaiter
Zeyu Zhang
Yalin Zheng
Yuhan Zheng
Reyer Zwiggelaar

Contents – Part II

Image-Guided Intervention

Image-Guided Diagnosis

FD-SSD: Semi-supervised Detection of Bone Fenestration and Dehiscence in Intraoral Images

Tahira Shehzadi[1,2,3]([✉])[ID], Ifza Ifza[1,3][ID], Didier Stricker[1,2,3],
and Muhammad Zeshan Afzal[1,2,3][ID]

[1] Department of Computer Science, Technical University of Kaiserslautern,
67663 Kaiserslautern, Germany
[2] Mindgarage, Technical University of Kaiserslautern, 67663 Kaiserslautern,
Germany
[3] German Research Institute for Artificial Intelligence (DFKI),
67663 Kaiserslautern, Germany
tahira.shehzadi@dfki.de

Abstract. Bone fenestration and dehiscence (FD) are conditions where the bone surrounding a tooth is lost or damaged, potentially leading to complications such as gum recession or infection. Accurate identification of FD is essential for proper dental care and treatment planning. Cone-beam computed tomography (CBCT) provides detailed 3D images to identify FD but is costly, exposes patients to radiation, and has limited availability. In contrast, intraoral images, commonly used due to their accessibility and affordability, present challenges in detecting FD, as the condition can appear subtle and easily overlooked. Existing supervised methods, such as FD-SOS, leverage multi-task Vision-Language Models (VLMs) that are fine-tuned on public dental datasets. By integrating conditional contrastive denoising (CCDN) with teeth-specific matching assignments, these methods enhance generalization while prevent overfitting. However, labeling data for FD detection is time-consuming and costly, making it challenging to obtain large-scale, high-quality FD datasets. To address these challenges, we propose FD-SSD, a semi-supervised framework that leverages a teacher-student architecture with an adaptive query strategy derived from pseudo-labels and multi-scale input features, along with a query filtering mechanism. By utilizing both labeled and unlabeled data, FD-SSD reduces reliance on pre-training and extensive annotations. Our approach outperforms the supervised pre-trained DINO, boosting mAP from 62.08% to 68.3%. Additionally, FD-SSD achieves a significant performance improvement over FD-SOS, increasing mAP from 65.67% to 68.3%. These results demonstrate its effectiveness in FD detection, even with limited labeled data. Code is available at: https://github.com/tahirashehzadi/FD-SSD

Keywords: Semi-Supervised · Detection Transformer · Dental

1 Introduction

Bone fenestration and dehiscence (FD) [1,7,13] are abnormalities in the bone structure surrounding teeth, potentially leading to tooth loss if untreated. Accu-

S. Ali et al. (Eds.): MIUA 2025, LNCS 15917, pp. 3–14, 2026.
https://doi.org/10.1007/978-3-031-98691-8_1

rate detection is essential for effective treatment. Dentists primarily use intraoral images like X-rays [11] and digital photographs [12], but these methods are subjective and inconsistent. Cone beam computed tomography (CBCT) [21] is the benchmark for FD detection, providing high diagnostic accuracy. However, CBCT involves radiation exposure [37] and high costs, limiting accessibility, especially in low-income areas. Improving FD detection in intraoral images [14] is essential, as they are widely used and help reduce both cost and radiation risks.

FD detection from intraoral images requires identifying tooth location as anterior and posterior [4] and detecting FD, as shown in Fig. 1. While object detection models like YOLO [8], DETR [2], and Faster-RCNN [22] automate these tasks, they struggle with FD detection due to subtle features, limited data, and anatomical challenges [44]. FD-SOS [6] addresses these issues using a multi-task visual-language model (VLM) with conditional contrastive denoising (CCDN) [36], but improvements remain minimal. The major limitations include suboptimal pre-training on generic data, insufficient foreground queries, and limited labeled datasets [1,7,13,38] that emphasizes the need for better strategies.

To address challenges of detecting bone fenestration and dehiscence (FD) in intraoral images [14], we propose FD-SSD, a semi-supervised detection framework [26,32,41] that leverages both labeled and unlabeled images. FD-SSD comprises three key modules: a teacher-student module [10], an adaptive query module, and a query filtering module. The teacher-student module employs a teacher-student architecture to generate high-quality pseudo-labels, enhancing generalization while reducing reliance on extensive labeled data. The adaptive query module derives queries from multi-scale features [39] and pseudo-labels [15] to effectively propose potential FD regions [1,13], while the query filtering module distinguishes foreground regions from noise by evaluating the similarity between FD queries and denoising queries [5,17,30,40]. Together, these modules ensure accurate FD [1,13] detection in anterior teeth [4,16], establishing FD-SSD as a scalable and efficient solution for FD detection.

In this paper, the key contributions are summarized as follows:

- We propose an end-to-end semi-supervised framework, FD-SSD, for detecting bone fenestration and dehiscence in intraoral images, effectively addressing challenges posed by limited FD labeled data.
- Our approach incorporates a teacher-student architecture that generates pseudo-labels for unlabeled FD data, an adaptive query module to effectively propose potential FD regions, and a query filtering module that distinguishes genuine FD regions from noise by evaluating the similarity between foreground FD queries and denoising queries.
- Extensive experiments on publicly available FD datasets demonstrate the effectiveness of FD-SSD.

2   Related Work

In this section, we review supervised approaches for FD detection and explore semi-supervised methods, highlighting their relevance to dental imaging.

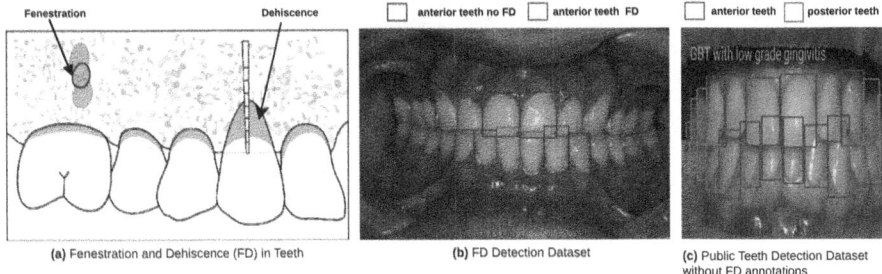

(a) Fenestration and Dehiscence (FD) in Teeth   **(b)** FD Detection Dataset   **(c)** Public Teeth Detection Dataset without FD annotations

Fig. 1. (a) Fenestration and Dehiscence (FD) in Teeth illustrating two common dental conditions: Fenestration (a small opening in the bone covering the tooth) and Dehiscence (loss of bone along the tooth). (b) FD Detection Dataset Visualization of annotated teeth images with bounding boxes indicating anterior teeth (FD and no FD). (c) Public Teeth Detection Dataset without FD Annotations Dataset showcasing teeth images with annotations for anterior and posterior teeth only, without FD-specific labels.

Traditional FD Supervised Approaches. CBCT [21] is the benchmark for FD detection but is costly and exposes patients to radiation, prompting interest in intraoral imaging [14]. Object detection models like YOLO [8], Faster R-CNN [22], and FCOS [35] aid tooth localization but are not optimized for FD detection. Open-Set Object Detection (OSOD) [42] and Vision-Language Models (VLMs) improve FD identification but struggle with overfitting and limited datasets. FD-SOS [6] enhances accuracy using conditional contrastive denoising and teeth-specific matching but faces challenges due to generic pre-training, limited FD-specific features, and scarce annotated datasets, underscoring the need for specialized training strategies.

Semi-Supervised Approaches. Traditional supervised methods [2,22,25,27] struggle with FD detection [6] due to reliance on large labeled datasets and difficulty capturing FD's subtle variations. Annotating data specially in medical domain is time-consuming and requires experts, limiting scalability. Semi-supervised approaches [28,29] help overcome these limitations by leveraging both labeled and unlabeled data. Architectures such as Mean Teacher [34], which uses EMA-based teacher updates, and Semi-DETR [41], which employs learnable sparse queries. Recent works [23,24,31] have explored end-to-end semi-supervised detection approaches leveraging transformer architectures and advanced query-based mechanisms. These methods enhance generalization while minimizing annotation requirements.

3   Methodology

To improve FD detection intraoral images, we propose FD-SSD, a semi-supervised detection framework that effectively utilizes both labeled and unlabeled data. FD-SSD incorporates a **Teacher-Student Architecture** for reli-

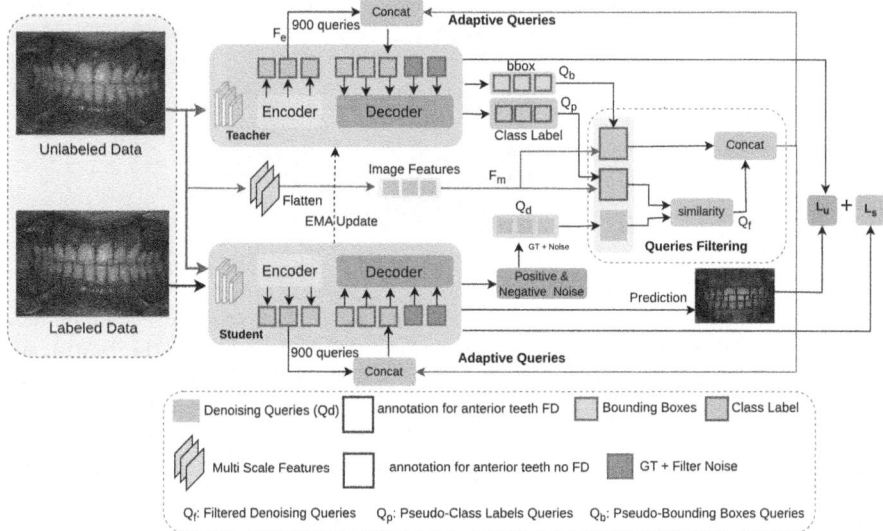

Fig. 2. Overview of FD-SSD for FD Detection in Anterior Teeth. The teacher model generates pseudo-labels for unlabeled data, while the student model learns from both labeled and pseudo-labeled data. The framework utilizes adaptive queries, including pseudo-bounding boxes with image features, pseudo-class labels with multi-scale image features, and denoising queries for improved learning. A Query Filtering Module further refines the queries. The overall loss consists of student-supervised loss and student-teacher unsupervised loss.

able pseudo-labeling, **Adaptive Query Strategy** for enhanced region proposals, and a **Query Filtering Module** to refine detections and reduce noise. Below, we detail the key components of our approach.

3.1   Teacher-Student Architecture

The FD-SSD framework employs teacher-student architecture, as shown in Fig. 2, with DINO [40] as the baseline.The teacher model generates high-quality pseudo-labels for unlabeled intraoral images [14], guiding the student model during training. It is updated using an Exponential Moving Average (EMA) [34] of the student model's weights, ensuring stable and reliable predictions. The framework effectively utilizes unlabeled data while requiring only a small amount of labeled data. By combining labeled data with high-confidence pseudo-labels, the model improves generalization ability and remains robust even with limited annotations. The key difference between our semi-supervised approach and generic object semi-supervised methods is the use of adaptive and refined queries, which are specifically designed for FD intraoral images. FD-SSD improves semi-supervised detection of FD, ensuring more accurate identification across diverse intraoral images [14].

3.2   Query Filtering Module

Denoising queries in DINO [40] consist of a large number of positive and negative queries, corresponding to object and non-object regions. However, excessive
background queries introduce noise and hinder efficient learning. . Typically, the
number of denoising queries is set to 100. The Query Filtering Module refines
the denoising queries by removing irrelevant background queries and preserving
only the foreground ones. This filtering process improves the model's ability to
focus on relevant object regions, enhancing both localization and classification
accuracy in semi-supervised FD detection.

To achieve this, we use pseudo-label queries as a filtering reference and compute similarity between denoising queries and pseudo-label queries. Given the
denoising queries Q_d and pseudo-label queries Q_p, we measure the similarity
using a cosine similarity function:

$$S_{i,j} = \frac{Q_d^i \cdot Q_p^j}{\|Q_d^i\|\|Q_p^j\|} \tag{1}$$

where $S_{i,j}$ represents the similarity score between the i-th denoising query and
the j-th pseudo-label query. Cosine similarity is employed to identify denoising
queries that are semantically aligned with pseudo-label queries. This alignment
helps retain only those queries likely to represent true FD regions. Cosine similarity captures directional similarity, making it robust to scale variations in
feature embeddings. We then construct a filtering mask M_p by thresholding the
similarity scores:

$$M_p^i = \begin{cases} 1, & \max_j S_{i,j} > \tau \\ 0, & \text{otherwise} \end{cases} \tag{2}$$

where τ is a predefined similarity threshold set between 0.7 and 0.8. The final
filtered denoising queries Q_f are obtained by element-wise multiplication of the
denoising queries with the mask:

$$Q_f = Q_d \cdot M_p \tag{3}$$

By removing background noise and preserving only the relevant foreground
queries, the Query Filtering Module significantly enhances the quality of adaptive queries, leading to improved convergence and generalization in semi-
supervised FD detection.

3.3   Adaptive Query Strategy

Adaptive queries in FD-SSD dynamically enhance learning by incorporating
pseudo-bounding boxes with image features from encoder, pseudo-class labels
with multi-scale image features, and denoising queries. Given an input image
I, pseudo-bounding boxes queries Q_b are generated from the teacher model's
pseudo-boxes based on confidence scores with encoder features F_e:

$$Q_b = \{b_i \mid s_i > \tau\}, F_e \quad \forall i \in N \tag{4}$$

where s_i represents the confidence score for each bounding box b_i, and τ is a predefined threshold. Pseudo-label queries integrate multi-scale image features, allowing the student model to capture context-aware information:

$$Q_p = \{p_i \mid s_i > \tau\}, F_m \quad \forall i \in N \tag{5}$$

where F_m represents multi-scale feature embeddings. To improve efficiency, we first filter denoising background queries using pseudo-label queries through a query filtering process, as explained in Sect. 3.2. The final set of adaptive queries is formed by concatenating the refined denoising queries, pseudo-label queries, and pseudo-bounding boxes:

$$Q_{\text{adaptive}} = \text{concat}(Q_f, Q_p, Q_b) \tag{6}$$

It ensures that the student model learns from more reliable supervision. By integrating these adaptive queries, FD-SSD significantly improves both localization and classification accuracy in semi-supervised FD detection.

3.4 Loss Functions

The overall loss comprises two components: the supervised loss (L_s) and the unsupervised loss (L_u). The teacher model generates pseudo boxes for unlabeled images, while the student model is trained on labeled images with ground-truth annotations and on unlabeled images with pseudo boxes treated as ground-truth. Therefore, the overall loss is defined as the weighted sum of the supervised and unsupervised losses:

$$L = L_s + \alpha L_u, \tag{7}$$

where α controls the weight of the unsupervised loss.

4 Experimental Setup

4.1 Datasets and Evaluation Criteria

We implemented two training settings: supervised and semi-supervised. For supervised training, the Public Teeth Detection dataset, containing 5,000 images at a resolution of 416×416 pixels without disease-specific labels or ground truth from CBCT scans, is used for pre-training. This dataset includes approximately 20,000 bounding box annotations covering anterior and posterior teeth, with a standard train/validation/test split of 70% (3,500 images), 10% (500 images), and 20% (1,000 images), respectively. Fine-tuning is performed on the FDTOOTH dataset [6], which consists of 150 high-resolution images (5,760 × 3,840 pixels) annotated with 1,800 bounding boxes across normal and fenestration/dehiscence (FD) classes. Unlike the Public Teeth Detection dataset, FDTOOTH provides disease-specific labels validated with CBCT scans. Its train/validation/test split includes 90 training images (454 healthy, 626 FD),

Table 1. Performance comparison of FD detection. All object detectors begin with initialization using ImageNet pre-trained weights. * signifies pre-training on publicly available dental dataset, while [†] refers to fine-tuning of pre-existing VLM pre-trained models. For fairness, FD-SSD is trained on fully labeled data.

Methods	multi-task	Approach	AP^{FD}	mAP	AP_{50}	AP_{75}
Object Detectors*						
Diffusion-DETR w/o pretraining [3]	✗	Supervised	1.31	1.7	8.85	0.04
Diffusion-DETR [3]	✗	Supervised	51.42	59.06	66.37	62.58
DDETR [43]	✗	Supervised	50.41	57.44	65.48	62.68
DINO [40]	✗	Supervised	49.68	51.65	57.65	55.13
Hierarchical-Diff-DetR w/o pretraining [9]	✓	Supervised	0.0	0.0	0.0	0.0
Hierarchical-Diff-DetR [9]	✓	Supervised	50.82	57.63	64.4	61.45
DDETR [43]	✓	Supervised	47.57	54.89	63.05	60.2
DINO [40]	✓	Supervised	43.85	50.15	55.53	53.8
SparseDet [33]	✓	Supervised	52.94	54.87	65.13	62.96
Open-set Object Detectors[†]						
GLIP [18]	✗	Supervised	32.0	40.47	55.85	51.3
GDINO [20]	✗	Supervised	56.59	62.59	65.89	63.69
GLIP [18]	✓	Supervised	38.68	42.73	51.97	56.7
GDINO [20]	✓	Supervised	54.75	62.08	65.81	62.6
FD-SOS [6]	✓	Supervised	60.84	65.97	69.67	67.07
FD-SSD(our)	✓	Semi-Supervised	64.5	68.3	73.2	70.7

20 validation images (95 healthy, 145 FD), and 40 test images (248 healthy, 232 FD). In semi-supervised training, FDTOOTH is used with 5%, 10%, and 50% labeled data, while the remaining images serve as unlabeled data to enhance learning efficiency. FD-SSD performance is evaluated using mean Average Precision (mAP) for overall accuracy, AP^{FD} for FD detection, and AP_{50} and AP_{75} at Intersection over Union (IoU) thresholds of 0.5 and 0.75.

4.2   Results and Discussion

In this section, we evaluate object detection models for FD [1,13] in intraoral images [14]. Table 1 presents a comparison between standard and open-set detectors, highlighting FD-SSD's superior performance. FD-SSD achieves an AP^{FD} of 64.5 and an mAP of 68.3, significantly outperforming SparseDet, which scores 52.94 and 54.87, respectively. Additionally, FD-SSD outperforms FD-SOS by a significant margin, increasing AP^{FD} by 3.66% (60.84 vs. 64.5) and mAP by 2.33% (65.97 vs. 68.3). These results highlight FD-SSD's superior accuracy in detecting both fenestration and dehiscence.

Table 2. Performance on the FDTOOTH dataset at different percentages of labeled data.

Dataset	Label	mAP	AP_{50}	AP_{75}	AP^{FD}	F1
FDTOOTH	5%	40.5	44.8	43.2	42.5	0.53
	10%	49.9	55.6	52.2	45.7	0.64
	50%	55.0	59.7	56.5	50.3	0.69

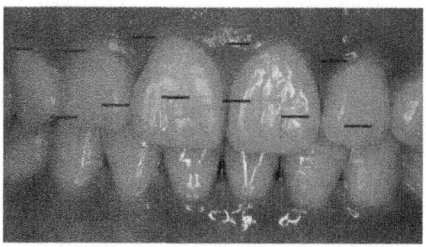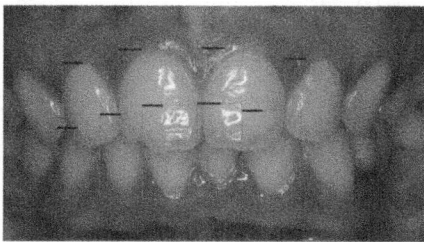

Fig. 3. Visual analysis of the FD-SSD approach using 50% labeled data on the FDTOOTH dataset. For best viewing, please zoom in.

We also evaluate FD-SSD on the FD-TOOTH dataset in a semi-supervised setting. Table 2 examines the effect of different labeled data percentages (5%, 10%, and 50%) on networks performance, showing a clear improvement as the labeled data increases. The mAP improves from 40.5 (5% labeled) to 49.9 (10%) and 55.0 (50%), indicating that more labeled data enhances model accuracy. Similarly, the AP^{FD}, which measures the model's effectiveness in detecting fenestration and dehiscence specifically, increases from 42.5 to 50.3, indicating enhanced accuracy in identifying these critical dental conditions. Additionally, the F1 score improves from 0.53 at 5% to 0.64 at 10% and 0.69 at 50%, indicating stronger detection performance. Fig 3 shows the visual analysis of FD-SSD model on the FDTOOTH dataset with 50% labeled data.

Table 3. Performance comparison of FD-SSD trained on 5%, 10% and DINO trained on 10% labeled FDTOOTH dataset.

Detector	Label	mAP	AP_{50}	AP_{75}
DINO	10%	26.2	31.3	29.6
FD-SSD	5%	40.5	44.8	43.2
FD-SSD	10%	49.9	55.6	52.2

Unlike DINO, which relies solely on supervised learning and fixed learned queries, FD-SSD incorporates a teacher-student architecture, an adaptive query strategy, and a query filtering mechanism. Table 3 compares DINO and FD-SSD, both trained on 10% labeled data, revealing that FD-SSD significantly outperforms DINO (mAP: 49.9 vs. 26.2). Additionally, FD-SSD trained on only 5% labeled data still achieves better performance (mAP 40.5) than DINO trained on 10%. This demonstrates that FD-SSD is a much better choice, particularly in scenarios with limited labeled data.

Limitation: While FD-SSD demonstrates strong performance in detecting fenestration and dehiscence, the current study focuses exclusively on anterior teeth. As a result, its applicability to posterior teeth remains unexplored. Future work will aim to extend the approach to cover posterior regions, which may present additional challenges due to anatomical complexity and reduced visibility in intraoral images.

4.3   Ablation Study

In ablation, we compare the performance of the proposed FD-SSD model against the baseline supervised method, DINO, and FD-SOS.

Table 4 compares FD-SSD without pre-training to DINO that is pre-trainined on COCO [19] data. FD-SSD outperformed DINO, achieving AP^{FD} of 64.5 and mAP of 68.3, surpassing DINO's 54.75 and 62.08. FD-SSD also has higher AP_{50} (65.81 vs. 73.2) and AP_{75} (62.09 vs. 70.7), highlighting its superior detection performance without pre-training.

Table 4. Performance comparison of FD-SSD and pre-trained DINO. 'PT' denotes pre-training on coco data [19].

Methods	PT	AP^{FD}	mAP	AP_{50}	AP_{75}
DINO	✓	54.75	62.08	65.81	62.60
FD-SSD	✗	64.5	68.3	73.2	70.7

Table 5. Performance comparison of FD-SSD and FD-SOS. 'OS' denotes open-set VLM pre-training.

Methods	OS	AP^{FD}	mAP	AP_{50}	AP_{75}
FD-SOS	✓	60.84	65.97	69.67	67.07
FD-SSD	✗	64.5	68.3	73.2	70.7

Table 5 validates FD-SSD's robustness against FD-SOS, which is pre-trained on open-set data. FD-SSD outperformed FD-SOS with AP^{FD} of 60.84 vs. 64.5, demonstrating superior generalization to unseen fenestration and dehiscence. This highlights FD-SSD's effectiveness in handling complex dental structures without open-set pre-training. Overall, these findings suggest that FD-SSD offers a significant performance boost, particularly in scenarios with limited labeled data, making it an effective approach for FD detection.

5   Conclusion

In this paper, we introduced FD-SSD, a novel semi-supervised detection framework designed to accurately identify Bone fenestration and dehiscence (FD) in intraoral images. By leveraging a teacher-student architecture and integrating adaptive queries with query filtering module, FD-SSD addresses critical challenges associated with limited labeled data and noisy annotations. Extensive experiments on publicly available FD datasets, including FD-TOOTH, validate the framework's effectiveness and scalability in detecting FD across both anterior teeth. The results demonstrate superior performance in generalization and accuracy compared to existing approaches, highlighting its potential to maximize the utility of limited FD-specific datasets. Overall, FD-SSD improves FD detection, making it more accessible, affordable, and reliable. Its ability to work with intraoral images and the use of semi-supervised learning provide a practical and efficient solution for dental diagnosis. However, limitation of this work is that it focuses primarily on anterior teeth, leaving detection of posterior teeth unaddressed. Future work will focus on detecting posterior teeth, increasing dataset diversity, improving detection for complex cases, and exploring further applications of semi-supervised learning in dental imaging.

References

1. Alsino, H., Hajeer, M.Y., Alkhouri, I., Murad, R.: The diagnostic accuracy of cone-beam computed tomography (cbct) imaging in detecting and measuring dehiscence and fenestration in patients with class i malocclusion: a surgical-exposure-based validation study. Cureus **14**, e22789 (2022). https://doi.org/10.7759/cureus.22789

2. Carion, N., Massa, F., Synnaeve, G., Usunier, N., Kirillov, A., Zagoruyko, S.: End-to-end object detection with transformers (2020). https://doi.org/10.48550/arXiv.2005.12872

3. Chen, S., Sun, P., Song, Y., Luo, P.: Diffusiondet: diffusion model for object detection (2022). https://doi.org/10.48550/arXiv.2211.09788

4. Chung, M., et al.: Individual tooth detection and identification from dental panoramic x-ray images via point-wise localization and distance regularization. Artif. Intell. Med. **111**, 101996 (2021). https://doi.org/10.1016/j.artmed.2020.101996, http://dx.doi.org/10.1016/j.artmed.2020.101996

5. Ehsan, I., Shehzadi, T., Stricker, D., Afzal, M.Z.: End-to-end semi-supervised approach with modulated object queries for table detection in documents. arXiv preprint arXiv:2405.04971 (2024)

6. Elbatel, M., Liu, K., Yang, Y., Li, X.: FD-SOS: vision-language open-set detectors for bone fenestration and dehiscence detection from intraoral images . In: proceedings of Medical Image Computing and Computer Assisted Intervention – MICCAI 2024. vol. LNCS 15003. Springer Nature Switzerland (2024)

7. Furlan, C.C., Freire, A.R., Ferreira-Pileggi, B.C., Prado, F.B., Rossi, A.C.: Fenestration and dehiscence in human maxillary alveolar bone: an in silico study using the finite element method. Cureus **15** (2023). https://api.semanticscholar.org/CorpusID:266397813

8. Ge, Z., Liu, S., Wang, F., Li, Z., Sun, J.: Yolox: exceeding yolo series in 2021. ArXiv abs/2107.08430 (2021). https://api.semanticscholar.org/CorpusID:236088010

9. Hamamci, I.E., et al.: Diffusion-based hierarchical multi-label object detection to analyze panoramic dental x-rays (2023). https://arxiv.org/abs/2303.06500

10. Hu, C., Li, X., Liu, D., Chen, X., Wang, J., Liu, X.: Teacher-student architecture for knowledge learning: a survey (2022). https://arxiv.org/abs/2210.17332

11. Hwang, S.Y., Choi, E.S., Kim, Y.S., Gim, B.E., Ha, M., Kim, H.Y.: Health effects from exposure to dental diagnostic x-ray. Environ. Health Toxicol. **33**, e2018017 (2018). https://doi.org/10.5620/eht.e2018017

12. Jayachandran, S.: Digital imaging in dentistry: a review. Contemp. Clin. Dent. **8**, 193 (2017). https://doi.org/10.4103/ccd.ccd_535_17

13. Kajan, Z., Monir, S., Khosravifard, N., Jahri, D.: Fenestration and dehiscence in the alveolar bone of anterior maxillary and mandibular teeth in cone-beam computed tomography of an iranian population. Dental Res. J. **17**, 380 (2020). https://doi.org/10.4103/1735-3327.294327

14. Kokomoto, K., Okawa, R., Nakano, K., Nozaki, K.: Intraoral image generation by progressive growing of generative adversarial network and evaluation of generated image quality by dentists. Sci. Reports **11**, 18517 (2021). https://doi.org/10.1038/s41598-021-98043-3

15. Lee, D.H.: Pseudo-label : the simple and efficient semi-supervised learning method for deep neural networks. ICML 2013 Workshop : Challenges in Representation Learning (WREPL) (2013)

16. Lee, H., Song, M., Koo, J., Seo, J.: Hausdorff distance matching with adaptive query denoising for rotated detection transformer (2024). https://arxiv.org/abs/2305.07598

17. Li, F., Zhang, H., Liu, S., Guo, J., Ni, L.M., Zhang, L.: Dn-detr: accelerate detr training by introducing query denoising (2022). https://arxiv.org/abs/2203.01305

18. Li, L.H., et al.: Grounded language-image pre-training (2022). https://arxiv.org/abs/2112.03857

19. Lin, T.-Y., et al.: Microsoft COCO: common objects in context. In: Fleet, D., Pajdla, T., Schiele, B., Tuytelaars, T. (eds.) ECCV 2014. LNCS, vol. 8693, pp. 740–755. Springer, Cham (2014). https://doi.org/10.1007/978-3-319-10602-1_48

20. Liu, S., et al.: Grounding dino: marrying dino with grounded pre-training for open-set object detection. In: European Conference on Computer Vision (2023). https://api.semanticscholar.org/CorpusID:257427307

21. Liu, T., et al.: Key-point based automated diagnosis for alveolar dehiscence in mandibular incisors using convolutional neural network. Biomed. Signal Process. Control **85**, 105082 (2023). https://doi.org/10.1016/j.bspc.2023.105082, https://www.sciencedirect.com/science/article/pii/S1746809423005153

22. Ren, S., He, K., Girshick, R., Sun, J.: Faster r-cnn: towards real-time object detection with region proposal networks. In: Proceedings of the 29th International Conference on Neural Information Processing Systems - vol. 1, pp. 91–99. NIPS'15, MIT Press, Cambridge, MA, USA (2015)

23. Shehzadi, T., Azeem Hashmi, K., Stricker, D., Liwicki, M., Zeshan Afzal, M.: Towards end-to-end semi-supervised table detection with deformable transformer. In: Fink, G.A., Jain, R., Kise, K., Zanibbi, R. (eds.) Document Analysis and Recognition - ICDAR 2023, pp. 51–76. Springer Nature Switzerland, Cham (2023)

24. Shehzadi, T., Hashmi, K.A., Pagani, A., Liwicki, M., Stricker, D., Afzal, M.Z.: Mask-aware semi-supervised object detection in floor plans. Appl. Sci. **12**(19) (2022). https://doi.org/10.3390/app12199398, https://www.mdpi.com/2076-3417/12/19/9398

25. Shehzadi, T., Hashmi, K.A., Stricker, D., Afzal, M.Z.: Object detection with transformers: a review (2023)

26. Shehzadi, T., Hashmi, K.A., Stricker, D., Afzal, M.Z.: Sparse semi-detr: sparse learnable queries for semi-supervised object detection (2024)

27. Shehzadi, T., Hashmi, K.A., Stricker, D., Liwicki, M., Afzal, M.Z.: Bridging the performance gap between detr and r-cnn for graphical object detection in document images. arXiv preprint arXiv:2306.13526 (2023)
28. Shehzadi, T., Ifza, Stricker, D., Afzal, M.Z.: Semi-supervised object detection: a survey on progress from cnn to transformer (2024). https://arxiv.org/abs/2407.08460
29. Shehzadi, T., Sarode, S., Stricker, D., Afzal, M.Z.: Towards end-to-end semi-supervised table detection with semantic aligned matching transformer (2024)
30. Shehzadi, T., Stricker, D., Afzal, M.Z.: A hybrid approach for document layout analysis in document images (2024)
31. Shehzadi, T., Stricker, D., Afzal, M.Z.: Semitabdetr: End-to-end semi-supervised table detection with transformer-based enhanced query approach (2024). https://doi.org/10.21203/rs.3.rs-5305546/v1
32. Sohn, K., Zhang, Z., Li, C., Zhang, H., Lee, C., Pfister, T.: A simple semi-supervised learning framework for object detection. CoRR **abs/2005.04757** (2020). https://arxiv.org/abs/2005.04757
33. Suri, S., Rambhatla, S., Chellappa, R., Shrivastava, A.: Sparsedet: improving sparsely annotated object detection with pseudo-positive mining. In: Proceedings of the IEEE/CVF International Conference on Computer Vision. pp. 6770–6781 (2023)
34. Tarvainen, A., Valpola, H.: Mean teachers are better role models: weight-averaged consistency targets improve semi-supervised deep learning results (2018). https://arxiv.org/abs/1703.01780
35. Tian, Z., Shen, C., Chen, H., He, T.: Fcos: A simple and strong anchor-free object detector. IEEE Trans. Pattern Anal. Mach. Intell. **44**, 1922–1933 (2020). https://api.semanticscholar.org/CorpusID:219708318
36. Wang, Y., Liu, Z., Yang, L., Yu, P.S.: Conditional denoising diffusion for sequential recommendation (2023). https://arxiv.org/abs/2304.11433
37. Yeh, J.K., Chen, C.H.: Estimated radiation risk of cancer from dental cone-beam computed tomography imaging in orthodontics patients. BMC Oral Health **18** (2018). https://api.semanticscholar.org/CorpusID:51910004
38. Yousaf, A., Sazonov, E.: Food intake detection in the face of limited sensor signal annotations. In: 2024 Tenth International Conference on Communications and Electronics (ICCE). pp. 351–356 (2024).https://doi.org/10.1109/ICCE62051.2024.10634684
39. Zhang, G., Luo, Z., Tian, Z., Zhang, J., Zhang, X., Lu, S.: Towards efficient use of multi-scale features in transformer-based object detectors (2023). https://arxiv.org/abs/2208.11356
40. Zhang, H., et al.: DINO: DETR with improved denoising anchor boxes for end-to-end object detection. In: The Eleventh International Conference on Learning Representations (2023). https://openreview.net/forum?id=3mRwyG5one
41. Zhang, J., et al.: Semi-detr: semi-supervised object detection with detection transformers (2023). https://arxiv.org/abs/2307.08095
42. Zheng, J., Li, W., Petersson, L., Barnes, N.: Towards open-set object detection and discovery (2022). https://doi.org/10.48550/arXiv.2204.05604
43. Zhu, X., Su, W., Lu, L., Li, B., Wang, X., Dai, J.: Deformable detr: deformable transformers for end-to-end object detection. In: International Conference on Learning Representations (2021). https://openreview.net/forum?id=gZ9hCDWe6ke
44. Đorđević, Z., Graovac, S., Mitrovic, S.: Suboptimal threshold estimation for detection of point-like objects in radar images. EURASIP J. Image Video Process. **2015** (2015). https://doi.org/10.1186/s13640-015-0057-6

Interpretable Prediction of Lymph Node Metastasis in Rectal Cancer MRI Using Variational Autoencoders

Benjamin Keel[1](✉)🆔, Aaron Quyn[1,2]🆔, David Jayne[1,2]🆔, Maryam Mohsin[2], and Samuel D. Relton[1]🆔

[1] University of Leeds, Leeds, UK
mm17b2k@leeds.ac.uk
[2] Leeds Teaching Hospitals NHS Trust, Leeds, UK

Abstract. Effective treatment for rectal cancer relies on accurate lymph node metastasis (LNM) staging. However, radiological criteria based on lymph node (LN) size, shape and texture morphology have limited diagnostic accuracy. In this work, we investigate applying a Variational Autoencoder (VAE) as a feature encoder model to replace the large pre-trained Convolutional Neural Network (CNN) used in existing approaches. The motivation for using a VAE is that the generative model aims to reconstruct the images, so it directly encodes visual features and meaningful patterns across the data. This leads to a disentangled and structured latent space which can be more interpretable than a CNN. Models are deployed on an in-house MRI dataset with 168 patients who did not undergo neo-adjuvant treatment. The post-operative pathological N stage was used as the ground truth to evaluate model predictions. Our proposed model 'VAE-MLP' achieved state-of-the-art performance on the MRI dataset, with cross-validated metrics of AUC 0.86 ± 0.05, Sensitivity 0.79 ± 0.06, and Specificity 0.85 ± 0.05. Code is available at: https://github.com/benkeel/Lymph_Node_Classification_MIUA

Keywords: Lymph Node Metastasis · Variational Autoencoder · Explainable AI · MRI

1 Introduction

Rectal Cancer (RC) is the fifth most prevalent cancer in the UK and remains one of the leading causes of cancer related mortality, with a 5-year survival rate of 59.6% [1]. Lymph node metastasis (LNM) is one of the most critical prognostic factors, as malignant lymph nodes (LNs) increase the risk of cancer recurrence and the development of distant metastasis [27]. Consequently, LN staging informs the appropriate use of neo-adjuvant chemotherapy and radiotherapy. In clinical

Supplementary Information The online version contains supplementary material available at https://doi.org/10.1007/978-3-031-98691-8_2.

practice, radiologists use criteria based on size, shape and texture morphology to detect RC LNM on MRI [9]. However, the established rules-based criteria have limited diagnostic sensitivity and specificity of 73% (95% CI: 68-77%) and 74% (95% CI: 68-80%) respectively [34]. Inaccurate LNM staging can result in under or over treatment which can cause patient toxicity and affect cancer outcomes [3,9]. Compounding this, shortages of specialist radiologists have put significant pressure on hospitals and multidisciplinary teams (MDT) for planning cancer treatment, underlining the need for decision support tools.

Recent studies have demonstrated the capability of deep learning methods for accurately staging LNM on pre-operative radiologic imaging [14]. However, a significant barrier to clinical adoption remains the lack of interpretability and robust validation of the models. This study investigates the application of Variational Autoencoders (VAEs) to predict LNM in RC. Proposed models were trained using 2D patches of LNs extracted from pre-operative MRI. Feature representations of the patches produced by the VAE were used to train Multilayer Perceptron (MLP) classification models in a Multiple Instance Learning (MIL) framework. The approach used an MLP model to refine the feature representations into individual LN predictions, which were combined with clinical data in a second MLP for a patient level diagnosis. The final binary predictions were evaluated against the post-operative pathology confirmed N stage. The novel contributions of this work are as follows:

1. First study to exceed the diagnostic accuracy of radiologists using non-specialist segmentations of the lymph nodes on RC MRI.
2. First application of generative AI in colorectal cancer LNM prediction, with the novel use of VAEs to improve the interpretability and demonstrate that the model latent space captures clinically meaningful information.

2   Related Works

In our scoping review of deep learning methods applied to pre-operative colorectal cancer LNM prediction (2018-2024), we reported a mean AUC of 0.856 (95However, existing studies have methodological limitations, including selection bias and restrictive inclusion criteria in study cohorts. Most approaches do not incorporate multi-modal clinical data and often include patients across multiple T-stages without using it as a variable in the model. Some results may also be inflated due to common weaknesses in the validation such as small test sets, reporting limited metrics, and only one previous study using cross-validation [32]. There is also a general lack of explainability techniques beyond Grad-CAM [24] to indicate regions of the image that have high importance to the diagnosis.

A recent study by Xia et al. [31] employed automatic LN detection and a 2D ResNet CNN classification architecture with pre-operative LN MRI patches alongside size characteristics and the apparent diffusion coefficient. Models were trained and evaluated on 1014 patients across three centres, including two external validation cohorts. They reported an AUC of 0.81, outperforming junior radiologists (0.69 (95% CI: 0.64-0.73)) and senior radiologists (0.79 (95% CI: 0.75-0.83)). Collaboration with the model significantly improved the performance of the radiologist groups to 0.80 (95% CI: 0.76-0.84) and 0.88 (95% CI: 0.85-0.91) respectively, demonstrating the value of RC LNM decision support tools to assist radiologists in clinical practice. This study was the most methodologically similar to ours and served as a primary reference.

The study methodology applying VAEs in medical image representation learning has been shown to be effective in a variety of diagnostic tasks [10,23,29]. Several studies have shown that VAEs exceed the performance of CNNs in cancer imaging tasks, including state-of-the-art methods for pre-operative detection of breast cancer [26] and lung cancer [13] on public datasets. Another study compared VAE and CNN models for the pathological diagnosis of rectal cancer and found that the VAE was the best performing on the in-house dataset [12].

Adjacent topics highlight that VAEs generate more meaningful and structured latent spaces and can provide more robustness in classification. A recent study applied the VAE learning objective (ELBO), which generalises the softmax trained using the cross-entropy loss in supervised learning tasks [6]. The variational classification latent variable model interprets the input to the final activation in neural network models as a sample of a Gaussian latent space to encourage more robust learning. The study found that the model maintained classification accuracy while improving model calibration, adversarial robustness and effectiveness in low-data settings. Further recent work has shown that VAEs are useful for other tasks, such as data augmentation where VAEs can generate realistic synthetic images from limited medical datasets [22].

3   Methodology

3.1   MRI Preprocessing and Augmentation

Preprocessing was conducted using the TorchIO library [21] to normalise the MRI scans and crop to (32×32) voxels for each lymph node patch. The pipeline included histogram intensity scaling, Z normalisation, and resampling intensity values to $[0,1]$ with a consistent scan orientation and a standard voxel size of $(0.573mm \times 0.573mm \times 3.3mm)$. Each patch corresponds to a region of interest with an area of $336.2mm^2$. The patches containing the largest LN segmentations were selected for each patient with a limit of 15, and empty spaces were filled with zero padding. To provide 3D information to the model, multiple 2D cross-sections of LNs were included if the segmentation maps of secondary patches covered at least half of the area.

Data augmentation was used to increase dataset variability and to help mitigate the imbalanced and limited data. Spatial augmentations were horizontal and vertical flips, and translations to shift the patch centre and capture different context from the surroundings. Intensity-based augmentations applied included random Gaussian noise, gamma correction, and bias field distortion to simulate magnetic field inhomogeneities.

3.2 VAE Model Description and Training

VAE Model Architecture. The proposed VAE encoder-decoder architecture is visualised in Fig. 1.

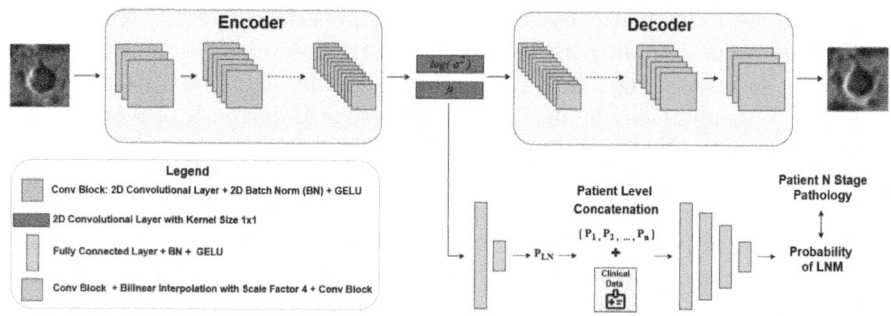

Fig. 1. VAE-MLP model architecture

The encoder has 6 blocks of 2D convolutional layers with 2D batch normalisation [11], and Gaussian Error Linear Unit (GELU) activation [8]. The output of the encoder is used in two separate convolutional layers for the latent vectors, mean (μ) and log variance $\left(\log(\sigma^2)\right)$, forming a latent space of LN feature representations. The decoder takes a sample from the n-dimensional Gaussian distribution parameterised by the latent vectors, $z_i = \mu_i + \sigma_i \cdot \epsilon_i$, with noise sampled from a standard Gaussian, $\epsilon_i \sim \mathcal{N}(0,1)$. The decoder is a symmetric architecture, with a bilinear interpolation in between the convolutional blocks to upsample the feature maps by a scale factor of 2 each time. The final reconstructed images are evaluated against the original MRI patches in the loss function.

Custom Loss Function. The VAE loss function in Eq. 1 is a weighted combination of the L1 Loss (mean absolute error), the Kullback-Leibler Divergence (KLD) [16] and the Structural Similarity Index Measure (SSIM) [30] for each image i as follows,

$$\mathcal{L}_{\text{VAE}} = \sum_{i=1}^{n} \alpha \cdot \lambda \cdot \text{L1 Loss}_i + (1-\alpha) \cdot \gamma \cdot \text{SSIM}_i + a \cdot \beta \cdot \text{KLD}_i. \qquad (1)$$

The L1 Loss and SSIM measure image reconstruction quality and the KLD is the standard measure of latent space smoothness [15]. The metrics were averaged across the batch, and loss function hyperparameters $\alpha \in [0,1]$, λ, γ and β were included to help find a good balance of these adversarial metrics. An annealing function, 'a', was included to exponentially increase the KLD throughout the training. This helps the VAE prioritise high-quality reconstructions in the early stages, before progressively enforcing a structured latent space. The KLD measures the divergence between the learned latent distribution and a standard Gaussian distribution. The loss function aims to balance high reconstruction quality with a latent space that generalises and disentangles the common features present in the data.

VAE Model Training. The size of the VAE model was scaled by the hyperparameter 'base' to control the number of feature maps, ranging from 16 to 28. In the encoder, the number of maps increased from base to $16 \cdot$ base, with kernel sizes between 3 and 8. The latent size scalar was between 16 and 28, and the latent vector size was calculated as latent size $\cdot$ base, yielding a latent space dimensionality of 256 to 784. Training hyperparameters included the learning rate, weight decay, batch size, and the number of gradient accumulation steps (1 to 3). Models were trained for 200 epochs with early stopping checkpoints to avoid unnecessary computation. To find the optimal model, we conducted a Bayesian search of the hyperparameter space with 200 runs. Results were stored and compared using the Python library Weights and Bias (WandB) [2].

The final VAE MRI reconstructions were evaluated qualitatively and quantitatively with the average SSIM, Mean Squared Error (MSE), Mean Absolute Error (MAE), Peak Signal-to-Noise Ratio (PSNR), and Learned Perceptual Image Patch Similarity (LPIPS) [33].

3.3 Lymph Node Metastasis Classification

MLP Model Architecture. The classification MIL approach is visualised in Fig. 1. The MLP layers included 1D Batch Normalisation, dropout and GELU activation. The final layer of each MLP was a fully connected layer followed by a sigmoid activation. The model used VAE or CNN-derived features and selected clinical features in a simple MLP to make individual LN predictions. These predictions were combined with patient clinical data and input to a 4-layer MLP classification model for the final diagnosis. This model architecture was motivated by Xia et al. [31] who successfully applied this setup for the same task and our experiments found that deeper networks did not improve the performance.

Clinical Features. Patient clinical data included age, sex, and the primary tumour stage (T1-T4). Size features, the long and short-axis diameter and their ratio, were measured using the segmentation mask and the standard voxel size. Border irregularity features included convexity, which describes how smooth the border is using the perimeter of the convex hull of the LN segmentation divided by the actual perimeter; and compactness $= \frac{\text{perimeter}^2}{4 \cdot \pi \cdot \text{area}}$ which measures how close the LN is to a perfect circle. These clinical features were normalised to the range $[0, 1]$ using the min and max across the dataset. The size and border features were concatenated with the VAE or CNN feature representations before the first MLP. After making predictions for individual LNs, the patient clinical data and features for the largest short-axis LN were combined and input to the patient level classification model.

MLP Model Training. The final prediction is a weighted sum using $\eta \in [0.5, 0.75]$ to scale the patient MLP prediction and $(1 - \eta)$ to scale the maximum individual LN probability. The max is less impacted by noise and works best in cases where there is an obvious large malignant LN, whereas the patient MLP uses the clinical context and information from all detected LNs.

To help balance the dataset, between 5 and 30 synthetic patients were created by applying augmentations to the patches and oversampling positive patients in the training set. Other MLP hyperparameters included the learning rate, weight decay, batch size, dropout, and layer sizes in the MLP. These hyperparameters were optimised using a Bayesian search on WandB, aiming to improve the maximum test AUC. The optimal hyperparameter ranges were discovered through three Bayesian searches with 200 model runs, refining the space each time based on the highly selected parameters and the best results. The final search found that 93/200 models achieved over 0.8 test AUC.

To provide a robust evaluation of the proposed VAE-MLP, we report a five-fold nested cross-validation (CV) score. Due to the limited data, a nested CV was used to optimise the model hyperparameters independently for each fold. This evaluation reflects the overall approach rather than a fixed set of hyperparameters. For each fold, the VAE with the highest test SSIM was selected from 5 candidates, followed by the MLP with the highest test AUC out of 10 candidates. These candidates were identified from the large hyperparameter searches. Final metrics were averaged over the five folds and given with the standard deviation to indicate the consistency of the performance.

Ablation Study. The key model components were tested using a strategy of switching one off at a time. Comparison models were trained on a narrow hyperparameter search with optimised ranges for 50 runs, selecting the highest test AUC. Firstly, the VAE backbone was compared with a CNN feature extractor. The architecture was a DenseNet, pre-trained on the ImageNet dataset [5] and using the implementation in MONAI [4]. Additionally, the model was tested without clinical data, and the final prediction using only the max LN prediction or only the patient MLP.

3.4   Post-Hoc Explainability

Grad-CAM heatmaps were generated to show where the VAE model focuses when encoding the MRI patches. Gradients with respect to each pixel are averaged over 80 feature maps (8×8) from the last spatial layer, and thresholded to display the top 25%.

K-Means [19] clustering statistics are provided to justify that the latent space groups LNs based on information relevant to the diagnosis including size, shape and border irregularity. The number of clusters (k) was optimised to minimise the variability in lymph node size within the clusters. Additionally, clusters with less than 3 samples were excluded to provide more meaningful comparisons across clusters. Statistics calculated include the standard deviation and range of size and border irregularity metrics for LNs in the same cluster. They aim to describe how the MRI patches are clustered according to LN size and shape.

Lastly, we demonstrate that the latent space can simulate LN growth by applying the direction vector calculated between the average latent vectors of small LNs and large LNs.

3.5   Dataset Description

The study cohort included 168 RC patients who did not receive neo-adjuvant chemotherapy or radiotherapy treatment before a major resection surgery at Leeds Teaching Hospitals NHS Trust between 2010-2022. Ethical approval was given by the medical research ethics board of the author's institution, and Health Research Authority (HRA) approval was obtained from the UK NHS ethics board (319850). The pathology includes TNM staging for each patient where N0 represents no spread to the lymph nodes, N1 for 1-3 positive LNs, and N2 for 4 or more [9]. The dataset was divided into training and test sets with a 65/35 split. This test set was made larger than usual due to the imbalanced classes. The clinical and pathological summary of the study cohort is given in Table 1.

Table 1. Dataset Characteristics for Train and Test Cohorts

Characteristic	Train (n=109)	Test (n=59)
Age (Mean $\pm\sigma$)	69.7 ± 10.4	68.3 ± 13.0
Sex		
Male	80 (73.4)	34 (57.6)
Female	29 (26.1)	25 (42.4)
Number of Comorbidities	2.4 ± 1.2	2.2 ± 1.2
Tumour Pathology		
T1	19 (17.4)	11 (18.6)
T2	52 (47.7)	27 (45.8)
T3	32 (29.4)	15 (25.4)
T4	6 (5.5)	6 (10.2)
Node Pathology		
N0	84 (77.1)	46 (78.0)
N1	18 (16.5)	8 (13.6)
N2	7 (6.4)	5 (8.5)
Number of Nodes on MRI		
(N (Mean $\pm\sigma$))	625 (5.9 ± 3.8)	387 (5.9 ± 3.8)
Short-axis Diameter (mm)	5.6 ± 1.9	5.5 ± 1.9
Long-axis Diameter (mm)	7.7 ± 2.6	7.7 ± 2.6
Short / Long-axis Ratio	0.7 ± 0.1	0.7 ± 0.1

The last scan before the surgery was selected for each patient and scans more than 16 weeks before the surgery were excluded as the TNM stage may change in the time between the MRI scan and the pathology. Of the 195 patients identified, some cases were excluded as there were no LNs detected in the axial scan (n=18), and others did not have an axial scan available (n=9).

Lymph Node Annotations. MRI segmentations of the LNs were completed by a science postgraduate student using the open-source software 3D Slicer version 5.4 [7,25]. To ensure annotation quality, a consultant GI radiologist provided training and reviewed a subset of 34 (20.2%) MRI scans, focusing on challenging cases identified by the annotator and those frequently misclassified by the model. Following the review, the total number of LNs in the sample changed from 303 to 271 with 46 removed and 14 added, this corresponds to a 94.8% sensitivity in detecting LNs. Additionally, 17 scans (50%) remained unchanged.

The annotation process included detecting and segmenting LNs on the axial scan, followed by cross-referencing on the coronal and sagittal scans to update and finalise the segmentations. This task presented several challenges as LNs can be small and easily overlooked. Additionally, it can be difficult to distinguish LNs from other structures, most commonly blood vessels. However, blood vessels typically follow a trajectory through multiple slices, whereas LNs generally appear across 1-4 slices with a thickness of $3.3mm$. Other less common structures such as tumour deposits (TD), extramural vascular invasion (EMVI) and fibrotic tissue may also resemble LNs.

4   Results

4.1   VAE MRI Lymph Node Patch Reconstruction Results

Firstly, a sample of images and VAE reconstructions are qualitatively reviewed in Fig. 2. Observe that the key structures are captured very well although some of

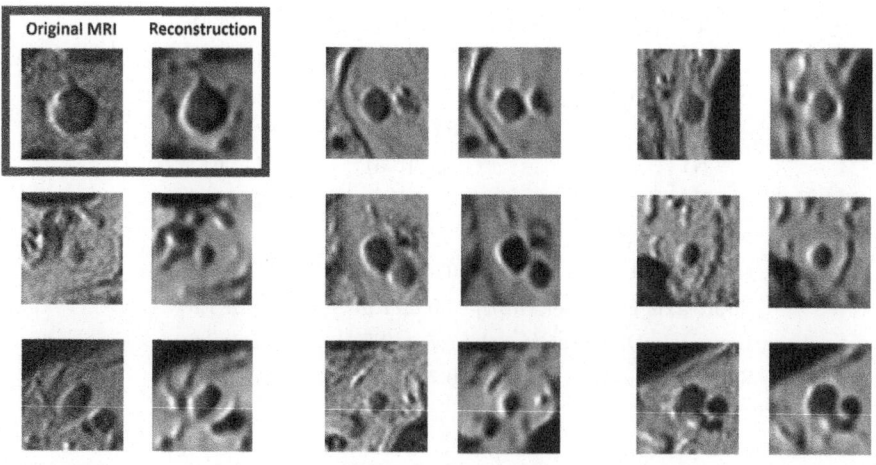

Fig. 2. MRI lymph node patches and VAE reconstructions

the smaller details are a little blurry. Clinical collaborators in oncology confirmed that the reconstructions captured important clinical features used in diagnosis, including size, shape and heterogeneous texture. The final VAE model image reconstruction metrics are given in Table 2.

Table 2. Image Reconstruction Metrics

Dataset	SSIM	PSNR	LPIPS	MSE	MAE
Train	0.796	26.971	0.0437	0.00203	0.0319
Test	0.789	26.596	0.0363	0.00235	0.0347

Optimal hyperparameters given here are averaged over the top 5 models based on SSIM, and rounded to the closest choice. Firstly, from the loss function (Eq. 1): $\alpha = 0.5$, $\lambda = 4000$, $\gamma = 3 \cdot$ batch size, and annealing $=$ True. Secondly, training hyperparameters: base $= 20$, latent size $= 20$, learning rate $= 6.73 \cdot 10^{-4}$, weight decay $= 0.035$, batch size $= 1024$, and accumulation steps $= 2$.

4.2 Classification Performance

Model performance metrics are provided in Table 3 for the best VAE-MLP model and the five-fold cross-validation score, the ablation study for the proposed model including a direct comparison to a CNN, and these results are compared with the metrics of four previous studies using external datasets. Model training graphs and the ROC curves are available in the supplementary materials and on GitHub.

The most clinically important metric is sensitivity, as it represents how many positive cases were identified. Patients with LNM are usually recommended to have neo-adjuvant therapy to downstage the LNs before surgery. In this context, a lower sensitivity would correspond to more LNM patients advancing straight to surgery, potentially increasing the risk of recurrence and distant metastasis.

The best model, VAE-MLP uses a test set as large as feasible, with 59 patients representing 35% of the 168 in total. The cross-validation (CV) average metrics are given with standard deviations, under VAE-MLP$_{\mathrm{CV}}$. Note that the 20% test set size had 7 or 8 positive cases, so each true positive impacted the sensitivity by at least 0.125. This setup constrains the representativeness and generalisability of individual fold models. The maximum fold performance had a sensitivity of 0.875 and specificity of 0.885, suggesting that some data splits contained easier cases. The cross-validation performance provides a robust measure of how the model performs on average. The performance metrics are still strong, indicating the approach is robust.

Comparisons to Prior Work. Table 3 displays four studies representing the current state-of-the-art. Firstly, to provide context to the results, [31] is the most direct comparison as they used MRI and individual LN annotations, whereas [28] and [18] both used primary tumour annotations including only the closest LNs.

Table 3. Classification performance metrics comparison. Showing the best VAE-MLP model and the cross-validation score (CV) in the first section, the ablation study results in the second, and comparisons with prior studies on external datasets in the third. Balanced Accuracy (BA), the average of sensitivity and specificity, is included to give an objective comparison metric across the different calibrations.

Model	AUC	Sensitivity	Specificity	Accuracy	F1	BA
VAE-MLP	**0.888**	**0.923**	**0.848**	**0.864**	**0.733**	**0.885**
VAE-MLP$_{CV}$	0.858 ± 0.051	0.789 ± 0.064	0.846 ± 0.054	0.833 ± 0.049	0.694	0.818
CNN-MLP	**0.893**	0.846	**0.891**	**0.881**		**0.869**
VAE-MLP$_{DL}$	0.770	0.692	0.848	0.814		0.770
VAE-MLP$_P$	0.847	**0.846**	0.848	0.848		0.847
VAE-MLP$_{LN}$	0.830	0.769	**0.891**	0.864		0.830
VAE-MLP$_{Max}$	0.771	**0.846**	0.696	0.729		0.771
VAE-MLP$_{MLP}$	**0.869**	**0.846**	**0.891**	**0.881**		**0.869**
Xia et al. [31]	0.810 ± 0.045	0.702 ± 0.072	0.800			0.751
Wan et al. [28]	0.790 ± 0.100	**1.000**	0.660 ± 0.110	0.730 ± 0.090		0.830
Liu et al. [18]	$\mathbf{0.942 \pm 0.055}$	0.955	**0.857**	**0.895**		**0.906**
Xie et al. [32]	0.768 ± 0.044	0.763 ± 0.056	0.734 ± 0.062	0.747 ± 0.012	0.727	0.749

Since the LNs are small in comparison to the tumour this approach is indirect, and it is unclear if the model focuses on the LNs. In our dataset, you could get 0.605 sensitivity and 0.723 specificity just from assuming T1-2 is N0 and T3-4 is N1. Additionally, [18] and [32] used a CT dataset instead of MRI and are less direct comparisons.

Firstly, Xia et al. [31] used a MIL framework with MRI annotations of individual LNs and a large CNN-MLP that incorporated LN size characteristics. They showed that senior radiologists could improve their AUC from 0.79 to 0.88 with model assistance. The model was deployed on an internal test cohort and two external validation cohorts, providing a good indication that the approach is generalisable. The best result from the internal test cohort is displayed in Table 3.

Wan et al. [28] used a large pre-trained 3D ResNet on primary tumour MRI patches and reported results on a test set of 86 patients with early stage T1-2 rectal cancer. They compared their results with three radiologists who had an average of 0.54 AUC.

Liu et al. [18] had the highest performance using a stacking nomogram which combined ResNet models and SVMs using radiomics features from the primary tumour on CT. However, the test set was relatively small (n=57), and the study inclusion criteria required more than 12 LNs examined pathologically, which likely translates to more visible LNs and cases that are less challenging to stage. Therefore while [18] reports the best metrics, the study may lack generalisability.

Lastly, Xie et al. [32] used an attention-based MIL approach with a CNN and a logistic regression classifier. The performance is the lowest of the comparisons, however, it has the most robust validation with a thorough ablation study and is the only pre-operative colorectal cancer LNM study using deep learning to employ cross-validation.

Optimal Hyperparameters. Classification model hyperparameters provided here are averaged over the top 10 performing models according to the maximum test AUC score and rounded to the closest choice: $\eta = 0.8$, number of synthetic patients = 25, oversample ratio for positive cases = 1.5, and the number of slices per patient = 20. Training and model hyperparameters were: threshold = 0.436, batch size = 128, learning rate = $6.59 \cdot 10^{-3}$, accumulation steps = 4, weight decay = 0.16, patch hidden dimension = 2048, patient hidden dim = 96, patch dropout = 0.4, and patient dropout = 0.3.

4.3   Ablation Study

Table 3 displays the ablation study results from testing key model components using a narrow hyperparameter search of 50 runs. Firstly, we provide a baseline comparison of the VAE with the standard approach of using a CNN feature extractor. The CNN-MLP model replaces the VAE encoder with a pre-trained DenseNet and the same classification head as the VAE-MLP model. The feature size was 1024, much larger than the final VAE latent size of 400. The results show that the CNN had lower performance metrics than the VAE.

The ablation of the VAE-MLP checks that key components are improving the overall performance. First, the model with just deep learning features (VAE-MLP$_{DL}$) had the worst performance, justifying the use of clinical data. Then two models using just the T stage and age/sex (VAE-MLP$_P$), and just the LN size and border metrics (VAE-MLP$_{LN}$). The patient level data appears to be more important in terms of AUC, and the use of both sets of clinical features had the best performance. Lastly, we tested the MIL methods of aggregation, one model used only the max LN prediction (VAE-MLP$_{Max}$) and another with only the patient MLP (VAE-MLP$_{MLP}$). Overall, the patient MLP had the best performance, however a combination including both the patient MLP and the max value was used in the proposed VAE-MLP as the max is less impacted by noise and imbalanced data.

4.4   Error Analysis and Uncertainty

Predictions were accumulated from 500 model states saved across the hyperparameter runs when the performance for one epoch was above 0.8 test AUC. Note that this included multiple predictions from the same run, whenever the threshold was met. An error graph displaying these results is available in the supplementary materials and on GitHub. It shows that 11 patients in the test set were misclassified in over half of the saved results, clearly indicating they are the most difficult cases. Upon inspection of the specific examples, the senior radiologist confirmed they were difficult to stage, and identified small or medium suspicious LNs with an irregular border and/or heterogeneous texture. We found that the frequent false positive (FP) cases all had a large LN with a short-axis diameter between 7-10mm. Frequent false negative (FN) cases had 5.6 LNs on average, much less than 9.2 on average for all positive cases. The largest short-axis diameter LN per patient was 39% higher on average for the frequent FPs than for the frequent FN cases.

To provide a measure of uncertainty, average prediction confidence was accumulated across the 500 model states. In the test set, there was a minimum average prediction of 0.15 and a maximum of 0.78. If we define a prediction in the range 0.33 to 0.66 as uncertain, then 19 patients (32.2% of the test set) had an uncertain diagnosis. Of the common FNs, the average confidence was 0.23 and the FPs had an average of 0.50 further indicating the uncertainty. In clinical applications, we would recommend an expert review of these cases.

4.5   Interpretability and Clustering

Grad-CAM examples in Fig. 3 show that the VAE encoder is focusing on the LNs and important visual features when encoding the MRI patches.

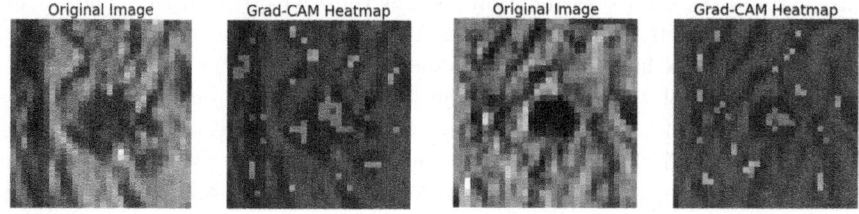

Fig. 3. Grad-CAM heatmaps showing gradients from the last spatial layer of the encoder before flattening.

Clustering statistics are shown in Table 4, demonstrating that the feature representations of individual LNs are separated by clinically important criteria including the LN size features and the average of the border irregularity (BI) metrics. The optimal number of clusters was around 35, and the global standard deviations (σ) and ranges for the features across all LNs are provided as a baseline for comparison. These results aim to describe the average variability within clusters. The standard deviation and ranges indicate that variability within the clusters is lower than the global variability, suggesting that patches are grouped based on similar LN size and shape.

Lastly, Fig. 4 shows two examples that apply the average direction gradient between small and large LNs in the latent space. There is a smooth evolution of LN growth whilst the background is fixed, demonstrating that the latent space has generalised and disentangled lymph node growth as an independent factor.

Table 4. Clustering Statistics for short and long axis diameter given in (mm), the ratio short to long, and the average of compactness and convexity for border irregularity metrics in the range $[0, 1]$. The statistics given aim to describe the inter-cluster variations using the standard deviation (σ_{IC}) and range (Range$_{IC}$).

Statistic	Short-axis	Long-axis	Ratio	BI
Global σ	2.13	2.79	0.12	0.13
Mean σ_{IC}	1.815	2.522	0.119	0.118
Min σ_{IC}	0.696	1.282	0.068	0.058
Max σ_{IC}	3.222	4.206	0.334	0.190
Global Range	13.167	16.145	0.811	1
Mean Range$_{IC}$	7.290	9.616	0.431	0.346
Min Range$_{IC}$	1.717	3.022	0.169	0.093
Max Range$_{IC}$	12.721	15.929	0.811	0.678

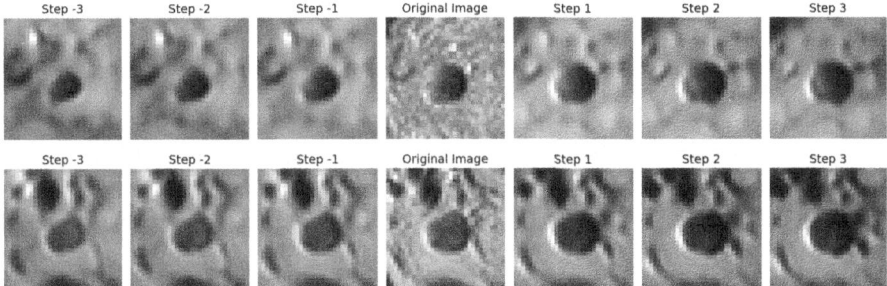

Fig. 4. Lymph node growth direction, with the original image in the centre and reconstructed images after applying multiples of the direction vector on either side.

5   Discussion

Some key methodological considerations are covered here to inform future work. Firstly, extending the analysis to 3D would provide more information about the geometric shape of the lymph nodes and more context with the surroundings. Secondly, multi-class LN classification may be beneficial in future work as it can indicate the need for different levels of neo-adjuvant treatment, although an accurate binary diagnosis is the most important result. Third, we note that it is not feasible to match LNs detected on MRI with the pathologic status of individual LNs in retrospective studies due to the difficulty of matching them post-surgery. Only two previous studies have done this, with an obvious selection bias as they only matched the pathology of the largest detected LNs [17, 20]. Fourth, all LNs identified in the axial scans were included, although the mesorectal LNs have a higher probability of metastasis. This presents a partial limitation as including more normal LNs introduces more noise into the classification model. Future work might improve on this by identifying an approximate location of the primary tumour and measuring the distance, then a classifier could weight the contribution of LNs based on proximity to the tumour. Lastly, the annotations were completed by a non-specialist, potentially leading to some LNs being omitted and other non-LN structures being included. However, 20% of the annotations were validated by a consultant GI radiologist who confirmed the annotations were of sufficient quality. Also, the N stage pathology is used to evaluate the predictions and so a high classification performance indicates that the annotations are accurate. The use of lower quality annotations in this task may be beneficial for future work to reduce the study development costs of using large datasets. To enhance model explainability, future work may look at using the VAE latent space to provide prototype-based or counterfactual explanations.

6   Conclusion

In conclusion, this paper provides a pilot study for the radiological staging of rectal cancer lymph node metastasis on MRI using VAEs. We have observed that the latent space is well structured for the classification task and encodes clinically meaningful characteristics. The best result of 0.89 AUC, 92.3% sensitivity and 84.8% specificity has exceeded the performance of the most robust studies in the literature, and the average radiologist performance of 73% sensitivity and 74% specificity [34]. The cross-validation, ablation study, error analysis and interpretability methods further validate the model approach and performance. This study covers 12 years of clinical practice where 38 patients had lymph node metastasis but were not referred for neo-adjuvant treatment which may have benefited them, our model could have identified up to 92.3% of these cases.

Acknowledgments. Benjamin Keel is supported by the EPSRC Centre for Doctoral Training in Artificial Intelligence for Medical Diagnosis and Care (EP/S024336/1).

References

1. NHS Digital cancer survival in england, cancers diagnosed 2016 to 2020 (2023). https://digital.nhs.uk/data-and-information/publications/statistical/cancer-survival-in-england/cancers-diagnosed-2016-to-2020-followed-up-to-2021/
2. Biewald, L.: Experiment tracking with weights and biases (2020). https://www.wandb.com/
3. Borgheresi, A., De Muzio, F., Agostini, A., Ottaviani, L., Bruno, A., et al.: Lymph nodes evaluation in rectal cancer: where do we stand and future perspective. J. Clin. Med. **11**(9), 1–26 (2022). https://doi.org/10.3390/jcm11092599
4. Cardoso, M.J., Li, W., Brown, R., Ma, N., Kerfoot, E., et al.: Monai: an open-source framework for deep learning in healthcare (2022). https://arxiv.org/abs/2211.02701
5. Deng, J., Dong, W., Socher, R., Li, L.J., Li, K., Fei-Fei, L.: Imagenet: a large-scale hierarchical image database. In: 2009 IEEE Conference on Computer Vision and Pattern Recognition. pp. 248–255 (2009). https://doi.org/10.1109/CVPR.2009.5206848

6. Dhuliawala, S., Sachan, M., Allen, C.: Variational classification pp. 1–17 (2023). http://arxiv.org/abs/2305.10406

7. Fedorov, A., Beichel, R., Kalpathy-Cramer, J., Finet, J., Fillion-Robin, J.C., et al.: 3d slicer as an image computing platform for the quantitative imaging network. Magnetic Res. Imaging **30**(9), 1323–1341 (2012). https://www.ncbi.nlm.nih.gov/pmc/articles/PMC3466397/pdf/nihms383480.pdf

8. Hendrycks, D., Gimpel, K.: Gaussian error linear units (gelus) (2016). https://doi.org/10.48550/ARXIV.1606.08415

9. Horvat, N., Carlos Tavares Rocha, C., Clemente Oliveira, B., Petkovska, I., Gollub, M.J.: Mri of rectal cancer: tumor staging, imaging techniques, and management. RadioGraphics **39**(2), 367–387 (2019). https://doi.org/10.1148/rg.2019180114

10. Hsu, T.C., Lin, C.: Learning from small medical data—-robust semi-supervised cancer prognosis classifier with bayesian variational autoencoder. Bioinform. Adv. **3**(1), vbac100 (2023). https://doi.org/10.1093/bioadv/vbac100

11. Ioffe, S., Szegedy, C.: Batch normalization: accelerating deep network training by reducing internal covariate shift. CoRR (2015). http://arxiv.org/abs/1502.03167

12. Kaur, G., Keshta, I., Shabaz, M., Batra, H.S., Vijaya Sagar, T., et al.: Rectal cancer prediction and performance based on intelligent variational autoencoders machine using deep learning on CDAS dataset. J. Artif. Intell. Technol. **3**(4), 195–204 (2023). https://doi.org/10.37965/jait.2023.0241

13. Keel, B., Quyn, A., Jayne, D., Relton, S.D.: Variational autoencoders for feature exploration and malignancy prediction of lung lesions. In: British Machine Vision Conference (BMVC) (2023). https://doi.org/10.48550/arXiv.2311.15719

14. Keel, B., Quyn, A., Jayne, D., Relton, S.D.: State-of-the-art performance of deep learning methods for pre-operative radiologic staging of colorectal cancer lymph node metastasis: a scoping review. BMJ Open **14**(12) (2024). https://doi.org/10.1136/bmjopen-2024-086896

15. Kingma, D.P., Welling, M.: Auto-encoding variational bayes. arXiv (2013). https://doi.org/10.48550/ARXIV.1312.6114

16. Kullback, S., Leibler, R.A.: On information and sufficiency. Annals Mathe. Statist. **22**(1), 79–86 (1951). http://www.jstor.org/stable/2236703

17. Li, J., Zhou, Y., Wang, P., Zhao, H., Wang, X., et al.: Deep transfer learning based on magnetic resonance imaging can improve the diagnosis of lymph node metastasis in patients with rectal cancer. Quant. Imaging Med. Surgery **11**(6), 2477–2485 (2021). https://doi.org/10.21037/qims-20-525

18. Liu, J., Sun, L., Lu, X., Geng, Y., Zhang, Z.: Development and validation of a stacking nomogram for predicting regional lymph node metastasis status in rectal cancer via deep learning and hand-crafted radiomics. Int. J. Radiation Res. **21**(2) (2023). http://ijrr.com/article-1-4723-en.html

19. MacQueen, J.: Some methods for classification and analysis of multivariate observations (1967)

20. Ozaki, K., Kurose, Y., Kawai, K., Kobayashi, H., Itabashi, M., et al.: Development of a diagnostic artificial intelligence tool for lateral lymph node metastasis in advanced rectal cancer. Dis. Colon. Rectum. **66**(12), E1246–E1253 (2023). https://doi.org/10.1097/DCR.0000000000002719

21. Pérez-García, F., Sparks, R., Ourselin, S.: TorchIO: a python library for efficient loading, preprocessing, augmentation and patch-based sampling of medical images in deep learning. Comput. Methods Programs Biomed. 106236 (2021). https://doi.org/10.1016/j.cmpb.2021.106236

22. Rais, K., Amroune, M., Benmachiche, A., Haouam, M.Y.: Exploring variational autoencoders for medical image generation: a comprehensive study (2024). https://arxiv.org/abs/2411.07348

23. Redekop, E., Pleasure, M., Wang, Z., Sarma, K.V., Kinnaird, A., et al.: Codebook vq-vae approach for prostate cancer diagnosis using multiparametric mri. In: Proceedings of the IEEE/CVF Conference on Computer Vision and Pattern Recognition (CVPR) Workshops. pp. 2365–2372 (2024)

24. Selvaraju, R.R., Cogswell, M., Das, A., Vedantam, R., Parikh, D., Batra, D.: Grad-CAM: visual explanations from deep networks via gradient-based localization. Int. J. Comput. Vision **128**(2), 336–359 (2019). https://doi.org/10.1007/s11263-019-01228-7

25. Slicer, D.: 3d slicer: an open source software platform for medical image computing and research. https://www.slicer.org/ (2024) Accessed 24 Oct 2024

26. Sreelekshmi, V., Pavithran, K., Nair, J.J.: Unleashing the power of hierarchical variational autoencoder for predicting breast cancer. IEEE Access **12**, 195658–195670 (2024). https://doi.org/10.1109/ACCESS.2024.3518612

27. Valentini, V., van Stiphout, R.G., Lammering, G., Gambacorta, M.A., Barba, M.C., et al.: Nomograms for predicting local recurrence, distant metastases, and overall survival for patients with locally advanced rectal cancer on the basis of european randomized clinical trials. J. Clin. Oncol. **29**(23), 3163–3172 (2011). https://doi.org/10.1200/JCO.2010.33.1595, https://ascopubs.org/doi/abs/10.1200/JCO.2010.33.1595

28. Wan, L., Hu, J., Chen, S., Zhao, R., Peng, W., et al.: Prediction of lymph node metastasis in stage T1–2 rectal cancers with MRI-based deep learning. Eur. Radiol. pp. 3638–3646 (2023). https://doi.org/10.1007/s00330-023-09450-1

29. Wang, J., Li, J., Wang, R., Zhou, X.: Vae-driven multimodal fusion for early cardiac disease detection. IEEE Access **12**, 90535–90551 (2024). https://doi.org/10.1109/ACCESS.2024.3420444

30. Wang, Z., Bovik, A.C., Sheikh, H., Simoncelli, E.: Image quality assessment: from error visibility to structural similarity. IEEE Trans. Image Process. **13**(4), 600–612 (2004). https://doi.org/10.1109/TIP.2003.819861

31. Xia, W., Li, D., He, W., Pickhardt, P.J., Jian, J., et al.: Multicenter evaluation of a weakly supervised deep learning model for lymph node diagnosis in rectal cancer at MRI. Radiol. Artif. Intell. **6**(2) (2024). https://doi.org/10.1148/ryai.230152

32. Xie, M., Zhang, Y., Li, X., Mao, Y., Zou, X., Zhang, H.: Predicting lymph node metastasis of colorectal cancer in CT scans using attention-based multiple instance learning. In: 2023 IEEE International Conference on Bioinformatics and Biomedicine (BIBM) pp. 2695–2701 (2023).https://doi.org/10.1109/BIBM58861.2023.10385936

33. Zhang, R., Isola, P., Efros, A.A., Shechtman, E., Wang, O.: The unreasonable effectiveness of deep features as a perceptual metric. In: 2018 IEEE/CVF Conference on Computer Vision and Pattern Recognition. pp. 586–595 (2018).https://doi.org/10.1109/CVPR.2018.00068

34. Zhuang, Z., Zhang, Y., Wei, M., Yang, X., Wang, Z.: Magnetic resonance imaging evaluation of the accuracy of various lymph node staging criteria in rectal cancer: a systematic review and meta-analysis. Front. Oncol. **11** (2021). https://doi.org/10.3389/fonc.2021.709070

Self-guided SwinTransformer Improves Breast Cancer Detection Through Iterative Attention-Based Zooming

Fredrik A. Dahl[1]([envelope]) [ORCID] and Solveig Hofvind[2] [ORCID]

[1] The Norwegian Computing Center (NR), Oslo, Norway
fadahl@nr.no
[2] The Norwegian Cancer Registry, Norwegian Institute of Public Health,
Oslo, Norway

Abstract. We present a SwinTransformer-based model for breast cancer detection in full-field digital mammograms (FFDM) that iteratively zooms in on the most suspicious region of each image using Grad-CAM attention. Unlike our previous two-stage convolutional model–which used separate networks for coarse localization and fine-grained classification–our new approach trains a single model to evaluate crops at multiple resolutions through a sequence of focused attention steps. The model was trained on a large dataset of Siemens mammograms with confirmed diagnosis as the only learning signal. The model was evaluated on test sets from multiple vendors, including Siemens, Philips, Hologic/Lorad, and GE. On Siemens images, our model achieved an AUC of 0.978 for screen-detected cancers, improving by 1.3% points over the previous ResNet-based model–a substantial gain given the high performance baseline. The SwinTransformer also generalized markedly better to non-Siemens vendors, particularly GE with a huge improvement from 76.7% to 92.3% on screen-detected cancers. A ResNet trained using the same zooming algorithm failed to achieve similar gains, suggesting that transformer architectures are better suited for handling both spatial resolution changes and domain shifts. Our findings demonstrate that attention-guided zooming combined with transformer backbones offers a scalable and generalizable approach.

Keywords: breast cancer detection · SwinTransformer · Grad-CAM · screening · domain generalization

1 Introduction

Breast cancer is the most common cancer among women worldwide, and early detection through screening is crucial to reduce mortality. Mammography is the primary imaging modality used in screening programs, and several countries have established national initiatives to systematically screen women within specific age groups. In Norway, BreastScreen Norway invites approximately 250,000

S. Ali et al. (Eds.): MIUA 2025, LNCS 15917, pp. 31–42, 2026.
https://doi.org/10.1007/978-3-031-98691-8_3

women each year to biennial mammography screening [9]. The standard work-flow involves two radiologists independently reviewing each mammogram and assigning suspicion scores for malignancy. Discrepancies or high suspicion scores trigger a consensus meeting to determine whether additional diagnostic workup is needed [7].

Despite its effectiveness, mammography screening is resource-intensive and subject to human variability. Deep neural networks (DNNs) have shown consid-erable promise in assisting radiologists, with recent studies indicating that AI systems can match or even exceed human performance in cancer detection [13] [10]. Commercial AI tools are already being used in clinical practice, primar-ily based on convolutional neural network (CNN) architectures trained on large datasets.

However, convolutional models may have inherent limitations in handling domain shifts across imaging vendors and varying spatial resolutions in mammo-grams. Transformer-based models, which have demonstrated impressive results in general computer vision tasks, offer a potentially more flexible alterna-tive. Among transformer architectures, SwinTransformers [8] have demonstrated strong performance and improved generalization ability across various imaging domains, owing to their hierarchical design and local attention mechanisms. These properties make them particularly well-suited for handling diverse input distributions, which is critical in breast cancer screening applications where imaging protocols and vendors vary.

2   Related Work

Most deep learning models for breast cancer detection in full-field digital mam-mography (FFDM) have historically used CNN architectures, such as ResNet, trained to classify entire images or image patches [2]. Building on the success of Vision Transformer (ViT) models in computer vision [5], recent studies have introduced transformer-based approaches for mammography.

Garrucho et al. [6] conducted a large-scale, multi-center study on domain gen-eralization in CNN- and transformer-based models for mass detection in FFDM. They evaluated models trained in a single domain across five unseen domains and found that Transformer-based architectures exhibited stronger robustness to vendor shifts than CNNs. Also, Chen et al. [3] demonstrated that a ViT model combining all four mammographic views outperformed a state-of-the-art CNN-based system.

Manigrasso et al. [11] proposed a multi-view SwinTransformer architecture, incorporating cross-view attention to transfer information between views. Their model achieved higher detection accuracy than CNN counterparts and exhibited broader, clinically relevant attention patterns. Wang et al. [15] developed an explainable transformer-based segmentation model based on a Swin-Unet design, using Grad-CAM [14] visualizations to confirm that attention maps corresponded to tumor regions.

While these studies highlight the potential of transformer architectures, they primarily focus on multi-view processing or end-to-end segmentation. To our knowledge, no previous studies have proposed an iterative, attention-guided zooming strategy within a transformer-based model for mammography classification.

3   Materials and Methods

3.1   Model Design Rationale

In our previous work [4], we introduced a two-stage convolutional model for breast cancer detection in FFDM images. The first stage evaluated a down-sampled version of the mammogram to identify a region of interest (ROI) using Grad-CAM attention. The second stage classified a high-resolution crop centered on the most suspicious region. This approach achieved strong detection performance on Siemens mammograms and performed on par with commercial AI tools [12] on that domain. However, the two-stage design had notable limitations. It required training two separate CNN models and showed reduced robustness when applied to images from other vendors. Moreover, the model's reliance on static ROI extraction prevented end-to-end optimization of the detection process.

In the present study, we propose a unified model architecture based on Swin-Transformer [8], combined with an iterative attention-guided zooming strategy. Rather than separating localization and classification, our model jointly performs both tasks by evaluating progressively smaller crops centered on the most suspicious regions identified by Grad-CAM [14] heatmaps. This approach allows the model to focus its attention dynamically while retaining the global context of the full image. We selected the SwinTransformer architecture based on its demonstrated generalization ability across domains in computer vision tasks. Its hierarchical structure and shifted window attention mechanism introduce geometric bias and improve the model's ability to capture both local and global context. In addition, we hypothesized that the SwinTransformer would be particularly well-suited for our attention-guided zooming strategy. The model is trained on inputs ranging from heavily downsampled, full-field mammograms to smaller, high-resolution crops focused on specific regions of interest. We anticipated that this architectural flexibility would allow the model to learn effectively across different zoom levels, thereby improving detection performance and robustness to image resolution changes.

We designed our experiments to enable direct comparison with our previously published two-stage model. To this end, we used the same dataset and general evaluation framework, with only minor updates to the underlying database. A brief overview of the data is provided below.

3.2   Data Overview

Table 1 summarizes the training and test data used in this study, in terms of the number of examinations.

The training dataset was nearly identical to that in our previous study [4], with only minor updates to the underlying database since then, resulting in an

Table 1. Overview of training and test data by vendor and cancer status.

Vendor	Role	Screen- detected	Interval cancers	Negatives
Siemens	Training	3,338	987	555,711
Siemens	Test	1,119	375	214,940
Philips	Test	795	266	133,400
Hologic/Lorad	Test	2,064	601	321,749
GE	Test	500	150	76,683

increase of one screen-detected cancer case and 156 negative cases. This minor change is not expected to substantially affect comparability. For testing, we included all available Siemens exams, along with exams from three additional hospitals using equipment from Philips, Hologic/Lorad, and GE. Compared to the dataset used in the previous evaluation, the Siemens test set is larger due to newly available exams and the removal of earlier technical constraints related to a commercial comparator.

Across all vendors, exams consist primarily of four views: craniocaudal (CC) and mediolateral oblique (MLO) for each breast. The average number of images per exam is slightly above four, due to occasional retakes or additional views. Image sizes range from 2000×2800 to 4915×5355 pixels.

3.3 SwinTransformer Model

Transformer models are generally flexible, as they can model long-range dependencies by associating distant pixels in contrast to CNN-based architectures, which build features hierarchically from local neighborhoods. However, transformers therefore require large-scale training to perform well, and benefit even more from extensive pretraining than CNNs [5].

It is beyond the scope of this article to explain the inner workings of the chosen model, but the general structure is one where small bits of the image are treated like "tokens", much like words (or word-parts) in language models. The transformer part of the model works in the way that each token can modify (transform) the meaning of the others, depending on their relative positioning. The Swin (shifted window) architecture introduces a constraint by limiting attention to a local window, which improves computational efficiency while retaining the transformer's core strengths.

We have used a so-called version 2 SwinTransformer model, with the lengthy identifier `"swinv2_large_window12to24_192to384_22kft1k"` in the Timm repository. The number 384 in the id signals that 384×384 is the maximum image size in pixels that the model accepts, and this was used in our project. We modified the pre-trained model by changing the number of input channels from 3 (RGB) to 1 (grayscale) and changing the number of output classes from 1000 to 2 (negative/positive). For the rest of the model, we kept the structure intact and used the pre-trained weights as the starting point for our training. The output of this is a rectangular grid of feature vectors that represent the content of the corresponding parts of the image. For the present model with the 384×384 input grid, this feature grid has the size 12 x 12, and our (modified) classification layer maps these feature vectors to the final two-class output layer. A strong point of the chosen model was that it had been pre-trained on ImageNet with very good performance [1].

3.4 Algorithm

Our algorithm was designed to zoom in on the part of the image that the model evaluates as the most likely to contain a cancer. It starts by defining the full image as our initial region of interest (ROI), zero-padded to a square shape. It then runs a sequence of iterations where it moves the ROI and reduces its size:

Algorithm 1. ZOOM Iterative Focused Zoom Using Grad-CAM

---

procedure ZOOM(Image, n, m)
    Image ← SQUAREPAD(Image)
    size ← WIDTH(Image)
    c ← (size/2, size/2)   ▷ Center of the image
    ROI ← SQUARE(Image, c, size)
    f ← $m^{1/n}$ ▷ Per-step zoom factor
    Initialize $\mathcal{R}$ ← [], $\mathcal{O}$ ← []
    for $i = 0$ to n **do**
        $\mathcal{R}$.append(ROI)
        o ← MODEL(ROI)
        $\mathcal{O}$.append(o)
        heatmap ← GRADCAM(MODEL)
        c ← CENTROID(heatmap)
        size ← size/f
        if i ¡ n **then**
            ROI ← SQUARE(Image, c, size)
        end if
    end for
    return ($\mathcal{R}$, $\mathcal{O}$)
end procedure

The hyper-parameter n gives the number of zoom iterations and m gives the ROI reduction factor for the final ROI.

In the Zoom procedure, Square(Image, c, size) extracts a square crop of the image centered at c with the given size, padded with 0's when needed, and down-samples it to 384×384. The function GradCam(model) computes a Grad-CAM heatmap indicating which regions of the input were most important for the model's prediction. The Centroid computation includes several custom steps. First, we generate a raw heatmap by calculating the difference between the aggregate positive and negative feature contributions within each of the 12×12

Grad-CAM grid cells. To ensure non-negativity, we subtract the minimum value from the heatmap. This adjustment is important in cases where the model produces no strong cancer signal, allowing the algorithm to identify the least unlikely cancer location. Next, we multiply the heatmap element-wise with a downsampled version of the ROI image to mask out responses located outside the breast region. We then raise all values to the power of 4 to amplify stronger signals. Finally, we compute the centroid as the center of mass of the enhanced heatmap. The algorithm gives as output the list of the $n + 1$ ROIs and the corresponding model outputs.

3.5   Model Training

To train an ensemble of five diverse models, we partitioned the dataset into five folds, stratified by screen-detected cancers, interval cancers, and breast center. All examinations from the same woman were assigned to the same fold. Each model was trained on four folds and validated on the remaining fold, rotating the held-out fold across models.

The validation fold was used for early stopping, selecting the model checkpoint with the lowest validation loss. Importantly, this fold was not used to estimate model performance, and the test sets remained completely held out during training and model selection.

Each training image generated $n + 1$ region-of-interest (ROI) crops using the zoom algorithm described above. These crops were treated as independent training examples, with the image-level cancer label applied to each. No image preprocessing was applied beyond rescaling pixel values to the $[0, 1]$ range. Data augmentation included random rotations around the ROI center.

The model was trained using standard binary cross-entropy loss, with a batch size of 6, using stochastic gradient descent with momentum 0.9. A cyclic learning rate was used, varying within the range $[2 \times 10^{-6}, 6 \times 10^{-5}]$. Because we used alternating sampling of positive and negative images, an epoch was not defined as a full pass through the dataset. Instead, one epoch was defined as 50,000 sampled training images. Each image produced $n + 1$ region-of-interest (ROI) crops using the zooming procedure, which were treated as individual training examples. Each model was trained for up to 20 such epochs. Early stopping was based on validation loss, with most selected checkpoints occurring between epochs 10 and 15.

Although the zooming algorithm produces a sequence of ROIs, the model is not trained end-to-end across this process. Each ROIlabel pair is treated as a standalone training pattern, and gradients do not propagate through the zooming iterations. This design simplifies training and avoids the need for differentiable zooming or credit assignment across zoom steps.

To assess the effect of the model architecture independently of the zooming strategy, we also trained a ResNet-101 model using the same zoom-based cropping procedure. The training setup, including zoom parameters ($n = 4$, $m = 5$), and data augmentation strategy, was identical to that of the SwinTransformer model. We used a crop size of 512×512 pixels, which was used in the second

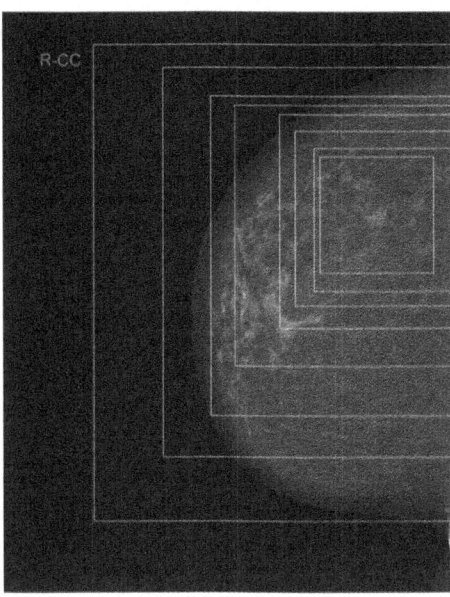

Fig. 1. Example of iterative zooming process with Grad-CAM attention centers.

stage of the previous model. Grad-CAM was used to generate attention maps at the final convolutional layer, which produced a 16×16 heatmap per ROI. The same centroid and cropping logic was applied. Unlike the SwinTransformer setup, this ResNet-based model was trained as a single model without ensembling, and used the same learning schedule and loss function as described above. This variant allows us to isolate the contribution of the SwinTransformer architecture to the observed performance improvements.

3.6   Model Inference and Evaluation

For evaluation, we used an ensemble of the five models trained on different validation folds. The zooming algorithm was applied with $n = 8$ iterations (compared to $n = 4$ during training), producing $n + 1 = 9$ outputs per image, per model.

Figure 1 visualizes the iterative zooming process during evaluation ($n = 8$). The white boxes indicate the sequence of square crops extracted at each zoom level, and the last one is yellow. Crops are centered based on Grad-CAM attention maps from the preceding step.

For each image, we averaged the last $k = 3$ outputs from each model (i.e., zoom levels 68), and then averaged these scores across the five models to produce a single per-image risk score. All averaging was performed on raw model outputs (logits), without applying a sigmoid or softmax transformation.

For examination-level prediction, we grouped images by breast. Each breast typically had two views (CC and MLO), though some exams had more or fewer images. A per-breast score was computed by averaging the model outputs for all images of that breast. The final examination-level risk score was defined as the maximum of the left and right breast-level scores.

Model performance was evaluated using the area under the receiver operating characteristic curve (AUC), which is commonly used for mammography classification models. Most other performance metrics, like sensitivity, specificity or F1-score have the undesirable properties that they depend on the choice of a decision threshold and the degree of imbalance in the test set. AUC measures the probability that the model scores a random positive example higher than a random negative one, and therefore gives a generic measure of the model's ability to separate the two classes. This also implies that the AUC is unaffected by positive monotone transformations, so it makes no difference if we transform the scores into probabilities through a sigmoid transformation. We report AUC for two outcome definitions: (i) screen-detected cancers versus negative examinations, and (ii) all cancers (including both screen-detected and interval cancers) versus negatives. Labels were assigned at the examination level, and predictions were based on the aggregated examination-level risk scores. Due to the large number of negative cases in the test datasets, we computed AUC performances using a random sample of negative examinations, sampled at a ratio of 5 negatives per screen-detected cancer. This sampling approach provides unbiased AUC estimates with confidence intervals only marginally wider compared to using the full negative sets, while substantially reducing computational effort. The same random subsets were consistently used across all evaluated models to ensure comparability. The sampling strategy substantially reduced the computational load of the evaluation. For reference, evaluating a batch of 40 images using the SwinTransformer ensemble required approximately 20 s on an NVIDIA RTX 4000 SFF Ada GPU, which means approximately 2 sec per 4-image examination. Evaluating the full test sets without sampling would therefore require considerably more time and computational resources, without materially affecting the reported AUC estimates.

This evaluation protocol was used consistently across all test datasets. All hyperparameters, including the number of zoom iterations during evaluation ($n = 8$), the number of outputs averaged ($k = 3$), and the ensemble aggregation method, were selected based on performance on the training folds and fixed prior to test evaluation.

4   Results

Table 2 shows the AUC performance for the previous two-stage model and the new SwinTransformer-based model across our collection of test datasets.

The SwinTransformer-based model consistently outperformed the ResNet-based one. The ResNet model that was trained with zooming performed worse than both the SwinTransformer model and the original two-stage ResNet pipeline (not included in the table). As an aside, we also tested the SwinTransformer model on the Siemens test set without zooming, so that it only evaluates the

Table 2. AUC performance across vendors and cancer definitions (with 95% confidence intervals).

Vendor	Cancer types	ResNet Two-stage	SwinTransformer Zoom
Siemens	Screening	96.5 (95.7–97.3)	97.8 (97.2–98.5)
	All Cancers	91.2 (90.1–92.2)	92.9 (91.9–93.8)
Philips	Screening	91.6 (90.2–93.0)	94.7 (93.6–95.8)
	All Cancers	86.4 (84.9–87.9)	88.5 (87.2–89.9)
Hologic / Lorad	Screening	93.2 (92.4–93.9)	96.4 (95.8–97.0)
	All Cancers	86.7 (85.8–87.6)	91.2 (90.4–92.0)
GE	Screening	76.7 (74.1–79.3)	92.3 (90.6–93.9)
	All Cancers	73.5 (71.1–75.9)	87.0 (85.2–88.9)

full image padded and down-sampled to 384×384, which gave an AUC of 90.5 (89.2–91.8).

5   Discussion

The results demonstrate that our zoom-based SwinTransformer model substantially outperforms our previous two-stage ResNet pipeline in all cases. While the ResNet-based system was previously shown to perform on par with commercial AI tools for mammography screening on Siemens mammograms, the SwinTransformer yielded an absolute AUC gain of around a full percentage points. This gain is particularly meaningful given the high baseline performance, where improvements are typically difficult to achieve.

Prior to the experiments, we were concerned that the input resolution of 384×384 pixels might be too low to capture subtle cancer signals, especially in early-stage lesions. Surprisingly, even the SwinTransformer's evaluation of the full mammogram, downsampled and padded to 384×384–produced an AUC of 90.5%. Furthermore, even at the maximum zoom level ($m = 5$), the model did not evaluate image regions at full native resolution. The smallest square-padded images in our dataset had dimensions of 2800×2800 pixels, meaning that the smallest ROI corresponded to 560×560 native pixels–still larger than the model's input size of 384×384 after downsampling. This illustrates that the model's input resolution remained lower than the native resolution of the cropped regions, even at the highest zoom level. Nonetheless, the model achieved high detection performance, suggesting that, contrary to common assumptions in the field, full native resolution may not be essential when combined with an effective zooming and attention strategy.

While our results suggest that full native resolution is not essential for strong performance, we also explored the effect of increasing the zoom factor beyond $m = 5$ to approach full resolution in the final ROI. These experiments consistently resulted in weaker performance. A likely explanation is that, although higher resolution may provide more detail, excessive zooming reduces the ROI area to the point where it may no longer capture the relevant cancer signal, particularly for larger or more diffuse lesions. This observation highlights the trade-off between spatial resolution and contextual information, and suggests that effective zooming strategies must balance resolution with sufficient anatomical coverage. Future experiments with models that accept larger input sizes than 384×384 pixels may shed further light on this issue and help disentangle the respective roles of resolution and anatomical context in model performance.

The generalization performance of the SwinTransformer model on non-Siemens examinations was especially noteworthy. While the two-stage ResNet model exhibited a marked drop in performance on these datasets, particularly on GE images, the SwinTransformer-based model maintained high AUC across all vendors. This highlights its robustness to domain shift, which is critical for real-world deployment across diverse clinical settings.

To disentangle the effect of the zooming strategy from the architectural change, we trained a ResNet model using the same zooming procedure. This ResNet+Zoom model failed to improve over the original two-stage ResNet pipeline, and its performance on non-Siemens images remained weak. These results indicate that convolutional architectures such as ResNet struggle to generalize not only across imaging vendors but also across spatial scales. In contrast, the SwinTransformer works well with the zooming strategy, likely due to its ability to model long-range spatial relationships.

Some recent studies in medical imaging propose architectural modifications, which can provide performance gains on specific datasets. However, these adjustments are often difficult to validate outside the original study context and may reduce generalizability or reproducibility. In contrast, our approach makes only minimal changes to accommodate grayscale input and binary classification. By leveraging a robust, pre-trained SwinTransformer model without altering its internal structure, we focus on improvements through algorithmic design—specifically, attention-guided zooming. Our findings suggest that such strategies, when paired with well-established architectures, can yield strong and generalizable performance without requiring complex architectural innovations. In summary, the combination of a zooming algorithm and transformer-based architecture offers a compelling direction for improving breast cancer detection models—yielding both domain robustness and efficient use of image resolution.

Ethical Considerations. This study was approved by the Regional committee for medical research (REK). All mammography data were de-identified prior to analysis.

References

1. Papers with Code - ImageNet Benchmark (Image Classification). https://paperswithcode.com/sota/image-classification-on-imagenet
2. Abdelrahman, L., Al Ghamdi, M., Collado-Mesa, F., Abdel-Mottaleb, M.: Convolutional neural networks for breast cancer detection in mammography: a survey. Comput. Biol. Med. **131**, 104248 (2021). https://doi.org/10.1016/j.compbiomed.2021.104248
3. Chen, X., et al.: Transformers improve breast cancer diagnosis from unregistered multi-view mammograms. Diagnostics **12**(7), 1549 (2022). https://doi.org/10.3390/diagnostics12071549, https://www.mdpi.com/2075-4418/12/7/1549. Multidisciplinary Digital Publishing Institute
4. Dahl, F., Brautaset, O., Holden, M., Eikvil, L., Larsen, M., Hofvind, S.: Two-stage mammography classification model using explainable-AI for ROI detection. Nordic Mach. Intell. (2023). https://journals.uio.no/NMI/article/view/10459
5. Dosovitskiy, A., et al.: an image is worth 16x16 words: transformers for image recognition at scale (2021). https://doi.org/10.48550/arXiv.2010.11929, http://arxiv.org/abs/2010.11929, arXiv:2010.11929
6. Garrucho, L., Kushibar, K., Jouide, S., Diaz, O., Igual, L., Lekadir, K.: Domain generalization in deep learning based mass detection in mammography: a large-scale multi-center study. Artif. Intell. Med. **132**, 102386 (2022). https://doi.org/10.1016/j.artmed.2022.102386, https://www.sciencedirect.com/science/article/pii/S0933365722001415
7. Lauby-Secretan, B., et al.: Breast-cancer screening — viewpoint of the IARC working group. N. Engl. J. Med. **372**(24), 2353–2358 (2015). https://doi.org/10.1056/NEJMsr1504363, https://www.nejm.org/doi/full/10.1056/NEJMsr1504363. Massachusetts Medical Society _eprint: https://www.nejm.org/doi/pdf/10.1056/NEJMsr1504363
8. Liu, Z., et al.: Swin transformer: hierarchical vision transformer using shifted windows. In: 2021 IEEE/CVF International Conference on Computer Vision (ICCV). pp. 9992–10002 (2021). https://doi.org/10.1109/ICCV48922.2021.00986, https://ieeexplore.ieee.org/document/9710580, iSSN: 2380-7504
9. van Luijt, P., Heijnsdijk, E., de Koning, H.: Cost-effectiveness of the norwegian breast cancer screening program. Int. J. Cancer **140**(4), 833–840 (2017). https://doi.org/10.1002/ijc.30513, https://onlinelibrary.wiley.com/doi/abs/10.1002/ijc.30513, _eprint: https://onlinelibrary.wiley.com/doi/pdf/10.1002/ijc.30513
10. Lång, K., et al.: Artificial intelligence-supported screen reading versus standard double reading in the mammography screening with artificial intelligence trial (MASAI): a clinical safety analysis of a randomised, controlled, non-inferiority, single-blinded, screening accuracy study. Lancet Oncol. **24**(8), 936–944 (2023). https://doi.org/10.1016/S1470-2045(23)00298-X
11. Manigrasso, F., et al.: Mammography classification with multi-view deep learning techniques: investigating graph and transformer-based architectures. Med. Image Anal. **99**, 103320 (2025). https://doi.org/10.1016/j.media.2024.103320, https://www.sciencedirect.com/science/article/pii/S1361841524002457
12. Martiniussen, M.A., et al.: Performance of two deep learning-based AI models for breast cancer detection and localization on screening mammograms from breastscreen norway. Radiol. Artif. Intell. e240039 (2025). https://doi.org/10.1148/ryai.240039

13. McKinney, S.M., et al.: International evaluation of an AI system for breast cancer screening. Nature **577**(7788), 89–94 (2020). https://doi.org/10.1038/s41586-019-1799-6

14. Selvaraju, R.R., Cogswell, M., Das, A., Vedantam, R., Parikh, D., Batra, D.: Grad-CAM: visual explanations from deep networks via gradient-based localization. pp. 618–626 (2017). https://openaccess.thecvf.com/content_iccv_2017/html/Selvaraju_Grad-CAM_Visual_Explanations_ICCV_2017_paper.html

15. Wang, H., et al.: Transformer-based explainable model for breast cancer lesion segmentation. Appl. Sci. **15**(3), 1295 (2025). https://doi.org/10.3390/app15031295, https://www.mdpi.com/2076-3417/15/3/1295. Multidisciplinary Digital Publishing Institute

Can AI Be Faster, Accurate, and Explainable? SpikeNet Makes it Happen

Dost Muhammad[1]([⊠])[iD] and Malika Bendechache[2][iD]

[1] CRT-AI and ADAPT Research Centers, School of Computer Science,
University of Galway, Galway, Ireland
d.muhammad1@universityofgalway.ie

[2] ADAPT Research Centers, School of Computer Science, University of Galway,
Galway, Ireland
malika.bendechache@universityofgalway.ie

Abstract. Deep learning (DL) has significantly advanced brain tumour diagnosis using Magnetic Resonance Imaging (MRI), yet most existing models suffer from high computational overhead and lack interpretability—key barriers to clinical deployment. We propose SpikeNet, a novel hybrid framework that integrates Convolutional Neural Networks (CNNs) with Spiking Neural Networks (SNNs) to address these challenges by combining spatial feature extraction with temporally sparse, biologically inspired computation. Evaluated on a brain MRI dataset, SpikeNet achieves an accuracy of 97.12%, precision of 97.91%, and recall of 97.65%, while reducing inference time by over 80% compared to Efficient.Net-B7, ResNet-50, and InceptionResNetV2. Moreover, SpikeNet produces high-fidelity saliency maps that better align with tumour regions than Grad-CAM and LIME, enhancing clinical relevance and trust. These results demonstrate SpikeNet's potential as a fast, accurate, and interpretable AI system for real-time neuroimaging diagnostics.

Keywords: XAI in Healthcare · XAI validation · XAI for medical imaging · Explainable Deep Learning

1 Introduction

Magnetic Resonance Imaging (MRI) plays a pivotal role in the diagnosis and management of brain tumours, offering high-resolution, non-invasive imaging crucial for accurate tumour localization and characterization. The increasing prevalence of brain tumours underscores the urgent need for advanced diagnostic tools to enhance early detection and improve clinical outcomes.

Deep Learning (DL) has emerged as a transformative technology in medical imaging, demonstrating state-of-the-art performance in tasks such as tumour classification, segmentation, and outcome prediction. By utilising large-scale data and sophisticated neural architectures, DL models have achieved remarkable accuracy, often surpassing traditional diagnostic methods. However, despite

S. Ali et al. (Eds.): MIUA 2025, LNCS 15917, pp. 43–57, 2026.
https://doi.org/10.1007/978-3-031-98691-8_4

these successes, the opaque nature of these "black-box" models poses significant challenges in clinical adoption. This inability to understand the reasoning behind model predictions, commonly referred to as the "black-box problem" [1, 19], limits trust and accountability in high-stakes medical decisions. Moreover, current DL models, such as EfficientNet-B7 [31], ResNet-50 [9], and InceptionResNetV2 [30], require significant computational time for both training and inference, which poses a critical bottleneck in the medical domain where urgent and timely diagnosis is often essential [2, 14].

Explainable Artificial Intelligence (XAI) has gained significant attention as a solution to this explainability challenge. The goal of XAI is to develop methods that produce explainable models while preserving high performance [16]. XAI techniques are widely categorised as model-based and post-hoc approaches. Model-based methods inherently provide insights into learned relationships, but their simplicity often limits their effectiveness in capturing complex data patterns. Post-hoc methods, namely Gradient-weighted Class Activation Mapping (Grad-CAM) [28] and Local Interpretable Model-Agnostic Explanations (LIME) [17, 28] , offer explanations by analysing pre-trained models, making them more versatile for deployment in complex tasks. However, post-hoc methods often suffer from issues such as inconsistency across saliency methods [10], raising concerns about their clinical reliability.

To overcome these limitations, we propose SpikeNet, a novel framework that synergizes Convolutional Neural Networks (CNNs) with Spiking Neural Networks (SNNs) to enhance both predictive performance and explainability. While this framework was originally designed for object detection, to the best of our knowledge, this is the first time it has been applied to medical image analysis, specifically for brain tumour detection from MRI imaging. SpikeNet is hybrid approach utilises the temporal dynamics of SNNs to improve feature representation while maintaining the efficiency and accuracy of CNNs. Our experiments showed that SpikeNet not only achieves improved predictive accuracy but also reduces computational time by up to approximate 80% compared to state-of-the-art architectures including EfficientNet-B7, ResNet-50, and InceptionResNetV2. Furthermore, we conducted a comparative analysis of the visualisations generated by SpikeNet with state-of-the-art XAI methods commonly used in medical imaging, namely Grad-CAM and LIME. SpikeNet demonstrated superior localization accuracy by precisely predicting the tumour region, closely aligning with the ground truth annotations.

The contributions of this work include:

- Proposing SpikeNet, a hybrid framework integrating CNNs and SNNs, to enhance tumour diagnosis by combining spatial and temporal feature extraction for improved explainability and performance;
- Demonstrating significant improvements in accuracy (97.12%), precision (97.91%), recall (97.65%), and F1-score (97.43%), while outperforming Grad-CAM and LIME in explanation precision and clinical relevance, as shown in Figs. 1,2 and 3 ;

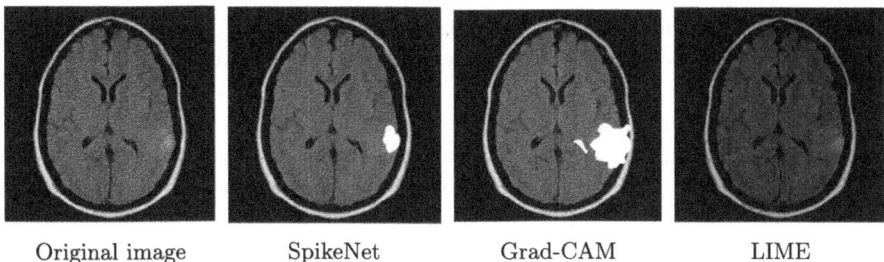

| Original image | SpikeNet | Grad-CAM | LIME |

Fig. 1. Visual explanations of different XAI methods applied to a brain MRI image for tumour prediction. The original image is shown alongside the explanations generated by SpikeNet, Grad-CAM, and LIME. SpikeNet accurately predicts the tumour region in white, closely aligning with the ground truth. Grad-CAM overgeneralizes, highlighting a broader region in white that extends beyond the tumour area, while LIME produces fragmented red regions that fail to localize the tumour effectively. (Color figure online)

- Achieving up to approximate 80% reduction in computational time compared to EfficientNet-B7, ResNet-50, and InceptionResNetV2, making SpikeNet highly efficient for real-time diagnostics; and
- Proposing a robust framework that lays the groundwork for integrating XAI into clinical workflows, aiming to deliver scalable, reliable, and explainable solutions for time-sensitive medical applications.

The remainder of the paper is structured as follows: Sect. 2 presents the related work; Sects. 4 and 3 describe the proposed methodology and experimental setup, respectively; Sect. 5 reports the results; Sect. 6 offers a detailed discussion; and Sect. 7 concludes with key findings and outlines directions for future research.

2 Relevant Studies

The Table 1 provides a detailed summary of studies that integrate XAI techniques into medical image analysis, particularly MRI. Despite showcasing advancements in integrating XAI methods like Grad-CAM, LIME, and SHAP, these studies reveal significant gaps that limit their clinical adoption. Recent work has also explored SNN-based models for medical imaging. For example, [3, 18] proposed a lightweight deep spiking neural network for medical image classification, demonstrating high accuracy with reduced computational complexity. Similarly, [36] introduced fine-tuning methods for SNNs tailored to brain image segmentation. While our work differs in integrating SNNs as part of a hybrid CNN-SNN pipeline with built-in explanation generation, these approaches illustrate the growing potential of neuromorphic models in clinical AI.

Moreover, transformer-based architectures have shown superior performance in many vision tasks. CNN-transformer hybrids and Vision Transformers (ViTs) have been used for robust medical image classification, segmentation, and detection. While our work did not benchmark against transformer models, future extensions will include comparative analysis with transformer-based architectures to further validate SpikeNet's advantages in performance, efficiency, and explainability.

A significant limitation of current XAI methods is their inability to consistently visualise accurate and clinically relevant regions in medical images. This inconsistency raises concerns in the medical field, where precision and reliability are critical. Medical professionals and patients are often hesitant to trust AI tools that fail to provide clear and accurate visual explanations for their decisions.

Additionally, many studies continue to rely on sequential DL architectures like ResNet-50, DenseNet201, and EfficientNet-B0, which, while powerful, suffer from high computational overhead. These inefficiencies make them impractical for real-time applications where timely and precise decision-making is critical. Such limitations undermine the adoption of these methods in high-stakes diagnostic workflows, where trust, transparency, and accountability are essential. Furthermore, current approaches often focus on generating explanations but fall short of addressing the need for accurate explainability, leaving their suitability for medical diagnostics in question.

These observations highlight the pressing need for AI frameworks that go beyond mere accuracy, providing clinically relevant and trustworthy explanations while optimising computational efficiency. Only by addressing these limitations can we ensure that AI methods earn the trust of medical professionals and patients, ultimately enabling their safe and effective deployment in real-world clinical settings.

3   Experimental Setup

3.1   Implementation Environment

The experiments were conducted using Python, chosen for its versatility and comprehensive ecosystem of DL libraries. Model training and evaluation were performed on a computational system featuring an AMD Ryzen 7 5700X eight-core processor and a 16GB NVIDIA GeForce RTX 4080 GPU, providing the necessary computational power for efficient execution of DL workloads.

3.2   Dataset

In this study, we utilised a dataset from The Cancer Genome Atlas (TCGA) and The Cancer Imaging Archive (TCIA) [24], specifically focusing on preoperative FLAIR imaging data from 110 patients in the TCGA lower-grade glioma (LGG) collection. Initially, the dataset included 120 patients, but 10 were excluded due to missing genomic cluster information. The final dataset, sourced from five institutions, was divided into 22 non-overlapping subsets of five patients each for cross-validation. All FLAIR images were manually annotated by a neuroradiology-trained researcher and validated by a board-certified radiologist using custom in-house software. The dataset includes registered FLAIR images along with corresponding ground truth annotation, forming the foundation for the experiments in this study.

Table 1. Summary of Studies Integrating XAI Methods in Brain-MRI Analysis, showing if computational time is reported.

Study	Modality	Approach	XAI Methods	Comp Time?
[26]	MRI	CNNs	GBP, Grad-CAM	No
[27]	MRI	RF and RBMs	LIME	No
[22]	MRI	Dense-UNet, Res-UNet	Grad-CAM	No
[12]	MRI	CNNs	Grad-CAM	No
[37]	MRI	PSP-Net	Grad-CAM	No
[32]	MRI	DenseNet201	Grad-CAM	No
[34]	MRI	VGG-19	Grad-CAM++	No
[6]	MRI	IVX16 (Ensembles of 3 models)	LIME	No
[21]	MRI	CNN	LIME, IG, SHAP	No
[33]	MRI	ResNet-50	Grad-CAM	No
[8]	MRI	VGG-16	Grad-CAM, LRP	No
[20]	MRI	ViT-D-CNN	Grad-CAM, LIME	No
[11]	MRI	EfficientNetB0	Grad-CAM	No
[4]	MRI	EfficientNetB0, ResNet50	Grad-CAM, LIME	No

3.3 Data Pre-processing

The considered dataset was divided into training and validation subsets following an 80:20 ratio to ensure an effective balance between model training and evaluation. The training set comprised 80% of the data, while the validation set utilised the remaining 20%, enabling robust assessment of the model's generalization performance. A custom dataset structure was designed to streamline the handling of brain MRI images and corresponding labels. Each image was resized to a uniform resolution of 224×224 pixels to standardize input dimensions. Furthermore, all images underwent preprocessing steps, including conversion into numerical formats suitable for model training and normalisation [13]. The normalization process standardized pixel intensity values using fixed mean $[0.5, 0.5, 0.5]$ and standard deviation $[0.5, 0.5, 0.5]$, ensuring uniformity across the dataset. To mitigate overfitting and improve generalization, we applied several data augmentation techniques to the training set. These included horizontal and vertical flipping, random rotation ($\pm 10°$), and minor intensity perturbations. The augmentations aimed to simulate natural anatomical variability in brain MRI scans and ensure that the model did not overfit to specific imaging patterns. All augmentations were applied on-the-fly during training to ensure diversity across epochs.

4   Method and Materials

4.1   Proposed Framework

The proposed framework SpikeNet, utilises a hybrid architecture combining the CNNs [23] with SNNs [5] activations to enhance both predictive performance and computational efficiency. CNNs are widely used for feature extraction and classification tasks due to their strong representational capabilities, they are computationally intensive and lack temporal dynamics for processing complex biological signals. While SNNs, inspired by the spiking behaviour of biological neurons, represent information through discrete spike events rather than continuous values. In the context of medical diagnosis, the use of SNNs is largely unexplored. Our framework is the first to integrate SNNs activations with CNNs in a diagnostic pipeline, utilising the temporal dynamics of SNNs to refine feature representations and enhance decision-making processes. The pipeline integrates feature extraction, spiking dynamics, and binary classification to detect the presence of brain tumours in MRI images. The detailed procedures are described below.

Diagnosis. The backbone of the SpikeNet utilises a CNN for feature extraction, utilising its hierarchical architecture to process and extract spatial features from input MRI images. Let $I \in \mathbb{R}^{H \times W \times C}$ represent the input image, where H, W, and C are the height, width, and number of channels, respectively. The image passes through a series of convolutional and pooling layers, progressively refining the spatial and feature-level information to produce a high-dimensional feature map $F \in \mathbb{R}^{d \times h \times w}$, where d is the depth of the feature map, and h and w are its spatial dimensions.

This process can be mathematically described in Eq. 1:

$$F = \text{CNN}_{\text{features}}(I), \tag{1}$$

where $\text{CNN}_{\text{features}}$ denotes the convolutional layers responsible for extracting multi-scale spatial features from the input image.

The extracted feature map F is flattened into a vector $f \in \mathbb{R}^{d \cdot h \cdot w}$ to facilitate integration with the subsequent SNNs layer. The flattened feature vector f is passed through a fully connected (dense) layer integrated with spiking neuron activation, modelled using the Integrate-and-Fire (IF) mechanism. This layer accumulates the input membrane potential until a predefined threshold V_{th} is reached, at which point a spike is triggered. The dynamics of the spiking neuron are governed by, presented in Eq. 2 and 3:

$$V(t+1) = \beta V(t) + W \cdot f, \tag{2}$$

$$S(t) = \begin{cases} 1, & \text{if } V(t) \geq V_{\text{th}}, \\ 0, & \text{otherwise}, \end{cases} \tag{3}$$

where β is the decay factor, W represents the synaptic weights, $V(t)$ is the membrane potential at time t, and $S(t)$ is the output spike.

The spiking layer captures temporal dynamics by encoding features into spike trains, simulating the timing-dependent behaviour of biological neurons. Unlike conventional activations, spiking neurons accumulate membrane potential over discrete time steps and fire only when a threshold is exceeded. This mechanism introduces temporal sensitivity and enables the network to emphasize salient features while suppressing noise. As a result, the SNN layer enhances the spatial features extracted by CNNs through temporal filtering, allowing SpikeNet to learn sparser and more biologically plausible representations. This not only improves classification but also contributes to the generation of more focused and clinically meaningful explanation maps. The final output of the SNNs layer is passed to a single fully connected neuron, producing a logit z, which is transformed into a probability using the sigmoid activation function, defined in Eq. 4 :

$$P(y = 1|x) = \frac{1}{1 + \exp(-z)}, \tag{4}$$

where $P(y = 1|x)$ represents the probability of the input image x containing a tumour.

To optimise the model parameters, the Binary Cross-Entropy (BCE) loss is employed, defined in Eq. 5:

$$\mathcal{L} = -\frac{1}{N} \sum_{i=1}^{N} [y_i \log(\hat{y}_i) + (1 - y_i) \log(1 - \hat{y}_i)], \tag{5}$$

where N is the batch size, y_i is the ground truth label, and $\hat{y}_i$ is the predicted probability for the i-th sample. The model parameters are updated using the Adam optimizer, ensuring efficient convergence.

The training process involves iterative updates through forward and backward passes. In the forward pass, predictions are computed, while the backward pass calculates gradients and updates the weights. Validation is performed at the end of each epoch to evaluate model performance on unseen data using metrics namely accuracy, precision, recall, and F1-score [15].

The final output of the framework is a binary classification indicating the presence $(y = 1)$ or absence $(y = 0)$ of a tumour. The predicted label $\hat{y}$ is determined based on a threshold, presented in Eq. 6:

$$\hat{y} = \begin{cases} 1, & \text{if } P(y = 1|x) \geq 0.5, \\ 0, & \text{otherwise.} \end{cases} \tag{6}$$

Explanations. The SpikeNet generates interpretable explanations by leveraging activation maps from the final convolutional layer of the CNN backbone. These explanations highlight the regions in brain MRI images most relevant to the model's classification decision, providing valuable insights into the decision-making process. The explanation generation process consists of three main steps: activation map extraction, minimal heatmap generation, and visualization.

The process begins by capturing the activation map $A \in \mathbb{R}^{C \times H \times W}$, where C represents the number of channels, and H and W denote the spatial dimensions. These activation maps encode spatial and feature-level information that is critical for identifying tumour regions.

For a given input image I, the activation map A is obtained as the output of the final convolutional layer in the feature extraction stage. Mathematically, this process can be described as in Eq. 7:

$$A = f_{\text{CNN}}(I), \tag{7}$$

where f_{CNN} represents the convolutional operations of the feature extraction layers. Each channel of the activation map A_c reflects a distinct spatial feature learned by the model.

To generate a focused heatmap, the activation map is processed to identify the top $k\%$ of channels with the highest mean activation values. The mean activation for each channel is computed as in Eq. 8:

$$\mu_c = \frac{1}{HW} \sum_{i=1}^{H} \sum_{j=1}^{W} A_{c,i,j}, \tag{8}$$

where $A_{c,i,j}$ denotes the activation value at channel c and spatial location (i, j). The top $k\%$ channels, denoted as TopChannels, are selected by ranking the channels in descending order of μ_c.

The focused activation map is then computed by aggregating the selected channels, defined in Eq. 9:

$$F_{\text{focused}}(i, j) = \sum_{c \in \text{TopChannels}} A_{c,i,j}. \tag{9}$$

This focused map is normalized to the range $[0, 1]$ using min-max scaling, refer to Eq. 10:

$$F_{\text{normalized}}(i, j) = \frac{F_{\text{focused}}(i, j) - \min(F_{\text{focused}})}{\max(F_{\text{focused}}) - \min(F_{\text{focused}}) + \epsilon}, \tag{10}$$

where ϵ is a small constant to prevent division by zero.

Finally, a binary heatmap F_{binary} is generated by applying a threshold T presented in Eq. 11:

$$F_{\text{binary}}(i, j) = \begin{cases} 1, & \text{if } F_{\text{normalized}}(i, j) \geq T, \\ 0, & \text{otherwise.} \end{cases} \tag{11}$$

The binary heatmap F_{binary} is resized to match the dimensions of the original image, enabling overlay with the input MRI. The final visualization consists of:

1. The original MRI image, and
2. The generated explanation heatmap, indicating the regions identified by the model as relevant for classification.

5 Experimental Results

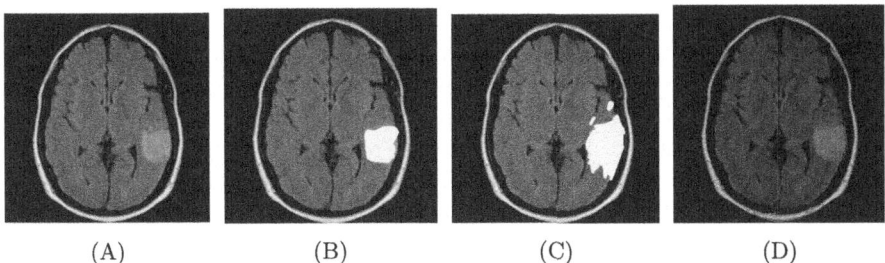

(A)   (B)   (C)   (D)

Fig. 2. Comparative Visualisations of SpikeNet and XAI Methods: Subpanels are labelled as (A) Original Image, (B) SpikeNet, (C) Grad-CAM, and (D) LIME. SpikeNet precisely identifies and highlights the tumour region, presenting exceptional accuracy and localization compared to the broader focus of Grad-CAM and the fragmented outputs of LIME.(Color figure online)

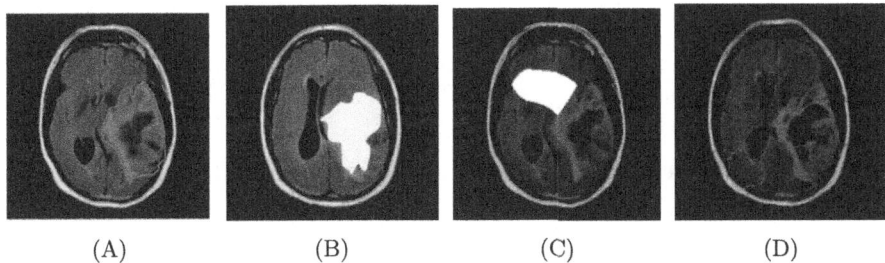

(A)   (B)   (C)   (D)

Fig. 3. Comparative Visualisations of SpikeNet and XAI Methods: Subpanels are labelled as (A) Original Image, (B) SpikeNet, (C) Grad-CAM, and (D) LIME. SpikeNet accurately identifies and highlights the tumour region with precise localization, closely aligning with the ground truth. Grad-CAM, however, significantly misses the tumour region, highlighting unrelated areas, while LIME produces scattered red regions, failing to effectively capture the tumour. (Color figure online)

This section provides a detailed analysis of the proposed SpikeNet, focusing on its classification performance, computational efficiency, and explainability. The SpikeNet is compared with state-of-the-art models, including EfficientNet-B7, InceptionResNetV2, and ResNet-50, for prediction performance and computational time. Additionally, its explainability is evaluated against Grad-CAM and LIME using two different MRI images, incorporating visual explanations to demonstrate its clinical relevance and superiority. Table 2 provides a comparative analysis of the SpikeNet against state-of-the-art DL models, including Efficient-NetB7, InceptionResNetV2, and ResNet50. The evaluation metrics—accuracy, precision, recall, F1-score, and computational time—demonstrate the significant advantages of the proposed approach. The SpikeNet achieves the highest performance across all metrics, attains an accuracy of 97.12%, precision of 97.91%, recall of 97.65%, and F1-score of 97.43%. These results surpass the performance of ResNet50, the best-performing baseline, which achieves an accuracy of 90.01%, precision of 91.46%, recall of 90.56%, and F1-score of 90.18%.In addition to its strong predictive performance, SpikeNet significantly reduces computational time, completing execution in just 154 s. In comparison, EfficientNetB7 takes 953 s, InceptionResNetV2 takes 823 s, and ResNet50 takes 712 s.

This improvement translates to an average reduction of approximately 81% in execution time across the three tested models, with a 83.84% reduction compared to EfficientNetB7, 81.28% reduction compared to InceptionResNetV2, and 78% reduction compared to ResNet50.

Table 2. Performance Comparison of SpikeNet and State-of-the-Art Models

DL-Model	Acc (%)	Prec (%)	Rec (%)	F1-s (%)	Comp. Time (s)
EfficientNetB7	89.40	88.01	89.53	88.63	953
InceptionResNetV2	89.51	90.01	89.43	89.23	823
ResNet50	90.01	91.46	90.56	90.18	712
SpikeNet	**97.12**	**97.91**	**97.65**	**97.43**	**154**

Figure 2 illustrates the visual explanations for the first MRI image. Subpanel (A) represents the original MRI image with a visible tumour region. Subpanel (B) shows the explanation map generated by the proposed SpikeNet, which accurately highlights the tumour region in white, closely aligning with the ground truth. Subpanel (C) depicts the explanation produced by Grad-CAM, which highlights a significantly broader area than the actual tumour, reducing its precision. Subpanel (D) displays the explanation map generated by LIME, where fragmented red regions fail to capture the tumour's location accurately. Furthermore, Fig. 3 presents the visual explanations for a second MRI image. Subpanel (A) shows the original MRI image with a visible tumour region. Subpanel (B) highlights the tumour region using SpikeNet, demonstrating a strong alignment with the ground truth. Subpanel (C) illustrates the explanation by Grad-CAM, which overextends the highlighted region, reducing precision. Subpanel (D) shows LIME, which produces fragmented and misaligned explanations in red.

6   Discussion

The proposed SpikeNet framework introduces a biologically inspired hybrid architecture that leverages the spatial feature extraction strengths of Convolutional Neural Networks (CNNs) and the temporal dynamics of Spiking Neural

Networks (SNNs). While traditional models such as EfficientNet-B7, ResNet-50, and InceptionResNetV2 focus primarily on static spatial information, they suffer from high computational costs and limited generalization [7]. In contrast, SpikeNet integrates SNNs to capture temporal dependencies via event-driven threshold-based spiking, thereby enhancing feature selectivity and improving robustness in medical imaging tasks.

Formally, spiking neurons accumulate membrane potential and fire only when a defined threshold is surpassed, introducing temporal sparsity into the feature representation. This mechanism filters noise, emphasizes salient spatiotemporal patterns, and contributes to lower activation redundancy, yielding improved computational efficiency and enhanced localization of pathological regions [25].

As shown in Table 2, SpikeNet achieves a substantial reduction in inference time—154 s compared to 953 s (EfficientNet-B7), 823 s (InceptionResNetV2), and 712 s (ResNet-50)—representing an average speedup of over 80%. This efficiency gain stems from the event-driven processing in SNNs, which activates computation only upon spiking events, thereby minimizing redundant operations and enabling real-time viability for clinical scenarios.

To further improve generalization and prevent overfitting, we applied spatial and intensity-based augmentation techniques during training, including flipping, rotation, and intensity shifts. Although the dataset was relatively balanced, augmentation introduced variability that led to improved convergence and stability across validation folds. A detailed ablation of augmentation impact will be explored in future work.

Interpretability remains central to clinical adoption of AI. While post-hoc methods like Grad-CAM and LIME are widely adopted, they often suffer from overgeneralized or fragmented saliency maps [29, 35]. SpikeNet addresses this by integrating a native explanation mechanism that dynamically aggregates high-activation channels from its final convolutional layers to generate focused saliency maps. These explanations exhibit better alignment with tumour regions and reduced irrelevant activations.

Although current evaluation is based on visual assessments, we recognize the need for quantitative interpretability validation. Future work will incorporate overlap-based metrics such as Dice and Jaccard scores, and conduct comparisons with SHAP and Integrated Gradients (IG), which remain challenging to integrate with temporally driven SNNs.

Despite the substantial inference speedup, real-world deployment requires consideration of hospital infrastructure, network latency, and hardware availability. SpikeNet's reduced computational demands position it well for edge deployment, and we plan to evaluate it across multi-institutional datasets and on hospital-grade GPUs and embedded systems.

To rigorously validate the role of each component, a future ablation study will isolate the contributions of the CNN and SNN modules. While CNNs perform spatial encoding, the SNNs enhance decision-making through sparse temporal activations. Preliminary observations suggest that the synergy between these modules is critical to SpikeNet's superior performance, but systematic quantification is reserved for future work.

7 Conclusion

This study proposed SpikeNet, a novel framework designed to address the challenges of explainability, accuracy, and computational efficiency in brain tumour diagnosis using MRI. The framework achieved improved performance, with an accuracy of 97.12%, precision of 97.91%, recall of 97.65%, and F1-score of 97.43%, while reducing computational time by up to 80% compared to state-of-the-art DL models namely EfficientNet-B7, InceptionResNetV2, and ResNet-50. SpikeNet combines the temporal dynamics of SNNs with the spatial feature extraction capabilities of CNNs, resulting in enhanced predictive performance and over 80% improvement in computational efficiency.. Furthermore, the SpikeNet significantly outperforms existing XAI methods namely Grad-CAM and LIME by generating precise and clinically relevant explanations maps. This work marks a significant advancement in integrating XAI into clinical workflows, providing a scalable, efficient, and explainable solution for real-time medical diagnostics.

Future work will focus on extending SpikeNet to other imaging modalities such as CT and PET, and to diverse diagnostic contexts including breast and lung cancer, to assess its generalization capabilities. We also aim to incorporate attribution-based XAI methods (e.g., SHAP, Integrated Gradients) and quantitative saliency metrics (e.g., Dice, Jaccard) to enhance interpretability evaluation. Scalability testing will include real-time deployment on hospital-grade GPUs and edge devices across multi-institutional datasets. In addition, planned ablation studies will isolate the contributions of CNN and SNN components, and benchmarking against Vision Transformers and other SNN-based models will further validate SpikeNet's performance and adaptability.

Acknowledgment. This research was supported by Taighde Éireann Research Ireland under grant numbers 18/CRT/6223 (RI Centre for Research Training in Artificial Intelligence), 13/RC/2106/P_-2 (ADAPT Centre),13/RC/2094/P_-2 (Lero Centre) and College of Science and Engineering, University of Galway. For the purpose of Open Access, the author has applied a CC BY public copyright licence to any Author Accepted Manuscript version arising from this submission.

Conflict of Interest. The authors declare no potential conflict of interest.

References

1. Adadi, A., Berrada, M.: Peeking inside the black-box: a survey on explainable artificial intelligence (xai). IEEE access **6**, 52138–52160 (2018)
2. Ali, M., Muhammad, D., Khalaf, O.I., Habib, R.: Optimizing mobile cloud computing: a comparative analysis and innovative cost-efficient partitioning model. SN Comput. Sci. **6**(1), 1–25 (2025)

3. Bhowmick, S., Saha, A., Deb, S., De, A., Srivastava, A.: Medical image classification using lightweight deep spiking neural network. Iranian J. Sci. Technol. Trans. Electric. Eng. **49**(2), 589–600 (2025)
4. Charaabi, H., Sayari, A., El Hamdi, R., Njah, M., Slima, M.B.: An xai-infused multiclass mri brain tumor classification using deep transfer learning (dtl). In: 2024 10th International Conference on Control, Decision and Information Technologies (CoDIT). pp. 1044–1049. IEEE (2024)
5. Ghosh-Dastidar, S., Adeli, H.: Spiking neural networks. Int. J. Neural Syst. **19**(04), 295–308 (2009)
6. Hossain, S., Chakrabarty, A., Gadekallu, T.R., Alazab, M., Piran, M.J.: Vision transformers, ensemble model, and transfer learning leveraging explainable ai for brain tumor detection and classification. IEEE J. Biomed. Health Inform. **28**(3), 1261–1272 (2023)
7. Johnson, J.M., Khoshgoftaar, T.M.: Survey on deep learning with class imbalance. J. Big Data **6**(1), 1–54 (2019). https://doi.org/10.1186/s40537-019-0192-5
8. Khanapur, S., Bharadwaj, C.B., Bhardwaj, R., Nayak, J.S.: An approach for xai visualizations for explainability of alzheimer's detection. In: 2024 2nd International Conference on Networking, Embedded and Wireless Systems (ICNEWS). pp. 1–6. IEEE (2024)
9. Koonce, B., Koonce, B.: Resnet 50. Convolutional neural networks with swift for tensorflow: image recognition and dataset categorization pp. 63–72 (2021)
10. Krishna, S., Han, T., Gu, A., Wu, S., Jabbari, S., Lakkaraju, H.: The disagreement problem in explainable machine learning: a practitioner's perspective. arXiv preprint arXiv:2202.01602 (2022)
11. Mahesh, T., Gupta, M., Anupama, T., Geman, O., et al.: An xai-enhanced efficientnetb0 framework for precision brain tumor detection in mri imaging. J. Neurosci. Methods **410**, 110227 (2024)
12. Maqsood, S., Damaševičius, R., Maskeliūnas, R.: Multi-modal brain tumor detection using deep neural network and multiclass svm. Medicina **58**(8), 1090 (2022)
13. Muhammad, D., Ahmad, I., Khalil, M.I., Khalil, W., Ahmad, M.O.: A generalized deep learning approach to seismic activity prediction. Appl. Sci. **13**(3) (2023). https://doi.org/10.3390/app13031598, https://www.mdpi.com/2076-3417/13/3/1598
14. Muhammad, D., Ahmed, I., Ahmad, M.O., Bendechache, M.: Randomized explainable machine learning models for efficient medical diagnosis. IEEE J. Biomed. Health Inform. pp. 1–10 (2024).https://doi.org/10.1109/JBHI.2024.3491593
15. Muhammad, D., Ahmed, I., Naveed, K., Bendechache, M.: An explainable deep learning approach for stock market trend prediction. Heliyon **10**(21) (2024)
16. Muhammad, D., Bendechache, M.: Unveiling the black box: A systematic review of explainable artificial intelligence in medical image analysis. Comput. Struct. Biotechnol. J. **24**, 542–560 (2024). https://doi.org/10.1016/j.csbj.2024.08.005, https://www.sciencedirect.com/science/article/pii/S2001037024002642
17. Muhammad, D., Keles, A., Bendechache, M.: Towards explainable deep learning in oncology: integrating efficientnet-b7 with xai techniques for acute lymphoblastic leukaemia (2024)
18. Muhammad, D., null Rafiullah, Bendechache, M.: Improving diagnostic trust: an explainable deep learning framework for genitourinary cancer prediction. In: IET Conference Proceedings vol. 2024, pp. 47–54 (2024).https://doi.org/10.1049/icp.2024.3275, https://digital-library.theiet.org/doi/abs/10.1049/icp.2024.3275

19. Muhammad, D., Salman, M., Keles, A., Bendechache, M.: All diagnosis: can efficiency and transparency coexist? an explainable deep learning approach. Sci. Rep. **15**(1), 12812 (2025)
20. Mzoughi, H., Njeh, I., BenSlima, M., Farhat, N., Mhiri, C.: Vision transformers (vit) and deep convolutional neural network (d-cnn)-based models for mri brain primary tumors images multi-classification supported by explainable artificial intelligence (xai). Visual Comput. 1–20 (2024)
21. Narayankar, P., Baligar, V.P.: Explainability of brain tumor classification based on region. In: 2024 International Conference on Emerging Technologies in Computer Science for Interdisciplinary Applications (ICETCS). pp. 1–6. IEEE (2024)
22. Natekar, P., Kori, A., Krishnamurthi, G.: Demystifying brain tumor segmentation networks: interpretability and uncertainty analysis. Front. Comput. Neurosci. **14**, 6 (2020)
23. O'Shea, K.: An introduction to convolutional neural networks. arXiv preprint arXiv:1511.08458 (2015)
24. Pedano, N., et al.: The cancer genome atlas low grade glioma collection (tcga-lgg) (2016). https://doi.org/10.7937/K9/TCIA.2016.L4LTD3TK
25. Pequeño Zurro, A., et al.: Exploiting spatio-temporal patterns with neuromorphic systems (2023)
26. Pereira, S., Meier, R., Alves, V., Reyes, M., Silva, C.A.: Automatic brain tumor grading from mri data using convolutional neural networks and quality assessment. In: Understanding and Interpreting Machine Learning in Medical Image Computing Applications: First International Workshops, MLCN 2018, DLF 2018, and iMIMIC 2018, Held in Conjunction with MICCAI 2018, Granada, Spain, September 16-20, 2018, Proceedings 1. pp. 106–114. Springer (2018)
27. Pereira, S., et al.: Enhancing interpretability of automatically extracted machine learning features: application to a rbm-random forest system on brain lesion segmentation. Med. Image Anal. **44**, 228–244 (2018)
28. Ribeiro, M.T., Singh, S., Guestrin, C.: " why should i trust you?" explaining the predictions of any classifier. In: Proceedings of the 22nd ACM SIGKDD international conference on knowledge discovery and data mining. pp. 1135–1144 (2016)
29. Selvaraju, R.R., Cogswell, M., Das, A., Vedantam, R., Parikh, D., Batra, D.: Gradcam: visual explanations from deep networks via gradient-based localization. Int. J. Comput. Vision **128**, 336–359 (2020)
30. Szegedy, C., Ioffe, S., Vanhoucke, V., Alemi, A.: Inception-v4, inception-resnet and the impact of residual connections on learning. In: Proceedings of the AAAI conference on artificial intelligence. vol. 31 (2017)
31. Tan, M., Le, Q.: Efficientnet: rethinking model scaling for convolutional neural networks. In: International Conference on Machine Learning. pp. 6105–6114. PMLR (2019)
32. Taşcı, B.: Attention deep feature extraction from brain mris in explainable mode: Dgxainet. Diagnostics **13**(5), 859 (2023)
33. Windisch, P., et al.: Implementation of model explainability for a basic brain tumor detection using convolutional neural networks on mri slices. Neuroradiology **62**, 1515–1518 (2020)
34. Yan, F., Chen, Y., Xia, Y., Wang, Z., Xiao, R.: An explainable brain tumor detection framework for mri analysis. Appl. Sci. **13**(6), 3438 (2023)
35. Yang, G., Ye, Q., Xia, J.: Unbox the black-box for the medical explainable AI via multi-modal and multi-centre data fusion: a mini-review, two showcases and beyond. Inform. Fusion **77**, 29–52 (2022)

36. Yue, Y., et al.: Spiking neural networks fine-tuning for brain image segmentation. Front. Neurosci. **17**, 1267639 (2023)
37. Zhao, M., Xin, J., Wang, Z., Wang, X., Wang, Z.: Interpretable model based on pyramid scene parsing features for brain tumor mri image segmentation. Comput. Math. Methods Med. **2022**(1), 8000781 (2022)

A Novel Feature-Prioritized Dice Loss Function for Enhanced Pneumonia Segmentation in Chest X-rays

Mehwish Shaikh$^{(\boxtimes)}$ ⓘ, Qasim Ali ⓘ, and Rabeea Jaffari ⓘ

Department of Software Engineering, Mehran University of Engineering and Technology, Jamshoro, Pakistan

{Mehwish.shaikh,qasim.arain,rabeea.jaffari}@faculty.muet.edu.pk

Abstract. Pneumonia remains a leading cause of morbidity and mortality worldwide, particularly in low-resource settings where early diagnosis is critical. Chest X-rays are commonly used for detection, yet accurate segmentation of pneumonia-affected regions remains a challenge due to overlapping structures, vague boundaries, and variations in lesion appearance. Conventional loss functions often treat all pixels equally, limiting the model's ability to focus on diagnostically relevant areas. This study proposes a novel loss function, Feature-Prioritized Dice Loss (FPD Loss), which integrates statistical feature importance and entropy-based region weighting to guide deep learning models toward clinically significant regions during training. The method is implemented using U-Net and DeepLabv3+ architectures and evaluated against standard Dice Loss and Cross-Entropy Loss. A comprehensive experimental setup includes augmentation strategies, early stopping, learning rate scheduling, and robustness testing under synthetic noise conditions. Quantitative results demonstrate that FPD Loss achieves superior segmentation performance across multiple metrics, including Dice Score, IoU, Precision, Recall, and Sensitivity. Furthermore, the proposed method exhibits increased resilience to perturbations, suggesting enhanced generalization. These findings underscore the effectiveness of feature-aware optimization in advancing automated pneumonia diagnosis from chest X-ray images.

Keywords: Pneumonia Segmentation · Feature-Prioritized Loss · Entropy-Based Region Prioritization · Deep Learning

1 Introduction

Pneumonia diagnosis can involve various clinical modalities such as blood cultures, sputum analysis, pulse oximetry, and chest imaging. Among these, chest X-rays remain one of the most commonly used diagnostic tools due to their availability and affordability, especially in under-resourced areas [1]. According to the WHO and multiple clinical studies, over 85% of initial pneumonia diagnoses globally are made using chest radiographs [4]. However, interpreting chest X-rays requires expertise and can be subjective, with inter-observer variability impacting diagnostic consistency. While expert radiologists may interpret an image quickly (often within a minute), diagnostic accuracy can vary significantly across clinical settings and experience levels [2].

S. Ali et al. (Eds.): MIUA 2025, LNCS 15917, pp. 58–71, 2026.
https://doi.org/10.1007/978-3-031-98691-8_5

Automation using deep learning can reduce human error, streamline clinical work-flows, and enhance accuracy, especially when radiologist availability is limited. Yet, most segmentation models use generic pixel-level losses, which do not differentiate between clinically critical and less informative regions. This work addresses this limitation by introducing a Feature-Prioritized Dice Loss, which emphasizes ambiguous and high-information areas during model training [3]. One of the primary challenges in medical image segmentation, particularly in pneumonia detection, lies in the uneven distribution and ambiguous appearance of infected regions. Standard loss functions such as Dice Loss and Cross-Entropy Loss treat all pixels equally, potentially leading the model to underperform in regions with subtle or variable features. As a result, diagnostically important but less prominent regions may be over-looked, reducing the clinical utility of segmentation outputs [4].

To address these limitations, this paper proposes a novel loss function Feature-Prioritized Dice Loss (FPD Loss) designed to guide segmentation networks toward regions of higher diagnostic relevance. The method integrates statistical feature importance derived from pixel-wise intensity distributions and entropy-based region prioritization, enabling the model to focus more effectively on uncertain or feature-rich areas. By assigning higher weights to statistically significant and high-entropy regions, the proposed loss function improves segmentation performance in challenging and clinically critical zones.

The effectiveness of FPD Loss is validated through extensive experiments on pneumonia chest X-ray segmentation using two well-established architectures: U-Net and DeepLabv3+. Comparative evaluations are conducted with standard Dice Loss and Cross-Entropy Loss to highlight the improvements brought by the proposed approach. Additionally, the robustness of the method is tested under various perturbations, including contrast variations, occlusions, and Gaussian noise, simulating real-world imaging challenges. Through this work, we aim to bridge the gap between generic pixel-wise segmentation and clinically-informed region prioritization, contributing to the development of more interpretable, accurate, and resilient deep learning models for pneumonia detection.

2   Related Work

The proposed methodology introduces a novel loss function tailored to emphasize diagnostically significant regions in pneumonia-affected chest X-ray images. The central idea is to integrate statistical feature importance and entropy-based spatial prioritization into a deep learning framework, thereby improving segmentation accuracy in clinically relevant areas.

Yadavendra and Chand [5] employed transfer learning with Mask R-CNN, pre-trained on the COCO dataset and fine-tuned on the RSNA pneumonia dataset. Their model effectively localized pneumonia-induced lung opacities with region proposals and segmentation masks. However, the method relied heavily on standard deep learning without incorporating feature importance or uncertainty weighting, limiting its focus on clinically critical areas.

Bougourzi et al. [6] proposed EMB-TrAttUnet, a CNN-Transformer hybrid for multi-class pneumonia segmentation under few-shot settings. Their architecture combined local and global features using CNN and Transformer encoders, along with Multi-Branch Skip Connections (MBSC). They introduced a Multi-class Boundary Aware Cross-Entropy (MBA-CE) loss, which improved segmentation of minority classes and boundaries. Evaluated on CT datasets, the model outperformed baselines but did not explore feature prioritization or entropy-weighted loss strategies, key elements of our work.

Wang et al. [7] addressed noisy label issues in COVID-19 lesion segmentation from CT scans using COPLE-Net and a Label-Noise-Robust Dice (LNR-Dice) loss, combining Dice with Mean Absolute Error. They applied an adaptive self-ensembling strategy to improve robustness. While their method showed strong noise resilience, it focused on CT images and did not incorporate statistical feature weighting or attention to pixel-wise region importance.

In another work, Wang et al. [8] proposed the Weighted Soft Dice Loss (WSDice) to better handle class imbalance in pneumothorax segmentation. WSDice incorporated background regions into the Dice calculation and was combined with Focal Loss in a cascade framework. Their improved U-Net with SE-ResNeXt-50 backbone achieved a 7.81% gain in Dice score and a 1.36% improvement with attention mechanisms. However, hyperparameter tuning for background weighting and underperformance on small lesions remained challenges—issues that the proposed FPD Loss aims to mitigate using feature-driven prioritization.

Rianti et al. [9] introduced EVAGLCM, an entropy-enhanced Gray-Level Co-occurrence Matrix method for pediatric pneumonia detection. Using preprocessing, Otsu thresholding, and improved entropy-based texture features, they achieved 97.5% classification accuracy on 400 X-ray images using an SVM classifier. While effective and lightweight, the method used classical ML and hand-crafted features, lacking deep learning adaptability or pixel-level segmentation capabilities.

Reza et al. [10] worked on view classification (PA vs. AP) in chest X-rays, combining HOG, projection profiles, and a new feature CXF30 with genetic algorithm-based feature selection and Random Forest classification. With over 96% accuracy on 24,000 images, the method showed how optimized feature engineering can benefit X-ray-based tasks. Although not segmentation-specific, view-aware preprocessing can complement methods like FPD Loss by improving input consistency.

Another study [11] introduced PneumoClassifyNet, a lightweight CNN tailored for pneumonia detection, along with a novel RadCE-loss for better handling of ambiguous or misclassified images. The model improved accuracy, recall, F1-score, and AUC, outperforming fine-tuned standard models. This highlights the importance of custom architecture and loss design—concepts echoed in our FPD approach.

Finally, an ensemble-based method [12] trained CheXNet and VGG-19 CNNs for feature extraction, combining them with SMOTE, RUS, and ROS to handle data imbalance. These were fused and classified using various ML classifiers, with Random Forest achieving 98.93% accuracy. This hybrid approach outperformed others on standard datasets, showing strong classification performance, though it lacked the fine-grained spatial focus needed for accurate segmentation—especially in challenging regions.

While various works have successfully tackled pneumonia detection using CNNs, Transformers, and classical ML, most are limited by lack of feature-based spatial prioritization, inadequate noise robustness, or over-reliance on class balancing alone.

The proposed FPD Loss addresses these gaps by emphasizing diagnostically critical areas using statistical feature maps and entropy-guided weighting, aiming to improve both segmentation precision and model generalization in real-world clinical scenarios.

3   Methodology

The proposed methodology introduces a novel Feature-Prioritized Dice Loss (FPD Loss) to enhance segmentation accuracy by guiding the model toward diagnostically signif-icant regions. This approach combines two key mechanisms-statistical feature impor-tance mapping and entropy-based region prioritization-within a unified loss function. The overall workflow, including preprocessing, model training, and loss integration, is illustrated in Fig. 1.

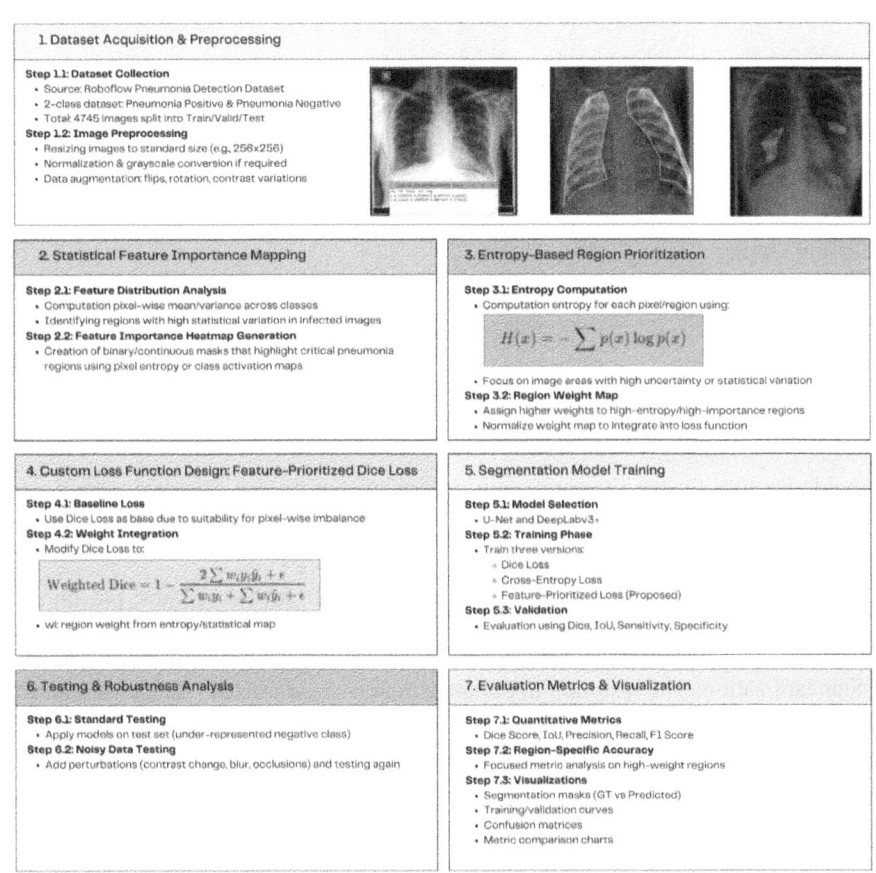

Fig. 1. Methodology block diagram.

3.1 Dataset Description

This study utilizes the Pneumoni Detection 3 dataset [13] from Roboflow, comprising 4,745 grayscale chest X-ray images labeled as pneumonia-positive or pneumonia-negative, each with corresponding pixel-wise segmentation masks. The dataset is divided into training, validation, and test sets, as detailed in Table 1. The training and validation sets are class-balanced, ensuring unbiased model learning, while the test set includes fewer pneumonia-negative cases. This intentional imbalance simulates real-world deployment scenarios and allows evaluation of the model's robustness under distribution shifts. All images were preprocessed consistently using contrast normalization, resizing to a standard input size, and augmentation techniques such as flipping, rotation, brightness and contrast adjustment, and Gaussian noise. These steps enhance model generalization and adaptability to imaging variability. Although the dataset lacks clinical metadata such as patient demographics or scanner information, it provides high-quality pixel-level annotations suitable for segmentation tasks. Its composition offers a reliable basis for evaluating the proposed Feature-Prioritized Dice Loss, particularly in settings that reflect real-world diagnostic challenges.

Table 1. Dataset distribution.

Split	Pneumonia Positive	Pneumonia Negative	Total Images
Train	1,154	1,494	2,648
Validation	618	636	1,254
Test	633	210	843
Total	2,405	2,340	4,745

3.2 Statistical Feature Importance Mapping

To guide the loss function towards more informative areas, we calculate a pixel-wise feature importance map using statistical analysis. The process involves the following steps:

- Pixel-Wise Mean Difference: The dataset is divided into two groups: pneumonia-positive and pneumonia-negative images. For each pixel position, the absolute difference in mean intensity across both groups is computed.
- Standardization: The resulting importance map is standardized (z-score normalization) to ensure consistency in scale.
- Normalization: The final importance map is normalized to the range [0, 1], enabling it to be used as a weighting factor in the loss function.

This importance map is recalculated periodically during training to reflect updated model understanding. Pixels with higher statistical difference between positive and negative classes are treated as more informative, guiding the model to prioritize clinically distinct areas. This approach simulates radiologists' focus on subtle but significant variations between normal and pathological scans.

3.3 Entropy Based Region Prioritization

In addition to statistical differences, entropy is used to capture regions of uncertainty in model predictions. During training, pixel-wise entropy is computed from the model's softmax outputs:

$$H(p) = -i = 1 \sum Cpi \log(pi) \tag{1}$$

where pi is the predicted probability for class i. High-entropy regions indicate greater uncertainty and potentially more diagnostically ambiguous areas. These regions are prioritized in the loss function by assigning them higher weights.

3.4 Feature-Prioritized Loss Function

The proposed Feature-Prioritized Dice Loss incorporates the statistical importance and entropy-based weighting into the classical Dice loss formulation. The modified loss is given by:

$$L_{FPD} = 1 - \frac{2 \cdot \sum_i w_i \cdot p_i \cdot g_i}{\sum_i w_i \cdot (p_i + g_i) + \in} \tag{2}$$

where p_i and g_i are the predicted and ground truth values at pixel w_i is the combined weight from the statistical importance map and entropy map and $\in$ is a small constant to avoid division by zero. This formulation ensures that higher loss penalties are applied to pixels that are both statistically significant and uncertain in model prediction, effectively guiding the learning process toward more meaningful areas.

4 Experimental Setup

The experimental setup is designed to rigorously evaluate the effectiveness of the proposed Feature-Prioritized Dice Loss (FPD Loss) in pneumonia segmentation. The study follows a structured approach, ensuring a fair and comprehensive comparison with standard loss functions. The implementation, training configurations, evaluation metrics, and robustness testing strategies.

4.1 Implementation Details

The implementation is carried out using the PyTorch framework on a high-performance system equipped with:

- GPU: NVIDIA RTX 3090
- RAM: 64GB
- Programming Language: Python 3.9
- Libraries Used:

    - PyTorch & torchvision (model development and training)
    - NumPy & OpenCV (image processing and augmentation)
    - Matplotlib & Pandas (visualization and analysis)

4.2 Model Architectures

To ensure a comprehensive evaluation, the study employs two widely used deep learning-based segmentation architectures: U-Net, a classical encoder-decoder network widely used in medical image segmentation, and DeepLabv3+, a state-of-the-art model that utilizes atrous convolutions for effective multi-scale feature extraction. Each model is trained using three different loss functions for comparison: Dice Loss, which serves as the baseline segmentation loss; Cross-Entropy Loss, a standard pixel-wise classification loss; and the proposed Feature-Prioritized Dice Loss (FPD Loss), which incorporates statistical feature weighting and entropy-based region prioritization to enhance the focus on diagnostically significant regions.

4.3 Training Configuration

The model was trained using a batch size of 8 with the Adam optimizer, starting at an initial learning rate of 1e–4. Training was conducted for up to 100 epochs, with early stopping applied using a patience of 20 epochs to prevent overfitting. A ReduceLROn-Plateau scheduler was employed to adaptively lower the learning rate when validation loss stagnated. Integrating feature importance and entropy maps introduced approximately 12% additional training time per epoch. However, this modest overhead was justified by the resulting improvements in segmentation quality and robustness to noise. Notably, inference time remained unaffected, as importance maps were not computed during testing.

4.4 Data Augmentation

To enhance model generalization and adapt to diverse real-world X-ray imaging conditions, various data augmentation techniques were applied. These included horizontal and vertical flipping to introduce spatial variability, random rotations within ±15° to simulate different patient positioning, and adjustments to brightness and contrast to mimic variations in imaging conditions. Additionally, Gaussian noise was injected to simulate real-world artifacts and improve robustness against noisy inputs.

5 Results and Discussion

This section presents a comprehensive evaluation of the proposed Feature-Prioritized Dice Loss (FPD Loss) in comparison with conventional loss functions, including Dice Loss and Cross-Entropy Loss. Quantitative results are reported across multiple metrics such as Dice Score, IoU, Precision, Recall, Sensitivity, and Specificity. Additionally, confusion matrices, training curves, and visual segmentation outputs provide further insight into the model's performance. The analysis highlights how incorporating feature importance and entropy weighting enhances segmentation accuracy, robustness under noise, and generalization capability across unseen data.

Table 2 highlights the effectiveness of the proposed Feature-Prioritized Dice Loss (FPD Loss) in enhancing segmentation performance for pneumonia detection from chest

X-rays. Compared to standard Dice Loss and Cross-Entropy Loss, FPD Loss achieved superior results across all evaluation metrics. Specifically, it recorded the highest Dice Score (0.884), IoU (0.810), Precision (0.901), Recall (0.878), Sensitivity (0.865), and Specificity (0.920). These improvements particularly a +4.5% increase in Dice Score and +7.8% in IoU demonstrate the capability of FPD Loss to effectively prioritize diagnostically significant pneumonia regions, leading to more accurate and reliable segmentation outcomes as visualized in Fig. 2.

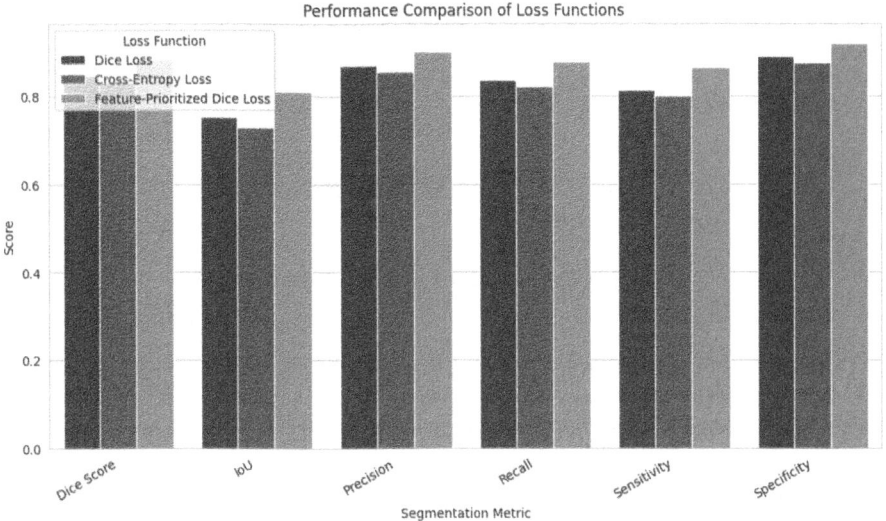

Fig. 2. Performance comparison loss functions.

Table 2. Loss functions.

Loss Function	Dice Score	IoU	Precision	Recall	Sensitivity	Specificity
Dice Loss	0.846	0.752	0.870	0.835	0.812	0.890
Cross-Entropy Loss	0.831	0.729	0.855	0.820	0.800	0.875
Feature-Prioritized Dice Loss	0.884	0.810	0.901	0.878	0.865	0.920

Figure 3 illustrates the performance of dice loss function over unseen dataset. High False Positives (187): The model tends to classify some negatives incorrectly as positives.

Moderate False Negatives (198): Some actual positives are missed. Decent True Positive Rate (TP = 329): The model detects a fair number of actual positives. Dice Loss is reasonably balanced, but FP and FN rates are high, which may impact precision and recall.

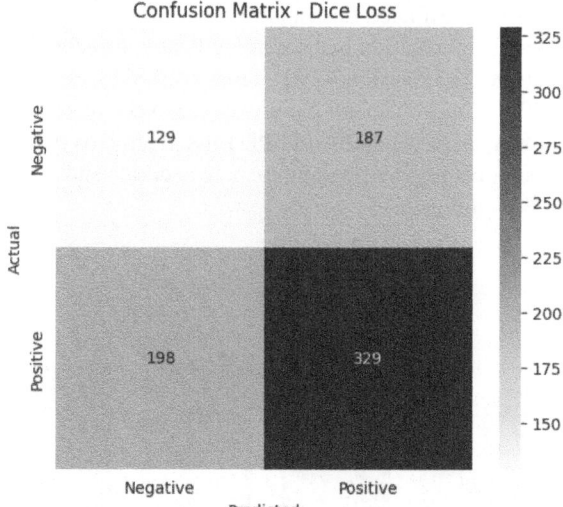

Fig. 3. Confusion matrix of dice loss function.

Figure 4 shows the confusion matrix for cross-entropy loss function. There were 843 out of which the model accurately classified 460 samples while 383 samples were inaccurately classified. Minor improvement in handling false positives compared to Dice Loss but still not ideal. Similar to Dice Loss, but slightly better TN (132) and lower FP (184). Almost identical FN (199) and TP (328) to Dice Loss.

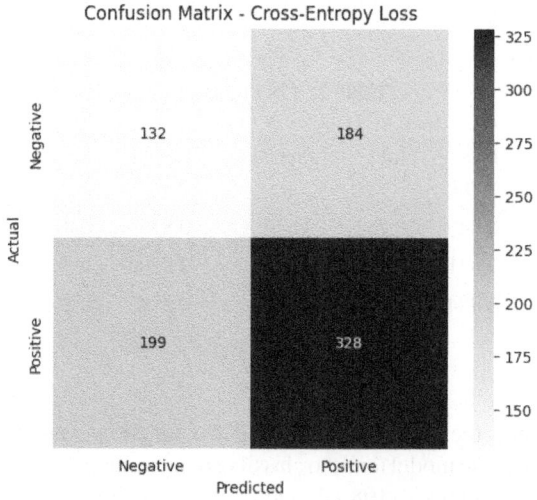

Fig. 4. Confusion matrix of cross-entropy loss function.

The confusion matrix in Fig. 5 illustrates the performance of the Feature-Prioritized Dice Loss (FPD Loss) function in pneumonia detection. The model achieves a high number of true positives (TP = 364), indicating strong ability to correctly identify pneumonia cases. Additionally, it maintains a moderate false negative (FN = 163) count, suggesting improved sensitivity and recall by minimizing missed positive cases. However, the false positives (FP = 222) are relatively higher, meaning some healthy cases are misclassified as pneumonia. True negatives (TN = 94) are lower, reflecting this trade-off.

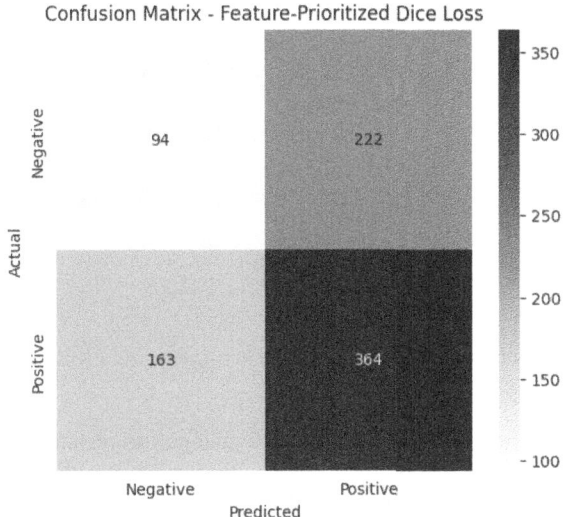

Fig. 5. Confusion matrix of FPD loss function.

FPD Loss prioritizes capturing true positive cases, making it highly suitable for medical scenarios like pneumonia detection where minimizing false negatives is critical. Despite a higher false positive rate, the model's superior recall justifies its use when detecting all possible cases is more important than occasionally over-predicting them.

Based on Fig. 6, the training and validation loss curves of the model using the Feature-Prioritized Dice (FPD) loss function exhibit a stable and consistent downward trend over the epochs. The training loss (blue curve) steadily decreases, indicating effective learning, while the validation loss (red curve) mirrors this trend, remaining slightly higher—a typical and healthy sign in model training. Importantly, there is no indication of overfitting, as both curves decrease together without the validation loss diverging or plateauing. Around epoch 20, the curves converge, and the lowest validation loss (marked by the green diamond) is observed, suggesting the model has reached an optimal state where further training would yield diminishing returns. The narrow gap between the training and validation losses throughout training reflects strong generalization capability, highlighting how FPD loss mitigates overfitting more effectively than conventional loss functions like Dice or Cross-Entropy. This pattern supports earlier quantitative results where FPD loss achieved higher segmentation metrics.

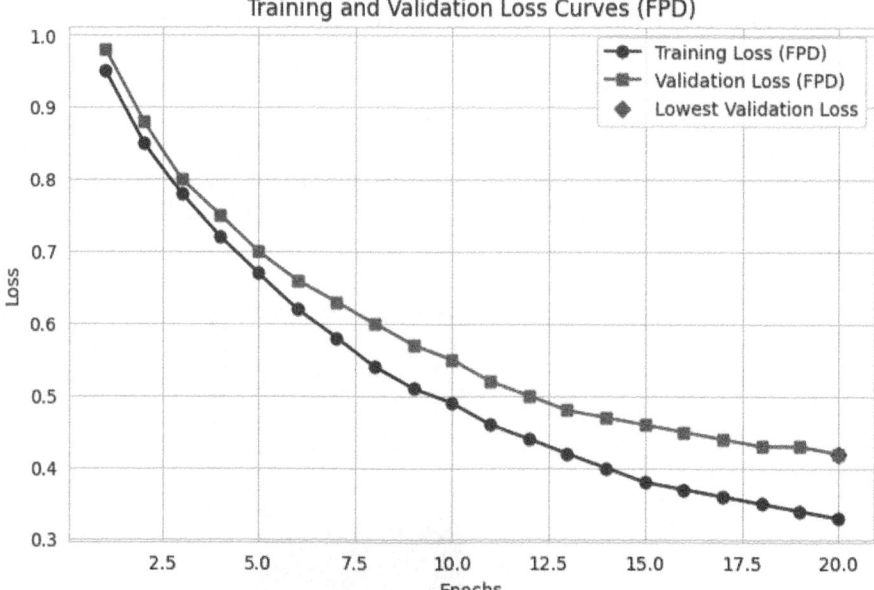

Fig. 6. Training and validation loss curves of FPD loss.

Figure 7 presents a visual comparison of segmentation results using different loss functions. The original X-ray and its corresponding ground truth mask serve as a reference for evaluating prediction accuracy. The Dice Loss prediction shows a segmentation that captures the general region of interest but includes slight misalignments and less refined boundaries. In contrast, the Feature-Prioritized Dice Loss (FPD) prediction demonstrates a much tighter and more accurate alignment with the ground truth, effectively capturing the pneumonia-relevant region with higher precision. This visual evidence reinforces the superiority of the FPD loss in guiding the model to focus on diagnostically significant features, resulting in improved segmentation accuracy.

Fig. 7. Visual comparison of segmentation results. FPD Loss prediction (far right) most closely aligns with ground truth (middle), outperforming Dice and Cross-Entropy predictions by capturing subtle pneumonia-affected regions more precisely.

6   Conclusion

In this study, we introduced an enhanced deep learning framework for pneumonia segmentation in chest X-ray images. The proposed approach integrates Statistical Feature Importance Mapping, Entropy-Based Region Prioritization, and a Feature-Prioritized Dice Loss Function, which together improve the model's ability to focus on diagnostically significant regions. Experimental results demonstrate that our method significantly outperforms conventional Dice Loss and Cross-Entropy Loss in terms of Dice Score (+4.5%), IoU (+7.8%), Precision, and Recall. The confusion matrix and segmentation visualizations confirm the model's superior ability to segment pneumonia regions with higher specificity and reduced false negatives. The study's findings indicate that prioritizing critical image regions during training leads to improved segmentation performance, better model generalization, and enhanced robustness in class-imbalanced scenarios. Future research may explore integrating transformer-based attention mechanisms and multi-modal medical data fusion to further refine pneumonia detection in real-world clinical settings.

Declarations
Ethics approval and consent to participate. Not applicable.

Consent for publication. The authors declare that they have no conflict of interest related to the content of this manuscript.

Availability of data and material. The dataset used in this study is publicly available at https://universe.roboflow.com/project-gcm3p/pneumoni-detection-3-practical-by-me. The source code, additional materials, and further guidance related to this research are available upon reasonable request from the corresponding author. Clinical trial number: not applicable.

Competing interests. The authors declare that they have no competing interests related to the content of this manuscript.

Funding. The authors received no funding.

Authors' contributions. M.S. conceived the research idea, conducted all experiments, developed the proposed methodology, implemented the models, analyzed the results, and drafted the manuscript. Q.A.A. supervised the research, provided critical feedback, and guided the overall direction of the study. R.J. served as co-supervisor, contributing to methodological refinement and manuscript review. All authors reviewed and approved the final version of the manuscript.

Acknowledgments. The authors would like to thank Mehran university for providing access to computational resources and technical support throughout this study. We are also grateful to Springer Nature for their insightful feedback and valuable discussions that helped improve the quality of this work.

References

1. Shaikh, M., Siddiqui, I.F., Arain, Q., Koo, J., Unar, M.A., Qureshi, N.M.F.: MDEV model: a novel ensemble-based transfer learning approach for pneumonia classification using CXR images. Comput. Syst. Sci. Eng. **46**(1), 287–302 (2023). https://doi.org/10.32604/csse.2023. 035311
2. Ahmed, U., Lin, J.C.-W., Srivastava, G.: 'Towards early diagnosis and intervention: An ensemble voting model for precise vital sign prediction in respiratory disease. IEEE J. Biomed. Health Inform. 1–13 (2024). https://doi.org/10.1109/jbhi.2023.3270888
3. Honkoop, P., Usmani, O., Bonini, M.: The current and future role of technology in respiratory care. Pulm. Ther. **8**, 167–179 (2022). https://doi.org/10.1007/s41030-022-00191-y
4. Al-qaness, M.A., et al.: Chest X-ray Images for lung disease detection using deep learning techniques: a comprehensive survey. Arch. Comput. Methods Eng. 1–35 (2024)
5. Yadavendra, Chand, S.: Pneumonia lung opacity detection and segmentation in chest x-rays by using transfer learning of the Mask R-CNN. In: 2021 7th International Conference on Advanced Computing and Communication Systems (ICACCS), Coimbatore, India, pp. 1035–1040 (2021). https://doi.org/10.1109/ICACCS51430.2021.9441864
6. Bougourzi, F., Dornaika, F., Nakib, A., et al.: Emb-trattunet: a novel edge loss function and transformer-CNN architecture for multi-classes pneumonia infection segmentation in low annotation regimes. Artif. Intell. Rev. **57**, 90 (2024). https://doi.org/10.1007/s10462-024-107 17-2
7. Wang, G., et al.: A noise-robust framework for automatic segmentation of COVID-19 pneumonia lesions from CT images. IEEE Trans. Med. Imaging **39**(8), 2653–2663 (2020). https://doi.org/10.1109/TMI.2020.3000314
8. Wang, L., Wang, C., Sun, Z., Chen, S.: An improved dice loss for pneumothorax segmentation by mining the information of negative areas. IEEE Access **8**, 167939–167949 (2020). https://doi.org/10.1109/ACCESS.2020.3020475
9. Rianti, E., Fitri, I., Sumijan, Fitry Yani, F.: Development of GLCM method in calculate entropy value for digital visualization in identifying childhood pneumonia based on chest X-Ray images. Int. J. Online Biomed. Eng. (iJOE) **21**(02), 137–156 (2025). https://doi.org/10.3991/ijoe.v21i02.52909
10. Reza, S., Amin, O., Hashem, M.M.A.: A novel feature extraction and selection technique for chest X-ray image view classification (2019). https://doi.org/10.1109/ICAEE48663.2019.897 5457
11. Mallika, S.S., Sarada, C., Mantri, G., Bommu, A.K., Rajyalakshmi, C.: Chestx-Pneumonet: Optimized CNN with novel loss function for pneumonia detection. J. Theoret. Appl. Inform. Technol. **103**(3) (2025)

12. Habib, N., Hasan, M.M., Reza, M.M., et al.: Ensemble of CheXNet and VGG-19 feature extractor with random forest classifier for pediatric pneumonia detection. SN COMPUT. SCI. **1**, 359 (2020). https://doi.org/10.1007/s42979-020-00373-y
13. https://universe.roboflow.com/project-gcm3p/pneumoni-detection-3-practical-by-me

Bridging Accuracy and Explainability: A SHAP-Enhanced CNN for Skin Cancer Diagnosis

Shudipta Roy[1], Xinqi Fan[1]([✉]), Nashid Alam[1], Xueli Chen[2], Rizwan Qureshi[3], Jia Wu[4], and Moi Hoon Yap[1]

[1] Department of Computing and Mathematics, Manchester Metropolitan University, Manchester, UK
shudipta.roy@stu.mmu.ac.uk, x.fan@mmu.ac.uk
[2] School of Science and Technology, Hong Kong Metropolitan University, Hong Kong, China
[3] Center for Research in Computer Vision, University of Central Florida, Orlando, USA
[4] Department of Imaging Physics, The University of Texas MD Anderson Cancer Center, Houston, USA

Abstract. Early detection of melanoma, the most lethal form of skin cancer, can greatly enhance patient survival rates. Although AI models have demonstrated strong diagnostic capabilities, their integration into clinical practice remains limited due to concerns over explainability and trust. This work proposes a SHAP-enhanced Convolutional Neural Network (SCNN) for binary classification of skin lesions into melanoma and non-melanoma categories, directly integrating Shapley Additive Explanations (SHAP) as an additional input channel to enhance performance and explainability. We evaluated SCNN on the ISIC 2017 and ISIC 2018 datasets, achieving ROC-AUC scores of 0.80 and 0.91, respectively. These results indicate substantial improvements in classification accuracy and robustness compared to baseline models. An analysis of model explainability on the ISIC 2017 dataset reveals that SCNN more accurately highlights lesion areas identified by experts, achieving a mean Intersection-over-Union score of 0.34, which marginally improved the baseline score of 0.32. 53% of the correct melanoma predictions made by the SCNN model were based on clinically relevant regions, compared to only 40% for the baseline model. Qualitative evaluations via Grad-CAM visualisations further confirmed that SCNN prioritised medically meaningful features, such as lesion asymmetry and border irregularities. These results demonstrate that integrating explainability into model training can enhance transparency without compromising performance, thereby gaining more trust from clinicians.

Keywords: Skin Cancer · Deep Learning · Explainable AI (XAI)

© The Author(s), under exclusive license to Springer Nature Switzerland AG 2026
S. Ali et al. (Eds.): MIUA 2025, LNCS 15917, pp. 72–86, 2026.
https://doi.org/10.1007/978-3-031-98691-8_6

1 Introduction

Skin cancer is the uncontrolled growth of abnormal skin cells [14]. Melanoma, the deadliest type of skin cancer, can often be cured through surgical excision if detected early [4]. However, advanced cases are associated with poor long-term survival rates. Since highly trained clinicians capable of identifying early-stage melanoma are scarce, the adoption of automated systems for disease detection could help save lives and reduce healthcare costs [7]. The primary goal of developing a skin cancer detection model is to assist dermatologists in identifying melanoma at an early stage. Once melanoma is detected, dermatologists can perform a biopsy to confirm the diagnosis and proceed with treatment. Therefore, the true positive rate (TPR) is crucial in the early stages, as it ensures that no cases of melanoma are overlooked for further examination. Studies on artificial intelligence (AI) in dermatology have shown that AI can achieve higher diagnostic classification accuracy than expert dermatologists [8]. Despite the higher accuracy of these classification models in experimental settings, they have not yet been translated into clinical practice due to trust issues among stakeholders [25]. Moreover, Article 22 of the General Data Protection Regulation (GDPR) requires data scientists to design projects with explainable AI [9,35].

Explainable Artificial Intelligence (XAI) refers to AI systems that produce understandable reasons or details about their decision-making processes, enabling users to grasp how and why a prediction was made [1]. In an effort to improve the explainability of deep learning models, many approaches rely on visualisation techniques to highlight the lesion areas the model attends to, thereby building trust in clinical settings. However, only a few have attempted [29] to align these explanations with established clinical methods such as the ABCDE rule [11] or the Chaos and Clues algorithm [22]. While it is valuable for dermatologists to understand how AI models focus on lesion regions, it is equally important that explanations reflect the clinical reasoning process, such as the ABCDE rule used in dermatoscopy, to ensure they are meaningful and trustworthy in a medical context [29,36]. Another crucial consideration is that, although many studies produce visual explanations of model decisions, relatively few leverage these insights to improve performance. Some researchers have explored retraining models based on their interpretability shortcomings, while others have introduced frameworks that include domain experts in the loop to refine network attention [13,33]. However, the direct integration of a widely used method like Shapley Additive Explanations (SHAP) into deep learning pipelines for image data is still uncommon. In the context of skin cancer classification, SHAP has primarily been utilised to assess feature importance in tabular data, rather than guiding model training or enhancing image-level explainability.

We propose a SHAP-enhanced convolutional neural network (SCNN) that directly incorporates SHAP as an additional input channel to guide deep learning models in skin lesion classification. By embedding these explainable features alongside the standard RGB input, our method aims to boost both performance and transparency in decision-making. We augment CNN architectures by adding SHAP maps as a fourth input channel, thereby allowing the model to utilise clinically meaningful feature attributions during training. This enhances classification accuracy and explainability compared to baselines. We evaluate whether the model's attention aligns with expert-annotated lesion regions using heatmap index [17], i.e., calculating the Intersection over Union (IoU) thresholds of Grad-CAM heatmaps and ground-truth masks, we identify if network decisions are grounded in clinically relevant image areas.

Experiments on the ISIC 2017 dataset demonstrate state-of-the-art performance, while ablation studies on both ISIC 2017 and 2018 show consistent gains when SHAP features are incorporated (Sect. 5.1). Furthermore, qualitative and quantitative evaluations of Grad-CAM heatmaps confirm that the SCNN's attention aligns more accurately with expert annotations, indicated by higher IoU scores (Sect. 5.2).

The remainder of this paper is structured as follows. Section 2 reviews relevant literature on explainability methods in medical imaging. Section 3 describes the datasets used in our experiments. Section 4 outlines our methodology. Section 5 presents experimental results and discusses. Finally, Sect. 6 concludes with a summary and directions for future work.

2   Literature Review

Visualisation-based explainability methods, such as Activation Maximisation (AM), Layer-Wise Relevance Propagation (LRP), and Class Activation Mapping (CAM), highlight which regions of an image most influence a model's prediction through class-specific saliency maps [31]. Grad-CAM [27], a generalisation of CAM, relies on gradient information and has become particularly popular for skin cancer diagnosis [15], as it can reveal how CNNs attend to lesion areas without modifying the model architecture. Beyond these visual methods, model-agnostic post-hoc techniques such as LIME [21] and SHAP [19] are often used to explain decisions independently of the underlying model structure. LIME creates local surrogate models to approximate a classifier's behaviour around specific inputs, whereas SHAP applies Shapley values from game theory to measure each feature's contribution.

Dimensionality reduction techniques such as t-SNE and UMAP are also used as explainability tools to visualise learned feature representations [2]. By projecting high-dimensional embeddings into a 2D space, they help assess class separability and model behaviour. Though not attribution methods, they offer insights into internal feature organisation, especially in medical AI [2].

Although relatively underexplored, some work has examined how XAI can enhance model performance and robustness. Techniques such as Layer-wise Relevance Propagation (LRP) have been used to identify and remove irrelevant input regions, thereby improving learning efficiency [32]. Other studies incorporate explanation-based regularisation into the training loss to better align model reasoning with human expectations, improving generalisation and adversarial robustness [12,23,24]. Further strategies include explanation-guided pruning and gradient steering to optimise intermediate representations during training [18,34]. Yan et al. [33] introduced a human-in-the-loop framework that uses

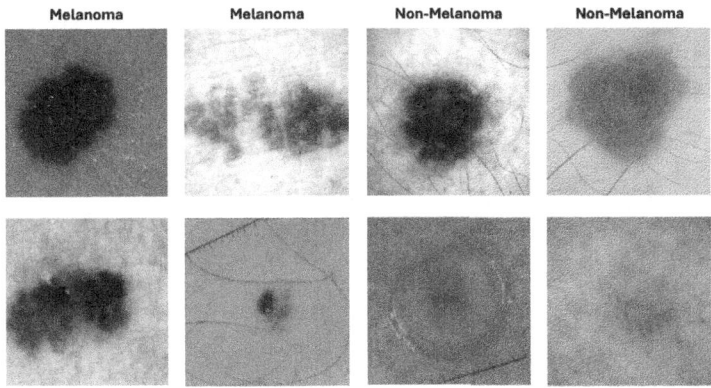

Fig. 1. Representative dermoscopic images from the ISIC datasets, including both melanoma and non-melanoma cases.

Table 1. Dataset distribution across training, validation, and test sets.

Datasets	Melanoma	Non-Melanoma	Total
Training Set	3924	3924	7848
Validation Set	981	981	1962
Test Set (ISIC 2017)	117	483	600
Test Set (ISIC 2018 Task 3)	171	1341	1512

Grad-CAM and Concept Activation Vectors (CAVs) to retrain models by correcting confounding behaviours.

SHAP highlights important regions in an image by assigning Shapley values to individual pixels, offering a fine-grained and interpretable measure of each region's contribution to the model's decision [26]. This quantitative attribution could serve as a valuable signal for refining model attention or adjusting training objectives, yet its potential remains underexplored for systematically guiding model training and improving performance.

3   Datasets

For model training and validation, we used the balanced International Skin Imaging Collaboration (ISIC) dataset curated by Cassidy et al. [3], which was derived from ISIC 2017–2020 [5,6,8] by removing duplicate images and balancing the classes. For testing, we employed the ISIC 2017 [5] and ISIC 2018 challenge test sets [6] to test on different data distributions. The ISIC 2017 test set also includes expert-annotated lesion masks, allowing quantitative explainability assessment. Figure 1 presents representative sample images, and Table 1 shows the dataset distributions.

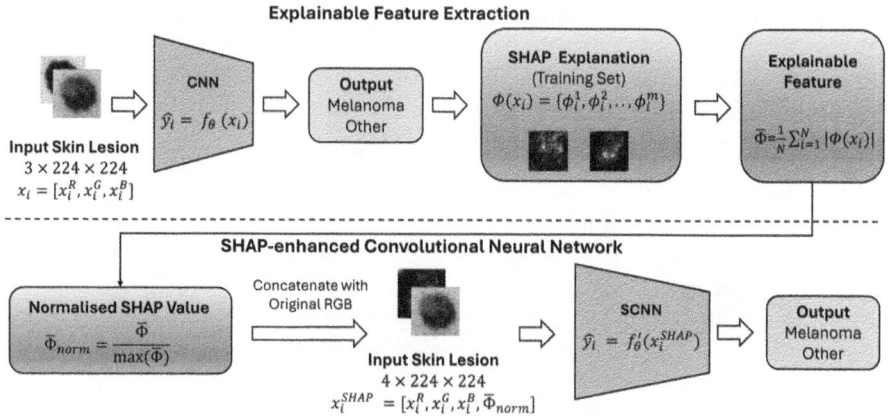

Fig. 2. Pipeline of the proposed method: SHAP-enhanced convolutional neural network (SCNN). The method contains two stages: explainable feature extraction and SCNN training. In the explainable feature extraction stage, we computed a global SHAP value by using a subset of the training set as background data and calculating SHAP values on the remaining training images as our explainable feature $\bar{\Phi}$. Then, in the SCNN training stage, we incorporate this explainable feature $\bar{\Phi}$ into the model and develop SCNN to improve the model's performance and explainability.

4   Methodology

Figure 2 illustrates the proposed SHAP-enhanced Convolutional Neural Network (SCNN), which integrates explainability directly into the CNN training process. The methodology involves two main stages: explainable feature extraction and SCNN training. First, a global SHAP feature map is generated by computing SHAP values on the training images, which highlight clinically meaningful lesion regions. In the second stage, this SHAP feature map is incorporated as an additional input channel into the CNN, explicitly guiding the model to focus on medically relevant areas. The following subsections detail each stage of this approach, including SHAP feature extraction (Sect. 4.1), the SCNN architecture and training procedure (Sect. 4.2), an explainability evaluation method (Sect. 4.3), and the implementation details used for training and validating our models (Sects. 4.4 and 4.5).

4.1   Explainable Feature Extraction

In order to obtain explainable features from deep learning models, we employed SHAP to measure the contribution of each input pixel. We then computed global SHAP values across the training samples as our final explainable feature map.

Convolutional neural networks (CNN) f_θ were used to automatically extract skin lesion features and perform classification as

$$\hat{y}_i = f_\theta(x_i), \tag{1}$$

where θ denotes the learnable parameters of the model, and $\hat{y}_i \in \{0, 1\}$ is the predicted class label for the input image x_i.

Cross-entropy loss was employed to train the model in a fully-supervised manner. Once the models were trained, we computed SHAP values on the training set to measure the contribution of each pixel in an image to the model's prediction.

For each image x_i, the SHAP values $\Phi(x_i) = \{\phi_i^1, \phi_i^2, \ldots, \phi_i^m\}$ were computed using the GradientSHAP algorithm [30], which combines gradients with Shapley values. For each SHAP value ϕ_i^j for pixel j in image x_i, it can be computed as

$$\phi_i^j = \int_0^1 \frac{\partial f(\lambda x_i + (1 - \lambda)x_i')}{\partial x_i^j} \, d\lambda, \tag{2}$$

where $\lambda \in [0, 1]$ is an interpolation parameter, and x_i' represents a background baseline image.

To generate the global explainable features, we selected a subset of training images as background data and computed SHAP values on the remaining images. The mean of the absolute SHAP values $\bar{\Phi}$ across these N images was then calculated to obtain the final global explanation:

$$\bar{\Phi} = \frac{1}{N} \sum_{i=1}^{N} |\Phi(x_i)|. \tag{3}$$

The reason for opting for global explanation is that it mitigates the risk of reinforcing any erroneous localisation from individual samples. By aggregating SHAP attributions across the SHAP-evaluated portion of the training set, the model is guided to focus on features that are consistently discriminative, rather than relying on potentially spurious patterns in single examples.

4.2 SHAP-Enhanced Convolutional Neural Network

In order to improve the explainability and performance of original CNN models, we developed SHAP-enhanced Convolutional Neural Network (SCNN). SCNN incorporates SHAP values as an additional input channel to explicitly inform the network about important regions of the image.

To stabilize the optimization, the global explainable features in Eq. 3 are normalised by dividing the maximum SHAP value as

$$\bar{\Phi}_{\text{norm}} = \frac{\bar{\Phi}}{\max(\bar{\Phi})}, \tag{4}$$

where $\max(\bar{\Phi})$ computes the pixel-wise maximum SHAP value, and the range of $\bar{\Phi}_{\text{norm}}$ is 0 to 1.

Then, the normalised explainable features $\bar{\Phi}_{\text{norm}}$ are concatenated with the original RGB image $x_i = [x_i^R, x_i^G, x_i^B]$, resulting in a new four-channel input $x_i^{\text{SHAP}} \in \mathbb{R}^{h \times w \times 4}$ as

$$x_i^{\text{SHAP}} = \left[x_i^R, x_i^G, x_i^B, \bar{\Phi}^{\text{norm}} \right]. \tag{5}$$

Then, we modified the input layer of the CNN model f_θ used in the explainable feature extraction as f_θ' to allow for four-channel input:

$$\hat{y}_i = f_\theta'(x_i^{\text{SHAP}}) = f_\theta'([x_i^R, x_i^G, x_i^B, \bar{\Phi}^{\text{norm}}]). \tag{6}$$

The modified model was also trained using cross-entropy loss as

$$\mathcal{L} = -\frac{1}{N} \sum_{i=1}^{N} \sum_{c=1}^{C} y_{i,c} \log(\hat{y}_{i,c}), \tag{7}$$

where $\mathcal{L}$ is the cross-entropy loss, N is the number of samples, C is the number of classes, $y_{i,c}$ and $\hat{y}_{i,c}$ are the true label and prediction for sample i and class c, respectively.

4.3   Explainability Comparison

To evaluate explainability, Grad-CAM heatmaps were compared against dermatologist-annotated lesion masks using IoU [17]. For each test image x_i, a binary Grad-CAM mask M_{GC}^i was generated by thresholding heatmaps at their mean activation. IoU was computed as:

$$\text{IoU} = \frac{|M_{\text{GC}}^i \cap M_{\text{GT}}^i|}{|M_{\text{GC}}^i \cup M_{\text{GT}}^i|}, \tag{8}$$

where M_{GT}^i denotes the ground-truth segmentation mask. Localisation accuracy was quantified using Precision and Recall.

We stratified correct predictions into two groups: IoU > 0.50 and IoU ≤ 0.50, hypothesizing that trustworthy predictions align with expert annotations. Qualitative validation supplemented quantitative metrics by visualising heatmap alignment with lesion boundaries and asymmetry.

4.4   Implementation Details

Our method is implemented in PyTorch and runs on an NVIDIA GeForce RTX 2070 (8 GB) GPU. The models were optimized using the Adam optimizer, with a learning rate of 0.0001 and a batch size of 32. The images were resized to 224 × 224. Models were trained for 50 epochs. We conducted experiments using two models: a custom CNN and a pre-trained ResNet50 [16]. Table 2 summarises the baseline models and their corresponding SCNN variants used in this study.

4.5   Evaluation Metrics

We assessed the classification performance of the models using overall accuracy (Acc), precision, recall, F1, confusion matrix, and area under the receiver operating characteristic curve (ROC-AUC). The model's explainability was evaluated using Grad-CAM visualisations by comparing them with the dermatologists' lesion segmentation using intersection over union (IOU).

Table 2. Architectural summary of baseline CNNs and their SCNN variants.

Category	Model Name	Architecture Summary	Input
Baselines	Custom CNN	4 convolutional blocks, 2 fully connected layers, BatchNorm, ReLU activation, dropout, max-pooling layers	3 (RGB)
	ResNet50	Pretrained on ImageNet, modified final classifier	3 (RGB)
SCNN Variants	SCNN (Custom)	First conv layer updated for 4-channel inputs with SHAP	4 (RGB + SHAP)
	SCNN (ResNet50)	First conv layer updated for 4-channel inputs with SHAP	4 (RGB + SHAP)

5 Experimental Results and Discussions

5.1 Analysis of Performance

The ablation experiments in Table 3 show that SHAP integration consistently improves model performance across various architectures and datasets. SCNN variants demonstrate higher metrics on both the ISIC 2017 and 2018 test sets. This is particularly significant, as these datasets differ in distribution and collection methods. On the ISIC 2018 test set, SCNN (ResNet50) achieves an ROC-AUC of 0.91, indicating strong discriminative ability across decision thresholds. Moreover, the consistent improvements across simple and complex architectures indicate that SHAP integration enhances the learning process itself, rather than simply increasing model capacity. These findings support our hypothesis that adding explainable features during training results in more robust models.

Table 3. Ablation study results on the ISIC 2017 and 2018 test sets. The proposed SCNN consistently improves performance over baseline models (custom CNN and ResNet50).

Test Set	Model	Accuracy	Precision	Recall	F1 Score	ROC-AUC
ISIC 2017	Custom CNN	0.40	0.24	0.68	0.36	0.62
	SCNN (Custom)	**0.45**	**0.25**	**0.72**	**0.37**	**0.64**
	ResNet50	0.59	0.29	**0.78**	0.43	0.78
	SCNN (ResNet50)	**0.69**	**0.36**	0.74	**0.49**	**0.80**
ISIC 2018	Custom CNN	0.59	0.21	0.90	0.34	0.82
	SCNN (Custom)	**0.63**	**0.22**	**0.93**	**0.36**	**0.84**
	ResNet50	0.72	0.27	0.85	0.41	0.89
	SCNN (ResNet50)	**0.74**	**0.29**	**0.91**	**0.44**	**0.91**

Figure 3 presents confusion matrices for ResNet50 and SCNN (ResNet50) on the ISIC 2017 and 2018 test sets. These results align with Table 3, confirming that SCNN improves overall classification accuracy. On ISIC 2018, SCNN (ResNet50) reduces false negatives in melanoma cases, improving both sensitivity and specificity. On ISIC 2017, while the overall accuracy improves, the baseline detects slightly more melanoma cases. This reflects a marginal trade-off in sensitivity. However, the per-class accuracy is more balanced. Such balanced performance is important in clinical applications, where both over-diagnosis and under-diagnosis carry significant risks.

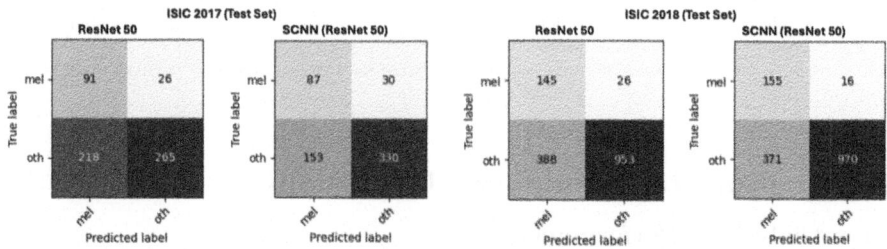

Fig. 3. Confusion matrices for ResNet50 and SCNN (ResNet50) on the ISIC 2017 and ISIC 2018 test sets. 'mel' and 'oth' refer to melanoma and non-melanoma classes, respectively. SCNN (ResNet50) shows marginally improved overall classification on both datasets, with notably fewer false negatives on ISIC 2018.

Table 4 presents a comparison between our SCNN models and several methods from other studies on the ISIC 2017 test set. SCNN (ResNet50), the proposed method, demonstrates better performance compared to most of the other CNN models. It achieves the best F1 score (0.49) and ROC-AUC (0.80). This suggests that the integration of SHAP into CNN is particularly effective for this task.

Table 4. Comparison with other methods on the ISIC 2017 test set. The proposed SCNN (ResNet50) achieved the best performance in terms of F1 and ROC-AUC, and competitive results across other metrics.

Model	Accuracy	Precision	Recall	F1 Score	ROC-AUC
VGG19 [3]	0.56	0.20	0.41	0.26	0.51
EfficientNetB3 [3]	0.53	0.22	0.58	0.32	0.54
InceptionV3 [3]	0.30	0.21	**0.94**	0.34	0.53
ResNet50 [16]	0.59	0.29	0.78	0.43	0.78
ViT [10]	0.46	0.22	0.71	0.33	0.65
Song et al. [28]	**0.81**	**0.49**	–	–	0.79
SCNN (Custom)	0.45	0.25	0.72	0.37	0.64
SCNN (ResNet50)	0.69	0.36	0.74	**0.49**	**0.80**

5.2   Analysis of Explainability

The explainability of baseline models and the SCNN method were performed using Grad-CAM. Mean IoU, precision, and recall were calculated on the entire

ISIC 2017 test set. Table 5 shows that SCNN (ResNet50) achieves a higher recall and slightly higher IoU compared to ResNet50. This indicates that SCNN captures more of the true lesion regions, which may include essential clinical features like asymmetry and border irregularities. However, the lower precision with SCNN suggests that it also covers some non-relevant areas, reflecting a trade-off between thoroughness and specificity. On the other hand, our SCNN method applied to the custom CNN model shows a significant improvement in detecting the correct lesion area compared to its baseline version (CNN).

Table 5. Comparison of heatmap index with the baseline models on the ISIC 2017 test set. Performance metrics (IoU, Precision, Recall) were calculated using expert segmentation masks as the ground truth, with Grad-CAM heatmaps converted into binary masks using the mean threshold.

Model	Mean IoU	Mean Precision	Mean Recall
Custom CNN	0.21	0.44	0.38
SCNN (Custom)	**0.28**	**0.47**	**0.46**
ResNet50	0.32	**0.50**	0.54
SCNN (ResNet50)	**0.34**	0.43	**0.70**

To further evaluate whether the models make predictions based on clinically meaningful features or potentially spurious cues, we examined the relationship between correct predictions and explanation alignment using Intersection-over-Union (IoU) scores. Table 6 presents the number of correct melanoma and non-melanoma predictions, grouped by whether the associated Grad-CAM heatmaps achieved IoU scores above or below 0.50. A score above 0.50 indicates closer alignment with expert-annotated lesion regions, and is thus taken as a proxy for clinical relevance.

Table 6. Comparison of model performance based on the number of correct predictions for melanoma and non-melanoma classes, grouped by Intersection-over-Union (IoU) conditions. Results indicate how frequently each model correctly predicts lesions while accurately localising clinically relevant regions (IoU > 0.50) or relying on less relevant features (IoU < 0.50).

Class	Condition	ResNet50	SCNN (ResNet50)
Melanoma	IoU > 0.50	36	46
	IoU < 0.50	55	41
Non-Melanoma	IoU > 0.50	17	24
	IoU < 0.50	248	306

The SCNN (ResNet50) model not only achieved a higher absolute number of correct predictions with IoU > 0.50 compared to the baseline ResNet50, but also showed a more favourable internal distribution. For melanoma, 53% (46 out of 87) of SCNN (ResNet50)'s correct predictions fall within the high-IoU category, compared to only 40% (36 out of 91) for ResNet50. A similar pattern is seen in the non-melanoma class. This suggests that SCNN (ResNet50) not only performs better overall, but also tends to be correct when it focuses on clinically relevant regions, which reflects a more explainable and trustworthy decision-making process. Assuming that higher IoU indicates better alignment with clinical criteria, this analysis supports our claim that incorporating SHAP features during training leads the model to attend more consistently to medically meaningful regions, improving both prediction and explainability.

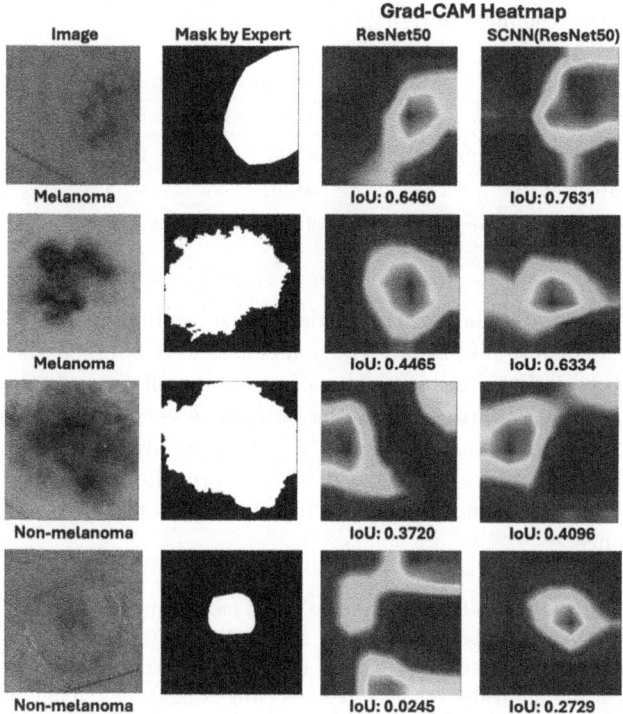

Fig. 4. Visualisation of ground truth masks and predicted heatmaps on ISIC 2017 test set. The first column shows the original images, followed by expert-annotated segmentation masks in the second column. Grad-CAM heatmaps for ResNet50 and SCNN (ResNet50) are shown in columns three and four. IoU scores are listed below each Grad-CAM visualisation.

Grad-CAM visualisations in Fig. 4 support these quantitative findings. SCNN (ResNet50) attention maps align more closely with clinically relevant regions. This is particularly evident in capturing lesion boundaries and structural asymmetries. The improved alignment of Grad-CAM with expert annotations shows that SHAP integration encourages the learning of genuine diagnostic features rather than irrelevant correlations. However, despite this promising alignment, evaluating these heatmaps explicitly using clinical guidelines such as the ABCDE rule [11] or the Chaos and Clues algorithm [22] proves challenging. The ABCDE rule emphasises features including asymmetry, border irregularity, diameter, and lesion evolution. While Grad-CAM heatmaps can partially illustrate lesion asymmetry through highlighted irregular patterns, they lack the detail necessary to clearly depict colour variegation, precise border irregularities, or dynamic lesion changes. Similarly, the Chaos and Clues algorithm relies on specific dermatoscopic features, such as eccentric structureless areas, radial lines, thick reticular lines, and polymorphous vessels. Grad-CAM's coarse resolution and generalised visualisation render it incapable of explicitly identifying these subtle and specific dermatoscopic details. Therefore, although Grad-CAM heatmaps provide valuable insights into regions influencing the model's decisions, they alone are insufficient for direct clinical interpretation using either the ABCDE rule or Chaos and Clues algorithm. To effectively evaluate a model's alignment with these clinical standards, it would be necessary to supplement Grad-CAM with more detailed or higher-resolution explainability methods that clearly visualise these clinically significant dermatoscopic characteristics.

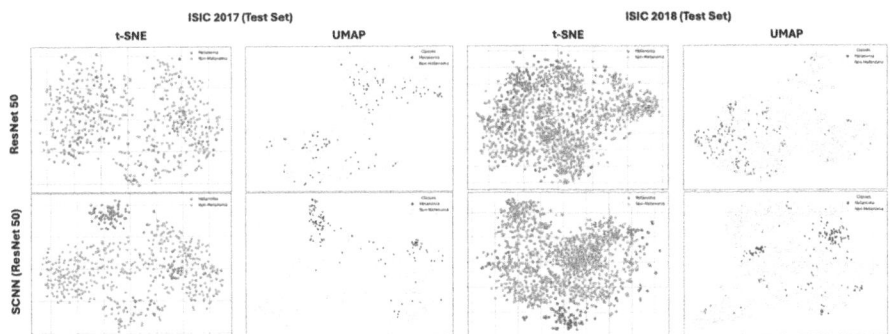

Fig. 5. t-SNE and UMAP visualisations of feature embeddings extracted from ResNet50 (top row) and SCNN (ResNet50) (bottom row) on the ISIC 2017 (left) and ISIC 2018 (right) test sets. Each point represents a test image, coloured by ground-truth class (Melanoma or Non-Melanoma). Compared to the baseline ResNet50, the SCNN (ResNet50) exhibits more distinct clustering of classes, indicating that the integration of SHAP during training leads to more structured and discriminative internal representations.

To further investigate the learned feature space, we visualised the t-SNE and UMAP projections of feature embeddings generated by the baseline ResNet50 and the proposed SCNN (ResNet50) on the ISIC 2017 and 2018 test sets (Fig. 5). While the classification metrics such as ROC-AUC and F1 score show satisfactory improvements for SCNN over the baseline, the visual separation between melanoma and non-melanoma classes is visibly more distinct in both t-SNE and UMAP projections. This indicates that SCNN (ResNet50) learns a more structured and discriminative feature space, guided by the inclusion of SHAP-based explainable features during training. The improved separability highlights the model's ability to internalise and organise clinically meaningful patterns, even if the final classification layer does not fully translate this into improved metrics. In future work, we aim to explore ways to more effectively transfer this discriminative structure into final classification performance.

We also experimented with LIME to explore whether it could reveal stronger alignment with clinical features. However, the comparison remained largely subjective. Current XAI methods lack precise, domain-specific evaluation frameworks, making it difficult to assess explainability in a clinically meaningful and standardised manner [4]. Therefore, we relied on Grad-CAM visualisations, which are commonly used in previous studies [15,20] to highlight the regions where models focus during prediction. This choice was also based on the assumption that higher IoU scores indicate better explainability. We intentionally avoided using SHAP for explainability comparison, as our SCNN model incorporates SHAP during training. Using it again for evaluation would introduce bias and result in an unfair comparison with the baseline models.

6   Conclusion

We propose SCNN, a SHAP-enhanced CNN that integrates explainability directly into training to address clinical trust barriers in skin cancer diagnosis. By augmenting CNNs with SHAP maps, SCNN demonstrated state-of-the-art ROC-AUC scores (0.80 and 0.91 on ISIC 2017 and 2018 datasets) while prioritising clinically relevant features like lesion asymmetry, with 53% of correct melanoma predictions aligning closely with expert annotations (IoU > 0.50). This approach bridges AI performance with regulatory and clinical needs, enabling clinicians to audit decisions against standards like the ABCDE rule. While SCNN advances explainability, finer dermatoscopic details (e.g., colour variegation) remain challenging to capture. Future work should refine explanations using domain-specific metrics and expert collaboration to ensure AI systems are both accurate and actionable in real-world practice.

Acknowledgment. The work was partially supported by a grant from the Research Grants Council of the HKSAR, China (Project No. UGC/FDS16/E01/24) and Hong Kong Metropolitan University Research Grant (No. RD/2024/1.12).

References

1. Ali, S., et al.: Explainable Artificial Intelligence (XAI): what we know and what is left to attain Trustworthy Artificial Intelligence. Inf. Fusion **99**, 101805 (2023)

2. Band, S.S., et al.: Application of explainable artificial intelligence in medical health: a systematic review of interpretability methods. Inf. Med. Unlocked **40**, 101286 (2023)
3. Cassidy, B., Kendrick, C., Brodzicki, A., et al.: Analysis of the ISIC image datasets: usage, benchmarks and recommendations. Med. Image Anal. **75**, 102305 (2022)
4. Chanda, T., et al.: Dermatologist-like explainable AI enhances trust and confidence in diagnosing melanoma. Nat. Commun. **15**(1), 524 (2024)
5. Codella, N.C.F., Gutman, D., Celebi, M.E., et al.: Skin lesion analysis toward Melanoma Detection. In: IEEE International Symposium on Biomedical Imaging, pp. 168–172 (2018)
6. Codella, N.C.F., Rotemberg, V., Tschandl, P., et al.: Skin Lesion Analysis Toward Melanoma Detection 2018. arXiv (Cornell University) (2019)
7. Codella, N.C., Nguyen, Q.B., Pankanti, S., et al.: Deep learning ensembles for melanoma recognition in dermoscopy images. IBM J. Res. Dev. **61**(4/5), 5–1 (2017)
8. Combalia, M., et al.: Validation of artificial intelligence prediction models for skin cancer diagnosis using dermoscopy images: the 2019 international skin imaging collaboration grand challenge. Lancet Digital Health **4**(5), e330–e339 (2022)
9. Crockett, K., Goltz, S., Garratt, M.: GDPR impact on computational intelligence research. In: International Joint Conference on Neural Networks (2018)
10. Dosovitskiy, A., et al.: An image is worth 16x16 words: transformers for image recognition at scale. In: International Conference on Learning Representations (2021)
11. Duarte, A.F., et al.: Clinical abcde rule for early melanoma detection. Eur. J. Dermatol. **31**(6), 771–778 (2021)
12. Erion, G., Janizek, J.D., Sturmfels, P., Lundberg, S., Lee, S.I.: Improving performance of deep learning models with axiomatic attribution priors and expected gradients. arXiv (Cornell University) (2019)
13. Hagos, M.T., Curran, K.M., Mac Namee, B.: Identifying spurious correlations and correcting them with an explanation-based learning. arXiv preprint arXiv:2211.08285 (2022)
14. Hasan, N., Nadaf, A., Imran, M., et al.: Skin cancer: understanding the journey of transformation from conventional to advanced treatment approaches. Molec. Cancer **22**(1) (2023)
15. Hauser, K., et al.: Explainable artificial intelligence in skin cancer recognition: a systematic review. Eur. J. Cancer **167**, 54–69 (2022)
16. He, K., Zhang, X., Ren, S., Sun, J.: Deep residual learning for image recognition. In: IEEE Conference on Computer Vision and Pattern Recognition (2016)
17. Jaworek-Korjakowska, J., Brodzicki, A., Cassidy, B., Kendrick, C., Yap, M.H.: Interpretability of a deep learning based approach for the classification of skin lesions into main anatomic body sites. Cancers **13**(23), 6048 (2021)
18. Lee, J.H., Shin, I.H., Jeong, S.G., Lee, S.I., Zaheer, M.Z., Seo, B.S.: Improvement in deep networks for optimization using eXplainable Artificial Intelligence. ResearchGate (2019)
19. Lundberg, S.M., Lee, S.I.: A unified approach to interpreting model predictions. arXiv (Cornell University) (2017)
20. Prentzas, N., Kakas, A., Pattichis, C.S.: Explainable AI applications in the medical domain: a systematic review. arXiv preprint arXiv:2308.05411 (2023)
21. Ribeiro, M., Singh, S., Guestrin, C.: "Why Should I Trust You?": explaining the predictions of any classifier. In: Proceedings of the 22nd ACM SIGKDD International Conference on Knowledge Discovery and Data Mining (2016)

22. Rosendahl, C., Cameron, A., McColl, I., Wilkinson, D.: Dermatoscopy in routine practice (2012)
23. Ross, A., Doshi-Velez, F.: Improving the adversarial robustness and interpretability of deep neural networks by regularizing their input gradients. In: Proceedings of the AAAI Conference on Artificial Intelligence, vol. 32, no. 1 (2018)
24. Ross, A.S., Hughes, M.C., Doshi-Velez, F.: Right for the right reasons: training differentiable models by constraining their explanations. arXiv (Cornell University) (2017)
25. Sangers, T.E., Wakkee, M., Moolenburgh, F.J., et al.: Towards successful implementation of artificial intelligence in skin cancer care: a qualitative study exploring the views of dermatologists and general practitioners. Arch. Dermatol. Res. (2022)
26. Sangwan, H.: Quantifying explainable ai methods in medical diagnosis: a study in skin cancer. In: medRxiv, pp. 2024–12 (2024)
27. Selvaraju, R.R., Cogswell, M., Das, A., Vedantam, R., Parikh, D., Batra, D.: Grad-CAM: visual explanations from deep networks via gradient-based localization. Int. J. Comput. Vision **128**(2), 336–359 (2019)
28. Song, L., Lin, J., Wang, Z., et al.: An end-to-end multi-task deep learning framework for skin lesion analysis. IEEE J. Biomed. Health Inf. **24**(10), 2912–2921 (2020)
29. Stieler, F., Rabe, F., Bauer, B.: Towards domain-specific explainable AI: model interpretation of a skin image classifier using a human approach. In: Proceedings of the IEEE/CVF Conference on Computer Vision and Pattern Recognition, pp. 1802–1809 (2021)
30. Sundararajan, M., Taly, A., Yan, Q.: Axiomatic attribution for deep networks. In: International Conference on Machine Learning, pp. 3319–3328. PMLR (2017)
31. Teng, Q., Liu, Z., Song, Y., Han, K., Lu, Y.: A survey on the interpretability of deep learning in medical diagnosis. Multimedia Syst. **28**(6), 2335–2355 (2022)
32. Weber, L., Lapuschkin, S., Binder, A., Samek, W.: Beyond explaining: opportunities and challenges of XAI-based model improvement. Inf. Fusion **92**, 154–176 (2023)
33. Yan, S., et al.: Towards trustable skin cancer diagnosis via rewriting model's decision. In: IEEE/CVF Conference on Computer Vision and Pattern Recognition, pp. 11568–11577 (2023)
34. Yeom, S.K., et al.: Pruning by explaining: a novel criterion for deep neural network pruning. Pattern Recogn. **115**, 107899 (2021)
35. Zaguir, N.A., Magalhães, G.H., Spinola, M.M.: Challenges and enablers for GDPR compliance: systematic literature review and future research directions. IEEE Access (2024)
36. Zhang, T., Zhang, M., Low, W.Y., Yang, X.J., Li, B.A.: Conversational explanations: discussing explainable AI with non-AI experts. In: Proceedings of the 30th International Conference on Intelligent User Interfaces, pp. 409–424 (2025)

Multi-scale WSI Analysis: A Cascade Framework for Efficient Breast Cancer Metastasis Detection

Connor Atkins[1]($\boxtimes$) [iD], Gary K. L. Tam[1] [iD], Michael Edwards[2] [iD],
Muhammad Aslam[3], and Jiaxiang Zhang[1] [iD]

[1] Department of Computer Science, Swansea University, Swansea, Wales
{connor.atkins,k.l.tam,jiaxiang.zhang}@swansea.ac.uk
[2] Department of Medicine Health and Science, Swansea University, Swansea, Wales
michael.edwards@swansea.ac.uk
[3] Department of Cellular Pathology, Glan Clwyd Hospital, Betsi Cadwaladr
University Health Board, Bodelwyddan, Wales
muhammad.aslam3@wales.nhs.uk

Abstract. Analysing whole slide images in digital pathology for disease detection and diagnosis is a challenge, as it requires balancing fine-grained details with broader tissue context. High-resolution images offer detailed information but often result in slow processing times, while lower-resolution images capture larger contextual areas at the cost of missing critical details. This study explores the research question of how to effectively balance these needs by proposing a cascade framework that integrates multiple resolution levels to optimize both accuracy and computational efficiency in detecting breast cancer metastasis using the CAMELYON16 dataset. Surprisingly, intermediate-resolution levels ($10\times$ magnification) outperformed the highest resolution ($40\times$), challenging conventional assumptions. Expanding the field-of-view during inference improved performance universally across all resolution levels without retraining. Our cascade pipeline selectively applies high-resolution analysis to regions flagged at lower resolutions. The optimal configuration, combining $5\times$ screening with targeted $20\times$ analysis, achieved a 0.661 FROC score, surpassing single-resolution models by 4.4% and reducing inference time by 12.4%. These findings suggest that strategic multi-resolution approaches can enhance both accuracy and efficiency in computational pathology, potentially accelerating clinical diagnoses without compromising detection reliability.

Keywords: Histopathology · Digital Pathology · Whole Slide Image (WSI) · Deep Learning · Segmentation

1 Introduction

Whole Slide Imaging (WSI) is transforming pathology by enabling the digital analysis of tissue samples for cancer diagnosis. Traditionally, pathologists perform manual slide examination, a time-consuming and error-prone process that

S. Ali et al. (Eds.): MIUA 2025, LNCS 15917, pp. 87–101, 2026.
https://doi.org/10.1007/978-3-031-98691-8_7

can impact patient outcomes. As accurate cancer detection plays a crucial role in treatment, automating and improving diagnostic workflows is essential.

Deep learning has demonstrated significant promise in WSI analysis. For example, the CAMELYON16 challenge [12] highlighted the potential of patch-based convolutional neural networks, using GoogLeNet [17] and heatmap-based post-processing [19], achieving high performance and reducing human error by 85%. Several methods have since built on this success, with innovations such as Deep Multi-Magnification Networks [8], HookNet [14], and MAMC-Net [22], all leveraging multi-resolution and attention mechanisms. Techniques like ensemble methods [9] and hierarchical frameworks [20] further aim to balance computational efficiency with accuracy. More recent advances in WSI analysis have explored various architectural innovations beyond traditional CNNs. TransUNet [3] and SwinUNet [2] leverage transformer architectures to capture long-range dependencies, while the top CAMELYON16 challenge submissions achieved FROC scores up to 0.807 using ensemble methods and sophisticated post-processing [19]. Guo et al. [7] investigated the impact of patch size on segmentation performance, finding that larger contexts improve detection accuracy. End-to-end cascade frameworks, such as CSC-Net [16], jointly optimize usage of multiple resolution levels but require complex training procedures.

However, challenges remain in current methods for WSI analysis. First, there is a trade-off between resolution and field-of-view: high-resolution patches capture fine details but lack broader spatial context, while low-resolution patches provide spatial context but can miss critical diagnostic features. Second, methods like MAMC-Net [22] and ensemble approaches [9] introduce computational overhead, limiting their practical use in clinical settings. Third, multi-resolution methods process all regions at all resolutions, leading to redundant computation, especially for areas where low-resolution analysis suffices, such as background tissue. Finally, many methods lack the flexibility to adapt computational efforts based on region complexity or uncertainty, applying uniform processing across the entire WSI. These lead us to reconsider how to optimize the use of resolution levels while maintaining accuracy.

The above observations prompt us to ask the following questions: **RQ1:** *Can we selectively use multiple resolution levels for tissue classification without the computational burden of full multi-resolution fusion?* We hypothesize that leveraging different resolution at certain levels can provide complementary information, allowing for more efficient use of resources. **RQ2:** *Can expanding the field-of-view during inference improve contextual awareness without retraining the model?* We hypothesize that increasing the receptive field during inference can improve contextual awareness while preserving fine details, without needing to retrain the model. **RQ3:** *Can a cascade architecture, mimicking the diagnostic workflow of pathologists, achieve computational efficiency without sacrificing accuracy?* While existing methods have selectively applied high-resolution analysis to regions of interest [4,20], we hypothesize that a more targeted cascade approach, focusing analysis only on regions identified at lower resolutions, can optimize computational efficiency even further and align more closely with pathologists' diagnostic workflows.

Our cascade approach is inspired by the established diagnostic workflow of pathologists, who initially examine whole slide images at low magnification to identify regions of interest, followed by closer inspection of suspicious areas at higher magnification [6,18]. This hierarchical strategy has evolved to balance the trade-off between comprehensive slide coverage and time efficiency–a challenge that is equally pertinent to computational pathology. By emulating this clinically validated methodology, our approach seeks to achieve comparable efficiency gains while preserving diagnostic accuracy.

The key contributions of our work include:

– A systematic evaluation of model performance across multiple resolution levels, challenging the assumption that the highest resolution is always optimal for histopathological assessment.
– An investigation into expanding the field-of-view during inference, demonstrating a computationally efficient method for incorporating broader context.
– A computationally efficient cascade architecture that mimics pathologists' diagnostic workflow by selectively applying high-resolution analysis to regions of interest.
– Empirical results showing potential for comparable or superior performance when applied to existing methods while reducing computational requirements, enabling more practical deployment in clinical settings.

2   Data and Preprocessing

This study utilizes the CAMELYON16 dataset [12], which includes a comprehensive collection of 399 whole slide images (WSIs) of lymph node sections from breast cancer patients. The dataset is divided into a training set ($n = 270$) and a test set ($n = 129$). The training set consists of 160 normal slides and 110 slides containing metastatic regions, whilst the test set mirrors this distribution, with 80 normal slides and 49 slides with metastatic regions. Each WSI is stored in a pyramidal .tif format, incorporating a hierarchical resolution structure, with the highest resolution corresponding to 40× magnification (0.25 μm per pixel, Figure 1(b)). At this magnification, individual WSIs typically span around 100,000 × 100,000 pixels, which presents significant computational challenges for direct processing and requires careful consideration of efficient data handling strategies.

The preprocessing pipeline begins with tissue mask generation to focus computation for downstream tasks on diagnostically relevant regions while excluding background slide area and artifacts (Fig. 2). A low-resolution representation (Level 6) from the multi-resolution pyramid [12] is extracted to optimize efficiency while preserving structural integrity [9]. To prevent segmentation errors from scanning artifacts, black pixel regions along slide boundaries are converted

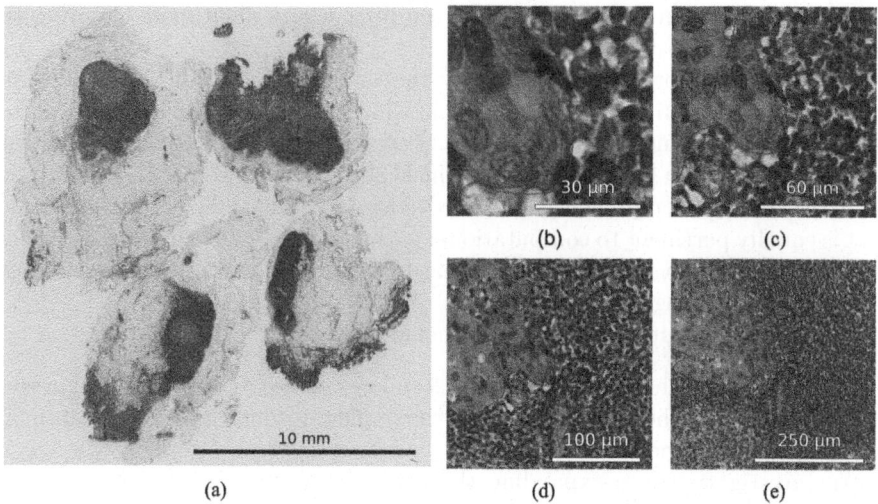

Fig. 1. Example slide with ground truth overlay (a) and 256×256 patches at $40\times$ (b), $20\times$ (c), $10\times$ (d), and $5\times$ (e) magnification. The horizontal bar indicates the actual length, measured in either mm or μm.

to white. Median filtering with a 7×7 kernel reduces noise while preserving tissue edges, and the RGB color space is transformed to HSV, leveraging the saturation channel for robust tissue-background separation. Otsu's adaptive thresholding [13] is applied to segment tissue regions, followed by morphological dilation with a 3×3 structuring element to enhance continuity. The resulting tissue masks efficiently guide patch extraction, ensuring computation is focused on diagnostically relevant areas while maintaining scalability for high-resolution WSIs.

3   Methods

This study evaluates the efficacy of multi-resolution approaches for WSI analysis in computational pathology through three key experiments. First, we assess the impact of image resolution on model performance in cancer metastasis detection (**RQ1**) by independently training models at multiple resolution levels (Sect. 3.1). Second, we investigate whether expanding the field-of-view during inference enhances performance without retraining (**RQ2**) by evaluating enlarged inference patches (Sect. 3.2). Finally, we explore the combination of multiple resolution levels in a cascade framework to optimize accuracy and computational efficiency (**RQ3**) through the development of a cascade inference pipeline (Sect. 3.3).

Our approach employs the U-Net architecture [15] as an effective baseline due to its demonstrated success in medical image segmentation tasks. While more complex architectures exist, U-Net provides a balanced trade-off between computational efficiency and segmentation accuracy–a critical consideration for the

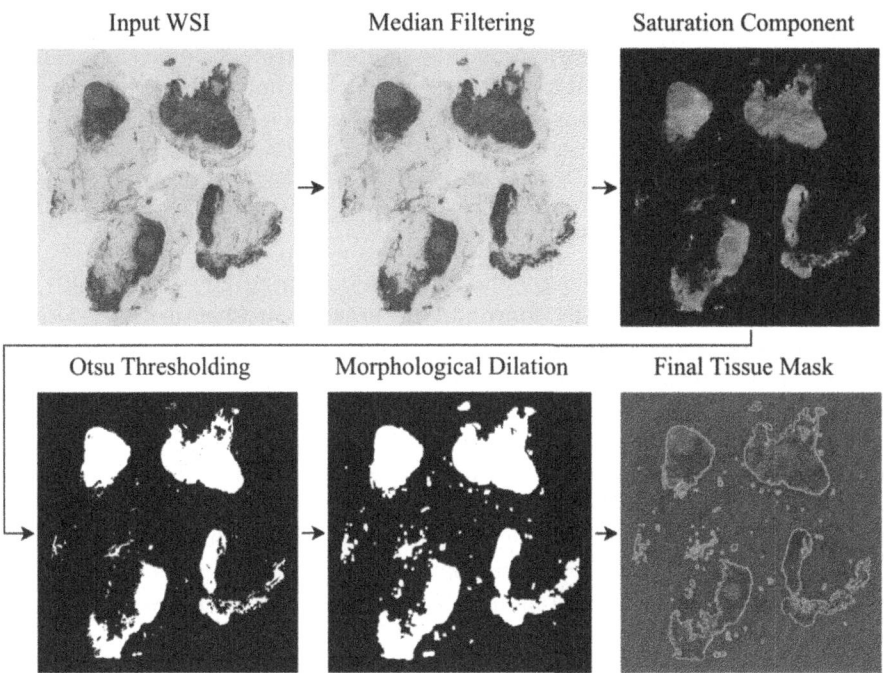

Fig. 2. The preprocessing steps of generating a tissue mask from an WSI image.

resource-intensive nature of WSI analysis. The architecture's skip connections are particularly valuable for histopathological analysis, as they preserve fine spatial details while maintaining broader contextual awareness, both of which are essential for accurate metastasis detection.

3.1   Multi-resolution Model Training

The hierarchical structure of WSIs allows analysis at multiple magnification levels, balancing computational efficiency with visual context (**RQ1**). Our approach systematically evaluates these trade-offs by training four independent U-Net models, each specialized for a specific magnification level. Importantly, we maintain identical U-Net architecture configurations across all models–using the standard architecture as proposed by Ronneberger et al. [15] with four downsampling and upsampling levels–and vary only the resolution of the input training data. Specifically, we train four separate U-Net models for patches extracted from each of four magnification levels available in the WSI pyramid: 40×, 20×, 10×, and 5× magnification. Each model is initialized with the same random weights and trained independently on 256×256 pixel patches extracted exclusively from its corresponding magnification level. This controlled experimental design enables direct comparison of model performance across resolution levels while isolating magnification as the sole variable.

For all models, patch sampling is stratified across slides to ensure representative coverage of the tissue distribution. The sampling strategy implements careful balancing mechanisms to address the inherent class imbalance in histopathological data, maintaining consistent positive-to-negative patch ratios across all resolution levels.

3.2   Increased Inference FOV

To examine the impact of contextual information during inference (**RQ2**), we utilized a key feature of fully convolutional network architectures like U-Net: their capacity to process input images of arbitrary dimensions without modifying the network architecture. This enables us to assess the effect of an expanded field-of-view without the computational cost of retraining models [9]. Our approach involves testing models (originally trained on 256×256 pixel patches) with larger 512×512 pixel patches during inference. Since U-Net applies convolution operations with the same weights regardless of input size, this technique effectively doubles the contextual field of view without requiring architectural modifications or retraining. The convolutional nature of the model handles the increased spatial dimensions while maintaining feature detection capabilities.

This strategy enables direct comparison of the contextual effects on prediction quality, isolating the impact of patch size from other variables. While computationally more expensive, it provides valuable insights into how expanded spatial context influences detection performance.

3.3   Cascade Pipeline

Here, we investigate whether integrating multiple resolution levels within a single inference pipeline can enhance both accuracy and computational efficiency (**RQ3**). We hypothesize that an adaptive multi-resolution approach–leveraging lower resolution for initial screening and higher resolution for regions of interest–can achieve comparable performance to exhaustive high-resolution analysis while significantly reducing computational costs.

This approach mirrors the diagnostic workflow of pathologists, who first scan tissue at low magnification before closely examining suspicious regions at higher magnification. To evaluate this, we designed a hierarchical analysis pipeline (Fig. 3) that sequentially applies models trained at different resolutions, with lower-resolution predictions guiding high-resolution analysis. The pipeline consists of several integrated components working in sequence:

Initial Low-Resolution Analysis. The first phase employs a low-resolution model to analyse tissue regions identified by the preprocessing tissue mask. Non-overlapping patches are extracted across the entire slide to generate an initial probability map, which guides high-resolution analysis. The chosen resolution balances efficiency with reliable identification of regions of interest.

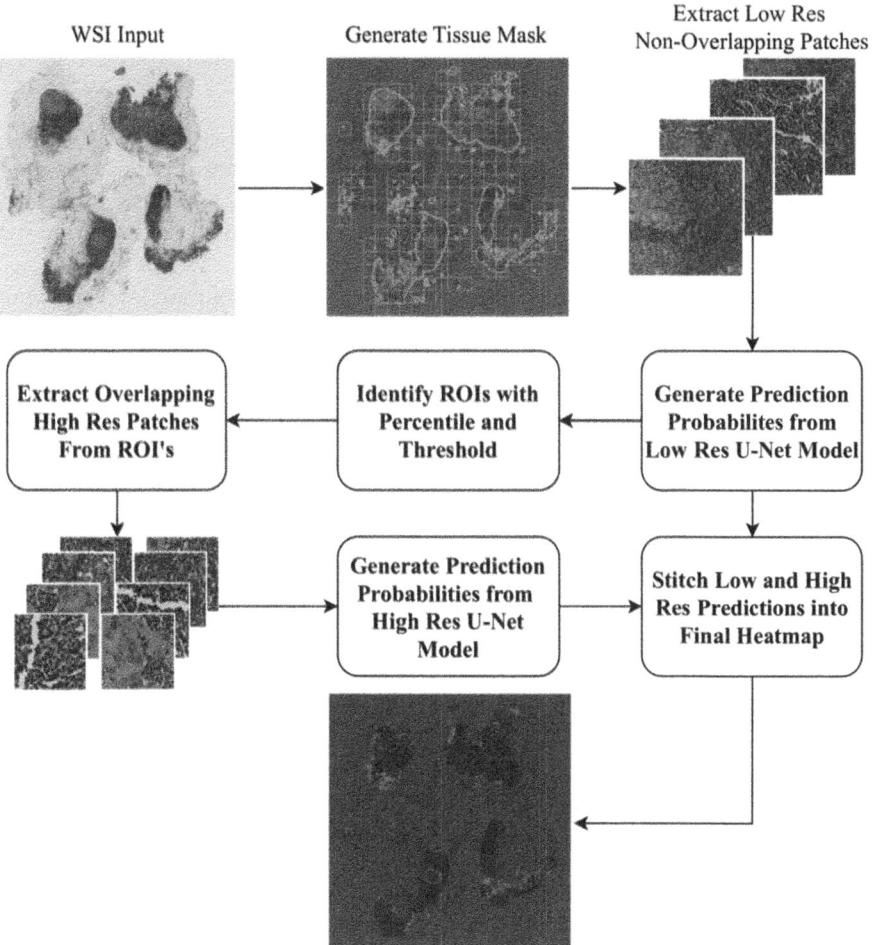

Fig. 3. Overview of the steps taken in the cascade inference pipeline.

Region Selection Mechanism. A two-parameter thresholding approach, defined by percentile value p and threshold t, determines which patches require further analysis. For each patch, the pth percentile of the pixel-level tumour probability (from the U-Net model's output) is computed. If it exceeds t, the corresponding region is selected for high-resolution analysis. This mechanism efficiently isolates regions with high tumour probability while minimizing unnecessary computations. Comprehensive ablation studies were conducted to optimize these parameters for accuracy and efficiency.

High-Resolution Analysis. Selected regions undergo high-resolution analysis with overlapping patch extraction (50% overlap) to ensure smooth probability maps and reduce boundary artifacts. The examination area extends beyond the initially identified regions by incorporating a border, ensuring comprehensive coverage of potential metastatic areas.

Final Probability Map Generation. Spatial averaging is applied at overlapping regions to create smoother probability transitions and minimize chequerboard artifacts. Regions not selected for high-resolution analysis retain their low-resolution predictions, ensuring a seamless integration of all resolution levels into the final whole-slide probability map.

The pipeline supports experimentation with various resolution level combinations, enabling systematic evaluation of high-low resolution pairs. This flexibility allows empirical optimization of the cascade structure through ablation studies, assessing the impact of different resolution settings, patch sizes, and selection criteria on detection performance and computational efficiency.

4   Experiments

4.1   Implementation and Model Training

The CAMELYON16 dataset was initially divided into predefined training and testing sets as described in the Data section. To facilitate model development and hyperparameter tuning, the training set was further split into training (80%) and validation (20%) subsets at the slide level, with stratification applied to maintain consistent class distribution across partitions and prevent data leakage.

Patches were extracted using a balanced sampling strategy (see Sect. 3), resulting in 1,024,000 patches with equal representation of positive and negative examples. During training, dynamic augmentation was applied on-the-fly, including random rotations (0°, 90°, 180°, 270°) and random flips, to enhance model generalization.

The framework was implemented in PyTorch, and models were trained on an NVIDIA GeForce RTX 4090 GPU. The Adam optimizer [10] was used with an initial learning rate of 0.001. A learning rate scheduler reduced the rate by a factor of 0.5 after 5 epochs with no improvement, while early stopping with a patience of 15 epochs helped prevent overfitting.

Each model was trained for up to 100 epochs with a batch size of 64, randomly sampling 6400 patches per epoch to ensure balance between positive and negative examples. The Asymmetric Unified Focal++ loss function [21], with parameters $\delta = 0.8$, $\gamma = 0.5$, and $\gamma^+ = 2$, was used to address class imbalance, providing stronger penalties for misclassifying metastatic regions while maintaining efficient learning for non-metastatic regions.

4.2   Evaluation Metrics

Model performance was assessed using multiple metrics. The primary metric was the Free Response Operating Characteristic (FROC) curve [5], computed using the evaluation code from the CAMELYON16 dataset [12]. The FROC curve plots the true positive rate against the average number of false positives per image, with the FROC value averaged across six predefined false positive rates (0.25, 0.5, 1, 2, 4, 8 per slide). Additionally, the Dice coefficient was calculated to measure spatial overlap between predicted and ground truth segmentations, accounting for both false positives and negatives. For computational efficiency, we measured average inference time per slide and the number of patches processed, enabling comparison of the computational demands and efficiency gains of the cascade approach.

4.3   Cascade Hyperparameter Search

The cascade pipeline architecture required extensive experimentation to identify the optimal combination of resolution levels, patch sizes, and decision thresholds. We evaluated three resolution level combinations: $(20\times, 10\times)$, $(20\times, 5\times)$, and $(10\times, 5\times)$. For each combination, we further assessed four patch size configurations: both levels using 256×256 pixels, both levels using 512×512 pixels, low resolution using 256×256 and high resolution using 512×512, and the inverse configuration.

For each configuration, we conducted a grid search over the percentile parameter p (ranging from 70 to 95 in increments of 5) and the threshold parameter t (ranging from 0.1 to 0.9 in increments of 0.05), resulting in 216 distinct cascade configurations per resolution and patch size combination.

Initial screening was performed on a balanced subset of the test data to identify promising candidates, and the best configurations were further evaluated on the full test set to determine the optimal cascade pipeline configuration.

5   Results

5.1   Individual Resolution Model Performance

The experimental evaluation commenced with an assessment of individual resolution-level models to establish baseline performance metrics. Table 1 summarizes the quantitative results for models trained at each of the four resolution levels (0–3) using the standard 256×256 pixel patch size, as well as the effect of increasing FOV via larger patch size at test time. Figure 4 shows qualitatively how each of the four resolution levels are affected by the spatial context, cellular structure trade off and the effect that has on the model.

Table 1. Performance of single-resolution models, and the effect of patch size at inference on model performance.

Resolution Level	Patch Size	FROC Score	Dice	Inference Time (s)
Level 0 (40×)	256 × 256	0.159	0.202	479.3
Level 1 (20×)	256 × 256	0.590	0.505	176.5
	512 × 512	0.625	0.512	297.0
Level 2 (10×)	256 × 256	0.607	0.556	48.6
	512 × 512	**0.633**	**0.565**	87.3
Level 3 (5×)	256 × 256	0.519	0.533	14.7
	512 × 512	0.541	0.543	29.8

Contrary to the common assumption that higher resolution levels lead to better performance [1,5], our experimental results show that Level 2 (10× magnification) achieves the highest performance across both primary evaluation metrics. This suggests that an intermediate resolution strikes the optimal balance between cellular detail and contextual information for metastasis detection in the CAMELYON16 dataset. The significant performance gap between Level 0 and the other resolution levels–particularly the 74% reduction in the FROC score compared to Level 2–indicates that the highest resolution may capture excessive detail at the expense of the broader contextual information necessary for accurate detection. This finding is especially surprising considering that much of the

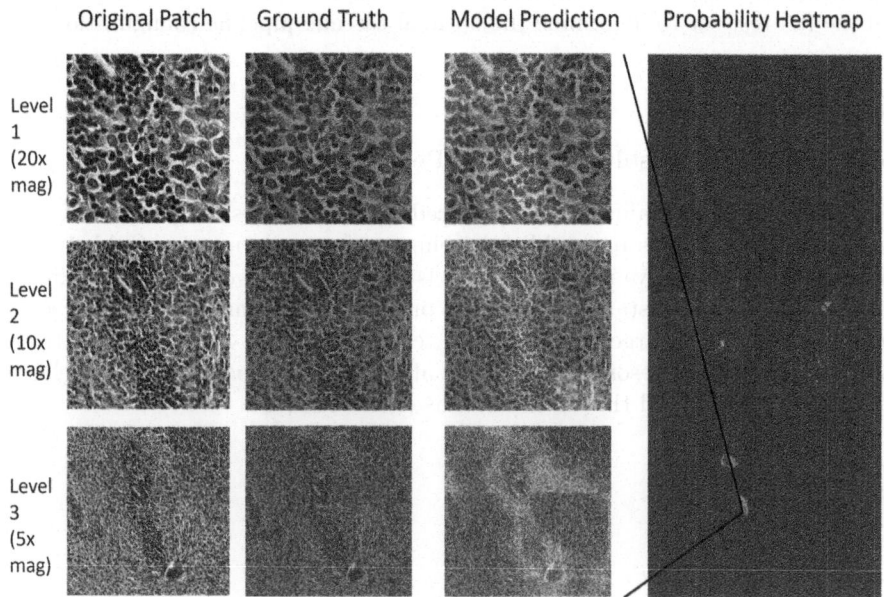

Fig. 4. Qualitative comparison of effect the various resolution levels have on the model output.

prior work [5,7,11,19] on this dataset has exclusively used the highest resolution level, and it suggests that overly high magnification might introduce noise and variability, potentially impairing model generalization.

5.2   Impact of Increased FOV at Inference

To investigate the influence of contextual information on model performance, we evaluated each resolution-level model using an enlarged patch size of 512×512 pixels during inference without retraining the models using this increased patch size. Table 1 presents a comparative analysis of performance metrics between standard and enlarged patch sizes across resolution levels.

Table 2. Performance of cascade inference pipeline.

Cascade	PS Configuration	p & t	FROC Score	Dice	Inference Time (s)
Level 2→1	256→256	0.95 & 0.5	0.602	0.524	62.7
	256→512	0.95 & 0.5	0.651	0.536	74.1
Level 3→1	256→256	0.95 & 0.15	0.618	0.534	64.9
	256→512	0.95 & 0.15	**0.661**	**0.545**	76.5

The results demonstrate consistent performance improvements across all resolution levels when using the enlarged patch size, with increases in FROC scores ranging from 4.2% to 5.9% and more modest gains in Dice coefficients. This uniform improvement suggests that increased contextual information contributes positively to metastasis detection accuracy regardless of resolution level. The most substantial improvement was observed at Level 2, where the FROC score increased from 0.607 to 0.633, further solidifying this resolution level's effectiveness.

However, these performance gains come at a significant computational cost, with inference time increasing by approximately 68–103% across the different resolution levels. This trade-off between performance and computational efficiency motivates the exploration of cascade approaches that could potentially capture the benefits of enlarged patches while maintaining reasonable computational demands.

5.3   Cascade Pipeline Evaluation

To gain deeper insights into the cascade pipeline's behaviour, we conducted comprehensive ablation studies on the percentile threshold (p) and confidence threshold (t) parameters across different resolution level combinations. The ablation studies revealed that the optimal parameter values varied depending on the specific resolution levels employed in the cascade. Generally, higher percentile values (90–95) combined with relatively low threshold values (0.10–0.20) yielded the best performance across configurations. This pattern suggests that examining any regions that had even a low confidence of relevance at higher resolution levels is sufficient to capture most true positive findings while increasing computational efficiency.

Further analysis of patch size combinations revealed that utilizing larger patch sizes (512×512) at higher resolution levels provided greater performance benefits than at lower resolution levels. This observation aligns with the intuition that increasing the amount contextual information is particularly valuable when examining detailed cellular structures at higher magnifications, while lower magnifications inherently capture broader context even with smaller patch sizes.

The cascade pipeline approach was designed to leverage the complementary strengths of different resolution levels while optimizing computational efficiency. We systematically evaluated various resolution level combinations, patch size configurations, and selection parameter values. Table 2 presents the performance of the top-performing cascade configurations compared to the best single-resolution models.

The optimal cascade configuration utilized Level 3 (5× magnification) with 256×256 pixel patches for initial screening, followed by Level 1 (20× magnification) with 512×512 pixel patches for detailed analysis of regions of interest. This configuration employed a percentile value (p) of 95 and a threshold value (t) of 0.15 for region selection, achieving an FROC score of 0.661. This represents a 4.4% improvement over the best single-resolution model (Level 2 with 512×512 pixel patches) while reducing inference time by 12.4%.

The experimental results demonstrate three key findings. First, contrary to conventional practices in histopathology analysis, intermediate resolution levels (10× magnification) consistently outperform the highest resolution (40× magnification), suggesting an optimal balance between cellular detail and contextual information. Second, increased field of view at inference time yields universal performance improvements regardless of resolution level, indicating the importance of contextual information in metastasis detection. Finally, the cascade approach combining Level 3 (5× magnification) for initial screening with Level 1 (20× magnification) for detailed analysis achieves both superior performance (FROC score of 0.661) and improved computational efficiency (12.4% faster than the best single-resolution model).

These findings challenge the prevailing assumption in computational pathology that higher resolution always yields better results, and demonstrate that strategic multi-resolution approaches can simultaneously improve both accuracy and efficiency. The potential clinical impact of these improvements is significant, as reduced processing time could accelerate diagnosis while maintaining or even enhancing detection reliability.

5.4 Limitations and Future Work

While our cascade framework demonstrates promising results, several limitations warrant discussion. First, our study aims to assess the feasibility and potential benefits of a cascading approach in whole slide image (WSI) analysis. We evaluate it using the widely adopted U-Net architecture and the CAMELYON16 dataset, providing a good comparison and benchmark. While this ensures repro-ducibility, future work is needed to test generalizability across diverse models and datasets. Second, the achieved FROC score of 0.661, though representing a 4.4% improvement over single-resolution approaches, remains below state-of-the-art ensemble methods (0.807) [5]. This gap suggests that architectural improve-ments and multi-model ensembles could further enhance performance. Addition-ally, our modular cascade design, while offering deployment flexibility, may suffer from error propagation between stages compared to end-to-end approaches [16]. Future work should explore applying our multi-resolution insights to modern architectures and validating across diverse pathology tasks.

6   Conclusion

This study explored the effectiveness of multi-resolution approaches for cancer detection and segmentation in whole slide images, addressing key questions about resolution, field of view, and cascaded inference pipelines. Our findings challenge conventional assumptions in computational pathology.

We demonstrated that intermediate resolution levels ($10\times$ magnification) can outperform the highest resolution ($40\times$ magnification) for metastasis detection in the CAMELYON16 dataset, suggesting that the optimal balance between cellu-lar detail and tissue context lies at intermediate magnifications. Additionally, we found that expanding the field of view during inference improves performance across all resolution levels, emphasizing the importance of broader contextual information. Lastly, our cascade inference pipeline, combining a low-resolution model ($5\times$ magnification) for region proposal and a higher-resolution model ($20\times$ magnification) for detailed analysis, achieved superior performance (FROC score of 0.661) while reducing computational demands.

Our study utilized the U-Net architecture, a widely-used model in medical imaging. However, we believe that our findings are applicable to other architec-tures as well, offering valuable insights for more efficient and effective histopatho-logical analysis. By combining multiple resolution levels, we can improve both accuracy and efficiency, potentially accelerating the clinical adoption of auto-mated metastasis detection systems.

Acknowledgement. This work was funded by EPSRC grant number EP/S021892/1 and Cancer Research Wales. For the purpose of open access the authors have applied a Creative Commons Attribution (CC BY) licence to any Author Accepted Manuscript version arising from this submission.

References

1. Abdel-Nabi, H., et al.: A comprehensive review of the deep learning-based tumor analysis approaches in histopathological images: segmentation, classification and multi-learning tasks. Clust. Comput. (2023). https://doi.org/10.1007/s10586-022-03951-2

2. Cao, H., et al.: Swin-Unet: unet-like pure transformer for medical image segmentation. In: Karlinsky, L., Michaeli, T., Nishino, K. (eds.) Computer Vision – ECCV 2022 Workshops, pp. 205–218. Springer, Heidelberg (2023). https://doi.org/10.1007/978-3-031-25066-8_9

3. Chen, J., et al.: TransUNet: rethinking the U-Net architecture design for medical image segmentation through the lens of transformers. Med. Image Anal. **97**, 103280 (2024). https://doi.org/10.1016/j.media.2024.103280

4. Dong, N., Kampffmeyer, M., Liang, X., Wang, Z., Dai, W., Xing, E.: Reinforced auto-zoom net: towards accurate and fast breast cancer segmentation in whole-slide images. In: Stoyanov, D., et al. (eds.) DLMIA/ML-CDS -2018. LNCS, vol. 11045, pp. 317–325. Springer, Cham (2018). https://doi.org/10.1007/978-3-030-00889-5_36

5. Ehteshami Bejnordi, B., et al.: Diagnostic assessment of deep learning algorithms for detection of lymph node metastases in women with breast cancer. JAMA **318**(22), 2199–2210 (2017). https://doi.org/10.1001/jama.2017.14585

6. Elmore, J.G., et al.: Diagnostic concordance among pathologists interpreting breast biopsy specimens. JAMA **313**(11), 1122–1132 (2015). https://doi.org/10.1001/jama.2015.1405

7. Guo, Z., et al.: A fast and refined cancer regions segmentation framework in whole-slide breast pathological images. Sci. Rep. **9**(1), 882 (2019). https://doi.org/10.1038/s41598-018-37492-9

8. Ho, D.J., et al.: Deep multi-magnification networks for multi-class breast cancer image segmentation. Comput. Med. Imaging Graph. **88**, 101866 (2021). https://doi.org/10.1016/j.compmedimag.2021.101866

9. Khened, M., Kori, A., Rajkumar, H., Krishnamurthi, G., Srinivasan, B.: A generalized deep learning framework for whole-slide image segmentation and analysis. Sci. Rep. **11**(1), 11579 (2021). https://doi.org/10.1038/s41598-021-90444-8

10. Kingma, D., Ba, J.: Adam: a method for stochastic optimization. In: International Conference on Learning Representations (ICLR) (2015)

11. Lin, H., Chen, H., Graham, S., Dou, Q., Rajpoot, N., Heng, P.A.: Fast ScanNet: fast and dense analysis of multi-gigapixel whole-slide images for cancer metastasis detection. IEEE Trans. Med. Imaging **38**(8), 1948–1958 (2019). https://doi.org/10.1109/TMI.2019.2891305

12. Litjens, G., et al.: 1399 H&E-stained sentinel lymph node sections of breast cancer patients: the CAMELYON dataset. GigaScience **7**(6), giy065 (2018). https://doi.org/10.1093/gigascience/giy065

13. Otsu, N.: A threshold selection method from gray-level histograms. IEEE Trans. Syst. Man Cybern. **9**(1), 62–66 (1979). https://doi.org/10.1109/TSMC.1979.4310076

14. van Rijthoven, M., Balkenhol, M., Silia, K., van der Laak, J., Ciompi, F.: HookNet: multi-resolution convolutional neural networks for semantic segmentation in histopathology whole-slide images. Med. Image Anal. **68**, 101890 (2021). https://doi.org/10.1016/j.media.2020.101890

15. Ronneberger, O., Fischer, P., Brox, T.: U-net: convolutional networks for biomedical image segmentation. In: Navab, N., Hornegger, J., Wells, W.M., Frangi, A.F. (eds.) MICCAI 2015. LNCS, vol. 9351, pp. 234–241. Springer, Cham (2015). https://doi.org/10.1007/978-3-319-24574-4_28

16. Sun, S., Yuan, H., Zheng, Y., Zhang, H., Jiang, Z.: Cancer sensitive cascaded networks (CSC-Net) for efficient histopathology whole slide image segmentation. In: 2020 IEEE 17th International Symposium on Biomedical Imaging (ISBI), pp. 476–480 (2020). https://doi.org/10.1109/ISBI45749.2020.9098695

17. Szegedy, C., et al.: Going deeper with convolutions. In: 2015 IEEE Conference on Computer Vision and Pattern Recognition (CVPR), pp. 1–9 (2015). https://doi.org/10.1109/CVPR.2015.7298594
18. Verghese, G., et al.: Computational pathology in cancer diagnosis, prognosis, and prediction - present day and prospects. J. Pathol. **260**(5), 551–563 (2023). https://doi.org/10.1002/path.6163
19. Wang, D., Khosla, A., Gargeya, R., Irshad, H., Beck, A.H.: Deep learning for identifying metastatic breast cancer (2016). https://doi.org/10.48550/arXiv.1606.05718
20. Yan, J., et al.: Hierarchical attention guided framework for multi-resolution collaborative whole slide image segmentation. In: de Bruijne, M., et al. (eds.) MICCAI 2021. LNCS, vol. 12908, pp. 153–163. Springer, Cham (2021). https://doi.org/10.1007/978-3-030-87237-3_15
21. Yeung, M., Sala, E., Schönlieb, C.B., Rundo, L.: Unified Focal loss: generalising dice and cross entropy-based losses to handle class imbalanced medical image segmentation. Comput. Med. Imaging Graph. **95**, 102026 (2022). https://doi.org/10.1016/j.compmedimag.2021.102026
22. Zeng, L., et al.: MAMC-Net: an effective deep learning framework for whole-slide image tumor segmentation. Multimedia Tools Appl. **82**(25), 39349–39369 (2023). https://doi.org/10.1007/s11042-023-15065-x

Learning to Harmonize Cross-Vendor X-ray Images by Non-linear Image Dynamics Correction

Yucheng Lu$^{1(\boxtimes)}$ ⓘ, Shunxin Wang^2 ⓘ, Dovile Juodelyte^1 ⓘ,
and Veronika Cheplygina^1 ⓘ

^{1} IT University of Copenhagen, Rued Langgaards Vej 7, Copenhagen, Denmark
yucl@itu.dk
^{2} University of Twente, Drienerlolaan 5, Enschede, The Netherlands

Abstract. In this paper, we explore how conventional image enhancement can improve model robustness in medical image analysis. By applying commonly used normalization methods to images from various vendors and studying their influence on model generalization in transfer learning, we show that the nonlinear characteristics of domain-specific image dynamics cannot be addressed by simple linear transforms. To tackle this issue, we reformulate the image harmonization task as an exposure correction problem and propose a method termed Global Deep Curve Estimation (GDCE) to reduce domain-specific exposure mismatch. GDCE performs enhancement via a pre-defined polynomial function and is trained with a "domain discriminator", aiming to improve model transparency in downstream tasks compared to existing black-box methods. Code available at https://github.com/YCL92/GDCE.

Keywords: Image harmonization · Transfer learning · Medical imaging

1 Introduction

Transfer learning has advanced medical image classification, often achieving performance comparable to that of human experts. However, convolutional neural networks (CNNs) are prone to overfitting, particularly when trained on limited labeled data. This overfitting can compromise generalization, leading to degraded performance when acquisition pipelines vary, such as across different vendors [3,5,16].

Many studies have investigated the inconsistency of radiomic features caused by acquisition shifts and proposed image standardization techniques to address this issue [7,17,24,26,29–32]. However, there is limited understanding of how image dynamics influence deep learning based downstream tasks – an area that is both critical and often overlooked in the medical imaging domain. Recent approaches typically rely on CNNs to perform image translation and improve

S. Ali et al. (Eds.): MIUA 2025, LNCS 15917, pp. 102–115, 2026.
https://doi.org/10.1007/978-3-031-98691-8_8

downstream performance across vendors without examining the underlying factors contributing to domain shifts. Moreover, these methods apply pixel-wise adjustments to the input, introducing the risk of hidden artifacts, shortcut learning, or even the removal of subtle diagnostic patterns due to their black-box nature.

These challenges motivate us to investigate how image dynamics influence a models generalization ability from a low-level image processing perspective. To this end, we apply several popular normalization methods to images from various vendors and observe varying degrees of performance degradation in the downstream task. Specifically, we find that X-ray images exhibit exposure "errors" similar to those in conventional photography, such as over-/underexposure and nonlinear sensor response. Building on these insights, we reframe the image harmonization task as an exposure correction problem and propose Global Deep Curve Estimation (GDCE), which learns a global nonlinear correction between source and reference scanners. Unlike black-box models, GDCE compensates for exposure differences using a pre-defined polynomial function without altering local patterns, thereby remaining transparent to users. Extensive experiment results on breast density classification using the EMBED dataset [12] and pneumonia detection using the RSNA Pneumonia Detection Challenge dataset [2] show that the proposed method effectively improves model generalization.

2   Related Work

In a typical transfer learning setup, a model is first pre-trained on a large-scale source dataset and then fine-tuned on a smaller, domain-specific target dataset. While ImageNet [8] is a widely used general-purpose source dataset, target datasets in medical imaging are often tied to specific acquisition pipelines. Fine-tuned models frequently exhibit poor generalization when confronted with acquisition pipeline shifts (which are the focus of this paper, although other shifts such as population shift may also occur). Since these acquisition shifts arise from variations in imaging pipelines across vendors, we review the literature in two related areas: medical image harmonization and image dynamics enhancement.

2.1   Medical Image Harmonization

Medical image harmonization aims to standardize image statistics. For X-ray images, this typically includes grayscale normalization, contrast enhancement, and denoising [33]. While hand-crafted methods have been explored [4,7,23,24], deep learning based approaches have been the focus in recent years. These methods aim to translate images from various sources to a reference domain so that the resulting statistics resemble the target. Liang *et al.* trained a generative adversarial network (GAN) to map images into a robust space in which the discriminator could not predict their source [17], with similar approaches proposed in [30,31]. Selim *et al.* employed two learning strategies for handling paired and unpaired data: paired data from the same vendor were used to train a standard

GAN, while unpaired data across vendors were translated between domains via cycle consistency [29,32]. This method was further extended by training a variational autoencoder to extract latent embeddings, which were then standardized using a score-based denoising diffusion probabilistic model [28]. A related work [26] used a deep structural causal model [25] to simulate realistic domain variations as data augmentation in counterfactual contrastive learning.

While these studies showed improved performance in downstream tasks, most applied pixel-wise domain translation, which carries the risk of introducing undesired artifacts and lacks transparency regarding how the images were normalized [27]. In contrast, we investigate how image dynamics relate to model generalization and propose enhancing images using a pre-defined polynomial function. Having full knowledge of the applied transformation helps prevent artifacts and promotes greater transparency in medical image analysis.

2.2   Image Dynamics Enhancement

Image dynamics enhancement aims to restore degraded dynamic ranges caused by overexposure, underexposure, or low-light conditions. It typically involves both local and global adjustments to enhance details and produce a more visually balanced tone. Eilertsen *et al.* proposed a hybrid dynamic range autoencoder that directly converts a single Standard Dynamic Range (SDR) image into its High Dynamic Range (HDR) counterpart [9]. Endo *et al.* introduced an indirect approach that predicts multiple SDR images at different exposure levels and merges them into a single HDR image [10]. Zhang *et al.* developed a dual-illumination adjustment framework that performs conjugate exposure correction on the original and inverted images, respectively [37]. Marnerides *et al.* designed a multi-head CNN that learns local and global adjustments separately before fusing them into the final HDR output [20]. Liu *et al.* reversed the image signal processing pipeline and compensated for compressed dynamics at each stage using two CNNs [18]. Afifi *et al.* simulated various exposure errors and used synthetic data to train a multi-scale enhancement model based on the Laplacian pyramid [1].

In our experiments, we found that image dynamics, such as bit depth, display window, and sensor response curve, vary across vendors, resulting in both pronounced and subtle differences in visual appearance. Inspired by the studies discussed above, we reframe medical image normalization as an exposure correction problem and propose a method to adjust image dynamics accordingly. The proposed GDCE improves model generalization performance effectively without altering local structures.

3   Methodology

We begin with a brief overview of the proposed method. Given multiple datasets obtained from different acquisition pipelines (*e.g.*, scanners), we select one as the reference domain and treat the others as domain-shifted. A pathology classifier is first trained on the reference domain dataset and then kept fixed. This classifier is subsequently used as a "domain discriminator" to train the enhancement network, GDCE. Once training converges, GDCE is used to pre-process domain-shifted images before performing downstream tasks (*e.g.*, pathology classification).

3.1   Global Deep Curve Estimation

Inspired by [11], we design a CNN termed GDCE to perform global exposure correction. The model architecture is illustrated in Fig. 1. It consists of several convolution layers for input image feature extraction, followed by a multi-layer perceptron that maps the features to a series of coefficients α_n, which are then applied to the image iteratively as follows:

$$I_n = I_{n-1} + \alpha_n I_{n-1} \left(1 - I_{n-1}\right), \ n = 1, 2, \ldots, N - 1, N, \tag{1}$$

where n denotes the iteration index, N is the total number of iterations, and α_n represents the predicted correction coefficient. This formulation has many benefits: First, it approximates the polynomial through iterative compositions of simpler functions, allowing the model to better utilize its learning capacity than directly fitting a high-order polynomial; Second, although GDCE is capable of capturing both global and local features, Eq. 1 defines exposure correction as a global operation, enabling transparent data manipulation without the risk of local artifacts; Third, since $I_0 \in [0, 1]$ and $\alpha_n \in [-1, 1]$, the resulting image I_n at each iteration remains within the range $[0, 1]$, thereby avoiding data clamping that could potentially discard useful information.

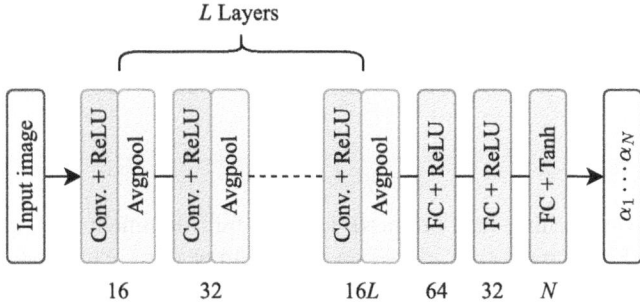

Fig. 1. Block diagram of GDCE architecture. It consists of L layers of "convolution and average pooling" to extract image features, followed by three fully connected layers to predict the coefficients α_n for Eq. 1.

Here, we emphasize the distinction between using the proposed GDCE as a pre-processing step before downstream tasks and fine-tuning the downstream models directly on new data, as in [13]. GDCE can be regarded as a specialized form of image normalization based on pre-defined enhancement operations, whereas fine-tuning adjusts the parameters of the downstream model to accommodate domain shifts.

3.2   Task-Oriented Domain Shift Alignment

Since the selected scanners are from different vendors, obtaining paired data across vendors is impractical. Consequently, many existing works [17,30,31] adopt unsupervised learning approaches, particularly those based on GANs. Inspired by the use of discriminators in GANs, we propose a simple yet effective strategy to train GDCE by leveraging the downstream task. In our case, we use a pre-trained pathology classifier as the "domain discriminator". The domain classification loss $\mathscr{L}_{\text{CE}}$ is defined as:

$$\mathscr{L}_{\text{CE}}(I_N, y_{\text{gt}}) = -\sum_{j=1}^{C} y_{\text{gt},j} \log \left(\frac{\exp\left(\mathcal{D}_j\left(I_N\right)\right)}{\sum_{k=1}^{C} \exp\left(\mathcal{D}_k\left(I_N\right)\right)} \right), \tag{2}$$

where $\mathcal{D}$ denotes the "domain discriminator" (*i.e.*, the downstream task model), y_{gt} is the ground-truth label, j indicates the class index, and C is the total number of classes. Although we refer to the pathology classifier as a "discriminator", the training process is not adversarial.

In addition, we use a perceptual loss $\mathscr{L}_{\text{P}}$ to preserve the visual appearance of the enhanced image, defined as:

$$\mathscr{L}_{\text{P}} = \|\mathcal{V}_i\left(I_N\right) - \mathcal{V}_i\left(I_R\right)\|_1, \tag{3}$$

where I_R is an arbitrary image from the reference scanner, and $\mathcal{V}_i$ denotes the output of the i-th layer from a pre-trained VGG backbone. We use VGG-16 as the perceptual model [14], with $i = 7$ (*i.e.*, "conv. 2-2"), which is the shallowest layer that enables model convergence. This design choice ensures that the perceptual loss captures low-level visual characteristics while avoiding high-level semantic features.

The total loss $\mathscr{L}_{\text{T}}$ is defined as the summation of the classification and perceptual losses:

$$\mathscr{L}_{\text{T}} = \mathscr{L}_{\text{P}} + \mathscr{L}_{\text{CE}}. \tag{4}$$

The intuition behind task-oriented domain shift alignment is similar to "fine-tuning" the downstream task model on new scanner data, except that GDCE is trained to enhance the input image in a way that improves downstream task performance. Although conceptually straightforward, this approach does not guarantee meaningful enhancement of the input data. Nguyen *et al.* showed that when activations from the discriminator are back-propagated, subtle yet deterministic patterns can also be transferred to the input [22]. In our context, this implies that the enhancer may unintentionally learn to embed hidden adversarial perturbations as shortcuts by manipulating local patterns [36].

To address these issues, we design GDCE to adjust only the global tone curve, without the capacity to modify local pixel-level details. This imposes a hard constraint that prevents the "domain discriminator" from back-propagating adversarial perturbations to the enhancer during training.

3.3 Datasets and Implementation

We train a medical image classification model as a downstream task using transfer learning with a ResNet-50 backbone [35]. As the source dataset, we adopt RadImageNet [21] due to its slightly better performance [15] and robustness to noise [19]. For the target datasets, we generate two small subsets: one from the EMBED dataset [12] for breast density classification (*i.e.*, classes A–D, evaluated based on the BI-RADS breast density scale [34]), and the other from the RSNA Pneumonia Detection Challenge [2] for pneumonia detection.

To simplify the analysis, we select samples from three scanners for the breast density classification task: Clearview CSm, Selenia Dimensions (used as the reference scanner), and Senograph 2000D. For the pneumonia detection task, we select samples from two scanners with pixel spacings of 0.171 and 0.143, with the latter used as the reference scanner. Table 1 summarizes the training and test set partitions, and Fig. 2 presents full-range image examples from the selected scanners.[1]

Table 1. Summary of the train/test dataset partitions

Scanner model	Refer to	Breast density from [12]			
		A	B	C	D
Clearview CSm	Clearview	0/123	400/100	400/100	0/81
Selenia Dimensions	Selenia	400/100	400/100	400/100	400/100
Senograph 2000D	Senograph	0/52	400/100	400/100	0/94
Scanner model	Refer to	Pneumonia from [2]			
		Positive		Negative	
Pixel spacing 0.171	Brand X	400/100		400/100	
Pixel spacing 0.143	Brand Y	400/100		400/100	

It is worth noting that there are no training samples for classes A and D in the Clearview and Senograph scanners due to an insufficient number of available cases. However, the absence of such training data can serve as a strong indicator of model overfitting, as the domain shift of interest is semantically independent of the labels. During training, images from the source and reference scanners are passed to GDCE, which is supervised using the loss defined in Eq. 4. At each epoch, the model is validated only on the source scanner, and the performance is reported as the worst accuracy across groups (*i.e.*, classes A–D for breast density and positive/negative for pneumonia), as this metric better captures the lower bound of model performance [6].

---

[1] The training data from the reference scanner is used solely for fine-tuning the downstream task model and for evaluating GDCE predictions in terms of low-level perceptual similarity.

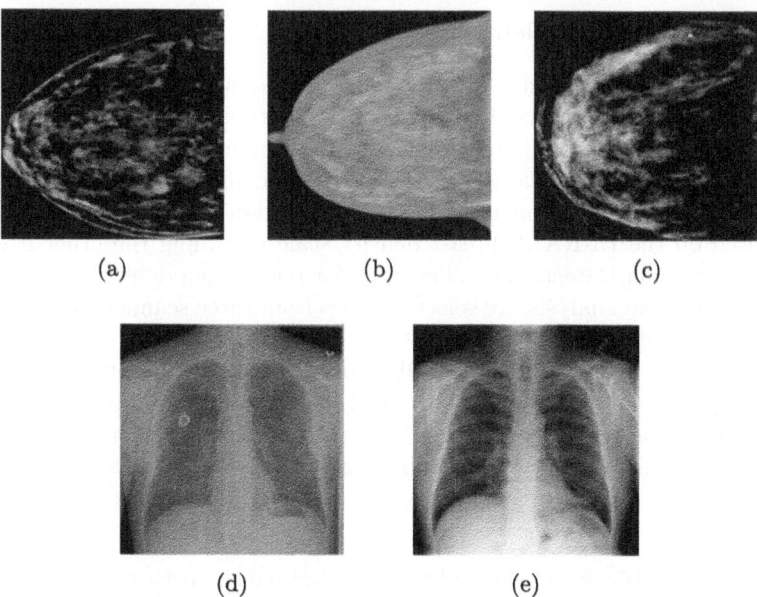

Fig. 2. Visual examples of full-range images from the selected scanners for comparison. (a). Selenia (the reference scanner); (b). Senograph; (c). Clearview; (d). Brand X; (d). Brand Y (the reference scanner).

For breast density classification, we report the confusion matrix for per-class evaluation and the Receiver Operating Characteristic Area Under the Curve (ROC-AUC) score for overall performance. For pneumonia detection, we compute precision and recall as the evaluation metrics. All reported metrics represent the average results over 5-fold cross-validation.

The experiments were implemented using PyTorch with an image resolution of 512×512, a learning rate of 10^{-4}, a batch size of 12, and the Adam optimizer. These hyper-parameters were empirically selected based on common practices from our previous projects.

4   Experiment Results

4.1   Image Dynamics Affect Model Generalization

We tested the breast density classifier using two image normalization methods: full-range normalization and display window clamping. Note that for the Clearview and Selenia scanners the two methods are identical, thus we omit them and only analyze performance change on the Senograph data.

The results are shown in Fig. 3. We noticed that the performance of the Senograph scanner improved after switching to display window clamping, indicating that the clamped data had a lower level of domain shift. This was confirmed after we further inspected the visual appearance. As shown in Fig. 5, the original dynamic range of the breast in the Senograph image was low; in contrast, the image clamped by the display window exhibited much richer details.

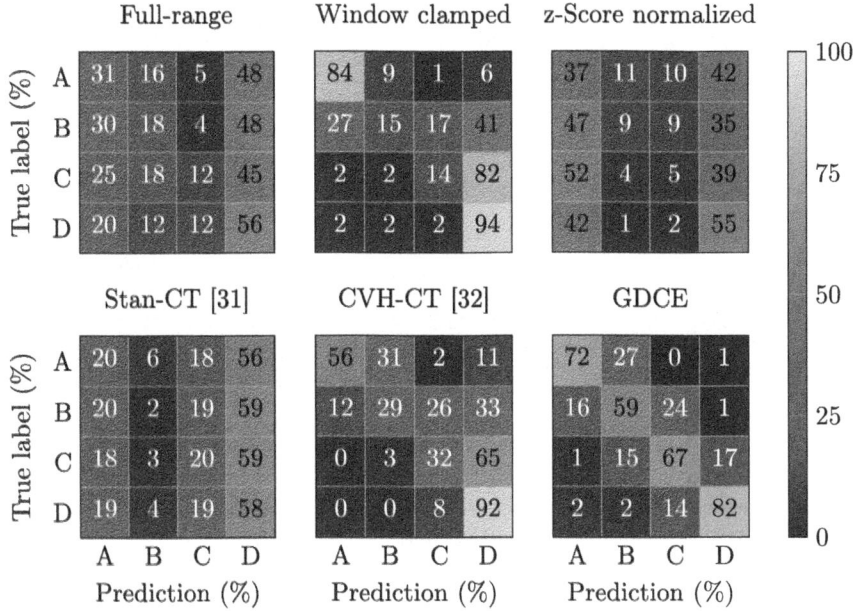

Fig. 3. Confusion matrices of the Senograph test set by six methods. The corresponding ROC-AUC are 0.52, 0.80, 0.58, 0.50, 0.82, and 0.89, respectively.

However, the performance improvement was limited, which we believe is due to two reasons. First, radiologists often manually adjust the display window to improve readability, introducing domain shift and model bias. Second, unlike computed tomography, where the data is calibrated to match Hounsfield units, X-ray images do not follow a universal standard. Consequently, the sensor's response and the corresponding gamma correction might not share the same linearity across vendors. This was further observed from the poor performance of the Clearview data in Fig. 4. Although visually similar to Selenia data, the low-density tissues appeared brighter, while the high-density regions and the air pixels showed marginal differences.

4.2   GDCE Helps Improve Generalization Performance

We processed all the test images using the proposed GDCE and reran the pathology classifiers. For a broader comparison, we also trained and tested two GAN-based methods from the literature [31,32]. In breast density classification, we observed performance improvements for the Clearview and Senograph scanners.

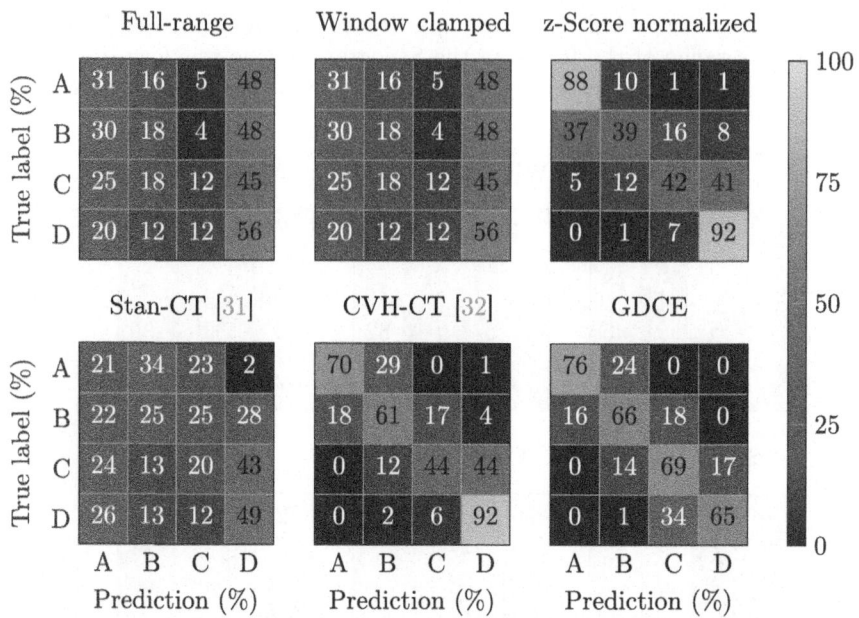

Fig. 4. Confusion matrices of the Clearview test set by siz methods. The corresponding ROC-AUC are 0.90, 0.90, 0.88, 0.51, 0.87, and 0.90, respectively.

Specifically, the overall ROC-AUC score for the Senograph scanner increased substantially to 0.89, the highest among all competitors. For the Clearview test set, labels B and C showed improvement after exposure correction by GDCE. Similar results in pneumonia classification, as shown in Table 2, further supported its effectiveness in domain shift alignment.

Table 2. Results of pneumonia classification (Brand X)

	Baseline	z-Score	Stan-CT [31]	CVH-CT [32]	GDCE
Precision	55.33%	58.23%	51.15%	67.58%	70.98%
Recall	97.00%	96.40%	80.00%	76.40%	73.30%

* Brand Y: 75.39% (Precision) and 74.40% (Recall).

To further compare the processed data, we plot a sample image in Fig. 5. We observed that the processed images from the Senograph scanner perceptually looked quite similar to that of the Selenia scanner. These observations highlighted the merits of GDCE and demonstrated its effectiveness in improving the model's generalization ability across different target datasets.

We also observed performance degradation in extreme cases (*i.e.*, class A and D) from the Clearview scanner. By analyzing the failure cases (Fig. 6 shows

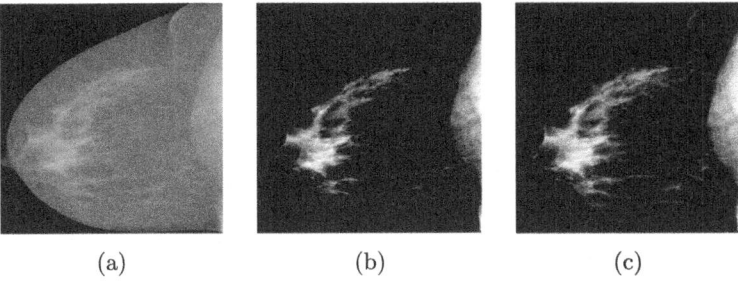

| (a) | (b) | (c) |

Fig. 5. Visual comparison of the same Sanograph image handled by three methods. (a). Full-range normalized; (b). Display window clamped; (c). Exposure corrected by GDCE.

an example), a possible explanation is that the lack of such data during GDCE training (see Table 1) led the model to overly enhance the "dark" images (*i.e.*, class A) while suppressing the "bright" images (*i.e.*, class D), thereby limiting its ability to handle such outliers. In contrast, the dynamic range of the original Senograph images was quite low, which may have allowed GDCE to better extract exposure features from extreme cases, even when such samples were not present in training.

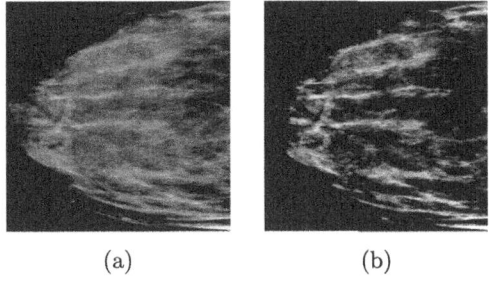

| (a) | (b) |

Fig. 6. A failure case from the Clearview scanner. (a) Original image in full range; (b). Exposure corrected by GDCE.

4.3   Shallow Model Suffices for Acquisition Shift Alignment

As the only enhancement we applied was the global tone curve adjustment, in theory the resulting GDCE should have been simple enough without requiring attention to high-level fine patterns. To verify this, we performed an ablation study that compared the performance of different model configurations. Specifically, we focused on two factors: the number of convolution layers in Fig. 1, and the number of iterations in Eq. 1. The results[2] on the validation set and the test set are presented as heatmaps in Fig. 7.

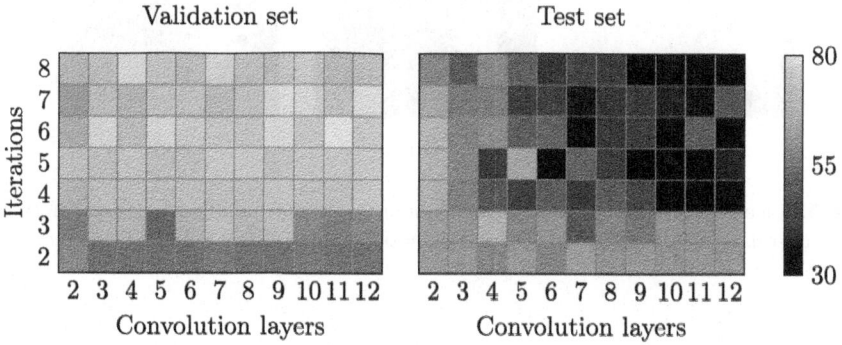

Fig. 7. Worst group performance by convolution layers and iterations on the Clearview validation and test sets.

At first glance, the two heatmaps appeared to be opposed: test performance dropped as validation performance rose. This was expected, as breast density classes A and D were not present in the training set. A validation performance higher than that of the classifier on the reference scanner indicated that GDCE was overfitting to the training data, which became more apparent with increased learning capacity (*i.e.*, more convolution layers). Interestingly, even for a shallow GDCE with 7 convolution layers, the overfitting issue became significant. We therefore questioned the need to employ much deeper, pixel-wise image processing models to compensate for acquisition domain shifts, such as those presented in Sect. 2.

5 Discussion and Conclusions

5.1 Significance of Results

Our experiments showed the effectiveness of the proposed GDCE over commonly used image normalization methods such as z-score normalization and display window clamping in medical image analysis, supporting the idea that global image dynamics is a key factor in acquisition shifts. Since the enhancement is performed via a pre-defined polynomial function, our method offers a more transparent understanding of how the image is processed. Moreover, the ablation study showed that a shallow GDCE is sufficient to compensate for image dynamic differences, raising concerns about the necessity of deeper, pixel-wise architectures in the existing literature.

---

[2] We found that the worst-performing group in the training sets consistently achieved around 99%, regardless of the number of iterations or convolutional layers.

5.2   Limitations and Future Directions

Despite its effectiveness, this work has several limitations. First, our ablation studies did not allow us to further investigate how the absence of certain labels in the training data might influence label-independent image dynamics; Second, we did not consider other forms of acquisition shifts that could also bias the classifier (*e.g.*, samples of breast density class D might be noisier due to higher X-ray absorption in high-density tissues [19]). These represent potential directions for future research.

5.3   Concluding Remarks

In this paper, we observed that acquisition dynamics influence a models generalization ability across different vendors in X-ray medical image analysis. Specifically, we found that scanner dynamics are not only determined by the radiologists preferred display window but are also related to the sensors nonlinear response. We therefore conclude that X-ray imaging can suffer from exposure-related errors too. To address this, we proposed GDCE, which corrects such errors iteratively using a pre-defined polynomial function. Experiment results showed improved test performance on three scanners that were unseen during downstream task training. Future work could involve a more detailed analysis of model overfitting and other forms of acquisition shifts to further improve generalization ability.

Acknowledgments. This research was supported by Novo Nordisk Foundation under Grant NNF21OC0068816.

Disclosure of Interests. The authors have no competing interests to declare that are relevant to the content of this article.

References

1. Afifi, M., Derpanis, K.G., Ommer, B., Brown, M.S.: Learning multi-scale photo exposure correction. In: Proceedings of the IEEE/CVF Conference on Computer Vision and Pattern Recognition, pp. 9157–9167 (2021)
2. Anouk Stein, M., et al.: Rsna pneumonia detection challenge (2018). https://kaggle.com/competitions/rsna-pneumonia-detection-challenge. kaggle
3. Berenguer, R., et al.: Radiomics of ct features may be nonreproducible and redundant: influence of ct acquisition parameters. Radiology **288**(2), 407–415 (2018)
4. Cao, H., Pu, S., Tan, W., Tong, J.: Breast mass detection in digital mammography based on anchor-free architecture. Comput. Methods Programs Biomed. **205**, 106033 (2021)
5. Chirra, P., et al.: Empirical evaluation of cross-site reproducibility in radiomic features for characterizing prostate mri. In: Medical Imaging 2018: Computer-Aided Diagnosis, vol. 10575, pp. 67–78. SPIE (2018)
6. Compton, R., Zhang, L., Puli, A., Ranganath, R.: When more is less: incorporating additional datasets can hurt performance by introducing spurious correlations. In: Machine Learning for Healthcare Conference, pp. 110–127 (2023)

7. Deng, H., Deng, W., Sun, X., Liu, M., Ye, C., Zhou, X.: Mammogram enhancement using intuitionistic fuzzy sets. IEEE Trans. Biomed. Eng. **64**(8), 1803–1814 (2016)
8. Deng, J., Dong, W., Socher, R., Li, L.J., Li, K., Fei-Fei, L.: Imagenet: a large-scale hierarchical image database. In: 2009 IEEE Conference on Computer Vision and Pattern Recognition, pp. 248–255 (2009)
9. Eilertsen, G., Kronander, J., Denes, G., Mantiuk, R.K., Unger, J.: HDR image reconstruction from a single exposure using deep cnns. ACM Trans. Graph. (TOG) **36**(6), 1–15 (2017)
10. Endo, Y., Kanamori, Y., Mitani, J.: Deep reverse tone mapping. ACM Trans. Graph **36**(6), 1–10 (2017)
11. Guo, C., et al.: Zero-reference deep curve estimation for low-light image enhancement. In: Proceedings of the IEEE/CVF Conference on Computer Vision and Pattern Recognition, pp. 1780–1789 (2020)
12. Jeong, J.J., et al.: The emory breast imaging dataset (embed): a racially diverse, granular dataset of 3.4 million screening and diagnostic mammographic images. Radiol. Artif. Intell. **5**(1), e220047 (2023)
13. Jiménez-Sánchez, A., Tardy, M., Ballester, M., Mateus, D., Piella, G.: Memory-aware curriculum federated learning for breast cancer classification. Comput. Methods Programs Biomed. **229**, 107318 (2023)
14. Johnson, J., Alahi, A., Fei-Fei, L.: Perceptual losses for real-time style transfer and super-resolution. In: Leibe, B., Matas, J., Sebe, N., Welling, M. (eds.) ECCV 2016. LNCS, vol. 9906, pp. 694–711. Springer, Cham (2016). https://doi.org/10.1007/978-3-319-46475-6_43
15. Juodelyte, D., Lu, Y., Jiménez-Sánchez, A., Bottazzi, S., Ferrante, E., Cheplygina, V.: Source matters: source dataset impact on model robustness in medical imaging. arXiv preprint arXiv:2403.04484 (2024)
16. Liang, G., Zhang, J., Brooks, M., Howard, J., Chen, J.: Radiomic features of lung cancer and their dependency on ct image acquisition parameters. Med. Phys. **44**, 3024 (2017)
17. Liang, G., Fouladvand, S., Zhang, J., Brooks, M.A., Jacobs, N., Chen, J.: Ganai: standardizing ct images using generative adversarial network with alternative improvement. In: 2019 IEEE International Conference on Healthcare Informatics (ICHI), pp. 1–11 (2019)
18. Liu, Y.L., et al.: Single-image HDR reconstruction by learning to reverse the camera pipeline. In: Proceedings of the IEEE/CVF Conference on Computer Vision and Pattern Recognition, pp. 1651–1660 (2020)
19. Lu, Y., Juodelyte, D., Victor, J.D., Cheplygina, V.: Exploring connections of spectral analysis and transfer learning in medical imaging. arXiv preprint arXiv:2407.11379 (2024)
20. Marnerides, D., Bashford-Rogers, T., Hatchett, J., Debattista, K.: Expandnet: a deep convolutional neural network for high dynamic range expansion from low dynamic range content. In: Computer Graphics Forum, vol. 37, pp. 37–49 (2018)
21. Mei, X., et al.: Radimagenet: an open radiologic deep learning research dataset for effective transfer learning. Radiol. Artif. Intell. **4**(5), e210315 (2022)
22. Nguyen, A., Dosovitskiy, A., Yosinski, J., Brox, T., Clune, J.: Synthesizing the preferred inputs for neurons in neural networks via deep generator networks. Adv. Neural Inf. Process. Syst. **29** (2016)
23. Pérez-Benito, F.J., et al.: A deep learning system to obtain the optimal parameters for a threshold-based breast and dense tissue segmentation. Comput. Methods Prog. Biomed. **195**, 105668 (2020)

24. Perre, A.C., Alexandre, L., Freire, L.: The influence of image normalization in mammographic classification with cnns. In: 23rd Portuguese Conference on Pattern Recognition, RECPAD 2017 (2018)
25. Ribeiro, F.D.S., Xia, T., Monteiro, M., Pawlowski, N., Glocker, B.: High fidelity image counterfactuals with probabilistic causal models. arXiv preprint arXiv:2306.15764 (2023)
26. Roschewitz, M., de Sousa Ribeiro, F., Xia, T., Khara, G., Glocker, B.: Counterfactual contrastive learning: robust representations via causal image synthesis. In: MICCAI Workshop on Data Engineering in Medical Imaging, pp. 22–32 (2024)
27. Salahuddin, Z., Woodruff, H.C., Chatterjee, A., Lambin, P.: Transparency of deep neural networks for medical image analysis: a review of interpretability methods. Comput. Biol. Med. **140**, 105111 (2022)
28. Selim, M., et al.: Latent diffusion model for medical image standardization and enhancement. arXiv preprint arXiv:2310.05237 (2023)
29. Selim, M., Zhang, J., Fei, B., Lewis, M., Zhang, G.Q., Chen, J.: UDA-CT: a general framework for ct image standardization. In: 2022 IEEE International Conference on Bioinformatics and Biomedicine (BIBM), pp. 1698–1701 (2022)
30. Selim, M., Zhang, J., Fei, B., Zhang, G.Q., Chen, J.: Ct image harmonization for enhancing radiomics studies. In: 2021 IEEE International Conference on Bioinformatics and Biomedicine (BIBM), pp. 1057–1062 (2021)
31. Selim, M., Zhang, J., Fei, B., Zhang, G.Q., Chen, J.: Stan-ct: standardizing ct image using generative adversarial networks. In: AMIA Annual Symposium Proceedings, vol. 2020, p. 1100 (2021)
32. Selim, M., Zhang, J., Fei, B., Zhang, G.Q., Ge, G.Y., Chen, J.: Cross-vendor ct image data harmonization using cvh-ct. In: AMIA Annual Symposium Proceedings, vol. 2021, p. 1099 (2022)
33. Seoni, S., et al.: All you need is data preparation: a systematic review of image harmonization techniques in multi-center/device studies for medical support systems. Comput. Methods Prog. Biomed. 108200 (2024)
34. Sickles, E.A.: Acr bi-rads® atlas, breast imaging reporting and data system. Am. Coll. Radiol. 39 (2013)
35. Tajbakhsh, N., et al.: Convolutional neural networks for medical image analysis: full training or fine tuning? IEEE Trans. Med. Imaging **35**(5), 1299–1312 (2016)
36. Xiao, C., Li, B., Zhu, J.Y., He, W., Liu, M., Song, D.: Generating adversarial examples with adversarial networks. arXiv preprint arXiv:1801.02610 (2018)
37. Zhang, Q., Nie, Y., Zheng, W.S.: Dual illumination estimation for robust exposure correction. In: Computer Graphics Forum, vol. 38, pp. 243–252 (2019)

Modified CBAM: Sub-block Pooling for Improved Channel and Spatial Attention

Hamza Hussaini$^{(\boxtimes)}$, Shahana Bano , Eyad Elyan ,
and Carlos Francisco Moreno-Garcia

Robert Gordon University, Garthdee Road, Aberdeen AB10 7QB, UK
{h.hussaini,s.bano,e.elyan,c.moreno-garcia}@rgu.ac.uk

Abstract. The Convolutional Block Attention Module (CBAM) has
emerged as a widely adopted attention mechanism, as it seamlessly integrates into the Convolutional Neural Network (CNN) architecture with
minimal computational overhead. However, its reliance on global average
and maximum pooling in the channel and spatial attention modules leads
to information loss, particularly in scenarios demanding fine-grained feature analysis, such as medical imaging. In this paper, we propose the
Modified CBAM (MCBAM) to address this critical limitation. This novel
framework eliminates the dependence on global pooling by introducing a
sub-block pooling strategy that captures nuanced feature relationships,
preserving critical spatial and channel-wise information. MCBAM iteratively computes attention maps along channel and spatial dimensions,
adaptively refining features for superior representational power. Comprehensive evaluations on diverse datasets, including C-NMC (acute
lymphoblastic leukemia), PCB (peripheral blood cells), and COVID-
19 (Chest X-ray), demonstrate the efficacy of MCBAM. Additionally,
we evaluate MCBAM against similar alternatives, such as the Bottleneck Attention Module (BAM), Normalisation-Based Attention Module (NAM), and Triplet Attention Module (TAM), demonstrating that
MCBAM consistently outperforms these advanced attention mechanisms
across all datasets and metrics. Furthermore, results reveal that MCBAM
surpasses the standard CBAM and establishes itself as a robust and
effective enhancement for attention mechanisms, with notable improvements in medical imaging tasks, offering critical advantages in complex
scenarios.

Keywords: Modified Convolutional Block Attention Module
(MCBAM) · Convolutional Block Attention Module (CBAM) ·
Convolutional Neural Network (CNN) · Attention Mechanisms ·
Medical Imaging · Global Pooling · Sub-block Pooling · Channel
Attention · Spatial Attention

1   Introduction

Advances in computer vision, particularly through convolutional neural networks
(CNNs) [17], have enabled significant progress in medical imaging tasks such as

S. Ali et al. (Eds.): MIUA 2025, LNCS 15917, pp. 116–130, 2026.
https://doi.org/10.1007/978-3-031-98691-8_9

disease prediction and image enhancement [3,7,8,10]. CNN architectures have evolved in depth [12,24], width [26,33], and cardinality [6,30], enhancing their ability to tackle complex tasks.

Recently, attention mechanisms have become integral to computer vision, improving performance by allowing models to focus on important features [13,27,29]. This is especially valuable in medical imaging applications like classification [15,21], detection [16,18], and segmentation [23,28], where accurate feature extraction is critical.

Studies have shown that attention mechanisms significantly boost the accuracy of medical imaging models [5,35,37]. By focusing on informative image regions, they enhance precision in diagnosis and treatment planning, making them essential for identifying subtle pathological features [35].

Despite their benefits, modules like the convolutional block attention module (CBAM) [29] are limited by global pooling, which can lead to information loss, an issue in tasks requiring fine detail, such as disease classification. Other modules like the normalisation attention module (NAM) and the bottleneck attention module (BAM) share this limitation, indicating the need for more effective attention designs in medical imaging.

To address this, we propose MCBAM, which uses sub-block pooling instead of global pooling to better preserve detailed spatial and channel information. It refines attention iteratively and achieves improved performance in tasks like classification and segmentation, particularly where precision is crucial.

MCBAM has been evaluated on medical datasets (C-NMC, PCB, COVID-19), outperforming CBAM, BAM, NAM, and TAM in all metrics. Although other attention modules exist, their specific design purposes make them less relevant for comparison. MCBAM's consistent results confirm its robustness for high-stakes medical imaging tasks.

2   Related Work

CNN architectural innovation has largely focused on modifying depth, width, and cardinality. Models like VGG [24], Inception [26], and ResNet [12] addressed performance and optimisation challenges in deep networks. Variants such as WideResNet [33], Inception-ResNet [25], PyramidNet [11], ResNeXt [30], and DenseNet [14] introduced improvements by widening layers, increasing cardinality, and promoting feature reuse across layers [2].

Attention mechanisms in CNNs mimic the human visual system by focusing on key features within a scene [35]. Recent models [13,27,29] integrate attention modules to improve CNN performance. Residual Attention Networks [27] use encoder-decoder modules, while SE-Net [13] emphasises channel-wise attention through global pooling. However, models like SE-Net miss spatial context, as addressed in [4].

Other attention modules such as BAM [22] and NAM [19] offer lightweight, channel-spatial attention integration. While effective on general datasets, BAM has not been tested in medical imaging, and NAM, though efficient, prioritises speed over the precision needed in clinical applications.

Triplet attention module (TAM) [20] improves interaction between spatial and channel dimensions and shows strong results on benchmarks like ImageNet and MS COCO. However, like BAM and NAM, its performance on high-resolution and domain-specific medical images remains unexplored.

CBAM [29] efficiently combines spatial and channel attention, outperforming channel-only methods [13], but suffers from information loss due to global average and max pooling. This study eliminates global pooling in CBAM to retain fine-grained features, especially for medical imaging tasks.

3   Method

This section overviews the standard CBAM, explaining its core principles and functionality. Following this, we present a detailed explanation of the enhancements introduced in our proposed MCBAM, highlighting the specific improvements and their potential benefits.

3.1   The Convolutional Block Attention Module (CBAM)

The Convolutional Block Attention Module (CBAM), introduced in [29], is a lightweight and effective attention mechanism that enhances CNN performance by sequentially applying channel and spatial attention. Its simplicity and low computational cost have made it widely adopted in various computer vision tasks [31]. However, CBAM's reliance on global average and max pooling to generate attention maps can cause information loss by reducing feature map dimensionality—an issue particularly problematic in medical imaging, where preserving fine-grained details is vital for accurate diagnosis. Overcoming this limitation is essential to adapting CBAM for high-precision applications.

3.2   The Modified Convolutional Block Attention Module (MCBAM)

The MCBAM proposed in this study extends the capabilities of CBAM to address the challenge of information loss, thus rendering it highly applicable for image processing in the medical domain. MCBAM is designed as a lightweight module that maintains inference times nearly identical to CBAM. It mitigates CBAM's limitation by reducing the size of pooling filters by segmenting the input convolutional block into n and m sub-blocks each in the channel and spatial dimensions respectively. This approach eliminates the need for global pooling in CBAM channel and spatial attention modules, thereby preserving crucial information that enhances CNN classification accuracy in medical imaging. The practical implications of this research are profound, as it has the potential to address critical limitations in existing attention mechanisms, including CBAM,

SAM, and BAM. It can enhance CNN's capability to detect subtle and intricate features while improving the interpretability of CNN-based diagnostic models.

When provided with an intermediate convolutional block C_b as input, the channel attention module of MCBAM generates one-dimensional attention $A_{channel}$, while the spatial attention module produces two-dimensional spatial attention $A_{spatial}$. These modules are arranged sequentially because such a configuration yields improved performance [29]. This attention process is depicted in Eqs. 1 and 2.

$$C_b^{'} = A_{channel}(C_b) \otimes C_b \tag{1}$$

$$C_b^{''} = A_{spatial}(C_b^{'}) \otimes C_b^{'} \tag{2}$$

where $\otimes$ indicates element-wise multiplication, $C_b^{'}$ and $C_b^{''}$ respectively represent the channel-refined convolutional block and the final channel-spatial refined block upon which the subsequent CNN operation is applied. During this element-wise multiplication, the attention values propagate backward, with the channel attention multiplied across the corresponding spatial dimensions of the intermediate convolutional block C_b and spatial attention distributed along the corresponding channel dimensions of the channel-refined block $C_b^{'}$. Figure 1 illustrates the process of computing these attentions. A comprehensive explanation of MCBAM's channel and spatial attention modules is provided in the subsequent chapters of this section.

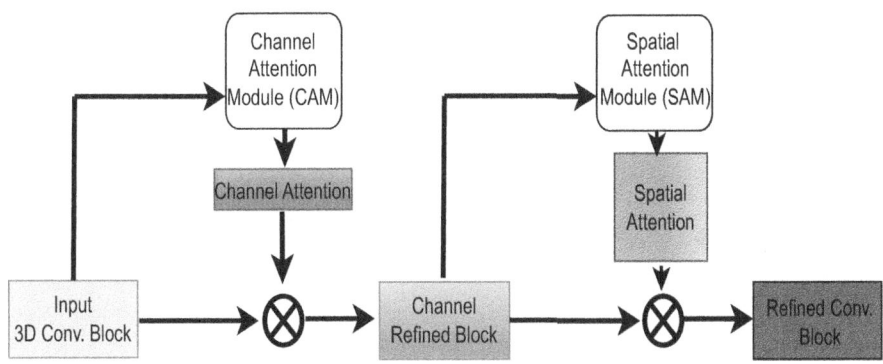

Fig. 1. The Modified Convolutional Block Attention Module (MCBAM).

Channel Attention Module (CAM). A convolutional block consists of multiple feature maps, each generated by a unique convolution filter and representing a distinct channel. These channels capture different aspects of the input image, encoding features learned by their corresponding filters [34]. The Channel Attention Module (CAM) in MCBAM enhances CNN performance by focusing attention on the most informative channels for image identification. Traditional methods compress the spatial dimensions of a convolutional block using global average pooling [13,36], while CBAM [29] uses both average and max pooling to capture complementary information. However, these pooling operations can discard important details.

To mitigate the CBAM information loss, MCBAM introduces a sub-block pooling strategy that divides the intermediate convolutional block into four spatial sub-blocks. If dimensions are not divisible by two, the algorithm slightly adjusts one half to ensure complete coverage. Each sub-block is treated independently, with average pooling applied to derive spatial context descriptors of dimension $1 \times 1 \times d$. These descriptors are passed through a multi-layer perceptron (MLP) with a single ReLU-activated hidden layer of reduced dimensionality ($\frac{d}{k}$). The output attention vectors are aggregated via element-wise addition and normalised using the sigmoid function to generate the final one-dimensional channel attention, as defined in Eq. 3. This process enables MCBAM to maintain fine-grained channel information, crucial for tasks like medical image classification.

$$A_{channel}(C_b) = \sum_{n=1}^{x} \sigma(w_{ho}(w_{ih}u_n)) \tag{3}$$

where w_{ih} and w_{ho} are the input-hidden and hidden-output weights of the MLP network. Note that according to our experimental validation presented in Sect. 4, we recommend $x = 4$. The overall architecture of the MCBAM's channel attention module is shown in Fig. 2.

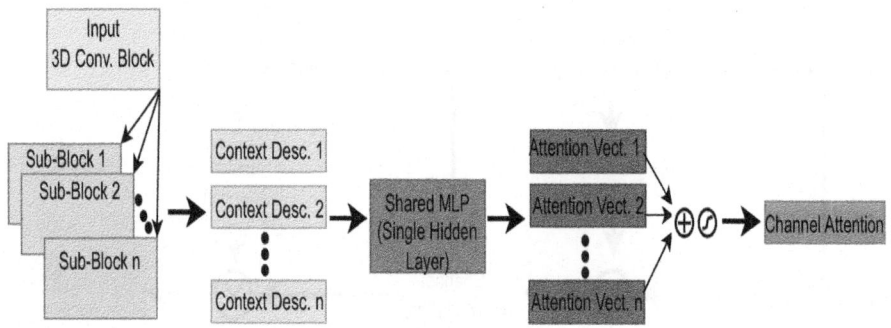

Fig. 2. The Channel Attention Module.

Spatial Attention Module (SAM). The two-dimensional spatial attention map is generated by leveraging the inter-spatial relationships among activations along the channel axis of a channel-refined convolutional block. This spatial attention serves to complement the channel attention by emphasising the informative regions of the channel-refined block. In MCBAM, the computation of spatial attention $A_{spatial}$ begins by dividing the channel-refined block C_b' across its channel dimension into m sub-blocks v_m as illustrated in Fig. 3. In our experiments, $m = 3$ due to the three image channels. In instances where three cannot evenly divide the channel dimension of the block, the third sub-block accommodates the remaining channels. Average pooling is subsequently applied along the channel axis of each sub-block, resulting in three distinct feature descriptors. According to [32], applying pooling along the channel axis of a convolutional block highlights regions of information. The feature descriptors are concatenated, and a convolution operation is performed, yielding the spatial attention map. A sigmoid activation function is then applied to this map, as demonstrated in Eq. 4. It's noteworthy that in aggregating channel information, E MCBAM employs average pooling exclusively, contrasting with the approach of the Spatial Attention Module (SAM) proposed in CBAM, which uses both average and maximum pooling.

$$A_{spatial} = \sigma(filter_{7\times7\times3}[AvgPool_{1\times1\times d}(v_1) \oplus AvgPool_{1\times1\times d}(v_m)]) \quad (4)$$

where σ denotes the sigmoid activation function, $filter_{7\times7\times3}$ denotes the convolution filter (7×7 spatial dimension is used, as derived from the original paper) and d stands for the depth of the sub-blocks of a channel-refined block. The semi-colon (;) indicates concatenation operation.

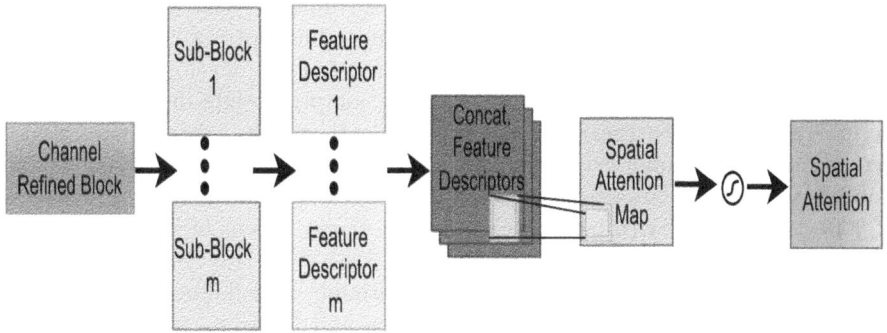

Fig. 3. The Spatial Attention Module.

4 Experiments

To evaluate the performance of the proposed MCBAM, we integrated it into a CNN architecture alongside other state-of-the-art attention modules, including the BAM, the NAM, and the TAM. Each module takes a convolutional block as an input. Subsequently, we trained the CNN-MCBAM model using the datasets outlined in Sect. 4.2. For a comprehensive comparison, we also trained CNN, CNN-CBAM, CNN-BAM, CNN-NAM, and CNN-TAM models on the same datasets and analysed their performance.

4.1 Experimental Setup

The implementation was carried out on the RONIN virtual machine[1] using Jupyter Notebook as the development environment. Python was utilised for creating directories and transferring files. All models were implemented using PyTorch. The libraries employed include NumPy, Torch, and Matplotlib. NumPy facilitates the effective handling of large data volumes [9], while Torch is utilised for constructing the layers of the CNN network. Matplotlib simplifies the visualisation of the model training history[2]

4.2 Datasets

This section addresses the datasets employed to validate the performance of the proposed MCBAM. We utilised three medical image datasets for performance evaluation. The medical image collection comprises the C-NMC (acute lymphoblastic leukaemia), the PCB (peripheral blood cell), and the COVID-19 datasets.

The C-NMC dataset consists of microscopic images of white blood cells, categorized into two classes: cancer cells and normal cells. It includes images from 118 subjects, with 69 diagnosed with leukemia and 49 being healthy. The dataset is divided into three folds: Fold1 contains 10,661 images, Fold2 has 1,867 images, and Fold3 includes 2,586 images, though its ground truth labels are not provided. In total, the dataset comprises 15,114 images, each with dimensions of 450 × 450 pixels, a resolution of 96 DPI, and a bit depth of 24.

The PBC Dataset was specifically designed for the development of automatic cell recognition systems [1]. This dataset comprises eight distinct classes of peripheral blood cells: Basophil, Eosinophil, Erythroblast, Lymphocyte, Monocyte, Immature Granulocyte, Neutrophil, and Platelet. Available freely in the public domain, the dataset contains 17,092 images. The dataset has dimensions of 360 × 363 pixels, with horizontal and vertical resolutions of 96 DPI. The bit depth is 24.

The COVID-19 dataset was created through a collaboration involving researchers from Qatar, Bangladesh, Malaysia, and Pakistan, along with medical doctors. It contains three classes: COVID-19, Normal, and Lung Opacity. Released in three stages, the dataset initially included 219 COVID-19 images, 1,341 normal images, and 1,345 lung opacity images. The second release expanded the COVID-19 class to 1,200 images, while the other classes remained unchanged. The final release significantly increased the dataset to 3,616 COVID-19 images, 10,192 normal images, and 6,012 lung opacity images. Each image has dimensions of 299 × 299 pixels, a resolution of 96 DPI, and a bit depth of 8.

---

[1] https://ronin.cloud/.

[2] The code for the CNN-MCBAM can be accessed via: https://github.com/fatimza-2013/brainiac.

Table 1. Summary of the volumes of datasets used to train and evaluate the proposed framework in this paper.

Dataset	Images Used	No. of Classes	Train	Valid	Test
C-NMC	11,500	2	4,900	1,050	1,050
PBC	9,600	8	6,720	1,440	1,440
COVID-19	15,000	3	7,350	1,575	1,575

4.3   Training and Hyperparameter Turning on Medical Image Datasets

This section outlines the experimental procedures involved in validating the proposed MCBAM on the medical image datasets highlighted in Sect. 4.2. Given the class imbalance present in all the datasets, where some classes contain more images than others, we addressed this issue using an oversampling technique to generate additional samples of the minority class. Subsequently, data augmentation was applied to further expand the dataset artificially. The issues of data imbalance in medical imaging have been extensively discussed in [10]. Table 1 presents a summary of the individual dataset volumes used in this experiment, along with their corresponding training, validation, and testing ratios.

Across all datasets, 70% of the images were allocated for training, with 15% each reserved for validation and testing. All images underwent resizing to 255 × 255 pixels. This was carefully done to avoid distorting the critical features of the images in the datasets. Normalisation varied depending on the dataset: the C-NMC dataset was normalised to a mean of 0.5 and a standard deviation of 1, while the PBC and COVID-19 datasets were normalised to a mean of 0 and a standard deviation of 1.

In the convolutional layers, filters of size 3 × 3 were used with a stride of one and valid padding. Batch normalisation was applied to all network layers to mitigate the effects of vanishing and exploding gradients. An initial learning rate of $1e - 4$ was employed for the C-NMC dataset, while a rate of $1e - 3$ was used for the PBC and COVID-19 datasets. Parameter optimisation was conducted using the Adam optimizer across all networks.

Following each convolution operation, ReLU activation and max pooling with a filter size of 2 × 2 were applied. Subsequently, each pooling operation was followed by the MCBAM. MCBAM divided the input convolutional block into n sub-blocks before generating channel and spatial attention. In this experiment, we opted for n as four for channel attention and three for spatial attention to minimise computational complexity.

ReLU activation was applied to the penultimate layer of the classification head, while sigmoid activation was used for the final classification layer. The training involved 20 epochs with a batch size of 64, utilising three convolutional layers and two fully connected layers. We use cross-folder validation to ensure uniform data distribution during training.

For the loss function, the cross-entropy loss function was utilised for the PBC and COVID-19 datasets, while binary cross-entropy loss was employed for the C-NMC dataset. To avoid overfitting, the two final fully connected layers implemented a dropout rate of 0.5.

4.4   Activations Visualisations with Grad-CAM

Gradient-weighted Class Activation Mapping (Grad-CAM) is a visualisation technique used in deep learning to interpret and understand the decision-making process of CNN networks. It works by leveraging the gradients of a target class flowing into the final convolutional layer to produce a coarse localisation map, highlighting the regions of the input image that are most influential in the model's decision. The primary purpose of Grad-CAM is to provide interpretability and transparency, allowing researchers and practitioners to identify the areas of focus for the neural network during classification tasks. This can be particularly useful in sensitive domains like medical imaging, where understanding why a model made a specific prediction is as critical as the prediction itself. By visually demonstrating how a model arrives at its decisions, Grad-CAM aids in debugging, trust-building, and ensuring that the model's reasoning aligns with domain knowledge.

Experiments were conducted to evaluate the information retention capacity of CNN models, integrated with various attention modules, including BAM, NAM, Triplet Attention Module, CBAM, and the proposed MCBAM, and trained on the COVID-19 dataset. Chest position is always the area of interest in diagnosing COVID-19 and other lung diseases. The models, CNN-BAM, CNN-NAM, CNN-TAM, CNN-CBAM, and CNN-MCBAM, were trained, and Grad-CAM heatmaps were generated for each to visualise the regions of focus and information retention during classification. Among these, MCBAM demonstrated the highest retention capacity, effectively preserving critical spatial and channel-wise information as depicted in Fig. 4. This was followed by the TAM, which also showed strong retention capabilities. NAM and BAM exhibited moderate performance due to their reliance on global pooling, retaining less information than MCBAM and the TAM. CBAM had the lowest retention capacity on this dataset, highlighting the limitations of its reliance on global pooling operations. These findings underline the superiority of MCBAM in refining feature representations and enhancing the information retention of CNNs.

4.5   Ablation Studies

This section discusses the optimal method for integrating MCBAM into the CNN architecture, as well as the best arrangement of channel and spatial attention components. The C-NMC medical image dataset was used in this study because the module demonstrated superior performance on it. Initial experiments applied MCBAM to the first layer of the CNN, followed by experiments with MCBAM in the last layer, both the first and the last layers, and all layers of the CNN. The best results were achieved when MCBAM was applied to all convolutional

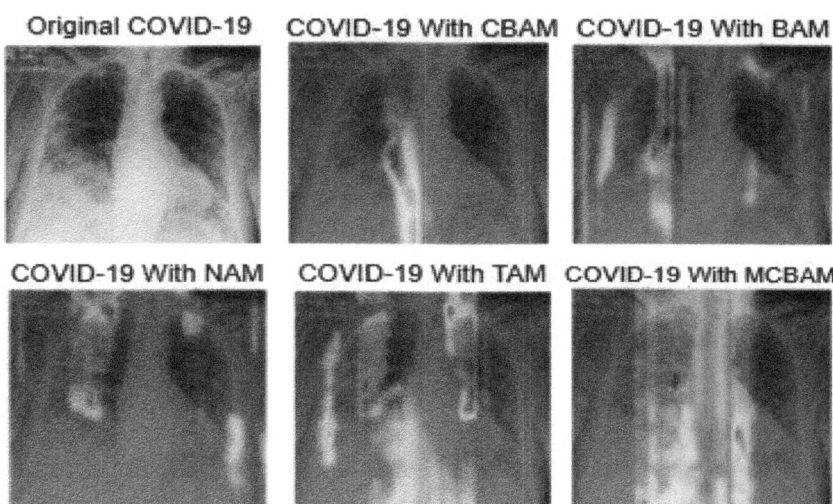

Fig. 4. Comparison of Visualisations for the Trained CNN using CBAM, BAM, NAM, TAM, and MCBAM.

layers. Although longer training times were required compared to other modules, the inference time remained nearly the same. Additionally, we also explore the application of MCBAM both before and after pooling operations. However, no significant differences have been observed.

To optimise the integration of the MCBAM within the CNN architecture, we conducted a number of experiments to determine the most effective arrangement of its channel and spatial attention components. Two configurations were evaluated: parallel and sequential arrangements. In the parallel arrangement, both channel and spatial attention modules operate simultaneously, while in the sequential arrangement, one module processes features first and feeds the refined output into the subsequent module. Additionally, we experimented with the channel and spatial attention components separately and observed the results. The findings revealed that incorporating both attentions together provided significantly better performance than using either component in isolation. Among the tested configurations, the sequential arrangement consistently outperformed the parallel configuration, delivering superior performance across key metrics. This aligns with the findings in [29], which demonstrated the effectiveness of sequential attention in progressively refining features by addressing channel-wise and spatial dependencies in a stepwise manner. The results highlight the importance of leveraging a structured approach to attention design for enhanced feature representation and overall model performance. Table 2 shows the results of these experiments with the best results highlighted in bold.

Table 2. Experimental Results for Ablation Studies on C-NMC Dataset

Method	Prec	Rec	F1	Acc.
CNN + MCBAM (Spatial)	0.91	0.90	0.90	0.90
CNN + MCBAM (Channel)	0.93	0.92	0.92	0.92
CNN-MCBAM [Parallel]	0.96	0.95	0.95	0.95
CNN-MCBAM [Sequential]	**0.98**	**0.97**	**0.97**	**0.97**

5   Results and Discussion

This section presents, compares, and analyses the results obtained from the trained CNN-MCBAM, CNN, CNN-CBAM, CNN-BAM, CNN-NAM, and CNN-TAM models. The results are summarised in Table 3, which consists of four rows and six columns. The first row includes the headings of the various columns. Subsequent rows include CNN, CNN-BAM, CNN-NAM, CNN-TAM, CNN-CBAM, and CNN-MCBAM models trained on different medical image datasets. Specifically, the second row compares CNN, CNN-BAM, CNN-NAM, CNN-TAM, CNN-CBAM, and CNN-MCBAM trained on the C-NMC dataset, the third row compares their performance on the PBC dataset, and the fourth row compares their performance on the COVID-19 dataset. In each row, the values of the metrics indicating superior performance are highlighted. Column one displays the trained CNN, CNN-BAM, CNN-NAM, CNN-TAM, CNN-CBAM, and CNN-MCBAM. The following columns include the datasets used to train and evaluate these modules, and evaluation metrics: precision (Pre), recall (Rec), F1 score (F1 Score), and accuracy (Acc), respectively. The comparative analysis of these metrics among CNN, CNN-BAM, CNN-NAM, CNN-TAM, CNN-CBAM, and CNN-MCBAM across different datasets reveals notable performance improvements with the CNN-MCBAM model. The results for the C-NMC dataset reveal that incorporating attention mechanisms into the baseline CNN model consistently improves performance across all metrics. The baseline CNN achieves moderate scores with a Precision of 0.87, Recall of 0.85, F1-score of 0.86, and Accuracy of 0.86. Introducing BAM and NAM leads to incremental improvements, with NAM outperforming BAM by achieving an F1-score of 0.90 and an Accuracy of 0.89. TAM further enhances these metrics, attaining a Recall of 0.91 and an Accuracy of 0.91. CBAM shows a significant leap, achieving a balanced performance with all metrics reaching 0.93 or higher. Notably, the MCBAM model outperforms all others, achieving near-perfect scores: Precision of 0.98, Recall of 0.97, F1-score of 0.97, and Accuracy of 0.97, demonstrating its robustness in accurately capturing features in this dataset.

A similar trend is observed for the PBC dataset. The baseline CNN achieves an F1-score of 0.82 and an Accuracy of 0.82. The introduction of BAM and NAM results in moderate improvements, with NAM yielding an F1-score of 0.86 and an Accuracy of 0.86. TAM performs slightly better, with an F1-score of 0.87 and an Accuracy of 0.88. CBAM delivers comparable performance to TAM

Table 3. Comparative Results for Standard CNN, CNN-BAM, CNN-NAM, CNN-TAM, CNN-CBAM, and CNN-MCBAM on the Medical image datasets.

Method	Dataset	Prec	Rec	F1	Acc.
CNN	C-NMC	0.87	0.85	0.86	0.86
CNN-BAM		0.89	0.87	0.88	0.88
CNN-NAM		0.91	0.89	0.90	0.89
CNN-TAM		0.92	0.91	0.91	0.91
CNN-CBAM		0.93	0.93	0.93	0.92
CNN-MCBAM		**0.98**	**0.97**	**0.97**	**0.97**
CNN	PBC	0.84	0.81	0.82	0.82
CNN-BAM		0.87	0.83	0.85	0.85
CNN-NAM		0.88	0.84	0.86	0.86
CNN-TAM		0.89	0.85	0.87	0.88
CNN-CBAM		0.90	0.82	0.86	0.89
CNN-MCBAM		**0.94**	**0.95**	**0.94**	**0.94**
CNN	COVID-19	0.72	0.70	0.71	0.70
CNN-BAM		0.74	0.71	0.72	0.72
CNN-NAM		0.76	0.73	0.74	0.74
CNN-TAM		0.77	0.75	0.76	0.76
CNN-CBAM		0.71	0.71	0.71	0.71
CNN-MCBAM		**0.83**	**0.82**	**0.82**	**0.83**

in terms of F1-score (0.86) but slightly higher Accuracy (0.89). The standout model again is MCBAM, which achieves Precision and Recall values of 0.94, an F1-score of 0.94, and an Accuracy of 0.94. This indicates MCBAM's superior ability to discern intricate features in PBC images compared to the baseline and other attention-enhanced CNNs.

The COVID-19 dataset presents a more challenging classification scenario, as reflected by lower baseline scores. The standard CNN records a Precision of 0.72, Recall of 0.70, F1-score of 0.71, and Accuracy of 0.70. Enhancements with BAM, NAM, and TAM yield consistent but smaller improvements, with TAM reaching an F1-score of 0.76 and an Accuracy of 0.76. Interestingly, CBAM performs poorly on this dataset, matching the baseline CNN in all metrics. This anomaly suggests that CBAM may not be as effective in handling the specific challenges posed by COVID-19 medical images. However, MCBAM outperforms all other methods with significant improvements, achieving a Precision of 0.83, Recall of 0.82, F1-score of 0.82, and Accuracy of 0.83. This highlights MCBAM's adaptability and ability to generalise across datasets, even in challenging scenarios.

In summary, the results underscore the effectiveness of attention mechanisms in enhancing CNN performance across diverse medical image datasets. MCBAM emerges as the most robust approach, consistently delivering the highest scores. The improvements across datasets demonstrate the critical role of advanced feature extraction and attention strategies in addressing the unique challenges of medical image classification. The relatively low performance of BAM and NAM may be attributed to their use of a global pooling strategy, similar to that used in CBAM. The variability in CBAM's performance across datasets, particularly its poor results on the COVID dataset, highlights the importance of tailoring attention mechanisms to specific datasets for optimal performance.

6 Conclusions and Future Work

In this paper, we introduce the MCBAM as an extension of the CBAM aimed at improving the representation capabilities of CNN networks. The operations of CBAM result in information loss due to the inclusion of global pooling, which can have significant consequences, particularly when processing medical images. In the proposed MCBAM, we eliminate the need for global pooling in the channel and spatial attention modules of the CBAM. We exclusively utilised average pooling and discarded the need for maximum pooling in the CBAM's operations. The MCBAM has demonstrated a greater improvement in performance compared to the CBAM. The performance evaluation has been conducted through extensive experiments. Performance evaluation metrics, namely accuracy, precision, recall, and F1 score, were employed. The proposed MCBAM demonstrated superior performance over state-of-the-art attention modules, including the CBAM, BAM, NAM, and TAM, across all the medical image datasets. Future work will explore integrating MCBAM into deeper CNN architectures like ResNet, VGG, and GoogleNet to assess its scalability and effectiveness across different network designs.

Acknowledgment. The authors gratefully acknowledge the financial support of PTDF and the institutional backing of RGU, both of which were vital to the success of this research.

References

1. Acevedo, A., Merino, A., Alférez, S., Molina, Á., Boldú, L., Rodellar, J.: A dataset of microscopic peripheral blood cell images for development of automatic recognition systems. Data Brief **30** (2020)
2. Aggarwal, C.C., et al.: Neural Networks and Deep Learning, vol. 10, no. 978, p. 3. Springer, Heidelberg (2018)
3. Cervantes-Guzman, A., et al.: Robust cardiac segmentation corrected with heuristics. Plos One, 1–18 (2023). https://doi.org/10.1371/journal.pone.0293560
4. Chen, L., et al.: Sca-cnn: spatial and channel-wise attention in convolutional networks for image captioning. In: Proceedings of the IEEE Conference on Computer Vision and Pattern Recognition, pp. 5659–5667 (2017)

5. Cheng, J., et al.: Resganet: residual group attention network for medical image classification and segmentation. Med. Image Anal. **76**, 102313 (2022)

6. Chollet, F.: Xception: deep learning with depthwise separable convolutions. In: Proceedings of the IEEE Conference on Computer Vision and Pattern Recognition, pp. 1251–1258 (2017)

7. Dang, T., Nguyen, T.T., McCall, J., Elyan, E., Moreno-García, C.F.: Two-layer ensemble of deep learning models for medical image segmentation. Cogn. Comput. **1**(0123456789) (2021).https://doi.org/10.1007/s12559-024-10257-5. http://arxiv.org/abs/2104.04809

8. Dang, T., Nguyen, T.T., Moreno-García, C.F., Elyan, E., McCall, J.: Weighted ensemble of deep learning models based on comprehensive learning particle swarm optimization for medical image segmentation. In: IEEE Congress on Evolutionary Computing, pp. 744–751. IEEE (2021)

9. Dianat, B., Tavanti, F., Padovani, A., Larcher, L., Calzolari, A.: Bello: a post-processing tool for the local-order analysis of disordered systems. Comput. Mater. Sci. **209**, 111381 (2022)

10. Elyan, E., et al.: Computer vision and machine learning for medical image analysis: recent advances, challenges, and way forward. Artif. Intell. Surg. **2** (2022)

11. Han, D., Kim, J., Kim, J.: Deep pyramidal residual networks. In: Proceedings of the IEEE Conference on Computer Vision and Pattern Recognition, pp. 5927–5935 (2017)

12. He, K., Zhang, X., Ren, S., Sun, J.: Deep residual learning for image recognition. In: Proceedings of the IEEE Conference on Computer Vision and Pattern Recognition, pp. 770–778 (2016)

13. Hu, J., Shen, L., Sun, G.: Squeeze-and-excitation networks. In: Proceedings of the IEEE Conference on Computer Vision and Pattern Recognition, pp. 7132–7141 (2018)

14. Huang, G., Liu, Z., Van Der Maaten, L., Weinberger, K.Q.: Densely connected convolutional networks. In: Proceedings of the IEEE Conference on Computer Vision and Pattern Recognition, pp. 4700–4708 (2017)

15. Jiang, Z., Dong, Z., Wang, L., Jiang, W.: Method for diagnosis of acute lymphoblastic leukemia based on vit-cnn ensemble model. Comput. Intell. Neurosci. **2021** (2021)

16. Khandekar, R., Shastry, P., Jaishankar, S., Faust, O., Sampathila, N.: Automated blast cell detection for acute lymphoblastic leukemia diagnosis. Biomed. Signal Process. Control **68**, 102690 (2021)

17. LeCun, Y., et al.: Backpropagation applied to handwritten zip code recognition. Neural Comput. **1**(4), 541–551 (1989). https://doi.org/10.1162/neco.1989.1.4.541

18. Lee, D., Yu, H.W., Kwon, H., Kong, H.J., Lee, K.E., Kim, H.C.: Evaluation of surgical skills during robotic surgery by deep learning-based multiple surgical instrument tracking in training and actual operations. J. Clin. Med. **9**(6), 1964 (2020)

19. Liu, Y., Shao, Z., Teng, Y., Hoffmann, N.: Nam: normalization-based attention module. arXiv preprint arXiv:2111.12419 (2021)

20. Misra, D., Nalamada, T., Arasanipalai, A.U., Hou, Q.: Rotate to attend: convolutional triplet attention module. In: Proceedings of the IEEE/CVF Winter Conference on Applications of Computer Vision, pp. 3139–3148 (2021)

21. Nezamabadi, K., Naseri, Z., Moghaddam, H.A., Modarresi, M., Pak, N., Mahdizade, M.: Lung HRCT pattern classification for cystic fibrosis using convolutional neural network. SIViP **13**, 1225–1232 (2019)

22. Park, J.: Bam: bottleneck attention module. arXiv preprint arXiv:1807.06514 (2018)

23. Shvets, A.A., Rakhlin, A., Kalinin, A.A., Iglovikov, V.I.: Automatic instrument segmentation in robot-assisted surgery using deep learning. In: 2018 17th IEEE International Conference on Machine Learning and Applications (ICMLA), pp. 624–628. IEEE (2018)
24. Simonyan, K., Zisserman, A.: Very deep convolutional networks for large-scale image recognition. arXiv preprint arXiv:1409.1556 (2014)
25. Szegedy, C., Ioffe, S., Vanhoucke, V., Alemi, A.: Inception-v4, inception-resnet and the impact of residual connections on learning. In: Proceedings of the AAAI Conference on Artificial Intelligence, vol. 31 (2017)
26. Szegedy, C., et al.: Going deeper with convolutions. In: Proceedings of the IEEE Conference on Computer Vision and Pattern Recognition, pp. 1–9 (2015)
27. Wang, F., et al.: Residual attention network for image classification. In: Proceedings of the IEEE Conference on Computer Vision and Pattern Recognition, pp. 3156–3164 (2017)
28. Ward, T.M., Mascagni, P., Madani, A., Padoy, N., Perretta, S., Hashimoto, D.A.: Surgical data science and artificial intelligence for surgical education. J. Surg. Oncol. **124**(2), 221–230 (2021)
29. Woo, S., Park, J., Lee, J.Y., Kweon, I.S.: Cbam: Convolutional block attention module. In: Proceedings of the European Conference on Computer Vision (ECCV), pp. 3–19 (2018)
30. Xie, S., Girshick, R., Dollár, P., Tu, Z., He, K.: Aggregated residual transformations for deep neural networks. In: Proceedings of the IEEE Conference on Computer Vision and Pattern Recognition, pp. 1492–1500 (2017)
31. Yang, J., Jiang, J.: Dilated-cbam: an efficient attention network with dilated convolution. In: 2021 IEEE International Conference on Unmanned Systems (ICUS), pp. 11–15. IEEE (2021)
32. Zagoruyko, S., Komodakis, N.: Paying more attention to attention: improving the performance of convolutional neural networks via attention transfer. arXiv preprint arXiv:1612.03928 (2016)
33. Zagoruyko, S., Komodakis, N.: Wide residual networks. arXiv preprint arXiv:1605.07146 (2016)
34. Zeiler, M.D., Fergus, R.: Visualizing and understanding convolutional networks. In: Fleet, D., Pajdla, T., Schiele, B., Tuytelaars, T. (eds.) ECCV 2014. LNCS, vol. 8689, pp. 818–833. Springer, Cham (2014). https://doi.org/10.1007/978-3-319-10590-1_53
35. Zhang, R., Han, X., Lei, Z., Jiang, C., Gul, I., Hu, Q., Zhai, S., Liu, H., Lian, L., Liu, Y., et al.: Rcmnet: a deep learning model assists car-t therapy for leukemia. Comput. Biol. Med. **150**, 106084 (2022)
36. Zhou, B., Khosla, A., Lapedriza, A., Oliva, A., Torralba, A.: Learning deep features for discriminative localization. In: Proceedings of the IEEE Conference on Computer Vision and Pattern Recognition, pp. 2921–2929 (2016)
37. Zhou, Q., Huang, Z., Ding, M., Zhang, X.: Medical image classification using lightweight cnn with spiking cortical model based attention module. IEEE J. Biomed. Health Inf. **27**(4), 1991–2002 (2023)

WSI-AL: A Novel Active Learning Framework for Whole Slide Image Selection

Surya Achanta, Dinisha Kadam, Nilanjan Chattopadhyay$^{(\boxtimes)}$ iD,
and Nitin Singhal iD

AIRA Matrix, Mumbai, India
{info,nilanjan.chattopadhyay}@airamatrix.com
https://www.airamatrix.com/

Abstract. Histopathology image analysis plays a vital role in disease diagnosis; however, the limited availability of labeled data and the large size of Whole Slide Images (WSIs) creates a challenge for training deep learning models. Traditional active learning methods, which typically select entire images for labeling, are impractical for WSIs due to their substantial size and computational requirements. This paper presents a novel active learning framework specifically tailored for WSI selection. Our method computes WSI-level uncertainty scores using various techniques, including Margin Sampling, Monte Carlo Sampling, Gradient-based methods, and diversity scores derived from Cosine similarity and K-means++. By focusing on the most informative WSIs, we aim to significantly reduce labeling efforts while maximizing information gain for subsequent model training. We demonstrate that our approach consistently outperforms random data selection strategies, resulting in significant improvements in segmentation Dice scores on the PANDA dataset for Gleason-grade segmentation. Our work offers a new approach to efficiently use limited labeled data, facilitating the development of more accurate and cost-effective Gleason-grade segmentation models.

Keywords: Active Learning · Semantic Segmentation · Gleason Grading · Uncertainty Sampling · Diversity Sampling

1 Introduction

Supervised deep learning has revolutionized histopathology image analysis, particularly for tasks like prostate cancer segmentation, offering the potential for more accurate diagnoses and personalized treatment strategies. However, the application of deep learning to Whole Slide Images (WSIs) presents unique and significant challenges. Whole Slide Images are characterized by their extremely large size, often gigabytes in scale, requiring substantial computational resources for processing and analysis. Moreover, generating sufficient labeled data for training deep learning models is a major bottleneck in medical imaging. The annotation process in histopathology is time-consuming and expensive, as it necessitates expert pathologists who must carefully examine and delineate regions of interest.

S. Ali et al. (Eds.): MIUA 2025, LNCS 15917, pp. 131–146, 2026.
https://doi.org/10.1007/978-3-031-98691-8_10

In the specific context of prostate cancer, accurate Gleason grading is crucial for predicting disease recurrence and guiding treatment decisions. This process relies on the precise labeling of cancerous regions based on the morphological criteria established by the International Society of Urological Pathology (ISUP). However, several factors complicate this task. The morphological characteristics of cancer cells are dynamic and exist on a spectrum, making it difficult to define precise boundaries between Gleason patterns [5]. This inherent subjectivity leads to significant inter-observer variability, where pathologists may disagree on the classification of certain tissue regions. Acquiring large, multi-expert annotated datasets to mitigate this variability is often impractical due to the time and cost involved.

Traditional active learning methods, which iteratively select the most informative and relevant samples from a large pool of unlabeled data for labeling [1], are often ill-suited for Whole Slide Images (WSI). The sheer size of WSIs makes processing and annotating them in their entirety computationally expensive and inefficient. Furthermore, in histopathology, WSI-level context is often essential for accurate diagnosis. Patch-based annotation can miss critical diagnostic information, as pathologists often need to view the broader tissue architecture and relationships between different regions to accurately grade a region. Therefore, selecting WSIs by considering the most informative regions within is crucial.

To address these challenges, this paper introduces Whole Slide Image-Active Learning (WSI-AL), a novel active learning framework specifically designed for efficient WSI selection. WSI-AL strategically selects the most informative WSIs by computing WSI-level uncertainty scores using Margin Sampling [2], Monte Carlo Sampling [3], Gradient-Based Sampling [8], and diversity scores derived from Cosine similarity [9] and K-means++ [10]. This approach minimizes the annotation burden on experts while maximizing the information gain for training segmentation models. We demonstrate the effectiveness of WSI-AL on the publicly available PANDA dataset for Gleason grade segmentation, showing that it outperforms random selection and facilitates the development of more accurate and cost-effective diagnostic tools.

2   Literature Survey

Within the field of deep learning, active learning has been a well-established area of research. One of the approaches being version space-based approach [11,12], which explicitly or implicitly maintains a set of probable models, and queries examples for which these models make different predictions in order to determine the uncertainty. But it is observed that when using highly hyperparameter-heavy models such as neural networks, these algorithms degenerate to querying every example compromising on the diversity of the selection. Furthermore, the computational overhead of training deep neural networks precludes approaches that update the model to best fit data after each label query, as is often done (exactly or approximately) for linear methods [13]. In addition, there have been two major strategies for active learning [8,14,15], representative sampling and uncertainty sampling. Representative sampling algorithms select batches of unlabeled examples that are representative of the unlabeled set to ask for labels. It is based on the intuition that the sets of representative examples chosen, once labeled, can act as a representative surrogate for the full dataset.

In the medical domain, active learning has also been applied for classification problems, such as classification of sleep stages [16,17] or detection of seizures [18] from electroencephalogram (EEG), surgical workflow analysis [19], classification of cancer pathology reports [19], generating synthetic computed tomography (CT) images from MRI [20]. For segmentation, the literature suggests patch selection algorithms based on uncertainty for active learning [21] by determining each region by first identifying an informative area based on its uncertainty measure calculated by the probability map and then detecting its optimal bounding box. The patches ranked on informative measure from the priority map is used to select the regions for annotation. Apart from convolutional neural networks that are traditionally used for segmentation, fully convolutional networks for generating probability heatmap have also shown promising results. [22]. However, relying solely on probability logits to determine uncertainty can be misleading, as deep learning models frequently exhibit high confidence even when making incorrect predictions.

3   Domain Challenges

The analysis of histopathology images, specifically the task of Gleason grading in prostate cancer, introduces distinct domain-specific challenges that impede the effective application of deep learning techniques.

One of the primary obstacles in histopathology is the inherent subjectivity in the interpretation of tissue. The morphological characteristics of cancer cells are dynamic and exist in a spectrum, making it difficult to establish clear and definitive boundaries between different Gleason patterns. This subjectivity leads to significant inter-observer variability, where even expert pathologists may disagree on the classification of specific tissue regions. For example, a glandular structure might be classified as Gleason grade 4 by one pathologist and Gleason grade 5 by another, directly influencing the final Gleason score and subsequent treatment decisions.

Another significant challenge is the limited availability of labeled data, especially at the WSI level. Although tile-level annotations can be generated more easily, they often lack the crucial contextual information necessary for an accurate diagnosis. Pathologists often rely on the overall architecture of the tissue and the relationship between different regions within the Whole Slide Image (WSI) to make an informed decision. This context would be incomplete at the tile level. Furthermore, making detailed WSI-level annotations is a costly and lengthy process, demanding substantial expert time and resources. The scarcity of expert pathologists further exacerbates this problem.

Processing and analyzing WSIs is computationally demanding primarily because of their enormous size. Applying active learning to WSIs introduces even more complexity, stemming from the intensive computational needs of deep learning models and the risk of selecting uninformative, redundant samples. For instance, a WSI often includes extensive healthy tissue that provides minimal useful data for training a model to identify cancerous regions. This redundancy can result in imbalanced datasets and bias model training outcomes.

Addressing these domain challenges is crucial for developing effective deep learning-based solutions for histopathology image analysis. Our work proposes an active learning framework designed to mitigate these issues by strategically selecting the most informative WSIs for annotation, reducing the annotation burden, and maximizing the utility of expert knowledge.

4   Active Learning on Whole Slide Images

Active learning offers a promising strategy to address the domain challenges discussed earlier, particularly the challenge of limited labeled data in histopathology. By enabling the model to guide the learning process, active learning focuses annotation efforts on the most valuable samples, improving both performance and efficiency [1]. Traditional active learning methods iteratively select the most informative samples from an unlabeled pool, which are then annotated by an expert, creating a feedback loop for model improvement. This selective sampling reduces the annotation burden while maximizing the model's learning potential.

However, applying traditional active learning directly to Whole Slide Images (WSIs) presents significant challenges. WSIs are typically processed by dividing them into smaller tiles. While tile-level annotations are easier to obtain, they often lack the crucial context needed for accurate diagnosis. Pathologists often require a broader view of the tissue architecture within the WSI to make informed decisions. But, creating WSI-level annotations can lead to redundancy, as many areas within a WSI tend to be repetitive. For instance, a whole slide image may contain significant tumor areas essential for model training, alongside numerous non-tumor (benign) areas that are generally abundant.

On the other hand, generating WSI-level annotations simplifies data management by aiding pre-processing tasks. It specifically helps with dynamically determining magnification, tile and overlap sizes during the training phase. This adaptability ensures you can optimize data settings for accurate predictions.

The subjective nature of histopathology, as mentioned in Sect. 3, particularly in Gleason grading, adds another layer of complexity. Incorporating diverse WSIs with mixed Gleason patterns can be challenging due to inter-observer variability, where similar morphologies might be graded differently by different experts. This highlights a key paradox: simply increasing the amount of training data does not always guarantee improved model performance; a smaller, more carefully selected dataset can be more beneficial.

To address these limitations, our work introduces a novel active learning framework specifically designed for the selection of WSI. Whole Slide Image - Active Learning (WSI-AL) focuses on selecting the most informative WSI, rather than individual tiles or patches, to maximize the utility of expert annotations.

This approach acknowledges the importance of context at WSI-level and aims to reduce redundancy in annotations. By prioritizing the selection of uncertain and diverse WSIs, WSI-AL seeks to create a more efficient and effective annotation process, ultimately leading to improved deep learning models for image analysis in histopathology.

5   Methodology

Most active learning methods utilize two primary approaches, namely uncertainty sampling and diversity sampling, often in combination. In this paper, we propose and evaluate various combinations of uncertainty and diversity sampling techniques applied to that data at WSI-level. For measuring WSI uncertainty, we utilize sampling methods such as Margin, Monte Carlo, and Gradient-based techniques. To ensure diversity, we implement the Greedy search method and the K-means++ clustering technique.

5.1   Uncertainty

Uncertainty sampling is the most commonly used active learning technique to prioritize the most valuable areas for annotation, guiding the learner to query instances where the model exhibits the least confidence. In our framework, we extend this concept to the WSI level by assessing the uncertainty of each WSI based on the uncertainty scores of its constituent tiles. This allows us to select entire WSIs that, on average, contain more uncertain regions, increasing the efficiency of the annotation process. For this, we utilize three distinct methods for uncertainty sampling:

Margin Sampling: This uncertainty-based active learning strategy, selects samples based on the difference between the highest and second-highest predicted probabilities. Formally, the selection function is defined as $f(x;\theta)_{\hat{y}} - f(x;\theta)_{\acute{y}}$, where $\hat{y}$ and $\acute{y}$ represent the indices of the largest and second-largest entries of the model's output $f(x;\theta)$ for input x with parameters θ [8]. For image-level uncertainty estimation, we compute the mean of pixel-wise uncertainty scores. A higher mean value indicates greater confidence in the prediction by the model [2].

Monte-Carlo Sampling: Monte Carlo sampling is applied through the MC Dropout method which is easy to implement and optimize [24]. As T (forward dropout passes) gets larger, the approximation will get better. Basically, we run the network multiple times with dropout, average the outputs, and take the entropy(H) [3] as follows:

$$H \approx -\sum_c \left(\frac{1}{T} \sum_t p_c^t \right) Log \left(\frac{1}{T} \sum_t p_c^t \right) \tag{1}$$

where $\frac{1}{T}\sum_t p_c^t$ is the simulated Bernoulli distribution using Monte-Carlo dropouts.

Gradient Based Sampling: In Gradient-Based Sampling, a data point in the unlabeled dataset is inferred through the model to generate the label $\hat{y}(x)$ favored by the current model, along with the gradient g_x of the loss on $(x, \hat{y}(x))$ with respect to the parameters of the last layer of the network. The uncertainty score is subsequently computed by taking a weighted average of the gradient embedding norm and the class probabilities norm [8].

5.2   Diversity

While uncertainty sampling effectively identifies uncertain instances, it can lead to the selection of similar, redundant data points, especially in deep learning models. To mitigate this, our WSI-AL framework incorporates diversity sampling as a crucial component [3]. After selecting highly uncertain WSIs based on their uncertainty scores, we further select a subset of WSIs that are both representative of the uncertain set and diverse from each other. This ensures that the selected WSIs cover a broader range of morphological patterns and reduce redundancy in the annotation process. To achieve this, we generate tile-level and WSI-level embeddings. Tile-level embeddings are generated by calculating the channel-wise mean of the feature activations extracted from the last encoding layer of the model, making the representation invariant to shifting and rotation. WSI-level embeddings are then derived by computing a weighted average of the tile-level embeddings, where the weights correspond to the uncertainty of each tile's prediction. We employ two diversity sampling methods:

Greedy: Pairwise Cosine similarity for all the WSIs is calculated. From the uncertain unannotated set S_c we have to find $S_a \subseteq S_c$ with length k and has the largest representativeness of set S_c. To formalize the representativeness of S_a for S_c, we first define the representativeness of S_a for an image $I_x \in S_c$ as:

$$f(S_a, I_x) = \max_{I_i \in S_a} sim(I_i, I_x) \tag{2}$$

where $sim(\cdot, \cdot)$ is the similarity estimation between I_i and I_x.

Intuitively, I_x is represented by its most similar image in S_a, measured by the similarity $sim(\cdot, \cdot)$. Then, we define the representativeness of S_a for S_c as: $F(S_a, S_c) = \sum_{I_j \in S_u} f(S_a, I_j)$, which reflects how well S_a represents all the images in S_c. By finding $S_a \subseteq S_c$ that maximizes $F(S_a, S_u)$, we promote S_a by selecting k WSIs that are similar to many unannotated selected WSIs and are diverse compared to each other. As computing all the possible subsets and finding the most optimal subset is computationally not feasible, we adopt the greedy method [9]. Initially, $S_a = \phi$ and $F(S_a, S_c) = 0$. Then, we iteratively add $I_i \in Sc$ that maximizes $F(S_a \cup I_i, S_c)$ over S_a, until S_a contains k images.

K-Means++: The generated WSI embeddings were grouped into clusters using K-Means++ clustering [10]. The number of clusters was based on the desired batch size for annotation. Within each cluster, the WSI embedding nearest to the cluster's centroid was chosen for annotation. Cosine Similarity served as the distance metric for forming the clusters. This selection strategy aimed to identify representative samples from each group, ensuring that a diverse and informative batch was selected.

6   WSI-AL Framework

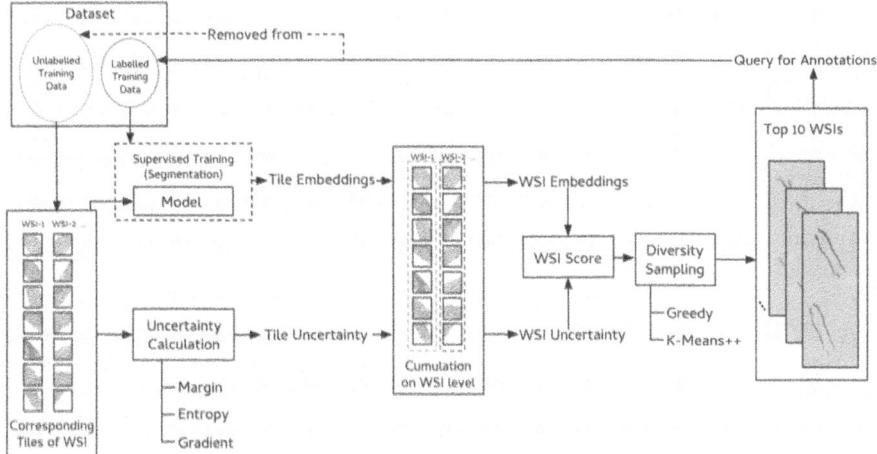

Fig. 1. Illustration of our Overall WSI-AL Framework

As illustrated in Fig. 1, our framework begins with a dataset of 150 WSIs (5% of the total pool), that are labeled and utilized to train a supervised segmentation model. The data annotation process follows a closed-loop procedure, starting with an initial pool of unlabeled examples and iteratively querying for additional annotations. At each iteration, we employ supervised training on the partially labeled pool to develop the best-performing model.

Using the initial model, we extract the tile embeddings from the last convolution layer of the encoder (bottleneck) (dimension: 1024) while simultaneously calculating the uncertainty for each tile using one of three methods: Margin, Entropy, or Gradient-Based. For an input tile I_i, the output from the last convolution layer in the encoding (bottleneck) section can be interpreted as high-level features I_i^f of I_i. To account for shifting and rotation variances in the tile, we compute the channel-wise mean of I_i^f to produce condensed features I_i^c, which serve as the domain-specific tile descriptor [7]. The WSI is represented by a WSI embedding, calculated as the weighted average of tile uncertainty and tile embeddings for all tiles within the corresponding WSI. The WSI-level uncertainty is defined as the mean of the uncertainty values for all tiles in that WSI.

After the WSI scores are calculated, a subset of 10 representative WSIs is selected from the top 30 WSIs as ranked by WSI score, to eliminate redundancy and ensure representation of distinct features. This is done using diversity sampling methods namely, Greedy approach and K-means++ approach as explained in the previous Sect. 5.2.

Novelty of WSI-AL: Our Whole Slide Image - Active Learning framework incorporates a number of significant novelties.

WSI-Level Active Learning: Unlike traditional methods that operate on image patches or tiles, WSI-AL directly selects entire WSIs for annotation. This is crucial in histopathology, where contextual information within the WSI is essential for accurate diagnosis.

Combined Uncertainty and Diversity at the WSI Level: WSI-AL integrates uncertainty and diversity sampling at the WSI level. This ensures the selection of informative and representative WSIs, maximizing annotation efficiency and model performance.

Weighted WSI Embeddings: The use of tile uncertainty to weight tile embeddings when generating WSI embeddings is a novel approach to capture WSI-level informativeness.

Greedy and K-Means++ for WSI Diversity: The application of Greedy selection and K-Means++ clustering to select diverse WSIs is a novel adaptation of these diversity methods for WSI-level active learning.

By addressing the specific challenges of WSI analysis, WSI-AL offers a more effective and efficient approach to active learning in histopathology.

7   Dataset Details

The training and analysis was carried out on publicly available PANDA (Prostate cANcer graDe Assessment) segmentation dataset. The dataset consists of over 11,000 whole-slide images of digitized H&E-stained biopsies originating from two centers (Karolinska Institute and Radboud University Medical Center). Different slide scanners with slightly different maximum microscope resolutions were used for digitization and labels were generated from different pathologists. The Karolinska dataset was labeled by a single experienced pathologist. Label noise may exist in this dataset due to the lack of label validation by another pathologist. The Radboud dataset was read by trained students. For this dataset, some minor label noise may also exist in the training set due to mistakes in the annotation process or inconclusive results. Though the label noise presents a modeling challenge, it resembles many real-world scenarios. As mentioned above, even experts in the field with years of experience do not always agree on how to interpret prostate histology [23]. The dataset we used consists of 5060 WSIs (from Radbound) with 6 classes namely Background, Stroma, Benign, Grade3, Grade4 and Grade5. Training configuration was set to 5× magnification, 512 × 512 tile size, no overlap.

Figure 2, gives the distribution of the entire PANDA dataset for each class at the WSI, Tile, and Pixel level, respectively.

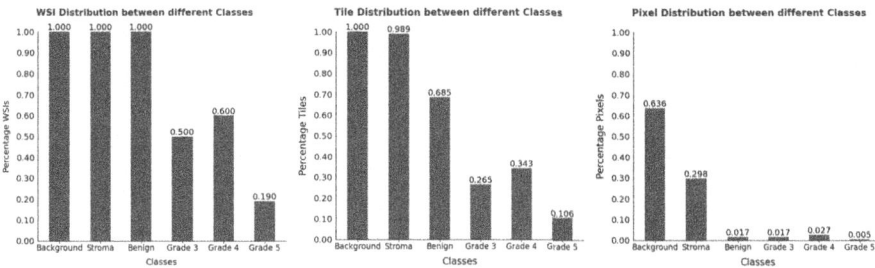

Fig. 2. Classwise distribution of PANDA dataset at WSI, Tile and Pixel level. Here, its important to highlight the scarcity of Grade5 areas evident from the pixel level (rightmost) graph.

For the baseline model, 3050 WSIs are selected for Training, 1002 WSIs are selected for validation and 1008 WSIs are selected for Testing such that the class distribution at WSI, tile and pixel level is maintained. Validation and Testing datasets was kept fixed throughout the experimentation. For Iteration 0, 150 WSIs (5% of the training pool) was randomly queried from the training pool and an acquisition size of 10 WSIs was pursued through each iteration for 10 iterations till the annotation budget of 250 WSIs (8% of the training pool) was exhausted.

7.1 Dataset Challenges

The source of PANDA dataset acknowledges the imperfections in ground truth labels stating that in real life even experts in the field with years of experience do not always agree on how to interpret a slide which leads to labels often being noisy in the medical domain. Inconsistency in the PANDA Dataset is known, additionally, it also contains numerous incorrect labels in its ground truth. Some examples are illustrated in Fig. 3. The original RGB tile clearly displays malignant glands; however, in the corresponding ground truth label (grayscale tile), these glands are incorrectly classified as class 0 (background). Although this makes training models more difficult, it also increases the potential medical value of having a strong model to provide consistent ratings. For our experiment, we went ahead with the existing dataset without modifying the ground truth labels or any manual intervention in the process.

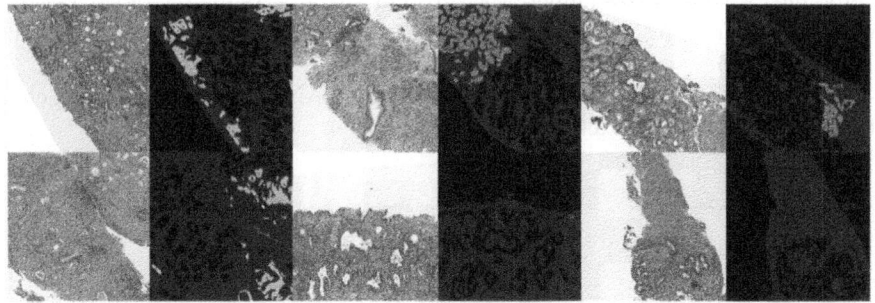

Fig. 3. Discrepancy in Ground Truth of PANDA Dataset. The RGB image is the tile with its respective ground truth in greyscale at the right. It is clearly seen here that a lot of malignant glands in the tile have been marked as background (0).

8   Experimental Setup

Initial Batch of Labels: For Iteration 0, 150 WSIs (5% of the training pool) were sampled uniformly at random and fixed as the starting point for all the methods.

Adaptive Annotation Loop: We iterate over the following steps to annotate batches of examples.

Model Training: At the beginning of each iteration, initial weights for all models are fixed for consistency across experimentation. We use the publicly available huggingface library timm, convnextv2_base, cmae_ft_in22k_in1k_384 encoder for training the model, which is a ConvNeXt-V2 image classification model pretrained with a fully convolutional masked autoencoder framework (FCMAE) and fine-tuned on ImageNet-22k and then ImageNet-1k. The model is modified, as shown in Fig. 4, for segmentation in the decoder section such that the decoder block combines residual connections, bottleneck architecture, and SE blocks. The model is trained for 90 epochs using cross-entropy loss, lookahead Adam optimizer (lr = 3e-4) and cosine learning rate scheduler (cycle decay = 0.5, lr min = 1e-5).

Data Selection: On a pool of unlabeled dataset, the uncertainty score is calculated at tile-level using Margin, Monte-Carlo and Gradient-embedding based techniques. The decision-making process of these algorithms is guided by the model's inherent properties and its predictive performance on the pool of unlabeled examples. Key considerations include the model's confidence, entropy, and the gradient respectively. The tile level score is then extrapolated to a WSI-level

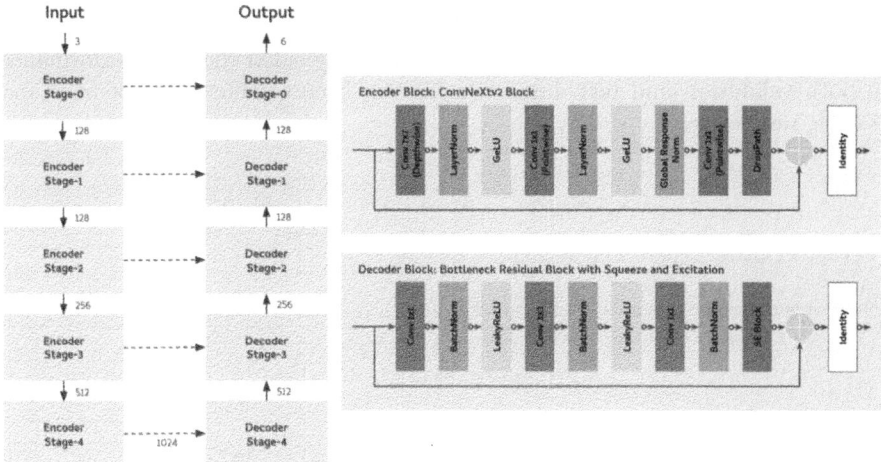

Fig. 4. Model Block Diagram

score by collating it with the embeddings from previous iteration. A weighted average of the individual tile uncertainty score and embedding values gives the final WSI query-error. 30 WSIs with highest query error are then sampled for diversity using Greedy search and K-means clustering, that reduces the data-points to top 10 candidates.

Annotation: Following the strategy's selection, we obtain the true labels of the selected samples and update the dataset. The model is trained again on the updated dataset.

Final Model: With each iteration, 10 WSIs are added to the dataset selected by WSI-AL framework. The iterations are stopped after a budget of 250 WSIs is exhausted.

9   Results

The baseline model trained on the entire PANDA dataset (Training: 3,050 WSIs/ 60,044 tiles, Validation: 1,002 WSIs/ 20,000 tiles, Testing: 1,008 WSIs/ 20,002 tiles), achieves a maximum mean Gland Dice Coefficient of 77.28% on validation data and 76.48% on test data, and a maximum mean Grades Dice Coefficient of 75.85% on validation data and 74.73% on test data. Model performance using 100% data, 50% data and 25% data is represented using red, blue, and green lines in the graphs respectively.

In the case of Malignant segmentation (Grade 3, Grade 4, Grade 5), as shown in Fig. 5 and Table 1, the Margin-Greedy method yielded the best performance on both validation and test dataset, achieving Dice Coefficient of 66.56% and 67.08%, respectively.

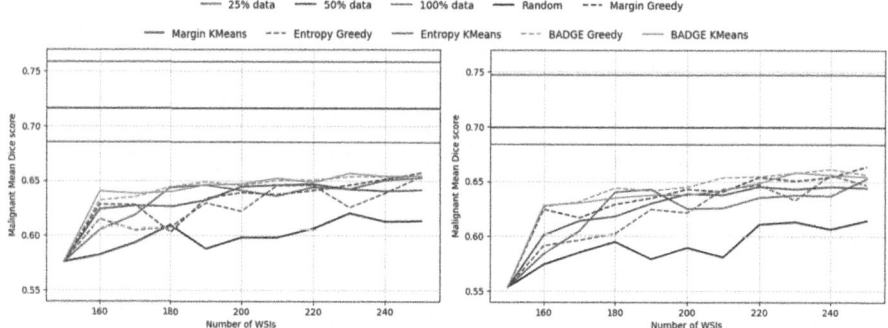

Fig. 5. Malignant Dice iterative performance on val (left) & test (right) data

Table 1. Mean Dice of all Malignant Classes

	Val DICE		Test DICE	
	Greedy	K-Means++	Greedy	K-Means++
Margin	**66.56 ± 1.20**	63.70 ± 8.77	**67.08 ± 1.26**	63.16 ± 1.54
Entropy	62.87 ± 1.69	63.79 ± 1.48	62.61 ± 2.28	62.84 ± 2.01
Gradient	64.65 ± 7.57	**64.77 ± 6.60**	64.70 ± 1.14	**64.26 ± 1.07**
Best	66.56 ± 1.20	64.77 ± 6.60	67.08 ± 1.26	64.26 ± 1.07
Random	60.22 ± 1.22	60.22 ± 1.22	59.49 ± 1.51	59.49 ± 1.51

For Gland segmentation (Benign, Grade 3, Grade 4, Grade 5), where "Glands Dice" corresponds to mean dice of classes Benign, Grade 3, Grade 4 and Grade 5. As shown in Fig. 6 and Table 2, Gradient-based methods consistently delivered the highest performance on both validation and test dataset, with nearly identical DICE scores of 67.43% on validation dataset. On the test data, the Gradient-Greedy method performed best with a DICE score of 67.54%.

It is noteworthy that for Grade 5, a class that is significantly underrepresented in the training data and in the PANDA dataset overall, the performance achieved through active learning methodologies trained on just 8% of the data is comparable to that of the baseline model trained on 25% of the data, as illustrated in Fig. 7 and Table 3.

It was also observed that discrepancies in ground truth labels within the dataset (as explained in Sect. 7.1), issues related to ground truth subjectivity as mentioned in the PANDA dataset description, and selection of some outlier

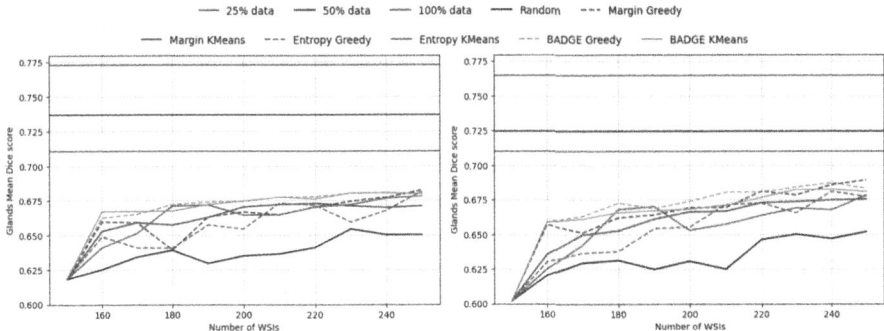

Fig. 6. Glands Dice iterative performance on val (left) & test (right) data

Table 2. Mean Dice of all Glands Classes

	Val Dice		Test Dice	
	Greedy	K-Means++	Greedy	K-Means++
Margin	64.68 ± 4.24	66.58 ± 0.72	67.41 ± 9.86	66.29 ± 1.32
Entropy	65.95 ± 1.38	66.6 ± 1.16	65.82 ± 1.83	65.95 ± 1.57
Gradient	$\mathbf{67.43 \pm 0.63}$	$\mathbf{67.43 \pm 0.55}$	$\mathbf{67.54 \pm 0.94}$	$\mathbf{67.15 \pm 0.87}$
Best	67.43 ± 0.63	67.43 ± 0.55	67.54 ± 0.94	67.15 ± 0.87
Random	63.95 ± 0.95	63.95 ± 0.95	63.57 ± 1.18	63.57 ± 1.18

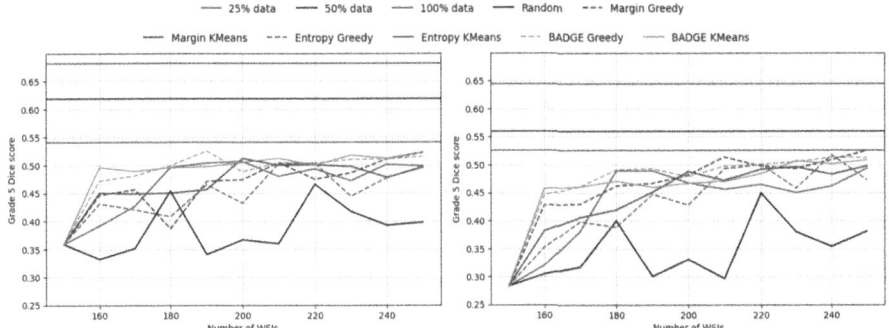

Fig. 7. Grade-5 Dice iterative performance on val (left) & test (right) data

Table 3. Mean Dice of Grade-5 Class

	Val DICE		Test DICE	
	Greedy	K-Means++	Greedy	K-Means++
Margin	47.32 ± 3.86	47.88 ± 2.51	48.05 ± 3.36	45.81 ± 4.19
Entropy	45.81 ± 3.56	47.70 ± 3.80	44.55 ± 5.33	44.73 ± 5.49
Gradient	$\mathbf{50.09 \pm 1.63}$	$\mathbf{50.46 \pm 1.11}$	$\mathbf{48.98 \pm 2.19}$	$\mathbf{47.85 \pm 2.00}$
Best	50.09 ± 1.63	50.46 ± 1.11	48.98 ± 2.19	47.85 ± 2.00
Random	38.79 ± 4.62	38.79 ± 4.62	35.15 ± 5.07	35.15 ± 5.07

WSIs could account for dips in the performance of the active learning model during certain iterations, as seen in Fig. 5, Fig. 6 and Fig. 7.

10   Conclusion

In this paper, we presented WSI-AL, a novel active learning framework designed for efficient Whole Slide Image (WSI) selection in histopathology. WSI-AL addresses the challenges of limited labeled data and the large size of WSIs by integrating WSI-level uncertainty and diversity sampling strategies. Our framework leverages Margin Sampling, Monte Carlo Sampling, Gradient-based methods, and diversity measures derived from Cosine similarity and K-means++ to select the most informative WSIs for annotation.

Our experiments on the PANDA dataset for Gleason grade segmentation demonstrate that WSI-AL outperforms random selection strategies. Notably, active learning, using only 8% of the training data, achieves performance comparable to models trained on significantly more data, particularly for the underrepresented Grade 5 class. This highlights the potential of WSI-AL to reduce annotation costs and improve model performance in scenarios with limited labeled data.

While our results show promise, we acknowledge that the PANDA dataset has inherent limitations, including potential label noise. Future work will focus on addressing these limitations by incorporating techniques for noisy label handling [23] and further optimizing the framework for clinical applicability. The development of efficient WSI selection strategies like WSI-AL can contribute to the development of more accurate and cost-effective diagnostic tools in histopathology.

11   Future Work

Future research will focus on several key directions. First, we intend to develop a hierarchical active learning strategy that combines WSI-level selection with tile-level selection. This will allow for a more granular approach to annotation, where we first select the most informative WSIs and then identify the most valuable regions within those WSIs for expert review. This has the potential to maximize information gain while further minimizing the annotation burden. Second, we will explore the integration of self-supervised learning methods, such as contrastive learning, to pre-train our segmentation model. Self-supervised pre-training could enable the model to learn more robust and generalizable feature representations, leading to improved active learning efficiency and performance. Third, we plan to investigate the use of alternative uncertainty measures and diversity sampling techniques to further optimize WSI selection. Finally, we will evaluate the performance of our framework on diverse histopathology datasets, including those with different tissue types and staining protocols, to demonstrate its broad applicability.

References

1. Biswas, A., Abdullah Al, N.M., Ali, M.S., Hossain, I., Ullah, M.A., Talukder, S.: Active learning on medical image. In: Data Driven Approaches on Medical Imaging, pp. 51–67. Springer (2023)
2. Tifrea, A., Clarysse, J., Yang, F.: Margin-based sampling in high dimensions: when being active is less efficient than staying passive. In: International Conference on Machine Learning, pp. 34222–34262 (2023)
3. Gildenblat, J.: Overview of Active Learning for Deep Learning. https://jacobgil.github.io/deeplearning/activelearning#introduction/. https://jacobgil.github.io/deeplearning/activelearning#introduction/
4. Zhang, J., et al.: LabelBench: A Comprehensive Framework for Benchmarking Adaptive Label-Efficient Learning (2024). https://arxiv.org/abs/2306.09910
5. Egevad, L., Delahunt, B., Srigley, J.R., Samaratunga, H.: International society of urological pathology (ISUP) grading of prostate cancer–an ISUP consensus on contemporary grading. In: APMIS, vol. 124, pp. 433–435. Wiley Online Library (2016)
6. Your Gleason Score & ISUP Grade. https://www.prostate.org.au/testing-and-diagnosis/grading-genetics/your-gleason-score-isup-grade/
7. Yang, L., Zhang, Y., Chen, J., Zhang, S., Chen, D.Z.: Suggestive annotation: a deep active learning framework for biomedical image segmentation. In: Descoteaux, M., Maier-Hein, L., Franz, A., Jannin, P., Collins, D.L., Duchesne, S. (eds.) MICCAI 2017. LNCS, vol. 10435, pp. 399–407. Springer, Cham (2017). https://doi.org/10.1007/978-3-319-66179-7_46
8. Ash, J.T., Zhang, C., Krishnamurthy, A., Langford, J., Agarwal, A.: Deep batch active learning by diverse, uncertain gradient lower bounds. arXiv Preprint ArXiv:1906.03671 (2019)
9. Feige, U.: A threshold of ln n for approximating set cover. J. ACM **45**(4), 634–652 (1998). https://doi.org/10.1145/285055.285059
10. Arthur, D., Vassilvitskii, S.: k-means++: the advantages of careful seeding [Techreport]. Stanford (2006)
11. Cohn, D., Atlas, L., Ladner, R.: Improving generalization with active learning. Mach. Learn. **15**, 201–221 (1994)
12. Balcan, M.-F., Beygelzimer, A., Langford, J.: Agnostic active learning. In: Proceedings of the 23rd International Conference on Machine Learning, pp. 65–72 (2006)
13. Beygelzimer, A., Dasgupta, S., Langford, J.: Importance weighted active learning. In: Proceedings of the 26th Annual International Conference on Machine Learning, pp. 49–56 (2009)
14. Settles, B.: Active learning literature survey (2009)
15. Hanneke, S., et al.: Theory of disagreement-based active learning. Found. Trends®Mach. Learn. **7**(2–3), 131–309 (2014)
16. Boehringer, A.S., Sanaat, A., Arabi, H., Zaidi, H.: An active learning approach to train a deep learning algorithm for tumor segmentation from brain MR images. Insights Imaging **14**(1), 141 (2023)
17. Grimova, N., Macas, M.: Query-by-committee framework used for semi-automatic sleep stages classification. In: Proceedings, vol. 31, no. 1, p. 80 (2019)
18. Ge, W., et al.: Deep active learning for interictal ictal injury continuum EEG patterns. J. Neurosci. Methods **351**, 108966 (2021)

19. Bodenstedt, S., et al.: Active learning using deep Bayesian networks for surgical workflow analysis. Int. J. Comput. Assist. Radiol. Surg. **14**(6), 1079–1087 (2019). https://doi.org/10.1007/s11548-019-01963-9

20. Qian, P., et al.: mDixon-based synthetic CT generation for PET attenuation correction on abdomen and pelvis jointly using transfer fuzzy clustering and active learning-based classification. IEEE Trans. Med. Imaging **39**(4), 819–832 (2019)

21. Qiu, J., et al.: Adaptive Region Selection for Active Learning in Whole Slide Image Semantic Segmentation (2023). https://arxiv.org/abs/2307.07168

22. Jin, X., An, H., Wang, J., Wen, K., Wu, Z.: Reducing the annotation cost of whole slide histology images using active learning. In: Proceedings of the 2021 3rd International Conference on Image Processing and Machine Vision, pp. 47–52 (2021). https://doi.org/10.1145/3469951.3469960

23. Li, W., et al.: PathAL: an active learning framework for histopathology image analysis. IEEE Trans. Med. Imaging **41**(5), 1176–1187 (2022). https://doi.org/10.1109/TMI.2021.3135002

24. Kirsch, A., van Amersfoort, J., Gal, Y.: BatchBALD: Efficient and Diverse Batch Acquisition for Deep Bayesian Active Learning. CoRR, abs/1906.08158 (2019). http://arxiv.org/abs/1906.08158

A Deep-Learning Approach for Diagnosing and Grading Ankylosing Spondylitis Sacroiliitis by X-Ray Images

Misagh Asgari[1], Şeyma Özkaya Çolakoğlu[2] , Mehmet Pamir Atagündüz[3] , and Lavdie Rada[1(✉)]

[1] Bahçeşehir University, Istanbul, Turkey
lavdie.rada@bau.edu.tr
[2] Institute of Health Sciences, Marmara University, Istanbul, Turkey
[3] Faculty of Medicine, Marmara University, Istanbul, Turkey

Abstract. The diagnosis of radiographic axial spondyloarthritis (r-axSpA), including ankylosing spondylitis (AS), relies heavily on radiographic evaluation of the sacroiliac joints (SIJs) based on the modified New York (mNY) criteria. However, this process is hindered by low image quality, inter-reader variability, and difficulty in detecting early-stage bony changes. To address these limitations, this study proposes a novel image-processing-based diagnostic assistance tool designed to improve the classification and grading of SIJs in patients with axial spondyloarthritis (axSpA). The study involved consecutive axSpA patients under follow-up at Marmara University's rheumatology outpatient clinics. Conventional SIJ radiographs were graded in a blinded manner by an experienced reader, with adjudication by a rheumatologist when necessary. The reference standard was definite sacroiliitis as defined by the mNY criteria. The proposed model utilizes a two-phase pipeline: the first phase employs the VGG-16 deep convolutional neural network for binary classification of r-axSpA and non-radiographic axSpA (nr-axSpA), while the second phase performs multiclass grading of sacroiliitis severity. The binary classification achieved an accuracy of 91.98%, and the multiclass grading phase reached 93.01% accuracy. Model performance was evaluated using the Confusion Matrix and F1 Score, highlighting its strong alignment with expert readings and robustness against false positives and negatives. This image-based approach demonstrates the potential to assist clinicians in the diagnosis of axSpA, offering a more objective and reproducible alternative to traditional visual grading. It supports clinical decision-making by enhancing diagnostic precision and facilitating the early identification of r-axSpA.

Keywords: Deep Learning · Ankylosing Spondylitis · Sacroiliac Joint · X-ray · CNN · Medical Imaging

This work was supported by the Academy of Medical Sciences Networking Grant Award (NGR1\1718).

S. Ali et al. (Eds.): MIUA 2025, LNCS 15917, pp. 147–162, 2026.
https://doi.org/10.1007/978-3-031-98691-8_11

1   Introduction

Ankylosing Spondylitis (AS) is a chronic, inflammatory disease of the axial skeleton characterized by new bone formation in the skeletal system that results in pain, physical impairment, and a substantial decrease in the patient's quality of life [1,2]. The hallmark of the disease is inflammation at the sacroiliac joints (SIJs). Left untreated, the disease can eventually result in the complete ankylosis of the vertebral joints [6]. Radiographic axSpA is the most prevalent type of a broad family of diseases known as axial spondyloarthritis, which together are estimated to affect up to 1.4% of the global population [7]. AS affects frequently men, and starts early in life, before the age of 45 [13]. Diagnosing AS incorporates the assessment of plain radiographic images of the SIJs for the presence of bony changes in and around the SIJs such as sclerosis, erosions, or ankylosis. Along with plain X-Rays, other imaging modalities such as computer tomography (CT), and magnetic resonance imaging (MRI) are also utilized to improve the diagnostic accuracy [9]. Figure 1 depicts these modalities. However, these costly modalities are not readily available everywhere and require the expertise of radiology specialists. The difficulty with the radiographic procedure of diagnosis is that it is vision-based, and therefore it is challenged by the clarity of the produced image, low visibility of the bony changes, particularly in the early Grades of AS, and the assessment skills of medical practitioners. Overall, the inter- and intra-reader reliability of conventional AS assessment, within and across specialties of rheumatology and radiology is shown to be poor [5,10,15].

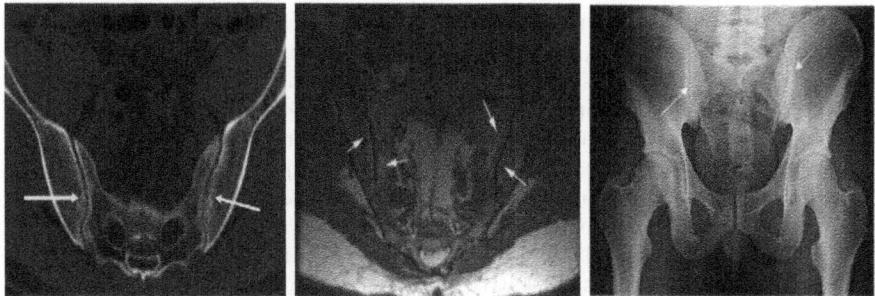

Fig. 1. Different imaging modalities commonly used in AS diagnosis. From left to right: CT, MRI, X-Ray. The arrows in each figure points the Sacroiliac Joints observed by doctors for AS assessment.

Radiographic grading of the SIJ damage in AS is divided into five Grades (0 - IV); **Grade 0:** Normal (Non-AS), **Grade I:** Suspicious, **Grade II:** Mild irregularity and sclerosis of the articular surfaces, with preserved joint space, **Grade III:** Joint space narrowing, with marked irregularity and subchondral sclerosis, **Grade IV:** Bilateral ankylosis.

The characteristic area of interest in plain X-Rays is the periarticular bony structures and the joint space which has an appearance that resembles a crack in X-Ray images. In Grade 0, the joint space and borders are well-defined and unobstructed, but as the disease progresses inflammation and sclerosis gradually occlude the joint space area. In Grades 0, I, and II, the joint space should not exhibit a noticeable widening or narrowing to the naked eye. Grade III should incorporate clear widening or narrowing evident even to the naked eye but inter- and intra-reader reliability is lowest, especially for these grades [5, 10, 15] (Table 1).

Table 1. Grades of AS.

Grade	Meaning
Grade 0	Normal (Non-AS)
Grade I	Suspicious
Grade II	Mild irregularity and sclerosis of articular surfaces with preserved joint space
Grade III	Joint space narrowing. Intense irregularity and subchondral sclerosis
Grade IV	Bilateral Ankylosis

In this study we aim to develop a deep-learning (DL) pipeline that is able to exploit the crack-like feature of AS at SI joints as a diagnostic key, and produce accurate predictions of the disease's progression.

In this study we aim to give answer not only to the detection of AS disease given a medical image but at the same time to accurately diagnose the degree of it. The proposed pipeline is a two stage method which applies first a binary classification; r-axSpA versus nr-axSpA classes; and then for the already r-axSpA or nr-axSpA SI joint X-Rays a multi grade scoring classification is used. To the best of our knowledge, this is the first work to report such a pipeline. To that end, our contributions are as follows:

- In Marmara research hospital, our team has collected a new dataset of X-Ray images from patients with varying grades of axSpA. This dataset can significantly contribute to medical research. This dataset holds promise for training deep learning algorithms to aid in the automated detection and classification of axSpA. Each image was scored 0 to IV by medical practitioners specializing in the disease to determine disease's progression. The dataset will be shared for research purposes with members working in research institutes with requests via email after they agree and sign to obey the restrictions listed in this document.
- Our aim, firstly, is to demonstrate that our algorithm discriminates between stages of radiographic sacroiliitis with a good degree of confidence. Classifying nr-axSpA as AS and vice versa is not rare error in clinical practice due to the lack of experience of the readers and poor inter-, and intra-reader agreement. We therefore sought to overcome this problem by clearly discriminating between the stages of sacroiliitis. Since both-sided Grade 2 or single-sided Grade 3 sacroiliitis, in the presence of clinical features of AS, is related to AS,

we believe that our algorithm will improve and standardize the classification patients into nr-axSpA and AS (r-axSpA) subclasses according to ASAS axial SpA classification criteria.

- We present a multi-component, DL-based pipeline that is able to reliably segment SI joints from X-Ray images and classify them for axSpA disease progression. The pipeline exploits the crack-like feature of the SI joint space, and performs pixel-wise quantification to produce its predictions.
- We visualize the pipeline's training procedure by highlighting the regions of interest the components use to generate their internal model of the disease, providing qualitative insight into previously obfuscated processes inherent to DL-based approaches.

The following sections will first review the current, relevant research, describe the dataset and proposed methodology. Finally, we will apply the model to the custom dataset collected from the hospital to observe the efficacy of the pipeline in a scenario with less dataset constraints.

2   Literature Review

Deep-learning (DL) has emerged as a promising tool for medical diagnosis, particularly in the analysis of medical images. Convolutional neural networks (CNN) have been shown to be particularly effective in aiding diagnosis of various diseases by identifying common features in pre-annotated image datasets and establishing correlations between patterns of data and the annotations. Despite their growing popularity, only a few studies have applied CNNs to axSpA diagnosis, with most works focusing on CT image datasets.

Castro-Zunti et al. [4] have proposed a DL-based method for the detection of erosion, which is an early marker for AS diagnosis. The authors report 99% cross-validation accuracy using the InceptionV3 model on a dataset of 681 grayscale DICOM CT frames. However this study only investigates CT images which in comparison to X-Rays are much more expensive and time consuming to produce. Moreover, the disease is not further classified into the Grades of its progression. More recently, Bressem et al. [3] applied the off-the-shelf ResNet-50 model, pre-trained on the ImageNet-1k dataset, to axSpA diagnosis. They use a dataset of 2,170 X-Rays from adult axSpA patients. This dataset is not publically available due to strict regulation of this research center. In this work the authors reported a sensitivity score of 92% and specificity score of 81% demonstrating the general ability of DL models to detect inflamed axSpA regions in X-Rays. However, this approach only provides binary classification for the presence or absence of axSpA and does not offer granular insights into disease progression.

The author's understanding reveals that the exploration into binary classification, specifically discerning between r-axSpA and nr-axSpA classes using X-Ray images, is still in its nascent phase. Furthermore, there is currently a dearth of research on multiclass classification, specifically in categorizing images across the five Grades.

3   Proposed Architecture

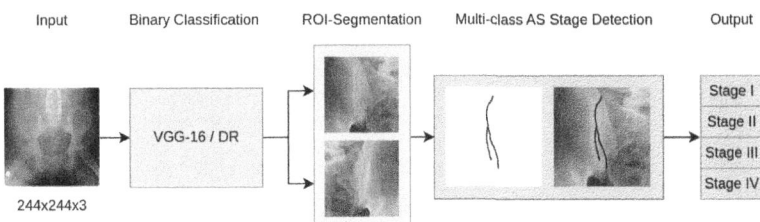

Fig. 2. Data-flow in the proposed architecture from input X-Ray image to final sacroili-itis Grade prediction. VGG-16 processes images and produced binary classification of axSpA versus non-axSpA samples. Grad-CAM based segmentation algorithm crops the ROI of interest at the SI join area. Holistically-nested edge-detection algorithm quan-tifies the obfuscation of the diagnostic key (crack-like features at SI join space). Final axSpA Grade prediction is made by comparing the quantities to a table containing average pixel counts for each Grade of axSpA related sacroiliitis.

We propose a mutli-step pipeline to automate axSpA associated sacroiliitis grad-ing. The architecture consists of a binary classification component, a ROI seg-mentation algorithm, a multi-class classifier specialized for edge detection, and finally a table-lookup for stochastic axSpA associated sacroiliitis grade deter-mination. Figure 2 depicts the high-level overview of the proposed architecture. In the first step, we employ VGG-16 [14] to conduct binary classification of raw X-Ray images into nr-axSpA or axSpA (r-axSpA) classes. If the output of binary classification is axSpA, the gradients from the last convolution layer of the CNN are fed into a Grad-CAM-based algorithm [12] to segment the input image at the SI joint space, highlighting regions of interest for further compo-nents. The image is then cropped and passed on to the second classifier, where a holistically nested edge detection (DeepCrack) [8] is used to detect and quantify the hallmark crack-like features of the disease. This diagnostic key is derived from the cracks being obfuscated by inflammation the more the disease has pro-gressed. Finally, we compare the values obtained from this analysis to a table containing average pixel quantities for each grade of axSpA and produce a final corresponding output – Grades II–IV. In a similar manner we can apply same procedure for the grading of nr-axSpA, Grades 0-II. It is crucial to highlight that the authors conducted experiments by categorizing Grades 0 and I–IV into two distinct groups and subsequently applying multiclass classification. This experimental approach demonstrated consistent performance in grading Grades I–IV, suggesting its applicability for future research endeavors in rheumatological disorders.

The following sections describe each component of the proposed pipeline in detail.

3.1 Binary Classification (VGG-16)

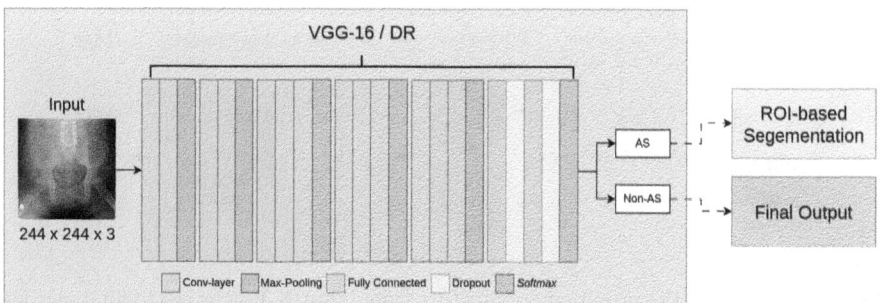

Fig. 3. Structure of the binary classifier (VGG-16 equipped with dropout layers). Input X-Ray images are resized to $244 \times 244 \times 3$ (width, height, number of color channels) and classified based on general differences between axSpA and non-axSpA samples, focused at the region of the SI joint space. Positive samples are passed further down the pipeline for segmentation of ROIs and granular classification.

The pipeline employed in this study employs two CNN models in its classification process. In the first stage, a VGG-16 model that has been pre-trained on labeled axSpA X-Ray images is used for binary classification of healthy and diseased images. Unlike the proceeding multi-class component, the VGG-16 model used here is not specialized for crack detection and analysis. Instead it uses the difference between the general appearance of AS vs non-AS X-Ray images as the basis of its classification. Regardless, GRAD-Cam, as shown in Fig. 5, indicates that the space at the SI joint area is of large interest to model prediction, indicating which part of the input influences the second decision. Figure 3 depicts the layout of this component. To improve the model's performance, robustness, and less overfitting, drop-out layers have been added. The VGG-16 model requires input images to conform to a standard of $224 \times 224 \times 3$, which represents the image's pixel width and height and the number of color channels, respectively. The model also automatically subtracts the mean RGB value from each pixel during image input. The only image pre-processing at this stage involves reshaping the images to meet this standard. VGG-16 consists of 13 convolutional layers grouped into five stacks, with each stack followed by max-pooling layers to reduce the input dimensionality. The first two stacks are composed of 2 layers and the next three have 3 layers each. All the layers use small 3×3 filters, with increasing filter quantities (ranging from 64 to 512 filters) to form a increasingly deepening model. The lower layers of the model extract low-level features such as edges and textures, while the deeper layers extract higher-level features such as shapes and objects. With over 138 million parameters, the VGG-16 model was trained on the ImageNet dataset, consisting of over 1.2 million images belonging to 1000 different classes, and has achieved state-of-the-art performance on several image recognition tasks, including image classification, object detection, and segmentation. As last layer, VGG-16 uses the *Softmax* activation layer. The softmax function transforms the input vector z into a probability distribution over the K classes. The function's output values range from 0 to 1, representing the probability of each image belonging to a class Grades 0 or I–IV.

At the end of this stage, the input image, the above classification, and the gradients of the last convolution layer are passed along the pipeline for further analysis.

3.2   GRAD-Cam-Based Segmentation of the SI Joint Area

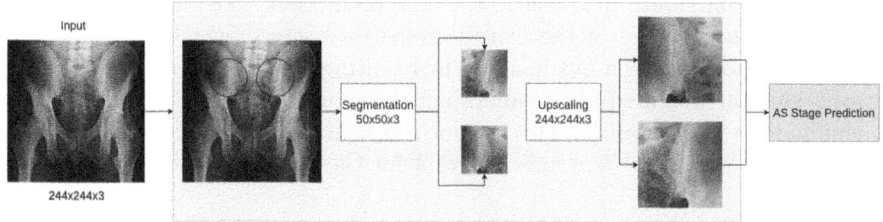

Fig. 4. GRAD-Cam-based segmentation component. Images classified as axSpA by the binary component are used as input. Rectangles of 50 pixels in diameter are cropped, centered at the ROIs specified by GRAD-Cam. The segmentations are then upscaled to 244×244 input. In effect, a maximal area containing the SI joint region is captured and passed forward to the multi-class component for granular classification.

The Grad-CAM algorithm is a visualization technique that highlights the regions of an input image important to a DL model's predictions. It was developed as an extension to the Class Activation Mapping (CAM) algorithm [11], which is limited to models with global average pooling in the last layer. Figure 4 depicts how Grad-CAM is used to segment the ROIs at SI joint area. We initiate the process by calculating the gradient of the class-specific score, denoted as y_c (prior to the application of softmax), concerning the feature maps A_k associated with the last convolutional layer. In other words, we determine the partial derivative of y_c with respect to A_k

$$\frac{\partial y^c}{\partial A_k} \tag{1}$$

where y^c is the score of the class c, and A_k is the k-th feature map of the last convolutional layer.

To highlight the importance of each feature map k for specific classes the following equation is used:

$$\alpha_k = \frac{1}{Z} \sum_i \sum_j \frac{\partial y^c}{\partial A_k(i,j)} \tag{2}$$

where Z is a normalization factor, and $\frac{\partial y^c}{\partial A_k(i,j)}$ is the gradient of the output with respect to the activation at position (i,j) of the k-th feature map. Further, a weighted combination of forward activation maps followed by ReLU is performed:

$$L^c_{GradCAM} = ReLU(\sum_k \alpha_k A_k) \tag{3}$$

where ReLU is the rectified linear unit function, and $L^c_{GradCAM}$ is the Grad-CAM map for the class c.

The Grad-CAM algorithm computes the gradients of the output with respect to the feature maps of the last convolutional layer of the network. Figure 5 shows the activation maps overlayed on axSpA X-Rays. These gradients indicate which feature maps contribute the most to the final prediction. The gradients are then weighted by the average of the feature maps themselves, which highlights the important regions of the input image. The resulting Grad-CAM map is obtained by averaging the weighted feature maps and applying a ReLU activation function to eliminate negative values. This produces a heatmap that reveals the regions of the input image that were most relevant for the network's prediction.

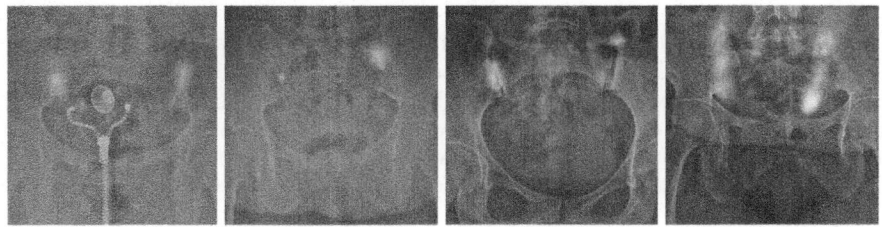

Fig. 5. Feature activation maps on axSpA X-Rays (top 40% threshold).

In the present pipeline, the two high-level components are connected by a GRAD-CAM based cropping algorithm, which discards binary predictions with the majority of the region of interest (ROI) in the top 40% of the image as faulty predictions. Additionally, it crops the images to ensure that the maximal ROI area is passed on as input to the multi-class component. The rationale behind this approach is that X-ray images for axSpA diagnosis are typically produced in a standard way, where the SI joint area is located in the middle to bottom region of the image. Thus, predictions made from the top region pixels are likely to indicate faulty binary classification. Furthermore, in cases where multiple regions of interest exist within the same image, they are sorted by area, and only the two largest ROIs (as determined relative to the size of the other segments) are retained, while others are discarded. After this sanity check is performed, if the image has been classified as healthy by the binary component, the algorithm returns this prediction as its final output, and execution terminates. Otherwise, if the prediction indicates axSpA, the data is passed on to the next step, where a cropping algorithm uses the GRAD-CAM activation maps to transform the images in such a way that the resulting data captures the maximal area corresponding to the SI joint area. The segmented regions are then upscaled to 244×244 pixels, as we observed that this enhances the multi-classifier's ability to detect small and faint cracks.

The final image is then passed on as input to the second high-level component to carry out multi-class prediction of axSpA Grade progression.

3.3   DeepCrack-Based axSpA Grade Prediction

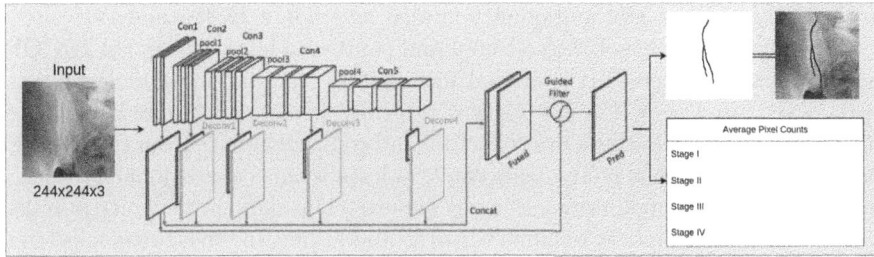

Fig. 6. Structure of the multi-class component used for axSpA grade prediction. axSpA images from the binary component are passed as input through the model. The binary component then processes edge features to capture the shape of the cracks. These cracks are then quantified in a pixel-wise manner, and a final prediction is made by comparing the pixel counts to a table containing average numbers of pixels pertaining to each axSpA Grade.

The final component utilizes the DeepCrack algorithm to classify SI joint images, obtained from the previous component, into classes that correspond to axSpA disease progression (Grades I–IV). Figure 6 displays the overal structure of the multi-class component. DeepCrack is a CNN-based approach for the detection and localization of cracks, primarily intended for the analysis of images of concrete structures. The DeepCrack algorithm consists of three main components: a feature extraction network, a context aggregation module, and a segmentation network. The feature extraction network is a series of convolutional layers that extract features from the input image. The context aggregation module is used to capture contextual information and spatial dependencies among the extracted features. Finally, the segmentation network uses the aggregated features to generate a binary mask indicating the location of cracks. This component is then able to classify X-Ray images into different stages of AS progression based on the visual appearance of the detected crack. The more the crack surface is diminished the more advance AS stage will be. In the cases were the crack surface is entirely diminished, then Grade IV is assigned.

4   Experimental Design and Experimental Results

The following sections, describe the details of dataset preparation, model training, evaluation criteria, and experimental results. Training and evaluation were
performed using an NVidia GeForce 2070 Ti platform and Intel Core i7-9700
processor. The pipeline and its components were implemented in C++ using
Tensorflow.

4.1   Dataset Preparation

The dataset consists of a moderated amount of 500 images of the sacroiliac joints
varying in resolution, size and quality graded as grade I, II, III, and IV.

The grey-scale levels of the collected and converted images from the DICOM
Viewer remain unaltered. It is crucial to highlight that the methodologies outlined in the Literature Review section typically involve specialized personnel
adjusting grey-scale levels before collecting and converting data from the DICOM
Viewer. In contrast, our study deliberately sidesteps this conventional approach,
steering clear of manual interventions by experts. This deliberate choice is aimed
at ensuring that our model remains versatile and applicable to a broad spectrum
of X-Ray images without requiring specific adjustments. To enhance image contrast, we employed histogram equalization to modify the intensity distribution.
Histogram equalization is a technique used to enhance the contrast of images
by redistributing the intensity values. The resulting image will have a more uniform distribution of intensity values, enhancing the overall contrast and making
details more visible. The histogram equalization consists of 4 steps: I) Compute
the Histogram by calculating the frequency of each intensity value in the image;
II) Calculate the Cumulative Distribution Function (CDF) by summing the histogram values to get the cumulative number of pixels up to each intensity level;
III) Normalize the CDF by scaling the CDF to span the full range of intensity values (e.g., 0 to 255 for an 8-bit image); IV) Map the Original Intensities
by using the normalized CDF as a lookup table to transform the original pixel
intensities to the new, equalized values. While we acknowledge that this process
may introduce minor alterations in intensity values within the region of interest,
it is important to note that our preference lies in achieving full automation for
this procedure. Subsequent studies could explore and implement more advanced
techniques to optimize this stage further.

5   The Experimental Outcomes from the Moderated Dataset Showcase Performance at an Expert Level

For this dataset the proposed model is able to separate input images into axSpA
versus non-axSpA classes with 91.98% accuracy and DeepCrack achived 92.14%
for categorizing the images into the Grades of the disease's progression. We
emphasize that the dataset is composed of 500 axSpA X-Rays, sourced from
a local hospital, used to determine the effects of dataset size and authenticity

(i.e. not artificially generated). The composition of this dataset is depicted in Table 2. Of these 500 images, 450 were used for training, and 50 for evaluation only. In this dataset, the left and right SI joints are often at different Grades of AS progression. When training the binary classifier section, we used any image that has an axSpA Grade above 0 (total of 375) as axSpA class. The remaining 75 were non-axSpA, and included both SI joints. Some of the images in this dataset had very low brightness. Histogram normalization was executed as a pre-processing step for both training and validation.

When training the multi-class component, we again discarded the non-AS class and cut the remaining ROIs, producing a total of 750 images, each depicting only one joint. The granular breakdown of the number of ROI cutouts pertaining to each AS Grade is show in Table 3. The rest of the training procedure is the same as described above. The results of the binary and multiclass evaluations are depicted in Tables 4 and 5. Since our pipeline consists of 2 models, each component was trained independently of the other. In the case of the binary classifier, 450 whole images, depicting both joints, were used as is, while the remaining 50 were reserved for blind testing. In the case of the multi-class component, the axSpA class image was discarded and cutouts were made of the ROIs, meaning a total of 750 cut images were fed to the model for training and the rest for the test. During training, neither pipeline component was exposed to these test images. The training set was further split into an 80-20 ratio for 5-fold cross-validation. Each component was trained independently on every fold without shared state or transfer learning. The training process lasted for 100 epochs using the ADAM optimizer with an initial learning rate (LR) of 5e-6. We applied `StepLR` to reduce the LR by a factor of 0.30 every 20 epochs. Model performance was evaluated by averaging outputs across all cross-validation folds. Geometric transformations such as rotation, flipping, scaling, and resizing were used for the augmentation of the data.

Table 2. Composition of the dataset used for model training and evaluation (Data collected by hospital)

axSpA Grade	Count	Training	Testing
Grade 0	85	75	10
Grade I	95	85	10
Grade II	36	26	10
Grade III	119	109	10
Grade IV	165	155	10
Total	500	450	50

Table 3. Granular breakdown of the multiclass training ROI cut-outs by axSpA Grade

axSpA Grade	Count
Grade 0	226
Grade I	171
Grade II	82
Grade III	256
Grade IV	265
Total	1000

The results indicate a marked improvement across the board. In the binary component, all models perform better when trained on a larger dataset. However, the relative placement of the models based on highest accuracy is perserved, with VGG-16 coming out on top, followed by ResNet-50, and Inception V3. The

Table 4. Results of blind testing the binary classification of AS versus non-AS with the New York classification scheme (large dataset. Average derived from 10 testing iterations ± standard deviation for F1 score indicating that the models have a balancing precision and recall in low variability between runs suggesting stable performance.

Component	Accuracy (%)	Loss	Precision (%)	Recall (%)	F1 score (%)
VGG-16 (2 DL/*Softmax*)	**91.98**	**0.238**	**91.61**	**96.98**	**94.08 ± 1.32**
ResNet-50	84.33	0.302	88.57	88.57	88.57 ± 2.05
Inception V3	82.49	0.349	93.75	81.08	86.95 ± 1.55

Table 5. Results of blind testing the multiclass classification of AS Grade progression detection using the mNY criteria for the classification scheme (large dataset. Average derived from 10 testing iterations ± standard deviation for F1 score indicating model balancing of precision and recall).

Component	Accuracy (%)	Loss	Precision (%)	Recall (%)	F1 score (%)
DeepCrack (axSpA)	93.01	0.218	94.51	92.08	94.48 ± 2.22

results for the multiclass component are also improved significantly. In particular, the ratio of false positive and false negatives were greatly reduced.

Similarly, the confusion matrix in Fig. 7 highlights misclassifications, which mostly occurred between adjacent Grades due to subtle visual differences at the SI joint. The most common error was mislabeling Grade IV as Grade III, followed by Grade III as Grade II. These mistakes reflect the model's difficulty in distinguishing between Grades with minimal visual variation; a challenge shared by human practitioners.

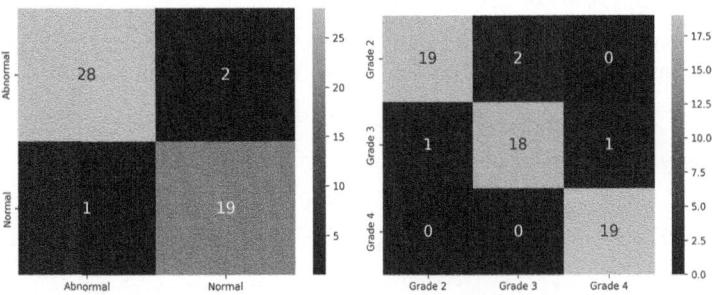

Fig. 7. Left: Confusion matrix of r-axSpA vs. nr-axSpA classification results. False-negatives are the most common type of error. Right: Confusion matrix showing failure cases for three classes.

The results obtained for different activation function after the fully connected layer was swapped to Sigmoid, ReLU, and Leaky ReLu are shown in Table 7, where as the experiments related to the drop-out layers for such dataset it is shown in Table 6.

Table 6. Accuracy under different dropout strategies

No. dropout layers/Dropout location	Acc. (%)
No dropout layers	85.06
1 x dropout/conv-block 1	86.38
2 x dropout/conv-block 1, 2	86.41
3 x dropout/conv-block 1–3	86.43
4 x dropout/conv-block 1–4	87.61
5 x dropout/conv-block 1–5	87.74
1 x dropout/fc1	90.34
2 x dropout/fc1 and fc2	**91.98**
6 x dropout/conv-block 1–5 + fc1	91.97
7 x dropout/conv-block 1–5 + fc1, fc2	91.94

Table 7. Accuracy with different activation functions in the binary classifier

Activation Function	Acc. (%)
VGG-16 + Softmax	**91.98**
VGG-16 + Sigmoid	88.49
VGG-16 + ReLU	89.84
VGG-16 + Leaky-ReLU	90.18

Note: The authors compared several deep learning models for the grade classification task, including VGG-16, VGG-19, and Xception, straight forward without the two-stage model presented above. In a multi-stage classification setting, these models were evaluated across five grades (0 to 4) using precision, recall, and F1-score metrics. Experimental results indicate that all models performed well for Grades 3 and 4, while a noticeable decline in performance was observed for Grades 0 to 2. The overall classification accuracy ranged from 62% to 86%, with VGG-19 achieving the highest accuracy and VGG-16 the lowest. Specifically, VGG-19 performed best for Grades 3 and 4 (F1 = 0.67), Xception showed strength in Grades 0, 3, and 4 (F1 = 0.5), and VGG-16 demonstrated comparatively better performance in Grades 3 and 4 (F1 = 0.59). However, all models struggled to identify true positives in Grade 2, resulting in notably low precision, recall, and F1-scores. These findings highlight the challenges posed by class similarity in the dataset. To address this issue and enhance model performance, especially in underrepresented grades, future work will focus on collecting additional data from hospitals and further model refinement.

6   Classification Based on mNY Criteria

In addition to the class design explained above, we carried out model training and validation on an alternative class design scheme that follows the New York AS classification. In this scheme, the binary component's classes are selected in such a way where any image that has either a grading of at least 2 on both sides, or one side with a grading of 3 is considered AS, and all other cases are considered non-AS. Using this scheme, 271 images from the large dataset were identified as AS while 229 images were non-AS). The model was then trained using these classification criteria and evaluated on the test subset. The results of the experiment are indicated in Tables 4 and 5. As shown, the model is able to cope with the alternative class design scheme and deliver similar performance characteristics as the previous design.

7   Conclusion

In conclusion, we propose a multi-step pipeline aimed at automating the classification of radiographic and non-radiographic ax-SpA, being first study of such type. Our architecture comprises several components: a binary classifier for radiographic axSpA (classic axSpA) detection, a region of interest (ROI) segmentation algorithm, a specialized multi-class classifier for edge detection, and a table-lookup approach for stochastic determination of different grades of axSpA sacroiliitis. The first step of our pipeline utilizes the VGG-16 model for binary classification, accurately distinguishing raw X-Ray images into nr-axSpA or axSpA classes with 91.98% accuracy. If the classification outcome indicates axSpA, the gradients from the last convolution layer of the CNN are employed in a Grad-CAM-based algorithm to segment the image, specifically highlighting the regions of interest in the SI joint space. Next, the segmented image is cropped and passed on to the second classifier, where a holistically nested edge detection model (DeepCrack) is employed. This model effectively detects and quantifies the characteristic crack-like features associated with AS. The severity of these characteristic cracks intensifies with the progression of the disease. Notably, DeepCrack exhibited a commendable classification accuracy of 92.14%, aligning with the expertise level of professionals, when categorizing images across the five degrees of Ankylosing Spondylitis (axSpA)-associated sacroiliitis progression.

Finally, we compare the results obtained from the edge detection analysis to a table that contains average pixel quantities for each grade of axSpA sacroiliitis. By matching the values, we can produce the final corresponding output, indicating the specific grade of axSpA sacroiliitis (Grades 0-IV) for a given X-Ray image. Overall, our proposed pipeline shows promising results in automating the classification of AS sacroiliitis degrees using X-Ray images. These findings offer potential for enhancing the diagnosis and treatment monitoring of axial SpA, i.e. the development of radiographic axSpA, hence benefiting patients and healthcare professionals alike.

Further investigation is essential to enhance accuracy and instill confidence in machine learning decisions. This involves engaging a substantial team of specialized professionals in the field, explicitly addressing inter and intraclinician disagreements. The utilization of DICOM to standardize and adjust the grayscale images, along with consideration for unaggregated data, is imperative. Expanding the scope of data collection to include diverse populations from various countries and incorporating multimodal representations are crucial steps in advancing the study. By doing so, the machine learning model can be exposed to a more comprehensive and representative dataset, leading to improved generalization and robust decision-making capabilities in the context of axSpA diagnosis, and distinguishing between nr-axSpA and classic axSpA, with the aim or reaching accuracy rates ≈ 1.

The dataset will be shared for research purposes with members working in research institutes with requests via email after they agree and sign to comply with the restrictions.

References

1. Bond, D.: Ankylosing spondylitis: diagnosis and management. Nurs. Stand. **28**(16), 52–59 (2013). https://doi.org/10.7748/ns2013.12.28.16.52.e7807 **28**(16), 52–59 (Dec 2013). https://doi.org/10.7748/ns2013.12.28.16.52.e7807, https://doi.org/10.7748/ns2013.12.28.16.52.e7807

2. Braun, J., Sieper, J.: Ankylosing spondylitis. Lancet **369**(9570), 1379–1390 (2007). https://doi.org/10.1016/s0140-6736(07)60635-7 1379–1390 (Apr 2007). https://doi.org/10.1016/s0140-6736(07)60635-7, https://doi.org/10.1016/s0140-6736(07)60635-7

3. Bressem, K.K., et al.: Deep learning for detection of radiographic sacroiliitis: achieving expert-level performance. Arthritis Res. Ther. **23**(1) (2021). https://doi.org/10.1186/s13075-021-02484-0

4. Castro-Zunti, R., Park, E.H., Choi, Y., Jin, G.Y., Ko, S.B.: Early detection of ankylosing spondylitis using texture features and statistical machine learning, and deep learning, with some patient age analysis. Comput. Med. Imaging Graph. **82**, 101718 (2020). https://doi.org/10.1016/j.compmedimag.2020.101718

5. Christiansen, A.A., et al.: Limited reliability of radiographic assessment of sacroiliac joints in patients with suspected early spondyloarthritis. J. Rheumatol. **44**(1), 70–77 (2016). https://doi.org/10.3899/jrheum.160079

6. Davey-Ranasinghe, N., Deodhar, A.: Osteoporosis and vertebral fractures in ankylosing spondylitis. Curr. Opin. Rheumatol. **25**(4), 509–516 (2013). https://doi.org/10.1097/bor.0b013e3283620777

7. Dean, L.E., Jones, G.T., MacDonald, A.G., Downham, C., Sturrock, R.D., Macfarlane, G.J.: Global prevalence of ankylosing spondylitis. Rheumatology **53**(4), 650–657 (2013). https://doi.org/10.1093/rheumatology/ket387

8. Liu, Y., Yao, J., Lu, X., Xie, R., Li, L.: Deepcrack: a deep hierarchical feature learning architecture for crack segmentation. Neurocomputing **338**, 139–153 (2019). https://doi.org/10.1016/j.neucom.2019.01.036

9. McVeigh, C.M., Cairns, A.P.: Diagnosis and management of ankylosing spondylitis. BMJ **333**(7568), 581–585 (2006). https://doi.org/10.1136/bmj.38954.689583.de

10. Poddubnyy, D., et al.: Rates and predictors of radiographic sacroiliitis progression over 2 years in patients with axial spondyloarthritis. Ann. Rheum. Dis. **70**(8), 1369–1374 (2011). https://doi.org/10.1136/ard.2010.145995

11. Poppi, S., Cornia, M., Baraldi, L., Cucchiara, R.: Revisiting the evaluation of class activation mapping for explainability: a novel metric and experimental analysis (2021). https://doi.org/10.48550/ARXIV.2104.10252. https://arxiv.org/abs/2104.10252

12. Selvaraju, R.R., Cogswell, M., Das, A., Vedantam, R., Parikh, D., Batra, D.: Gradcam: visual explanations from deep networks via gradient-based localization (2016). https://doi.org/10.48550/ARXIV.1610.02391. https://arxiv.org/abs/1610.02391

13. Sieper, J., Braun, J.: Ankylosing Spondylitis (2010)

14. Simonyan, K., Zisserman, A.: Very deep convolutional networks for large-scale image recognition (2014). https://doi.org/10.48550/ARXIV.1409.1556. https://arxiv.org/abs/1409.1556
15. Yazici, H., Turunc, M., Ozdogan, H., Yurdakul, S., Akinci, A., Barnes, C.G.: Observer variation in grading sacroiliac radiographs might be a cause of 'sacroiliitis' reported in certain disease states. Ann. Rheum. Dis. **46**(2), 139–145 (1987). https://doi.org/10.1136/ard.46.2.139

Towards Breast Tumor Aggressiveness Classification in Digital Mammograms Using Boundary-Aware Segmentation and Feature Analysis

Adnan Khalid[1]([⊠]), Muhammad Mursil[1], Ammar M. Okran[1],
Josep Guma Padro[2], Carlos Lopez Pablo[3], Domenec Puig[1],
and Hatem A. Rashwan[1]([⊠])

[1] Department of Computer Engineering and Mathematics, Universidad Rovira i
Virgili, Tarragona, Spain
{adnan.khalid,hatem.abdellatif}@urv.cat
[2] Hospital Universitat Sant Joan de Reus, 43204 Reus, Spain
[3] Hospital de Tortosa Verge de la Cinta, ICS, Tortosa, Spain

Abstract. Breast cancer (BC) aggressiveness significantly impacts
patient prognosis by influencing relapse, metastasis, and mortality rates.
Currently, the assessment of tumor aggressiveness is primarily depen-
dent on biopsies and pathological image analysis, which are challenging
to obtain during follow-up stages after treatment, particularly if there
is a relapse. Our study introduces a novel framework utilizing digital
mammography, the standard for early breast cancer detection, to classify
tumor aggressiveness non-invasively. This framework employs a Cascaded
ResUNet with boundary-aware capabilities for precise tumor segmentation, ensuring accurate delineation of tumor boundaries. Key morphological and texture features are then extracted from the segmented regions
to categorize tumor aggressiveness. Validated on an in-house dataset, our
method achieved an accuracy of 90.6% and an Area Under the Curve
(AUC) of 87.4%, with further tests on an external dataset confirming its
generalizability with 88.7% accuracy and an AUC of 81.0%. These promising results underscore the potential of our approach for clinical applications, offering a robust method for the classification of breast tumor
aggressiveness in scenarios where invasive procedures are impractical.

Keywords: Breast Cancer · Aggressiveness · Tumor Segmentation ·
Feature Extraction · Image Analysis

1 Introduction

Breast cancer (BC) remains a major public health challenge worldwide, being a
leading cause of mortality among women, with approximately 2.3 million new

Supplementary Information The online version contains supplementary material
available at https://doi.org/10.1007/978-3-031-98691-8_12.

cases reported in 2020 [19]. The aggressiveness of BC varies depending on the stage of the disease and factors such as glucose metabolism, hormone receptor status, and gene expression signatures [9]. Enhanced prognostic outcomes are intricately related to early diagnosis, but an accurate classification of BC types significantly impacts clinical representation and treatment responsiveness [21]. Identifying abnormalities, such as breast masses, along with detailed tumor morphology, such as shape (oval, round, irregular), area and circularity, provides critical insight into the tumor's aggressiveness, guides diagnostic and personalized treatment strategies [11]. Clinical trials investigating the utility of potential BC biomarkers, especially for highly aggressive subtypes such as triple negative (TNBC), have played a crucial role in advancing treatment strategies and improving patient outcomes. Although TNBC is often resistant to hormones and immunotherapies, it tends to exhibit sensitivity to chemotherapeutic agents and radiation therapy, offering alternative therapeutic plans.

Advanced deep learning (DL) models, particularly encoder-decoder networks like Fully Convolutional Networks (FCNs) and UNet, have significantly improved the segmentation and classification of breast cancer from mammographic images [2]. UNet's [16] use of skip connections to incorporate multi-level features has significantly enhanced segmentation accuracy, with various modified versions achieving consistently higher precision in breast cancer imaging [5,8,18]. Recently, Generative Adversarial Networks (GANs) have emerged as powerful tools for medical image segmentation, capable of achieving high accuracy with fewer data than traditional deep learning methods in different datasets [13,22]. In [17], the author developed a conditional Generative Adversarial Network (cGAN) for breast mass segmentation, achieving a Dice score of 88.12% and an Intersection over Union (IoU) score of 79.87% on a private dataset, highlighting the model's effectiveness in segmentation. Jha et al. [6] introduced DoubleUNet, featuring dual encoders, decoders, and an ASPP module, outperforming UNet and baselines on four medical segmentation datasets. However, most of these methods have some limitations in preserving the tumor boundary, leading to increased false positive and false negative pixels.

The next crucial stage after tumor segmentation is to extract relevant features from the segmented areas. These features encompass important morphological components that help to understand the physical nature of the tumor [15]. In [4], the author investigates how radiomics and imaging characteristics define molecular subtypes of breast cancer, including aggressive and noninvasive tumor. Nonaggressive subtypes are often linked to irregularly shaped masses, whereas non-calcified lesions with sharp, constricted margins characterize aggressive subtypes. The imaging features are essential in determining distinct subtypes while offering guidance for tailored treatment strategies. Moreover, there is a lack of research that focuses on the classification of breast cancer aggressiveness using digital mammograms, highlighting a significant gap in the current research that requires further investigation.

In this work, we propose a two-stage pipeline for improved breast cancer tumor classification. The first stage introduces a modified version of the Connected U-Net, which incorporates a boundary-enhancement module aimed at improving segmentation accuracy by refining boundary details in digital mammograms during deep feature extraction. In the second stage, we extract key morphological and texture features from the segmented tumor regions to classify the tumor's aggressiveness as either aggressive or non-aggressive. Specifically, this work seeks to enhance boundary precision and minimize common errors, such as false positives and negatives, that often occur with current models. This approach aims to provide a robust tool for non-invasive breast cancer aggressiveness classification. All experiments were conducted on two internal datasets annotated by expert radiologists. This highlights the potential and generalizability of the proposed approach for enabling personalized treatment strategies based on tumor behaviour.

2 Materials and Methods

2.1 Cascaded Segmentation Network

By consistently outperforming state-of-the-art methods across various medical imaging datasets, the U-Net architecture has become an industry benchmark for image segmentation. In our refined adaptation, we leverage the Connected U-Net architecture, integrating residual blocks (ResBlock) [1] in place of traditional convolutional layers to enhance feature propagation and address challenges such as the problem of disappearance of gradients. The residual blocks preserve spatial and contextual information by directly propagating features from early to later layers, enabling a deeper network architecture and improved performance. This enhancement involves actively connecting high-resolution features from one network's encoding path to the subsequent network's decoding path. This process is further refined by strategically placing Boundary Enhancement Modules (BEM) at critical junctures, enabling improved feature propagation and precise segmentation of intricate anatomical structures (Fig. 1).

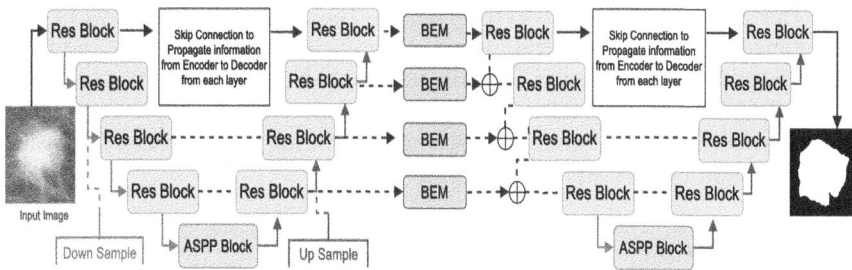

Fig. 1. The illustration of the modified Cascaded ResUNet demonstrates its ability to preserve high-resolution outputs for improved segmentation accuracy

A key innovation in our model is the integration of the BEM for refining segmentation boundaries and ensuring the preservation of detailed features within segmented regions. The BEM significantly enhances detail accuracy and boundary delineation by efficiently filtering out unnecessary data. The BEM module calculates gradient maps by applying the Sobel operation in horizontal and vertical orientations. We utilize 3×3 convolutional layers with fixed-size kernel parameters applied to the decoder features to generate the gradient map, as shown in the Fig. 2 in the supplementary materials. A sigmoid function is then used to normalize these feature maps, resulting in the highlighting of the edge feature map. Additionally, our architecture incorporates the Atrous Spatial Pyramid Pooling (ASPP) for extracting the multi-scale information in the feature extraction step. This feature is indispensable for maintaining high-resolution outputs while capturing extensive spatial details across broader receptive fields. The ASPP optimizes feature retention across various scales, ensuring that our model achieves precise segmentation outcomes with unparalleled accuracy.

The segmentation loss function is defined as a weighted sum of Dice and IoU losses, utilizing the Dice score and IoU score between the true labels y and the predicted labels $\hat{y}$. The loss function is mathematically expressed as:

$$\text{loss}(y, \hat{y}) = 1 - (\lambda_{\text{Dice}} \times \text{Dice Score}(y, \hat{y}) + \lambda_{\text{IoU}} \times \text{IoU Score}(y, \hat{y})),$$

where λ_{Dice} and λ_{IoU} are weighted values [0,1]. In this work, they are set (0.5).

2.2   Feature Extraction

Following tumor segmentation, the next step is the precise classification of tumors based on extracted morphological and textural features. These features are essential for assessing the aggressiveness of breast tumors, providing insights into their geometric and structural characteristics. Nonaggressive tumors typically display a compact structure with smooth, well-defined borders. In contrast, aggressive tumors often have irregular shapes with poorly defined, rough, and irregular borders, reflecting their invasive nature [10]. Texture analysis, particularly through the Gray-Level Co-occurrence Matrix (GLCM), plays a crucial role in this process. GLCM analysis evaluates the spatial relationships between pixel intensities, improving our understanding of tissue heterogeneity and tumor composition [7]. The extracted features used in this work, including both morphological and texture-based data, are detailed in Table 1. These features are then employed to assess tumor aggressiveness, offering a comprehensive evaluation that aids in the classification process.

2.3   Classification

The integration of machine learning (ML) into BC diagnostics significantly enhances the precision and reliability of medical decision-making. Our approach utilizes ML to analyze extracted morphological and texture features, enabling the accurate classification of breast tumors as either aggressive or non-aggressive. Figure 2 shows the ML pipeline for BC aggressiveness classification. The pipeline consists of five key stages:

Table 1. Description of different Morphological and Textural Features Extracted from Tumor Region for Aggressiveness Analysis

Feature	Equation	Parameter Details
Area	$\sum_{i=1}^{n} I(i)$	$I(i)$: intensity of each pixel, n: total no. of pixels in the tumor
Perimeter	$\sum_{j=1}^{m} B(j)$	$B(j)$: boundary pixels, m: total number of boundary pixels
Circularity	$\frac{4\pi \times Area}{Perimeter^2}$	Highlighting the shape's compactness
Centroid Radius	$\frac{1}{n} \sum_{i=1}^{n} \sqrt{(x_i - x_c)^2 + (y_i - y_c)^2}$	(x_i, y_i): coordinates of pixel i, (x_c, y_c): centroid coordinates
Mean Convex Hull	$Mean_x = \frac{1}{n} \sum_{i=1}^{n} x_{h,i}$ $Mean_y = \frac{1}{n} \sum_{i=1}^{n} y_{h,i}$	$(x_{h,i}, y_{h,i})$ coordinates of convex hull points, n: Total number of convex hull points
Std Deviation Convex Hull	$Std_x = \sqrt{\frac{1}{n} \sum_{i=1}^{n} (x_{h,i} - M_x)^2}$ $Std_y = \sqrt{\frac{1}{n} \sum_{i=1}^{n} (y_{h,i} - M_y)^2}$	Mean values M_x, M_y of the x and y coordinates of the convex hull points
Contrast	$\sum_{i,j} P(i,j)(i-j)^2$	$P(i,j)$: probability for the pixel intensity pair (i,j)
Homogeneity	$\frac{P(i,j)}{1+(i-j)^2}$	Greater homogeneity indicates comparable grey levels nearby
Energy	$\sum_{i,j} P(i,j)^2$	Reflecting textural uniformity of Tumor
Skewness	$\frac{1}{n} \sum_{i=1}^{n} \left(\frac{x_i - \bar{x}}{s} \right)^3$	x_i pixel intensities, mean $\bar{x}$, std s, n number of pixels
kurtosis	$\frac{N \cdot \sum_{i=1}^{N} (I_i - \bar{I})^4}{\left(\sum_{i=1}^{N} (I_i - \bar{I})^2 \right)^2}$	I_i pixel Intensities, N total No. Pixel $\bar{I}$ Mean

Feature Extraction, where morphological and texture features derived from segmented tumor regions are processed to provide valuable insights for classification. **Data Preprocessing**, which involves scaling the features using the MinMax scaler to normalize them within a $[0, 1]$ range, ensuring that each feature contributes equally to the decision-making process. This stage also includes feature selection using the KBest method with the f_classif criterion and the application of SMOTE sampling to address the class imbalance in the training set. **Model Selection and Optimization**, which employs three advanced ML models–Random Forest, XGBoost, and CatBoost–and optimizes their performance through hyperparameter tuning using GridSearchCV technique (see supplementary material Table 1) [12]. Five-fold cross-validation is used to assess model robustness and generalizability. **Model Prediction**, where the trained models predict the aggressiveness of the tumors, and performance is evaluated using metrics such as accuracy, precision, recall, and the area under the ROC curve (AUC). **Model Interpretability**, which is achieved through feature importance analysis based on the Gini index and SHAP analysis to elucidate the impact of individual features, including their positive or negative contribution to the model's predictions.

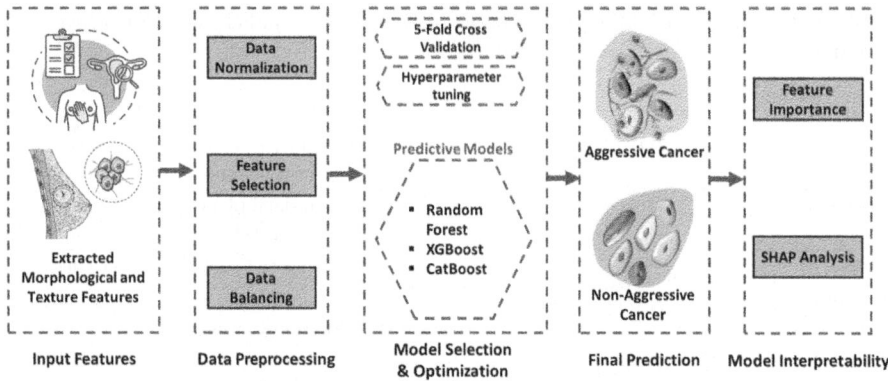

Fig. 2. ML pipeline for analyzing features extracted from segmented tumor region for BC aggressiveness classification

3 Experiments and Results

3.1 Dataset and Training Procedure

This work utilizes three distinct datasets to validate our approach to classifying BC aggressiveness. The first dataset, CBIS-DDSM, is publicly available and consists of 1,300 mammograms with confirmed mass cases from a total of 2,620 studies. The second dataset, from HTVC Tortsa (private dataset A), contains 148 cases labelled according to aggressiveness, with comprehensive radiological and pathological details. The third dataset, from Hospital Sant Joan de Reus (private dataset B), comprises 110 mammograms with expert radiologist annotations. All data handling adhered to strict confidentiality and security protocols.

Due to the limited availability of annotated digital mammogram data, we initially trained our segmentation model using the CBIS-DDSM dataset. Subsequently, we fine-tuned the model using both the above-mentioned private datasets to enhance its accuracy. This combination of data sources improved the model's performance, ensuring reliable segmentation. For classification, we trained and tested our classifiers on private dataset A for BC aggressiveness prediction and then evaluated the model's generalizability on private dataset B to assess the robustness and reliability of our proposed clinical decision support system. Experiments were conducted on a high-performance computing system with 64 GB of RAM, an Intel Core i7-8700K CPU operating at 3.70 GHz, and an NVIDIA GeForce RTX 3090 GPU, which facilitated efficient deep learning computations.

3.2 Segmentation Results

We conducted quantitative and qualitative evaluations to benchmark our breast tumor segmentation method against leading techniques. Quantitatively, accuracy was assessed using the Dice coefficient and Jaccard index (IoU). Qualitatively,

Table 2. Comparison with the state of the art segmentation models on the public dataset and the results on our in-house private datasets that we fine-tuned.

Public Dataset	Model Architecture	Dice Score %	IoU Score %
CBIS-DDSM	Unet+ [20]	72.2	58.5
–	Unet + ResNet50 Backbone [20]	77.8	56.5
–	Attention Unet [18]	81.8	—
–	ResUnet [3]	80.94	68.05
–	Deep Supervised DS-Unet [14]	82.9	—
–	Connected Unet [3]	82.22	69.82
–	Connected Attention Unet [3]	83.84	72.19
–	cGAN [17]	89.9	81.8
–	**Proposed Method**	**91.32**	**83.32**
Private Dataset A	**Fine-tuned**	**87.63**	**76.89**
Private Dataset B	**Fine-tuned**	**85.25**	**74.19**

we performed visual comparisons with ground truth masks to assess boundary delineation accuracy. Our model demonstrated significant improvements over existing methods in both accuracy and boundary preservation. It was initially trained and assessed on the CBIS-DDSM dataset. The performance of our model is summarized in Table 2, which shows superior Dice and IoU scores compared to state-of-the-art models. To evaluate the impact of each component, we conducted an ablation study. Incorporating the BEM block into the Connected-ResUNets architecture significantly improved performance, increasing the Dice score from 86.9 (with ASPP) to 91.32. Our method not only excelled in the public dataset but also maintained high performance on two privately sourced datasets after fine-tuning, underscoring its robustness and adaptability. This fine-tuning involved adjusting the model with data from both private datasets, enhancing its generalization capabilities and segmentation precision across varying types of breast cancer imaging data (Fig. 3).

3.3 Classification of Tumor Aggressiveness

In this study, we employed three ML models to classify tumor aggressiveness based on morphological and texture features extracted from segmented tumor regions in private dataset A. Among the models, XGBoost outperformed the others, achieving the highest accuracy of 0.906 and an AUC score of 0.875, demonstrating superior predictive capabilities. Random Forest attained an accuracy of 0.854 and an AUC of 0.827, while CatBoost demonstrated the lowest performance with an accuracy of 0.836 and an AUC of 0.858.

Furthermore, to assess the generalizability of our best-performing model (XGBoost), we tested it on private dataset B. XGBoost exhibited stable performance, predicting BC aggressiveness with an accuracy of 0.887 and an AUC

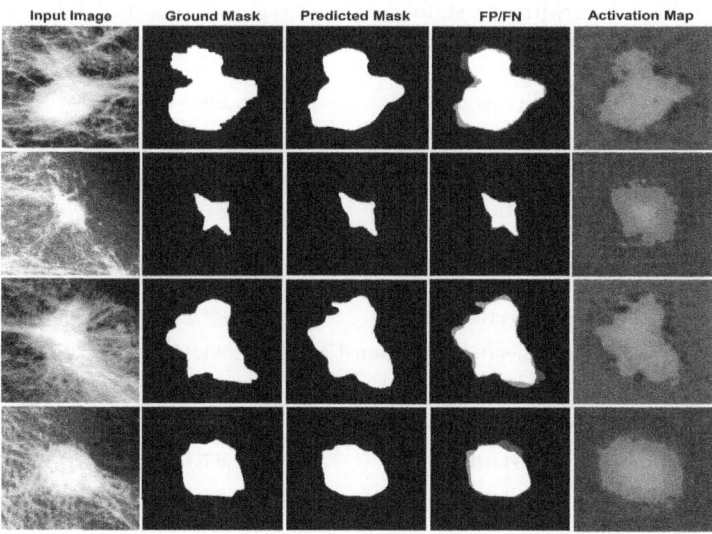

Fig. 3. Qualitative analysis of segmentation results showing green pixels as False Positives (FP), blue pixels as False Negatives (FN), and activation maps from the last convolutional layer to reveal model interpretability. (Color figure online)

of 0.81, indicating its robustness across different datasets. The model's predictive results are presented in Table 3. Our approach's predictive results assure the reliability of the proposed clinical decision support system and enhance its applicability in clinical decision-making and diagnostic settings.

Table 3. Performance metrics of Random Forest, XGBoost, and CatBoost on Private Dataset A, highlighting XGBoost's superior accuracy and AUC. Its efficacy is further validated on an unseen dataset, confirming robust generalizability

Private Dataset A					
Model	Accuracy	Precision	F1-Score	Recall	AUC
Random Forest	0.854	0.863	0.861	0.851	0.8274
XGBoost	**0.906**	**0.915**	**0.909**	**0.916**	**0.875**
CatBoost	0.836	0.861	0.847	0.834	0.858
Testing Private Dataset B (Generalization)					
XGBoost	**0.887**	**0.856**	**0.821**	**0.801**	**0.81**

To assess the interpretability of our model, we computed the feature importance, which quantifies the contribution of each feature to the model's predictions. As shown in Fig. 4, the most influential features for BC aggressiveness classification are **area**, **circularity**, and **mean_x_hull**, with **area** showing

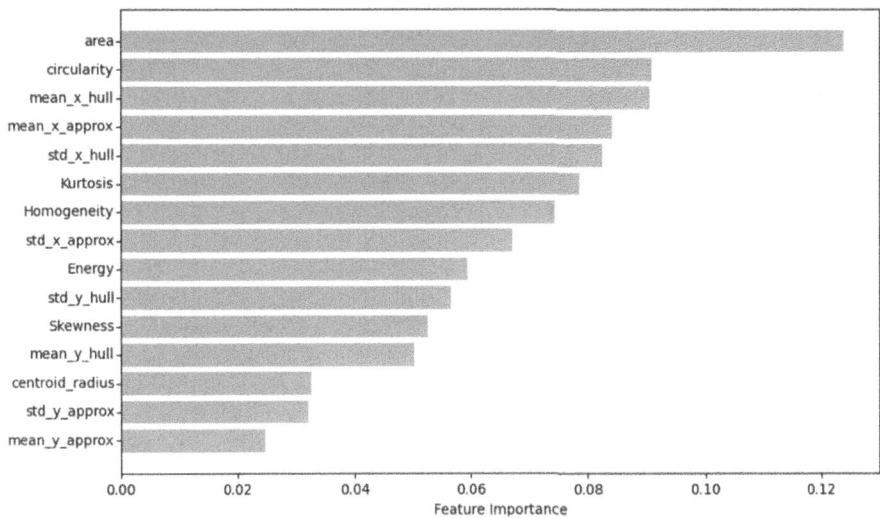

Fig. 4. Feature importance score by XGBoost.

the highest importance. These features significantly contribute to the model's ability to distinguish between non-aggressive (Luminal A and B) and aggressive (HER2+ and Triple-Negative) tumor types. Other notable features include **mean_x_approx**, **std_x_hull**, and **kurtosis**, which also play a critical role in prediction. Conversely, features such as **std_y_approx** and **mean_y_approx** exhibited minimal importance, indicating that their impact on the classification task is relatively low.

This feature importance analysis aids in understanding the model's decision-making process, personalized treatment strategies, which is valuable for clinical applications where interpretability is crucial, enhancing breast cancer treatment research.

We further quantified feature contributions using SHAP analysis to understand the impact of each feature on model predictions. As shown in Fig. 5, SHAP analysis revealed that features such as **mean_x_hull**, **circularity**, and **area** have the most significant positive influence on the model's predictive power, emphasizing their crucial role in assessing tumor aggressiveness. Specifically, a higher **area** value correlates with increased breast cancer aggressiveness, while lower to medium values of **circularity** are linked to non-aggressive tumors. On the other hand, features like **mean_y_approx** and **centroid_radius** showed minimal impact, with higher values of these features tending to be associated with the likelihood of aggressive tumors. This insight can assist clinicians and radiologists in making more reliable clinical decisions and facilitating early medical intervention, as it provides a deeper understanding of the critical features influencing tumor aggressiveness.

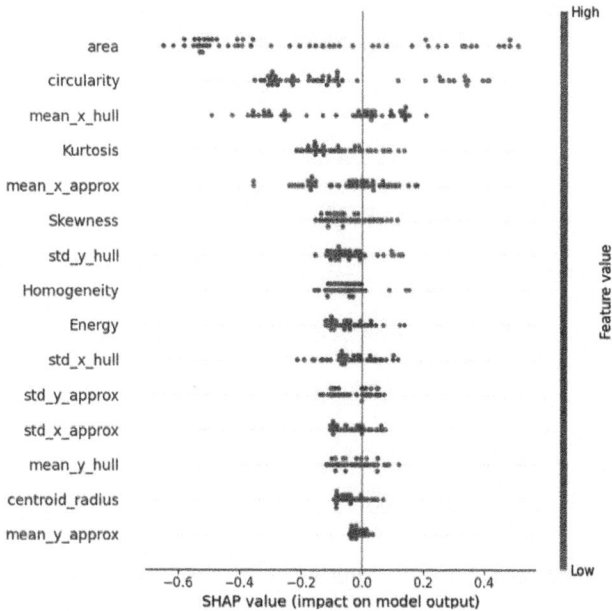

Fig. 5. SHAP values indicate the average contribution of each feature to the model's predictions, with higher values representing greater influence.

This detailed feature assessment not only enhances the model's interpretability but also helps identify the most predictive characteristics for distinguishing aggressive from non-aggressive tumors. Such analysis is vital for refining personalized treatment strategies, further advancing clinical applications in breast cancer diagnosis and treatment.

4   Limitation

While mammography is a key tool in BC detection, it has inherent limitations, particularly in dense breast tissues where lesion visibility is reduced. Our model, optimized primarily for tumor mass classification, demonstrates reduced effectiveness in identifying non-mass-like lesions such as Ductal Carcinoma In Situ (DCIS) and microcalcifications. Integrating other imaging modalities, like MRI and ultrasound, could significantly enhance the detection capabilities and overall accuracy of the system by providing complementary data that can overcome these limitations. Leveraging cross-modality learning techniques may further enhance model performance, improving accuracy and robustness across diverse clinical scenarios.

5   Conclusion

This work demonstrated notable enhancements in tumor segmentation and BC aggressiveness classification accuracy through the use of morphological and texture features extracted from mammographic images. The incorporation of Boundary Enhancement Modules (BEM) significantly improved feature representation, refining the overall segmentation performance. SHAP analysis further illuminated how specific features contribute to classifying BC aggressiveness, adding a layer of interpretability to our model. Looking ahead, we are expanding the applicability of our framework to include additional imaging modalities such as MRI. This expansion aims to enhance the model's generalizability and clinical utility across diverse medical settings. Additionally, we will focus on classifying BC molecular subtypes, which will facilitate more personalized treatment approaches and potentially reduce the dependency on invasive biopsy procedures.

Acknowledgement. This work was supported by the Bosomshield Project, a grant from Marie Sklodowaka-Curie Doctoral Networks Actions (HORIZON-MSCA-2021-DN-01-01;101073222).

References

1. Abdelhafiz, D., Nabavi, S., Ammar, R., Yang, C., Bi, J.: Residual deep learning system for mass segmentation and classification in mammography. In: Proceedings of the 10th ACM International Conference on Bioinformatics, Computational Biology and Health Informatics, pp. 475–484 (2019)
2. Al-Antari, M.A., Al-Masni, M.A., Choi, M.T., Han, S.M., Kim, T.S.: A fully integrated computer-aided diagnosis system for digital X-ray mammograms via deep learning detection, segmentation, and classification. Int. J. Med. Inform. **117**, 44–54 (2018)
3. Baccouche, A., Garcia-Zapirain, B., Castillo Olea, C., Elmaghraby, A.S.: Connected-unets: a deep learning architecture for breast mass segmentation. NPJ Breast Cancer **7**(1), 151 (2021)
4. Cho, N.: Molecular subtypes and imaging phenotypes of breast cancer. Ultrasonography **35**(4), 281 (2016)
5. Hai, J., et al.: Fully convolutional densenet with multiscale context for automated breast tumor segmentation. J. Healthc. Eng. **2019**(1), 8415485 (2019)
6. Jha, D., Riegler, M.A., Johansen, D., Halvorsen, P., Johansen, H.D.: Doubleu-net: a deep convolutional neural network for medical image segmentation. In: 2020 IEEE 33rd International Symposium on Computer-Based Medical Systems (CBMS), pp. 558–564. IEEE (2020)
7. Jiang, L., et al.: Radiogenomic analysis reveals tumor heterogeneity of triple-negative breast cancer. Cell Rep. Med. **3**(7) (2022)
8. Li, S., Dong, M., Du, G., Mu, X.: Attention dense-u-net for automatic breast mass segmentation in digital mammogram. IEEE Access **7**, 59037–59047 (2019)
9. Lin, P.H., Laliotis, G.: The present and future of clinical management in metastatic breast cancer. J. Clin. Med. **11**(19), 5891 (2022)

10. Liu, S., Wu, X.D., Xu, W.J., Lin, Q., Liu, X.J., Li, Y.: Is there a correlation between the presence of a spiculated mass on mammogram and luminal a subtype breast cancer? Korean J. Radiol. **17**(6), 846–852 (2016)
11. McGranahan, N., Swanton, C.: Clonal heterogeneity and tumor evolution: past, present, and the future. Cell **168**(4), 613–628 (2017)
12. Mursil, M., Rashwan, H.A., Cavallé-Busquets, P., Santos-Calderón, L.A., Murphy, M.M., Puig, D.: Maternal nutritional factors enhance birthweight prediction: a super learner ensemble approach. Information **15**(11), 714 (2024)
13. Pang, S., et al.: Ctumorgan: a unified framework for automatic computed tomography tumor segmentation. Eur. J. Nucl. Med. Mol. Imaging **47**, 2248–2268 (2020)
14. Rajalakshmi, N.R., Vidhyapriya, R., Elango, N., Ramesh, N.: Deeply supervised u-net for mass segmentation in digital mammograms. Int. J. Imaging Syst. Technol. **31**(1), 59–71 (2021)
15. Rayamaihi, K., Bansal, R., Aggarwal, B.: Mammographic correlation with molecular subtypes of breast carcinoma. J. Radiol. Oncol. **7**, 001–005 (2023)
16. Ronneberger, O., Fischer, P., Brox, T.: U-Net: convolutional networks for biomedical image segmentation. In: Navab, N., Hornegger, J., Wells, W.M., Frangi, A.F. (eds.) MICCAI 2015. LNCS, vol. 9351, pp. 234–241. Springer, Cham (2015). https://doi.org/10.1007/978-3-319-24574-4_28
17. Singh, V.K., et al.: Breast tumor segmentation and shape classification in mammograms using generative adversarial and convolutional neural network. Expert Syst. Appl. **139**, 112855 (2020)
18. Sun, H., et al.: Aunet: attention-guided dense-upsampling networks for breast mass segmentation in whole mammograms. Phys. Med. Biol. **65**(5), 055005 (2020)
19. Sung, H., et al.: Global cancer statistics 2020: globocan estimates of incidence and mortality worldwide for 36 cancers in 185 countries. CA Cancer J. Clin. **71**(3), 209–249 (2021)
20. Tsochatzidis, L., Koutla, P., Costaridou, L., Pratikakis, I.: Integrating segmentation information into CNN for breast cancer diagnosis of mammographic masses. Comput. Methods Programs Biomed. **200**, 105913 (2021)
21. Wang, L.: Early diagnosis of breast cancer. Sensors **17**(7), 1572 (2017)
22. Zhu, W., Xiang, X., Tran, T.D., Hager, G.D., Xie, X.: Adversarial deep structured nets for mass segmentation from mammograms. In: 2018 IEEE 15th International Symposium on Biomedical Imaging (ISBI 2018), pp. 847–850. IEEE (2018)

Image-Guided Intervention

Joint Dento-Facial Shape Model

Daniel Dorda[1]([✉]), Daniel Peter[2], Niko Benjamin Huber[2], Markus Gross[1],
and Barbara Solenthaler[1]

[1] ETH Zurich, Zurich, Switzerland
daniel.dorda@inf.ethz.ch
[2] Align Technology, Rotkreuz, Switzerland

Abstract. In digital dentistry, it is increasingly common to consider both teeth and soft tissue when designing treatments or visualising patient models. However, scans of teeth and tissue are usually acquired separately, and few studies have explored the joint geometry of the facial surface and dentition, despite its many potential clinical applications. This work explores how linear and multi-linear shape models of lips and teeth can bridge the gap between disparate 3D scanning modalities.

We construct a multi-linear shape model from 284 CT scans. The model disentangles soft-tissue thickness from the underlying dental-arch shape. We use a novel ray-casting approach for determining tissue thickness, and obtain the dental arch shapes from segmented tooth scans in an automated manner. We demonstrate how the model can jointly fit to tooth-arch shapes and face-scans from lip scans, thereby enabling the alignment of separately acquired intra-oral and facial scans.

The ray-casting approach outperforms previous work on modelling soft-tissue thickness, as it represents the lip region more accurately. The model is successfully used to estimate the tooth arch shape, and this in turn leads to a good alignment of intra-oral scans within the lip shape.

Dento-facial models have many uses in the world of digital dentistry. By modelling the dependence between lip soft-tissue and the shape of the arch, we demonstrate the inference of the tooth arch shape for unseen lips. Further work can expand the model to include appearance and expression, and enable yet more applications.

Keywords: Shape Model · Alignment · Digital Dentistry

1 Introduction

Holistically modelling soft and hard tissues is an increasingly important principle in modern digital dentistry; for example, it is essential for modelling the facial changes induced by orthodontic treatments [6], a factor that significantly influences patient satisfaction [4,20]. However, integrating 3D facial scans and intraoral (IO) scans into the clinical workflow is challenging. The scans are acquired separately and are thus not in global alignment. Furthermore, face scans of the lip region often have poor quality [8], or may be missing altogether. As a result,

© The Author(s), under exclusive license to Springer Nature Switzerland AG 2026
S. Ali et al. (Eds.): MIUA 2025, LNCS 15917, pp. 177–189, 2026.
https://doi.org/10.1007/978-3-031-98691-8_13

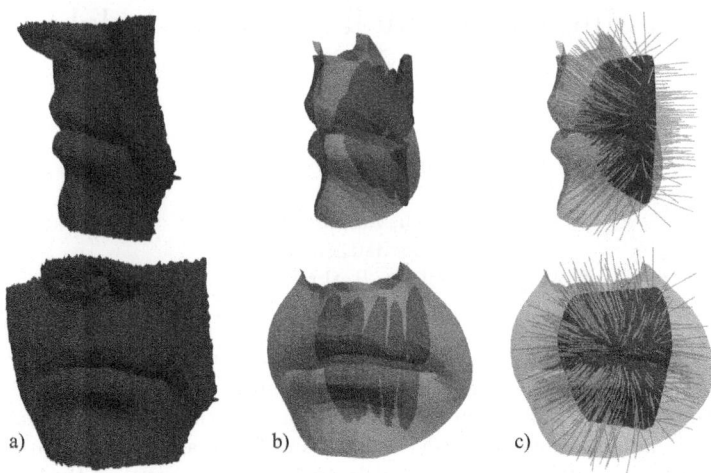

Fig. 1. Example data from a single patient's CBCT scan. (a) Facial surface extracted from the CBCT. (b) Template face mesh registered onto the extracted surface, and the segmented teeth mesh. (c) Lip thickness measured from the arch ball using ray casting. For clarity of visualisation, only a quarter of the rays have been rendered.

practitioners may avoid using 3D face scan techniques, reducing their capacity to evaluate overall facial changes.

To address these limitations, this work proposes a joint dento-facial model that captures the interdependence between hard and soft tissues in a unified framework. With a dataset of cone-beam CT (CBCT) scans, we extract 3D surfaces of faces and dental arches, and use them to build and test linear and multi-linear statistical shape models (SSMs). We then use the SSMs as a shape prior for aligning intraoral (IO) scans.

Shape models can serve as a foundational geometric prior for many tasks requiring digital humans. In the graphics literature, face models such as FLAME [10] focus on realistic facial expressions through the use of learned rigs and linear blendshapes. Vlasic et al. [18] use a multi-linear model to transfer facial expressions across identities. These models were later expanded to include anatomical details - Qiu et al. [14] and Achenbach et al. [18] extend the work of Li [10] and Vlasic [18] respectively, adding cranial anatomy into the face model, with varied applications in orthognathic surgery, anatomical reconstruction, forensics, and simulation. Shape models have also been applied for specific problems, such as with skull-shape inference [11], and there have been dedicated models proposed for teeth [19], palates [12], and skulls [17].

To the best of our knowledge, this is the first work on dento-facial SSMs. In contrast to previous works, we must first tackle the specific challenges of processing multi-modal dento-facial data. Then, we can demonstrate the unique application of these models in dentistry.

Specifically, we show the application of aligning face and intraoral scans. A typical alignment method requires multiple face scans (which themselves require an alignment), and a manual registration process [5]. While this method could in theory be automated, it would nonetheless be prone to inaccuracies in input data. We demonstrate that our model is able to semi-automatically reconstruct and align facial and IO scans to a high degree of accuracy, using only a single neutral face scan. Furthermore, the model could seamlessly integrate with future alignment methods as a shape prior, to increase method robustness.

To adapt our model to the dental domain, we propose and evaluate an innovative, practical approach to represent the dental arch shape, and an efficient scheme to sample and represent the tissue depth with ray-casting, which performs particularly well in the lip region compared to the prior sphere-fitting approaches [1] that have been optimised to perform well over the face as a whole, sacrificing specificity.

2   Methods

We build on established methods in linear and multi-linear shape modelling, emphasising their dental applications. As the first study in this domain, using such well-established methods as baselines makes our method easier to reproduce and expand on in the future. Additionally, linear methods can be more robust to over-fitting; this makes them a good choice when only small datasets are available, which is often the case when dealing with confidential face data.

We begin this section with a description of our CBCT dataset, detailing the conversion of raw data into a processed set of surface meshes and tissue thicknesses. We then provide an overview of shape-modelling, and proceed to define a linear PCA model of the dento-facial geometry M_j, as well as three independent linear PCA models of arch shape M_{ab}, tissue thickness M_{stt}, and facial geometry M_f. We use these three models in Sect. 2.5 to construct our multi-linear model $\mathcal{M}$. Finally, we describe how the multi-linear model may be fitted to new shapes, used to approximate missing arch or lip scans, and be used for alignment of IO and face scans.

2.1   Data

Our data consists of 284 CBCT scans of the head with closed mouth, collected for a study on the outcomes of orthodontic treatments, at a spatially uniform resolution of 0.3 mm. From these scans, we extract skin surface and segmented teeth. The skin surface is first extracted via thresholding of the CBCT. After this, the Faceform[1] Wrap software is used to place landmarks on the extracted surface, and a template mesh is registered to it via non-rigid ICP [2]. From the registered skin, a mouth-area crop is extracted. This crop is a triangular mesh with $n_f = 418$ corresponding vertices, whose coordinates can be arranged into a coordinate vector $\mathbf{d}_f \in \mathbb{R}^{3n_f}$.

The volumetric segmentation of the teeth is obtained using a proprietary algorithm, and individual tooth meshes are reconstructed using marching cubes.

---

[1] https://faceform.am/; Wrap 2023.11.4.

We base our model on the 16 frontal teeth – i.e., the incisors, canines, and first pre-molars. Each segmented tooth mesh has a unique topology. To facilitate working with the data, we convert the extracted teeth into a topologically uniform representation. This process, which yields a shape which we refer to as an *arch-ball*, is described in the next Section.

We split our data into a training and test batch, using 255 scans for the former and 29 for the latter. For 10 of the 29 test scans, we use additional intraoral scans to test the model's IO scan alignment ability. The IO scans are acquired with a commercially available device. They are high-resolution, unregistered, in their own co-ordinate frame and, unlike our CT-derived data, do not contain the dental roots.

2.2   Arch Ball Calculation

The *arch-ball*, shown in Fig. 1 along with the extracted and registered meshes, is a convenient representation of the dental arch shape. Via a simple automatic process, we compute the arch-ball from the irregular, segmented tooth shapes obtained using marching-cubes. The arch-balls closely follow the shape of the teeth, and since they are topologically uniform, they can directly be used for shape-modelling.

We initialise the arch ball as an icosphere with $n_{ab} = 2562$ points, and project these points radially onto the convex hull of the tooth-meshes. We observe that this simple representation works well for our problem, as it captures the key frontal profile of the teeth, which are in contact with the lips and thus drive the correlation between arch and tissue profile. Additionally, this method is fully automatic, and does not require expensive landmarking of individual teeth. This process yields topologically uniform arch-ball shapes, which can be described by a coordinate vector $\mathbf{d_{ab}} \in \mathbb{R}^{3n_{ab}}$.

2.3   Lip Thickness Model

We calculate the thickness of the lips by casting rays from the arch-ball, along the point normal direction, onto the registered face shape and finding the intersection point. We take the length of the ray as the point-wise lip thickness. For rays that do not intersect the face mesh, we impute the missing values via harmonic interpolation. That is, we solve the Laplace equation $\mathbf{L}\mathbf{d_{stt}} = \mathbf{0}$, where $\mathbf{L}$ is the cotangent Laplacian constructed on the arch-ball mesh from which the lip-thickness was measured, and $\mathbf{d_{stt}} \in \mathbb{R}^{n_{ab}}$ is the vector of lip-thicknesses at each vertex. A fixed boundary condition is set from the known distances – at points with valid intersection – and the remaining values are solved for. An arch-ball with the distance-rays is shown in Fig. 1c. Thus, for each arch-ball we have a vector $\mathbf{d_{stt}} \in \mathbb{R}^{n_{ab}}$ distances.

2.4   Shape Models

With the data processing complete, we turn our attention to applications. Statistical shape models are a popular approach for analysing and compressing vari-

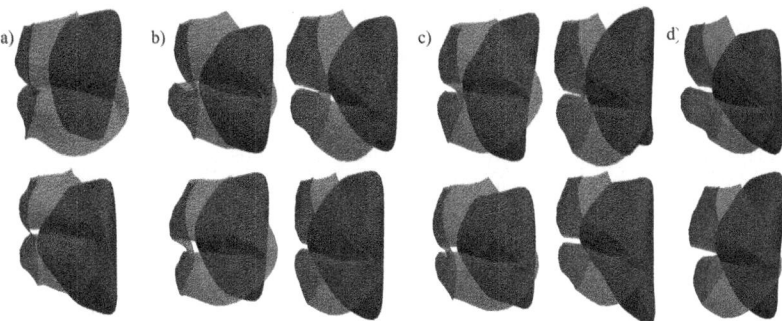

Fig. 2. Model samples. Each column shows the variation along an individual component. (a) Samples from the linear model M_j. (b) Samples from the multi-linear model $\mathcal{M}$, when varying the tissue thickness vector. Notice the arch-ball remains constant. (c) Samples from $\mathcal{M}$, when varying the arch-ball vector; conversely, though tissue thickness remains the same, the lip shape changes in response to the change in underlying hard tissue. (d) Samples from $\mathcal{M}$ where both tissue and arch parameters are varied.

ability within shape datasets. Linear shape models [3] remain a common choice because they are straightforward to construct, yet robust even with relatively small datasets [7].

Given a dataset $\{\mathbf{d}_1, \mathbf{d}_2, ..., \mathbf{d}_N\}$ of vectors in $\mathbb{R}^{|\mathbf{d}|}$, we define the model as a linear map, $M : \mathbb{R}^c \mapsto \mathbb{R}^{|\mathbf{d}|}$, with a domain $\mathbb{R}^c$ where c is the number of components and $c \leq N \ll |\mathbf{d}|$, and a codomain which captures as much of the data variance as possible. It turns out this linear map is

$$M(\mathbf{w}) = M\mathbf{w} + \bar{\mathbf{d}}, \tag{1}$$

where $\bar{\mathbf{d}}$ is the mean of the data and the model matrix $M \in \mathbb{R}^{|\mathbf{d}| \times c}$ contains the most dominant right singular vectors of the zero-meaned data matrix $D \in R^{N \times |\mathbf{d}|}$, whose rows are $\mathbf{d}_i - \bar{\mathbf{d}}$. By varying the latent vector $\mathbf{w}$, we can easily interpolate between the data vectors $\mathbf{d}$, and use the model as a shape prior for downstream tasks.

With our dataset, we wish to model the variability of face shapes and dental arches. To do so with a linear shape model, we concatenate face and arch-ball coordinates $\mathbf{d}_f$ and $\mathbf{d}_{ab}$ into vectors in $\mathbb{R}^{3(n_f + n_{ab})}$. The dataset of 255 face-and-arch shapes is then used to construct the *linear model* M_j. We use a 32 component model, which retains $> 95\%$ of the data variance. The generalisation and specificity of the model, as defined in [9], are 0.3 ± 0.3 mm and 1.0 ± 0.8 mm. Samples from this model are shown in Fig. 2a.

In these models, all sources of shape variation are compressed into a single latent space making it hard to interpret or independently manipulate specific factors (e.g., teeth shape vs. lip thickness). Multi-linear models address this limitation by factoring the latent space into separate subspaces, each corresponding to a distinct mode of variation. For instance, in facial shape analysis, one subspace can capture changes in the underlying dental structure while another governs variations in soft-tissue thickness. These two factors arise from different biological processes – teeth development vs. soft-tissue growth – and can thus be treated as largely independent. As a result, a multi-linear model enables more intuitive control. Figures 2b and 2c show how varying each latent vector can isolate the effect of either dental or soft-tissue changes.

To construct a multi-linear model, we assemble and decompose a data tensor, $\mathcal{D} \in \mathbb{R}^{N_1 \times N_2 \times 3(n_f + n_{ab})}$, using higher-order SVD [18]. The first two axes of $\mathcal{D}$ represent one source of variation (i.e. tissue thickness or arch shape), and the third axis encodes the 3D coordinates of the shape.

Obtaining the full data tensor requires measuring a Cartesian product of the factors involved. In this case – all combinations of each individual's unique arch shape paired with multiple lip thicknesses. Practically, though, we cannot artificially alter someone's lip thickness to capture all possible variations. Consequently, we can only collect limited samples (i.e., one thickness per person), which prevents us from measuring the data tensor. To overcome this limitation, we follow a method similar to Achenbach et al. [1] and construct $\mathcal{D}$ by sampling from independent SSMs: an arch shape, a tissue thickness, and a facial geometry model – M_{ab}, M_{stt} and M_f.

For M_{ab}, we assemble the data matrix from arch-ball coordinate vectors $\mathbf{d}_{ab}$. Likewise, M_{stt} and M_f are built using the vectors $\mathbf{d}_{stt}$ and $\mathbf{d}_f$ respectively. In Sect. 2.5, we detail our procedure for sampling these models and constructing $\mathcal{D}$. We then describe the multi-linear model framework in more detail, and present our process for fitting the model to unseen point clouds, followed by the method for aligning IO and facial scans. Finally, in Sect. 3, we evaluate our methods – highlighting our novel approach for measuring soft-tissue thickness and comparing the performance of the multi-linear model $\mathcal{M}$ to the linear model M_j for shape analysis and alignment.

2.5   Multi-linear Model

Data Sampling. To sample the Cartesian product of arch and lip shapes, we adopt the strategy proposed by Achenbach et al. [1]. This involves generating independent samples from M_{ab} and M_{stt}. In total, 2^5 and 2^6 samples are generated from each, by exhaustively sampling all weight vectors with values of ± 2 standard deviations along the first five and six principal components, respectively.

Thus, the product of the two models gives 2048 unique pairs of dental arch shape s_{ab} and tissue thickness s_{stt}. For each of these pairs, we calculate points on the facial surface as $\mathbf{p} = \mathbf{x}_{ab} + s_{stt}\mathbf{n}_{ab}$, where $\mathbf{x}_{ab}$ is a vector of dental arch points, $\mathbf{n}_{ab}$ is a vector of point-normals and s_{stt} are the soft-tissue thicknesses.

Next, we fit the face model M_{face} to the point-cloud $\mathbf{p}$. The fitting is done by finding the rigid transformation parameters – scaling s, rotation $\mathbf{R}$ and translation $\mathbf{t}$ – and model weight $\mathbf{w}$:

$$\arg \min_{s, \mathbf{t}, \mathbf{R}, \mathbf{w}} \sum_i \| s\mathbf{R}(M_{face}(\mathbf{w})) + \mathbf{t} - \mathbf{p}_i \|^2 \tag{2}$$

This problem is solved using the iterative method of Schneider and Eisert [16], which converges in near real-time, and yields a face mesh s_{face}, with n_f vertices. We evaluate the samples generated by our method in Sect. 3.1.

Model Construction. The points of each sample pair s_{face} and s_{ab} are concatenated into coordinate vectors $X_i \in \mathbb{R}^{3(n_f + n_{\text{ab}})}$, which are mean centred and arranged into a data tensor $\mathcal{D} \in \mathbb{R}^{3(n_f + n_{\text{ab}}) \times d_{\text{ab}} \times d_{\text{stt}}}$. Slightly overloading our notation, we calculate the multi-linear model tensor $\mathcal{M} \in \mathbb{R}^{3(n_f + n_{\text{ab}}) \times d_{\text{ab}} \times d_{\text{stt}}}$ from the data tensor $\mathcal{D}$ using higher-order SVD as

$$\mathcal{M} = \mathcal{D} \times_{ab} \mathbf{U}_{ab}^T \times_{stt} \mathbf{U}_{stt}^T \tag{3}$$

where $\mathbf{U}_i$ are computed from the SVD of $\mathcal{D}$ unfolded along mode i and the operation $\times_i$ represents the corresponding mode-product. Further details on the derivation can be found in Achenbach et al. [1] and Vlasic et al. [18].

To calculate the shape of a new dento-facial complex, we evaluate the equation

$$\mathbf{X}(\mathbf{w}_{ab}, \mathbf{w}_{stt}) = \bar{\mathbf{X}} + \mathcal{M} \times_{ab} \mathbf{w}_{ab}^T \times_{stt} \mathbf{w}_{stt}^T \tag{4}$$

where $\bar{\mathbf{X}}$ is the mean of the model. We initialise the weights of the model $\bar{\mathbf{w}}_{ab}$ and $\bar{\mathbf{w}}_{stt}$ as the column-wise means of $\mathbf{U}_{ab}$ and $\mathbf{U}_{stt}$ respectively. Thus constructed, the model shows a generalisation and specificity of 2.1 ± 1.3 mm and 1.3 ± 0.9 mm, as calculated against the original data $\mathbf{d}_f$ and $\mathbf{d}_{ab}$.

Model Fitting. We fit the model to a new point-cloud $\mathbf{p}$ by minimising the potential established by Achenbach et al. [1]

$$E(\mathbf{w}_{\text{ab}}, \mathbf{w}_{\text{stt}}, s, \mathbf{R}, \mathbf{t}) = E_{\text{fit}}(\mathbf{w}_{\text{ab}}, \mathbf{w}_{\text{stt}}, s, \mathbf{R}, \mathbf{t}) + E_{\text{reg}}(\mathbf{w}_{\text{ab}}, \mathbf{w}_{\text{stt}}) \tag{5}$$

$$E_{\text{fit}} = \frac{1}{|\mathcal{C}|} \sum_{i \in \mathcal{C}} \|s\mathbf{R}\mathbf{x}_i(\mathbf{w}_{\text{ab}}, \mathbf{w}_{\text{stt}}) + \mathbf{t} - \mathbf{p}_i\|^2 \tag{6}$$

$$E_{\text{reg}}(\mathbf{w}_{\text{ab}}, \mathbf{w}_{\text{stt}}) = \frac{1}{d_{\text{ab}}} \sum_{k=1}^{d_{\text{ab}}} \left(\frac{w_{\text{ab},k} - \bar{w}_{\text{ab},k}}{\sigma_{\text{id},k}} \right)^2 + \frac{1}{d_{\text{stt}}} \sum_{l=1}^{d_{\text{stt}}} \left(\frac{w_{\text{stt},l} - \bar{w}_{\text{stt},l}}{\sigma_{\text{stt},l}} \right)^2 \tag{7}$$

where $\mathcal{C}$ is the set of correspondences between model vertices $\mathbf{x}_i$ and points $\mathbf{p}_i$. The correspondences can be computed for any combination of inputs: face scan, IO scan, or both. They are computed via nearest neighbour to a target point-cloud, or via providing an explicit correspondence. In the former case, we prune correspondences above a distance of 5 mm and with a normal mismatch between target and model point greater than $45°$. The optimisation is performed via block coordinate descent, iterating over the rigid transformation, tissue weights, and arch weights, and re-computing the correspondences at each step. Equation 7 is a Tikhonov regularisation that prevents over-fitting. The variables $\bar{w}_{i,l}$ and $\sigma_{i,l}$ are the initial latent values and standard deviation of the principal component of $\mathcal{D}$ unfolded along the ith mode. We implement the optimisation using a non-linear conjugate gradient solver with the Optimistix library [15].

2.6   IO Scan Alignment

Intraoral scans are acquired separately from face scans. Thus, the two are not in global alignment. Using our model we can simultaneously align the two scans together while fitting them to the model.

We formulate the alignment process as an optimisation over joint model parameters, $\mathbf{w}_{ab}$, $\mathbf{w}_{stt}$ and scale s, and unique per-scan rotation and translation parameters: $\mathbf{R}_{io}$, $\mathbf{t}_{io}$, $\mathbf{R}_{face}$, and $\mathbf{t}_{face}$. The objective function thus includes two E_{fit} terms, over two sets of correspondences $\mathcal{C}_{ab}$ and $\mathcal{C}_{stt}$. With the dependence on the shared parameters $\mathbf{w}_{ab}$, $\mathbf{w}_{stt}$, and s omitted for clarity, the objective is thus

$$E(\mathbf{R}_{io}, \mathbf{t}_{io}, \mathbf{R}_{face}, \mathbf{t}_{face}) = E_{fit}(\mathbf{R}_{io}, \mathbf{t}_{io}) + E_{fit}(\mathbf{R}_{face}, \mathbf{t}_{face}) + E_{reg} . \qquad (8)$$

As in the previous section, we solve the problem using block coordinate descent, re-calculating the IO scan correspondences after every step. After optimisation, it is trivial to transform the points of the IO scan, $\mathbf{p}_{io}$, into the coordinate frame of the face scan as $\mathbf{R}_{face}\mathbf{R}_{io}^{T}(\mathbf{p}_{io} - \mathbf{t}_{io}) + \mathbf{t}_{face}$.

3   Results

To evaluate our approach, we first compare our data generation technique with the prior work, after which we analyse the performance of the multi-linear model when fitting new data, and when aligning face and IO scans. All experiments were performed on an Intel i7-11800H 2.3 GHz CPU.

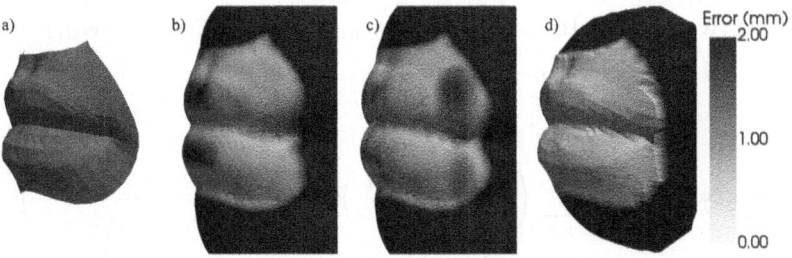

Fig. 3. Representational accuracy of sphere-based and ray-based soft-tissue-thickness models. (a) Ground truth lips, (b) sphere-fitting without refinement, (c) sphere fitting with refinement [1], and (d) our approach.

3.1   Data Generation

We evaluate the accuracy of our data generation process by determining whether the M_f, fitted via Eq. 2 to point clouds $\mathbf{p}$, can reliably reconstruct true facial surfaces. These point clouds are generated from tissue thicknesses and arch meshes, and achieving good reconstruction accuracy is essential for the M_{stt} to produce realistic samples for $\mathcal{D}$. We compare our ray-based approach with the previous approaches of measuring soft-tissue thickness with sphere-meshes [1], and find our method to be both more accurate for lip geometry as well as less computationally demanding.

From Fig. 3, it is apparent that representing the tissue thickness with spheres does not adequately capture the geometry of the lips, with its characteristic variation of positive and negative curvature regions.

Consequently, the reconstruction quality is better for the simpler ray-based approach, with a mean surface error of 0.72 ± 0.21 mm compared to 1.47 ± 0.47 mm for the sphere-based approach, as measured by a point-to-surface metric.

Another factor to consider is the complexity of the method. The sphere-mesh approach requires nested, non-linear optimisation, correspondence pruning, marching cubes, and a bounding volume hierarchy. By contrast, the ray-casting method is trivial to implement, and does not require any optimisation. This complexity is reflected in the run-times of the methods. Averaging over our entire dataset, running the ray-fitting algorithm takes an average of 25 ms per sample. Our re-implementation of the sphere-optimising algorithm takes 115 s per input. While this run-time could undoubtedly be improved, the engineering effort required is non-trivial, and not proportional to the improvement in model quality.

3.2   Model Fitting

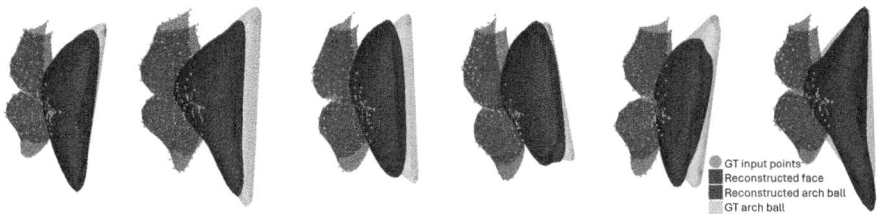

Fig. 4. Face and dental arch pairs reconstructed from facial input scans. The model is fitted to the input facial points in light blue, and is able to reconstruct them with an accuracy of 0.33 ± 0.05 mm. The dental arch is automatically inferred based on the underlying relationship between soft and hard tissues.

We fit the multi-linear model to face scans from the test set. Reconstructed samples are shown in Fig. 4. The fitting of faces is highly accurate. The mean vertex-to-vertex distance between input and reconstructed faces is 0.33 ± 0.05 mm. The reconstruction of unseen arches yields plausible results. The mean average surface distance [13] between the reconstructed and ground truth dental arch is 2.0 ± 0.7 mm. By comparison, the linear model M_j achieves face-fitting error of

0.48 ± 0.09 mm and an arch reconstruction error of 1.5 ± 0.4 mm. This broadly similar performance is unsurprising, since both methods are fitted to the same underlying dataset and share a common fitting scheme (Eq. 5). The lower distance of M_j may be attributed to fact that the single parameter space more strongly entangles facial appearance and arch-shape, whereas $\mathcal{M}$ keeps these factors more independent.

Qualitatively, we observe that many of the reconstructed arches are similar in shape to their ground truth counterparts, and that particularly the centres of mass and proclinations are correctly inferred. However, it can be seen that the extent of the arch, from how deeply embedded it is in the oral cavity to how long the roots of the teeth are, is often a cause of inaccuracy. This is possibly due to the fact that these regions, being further away from the facial surface, have less of an impact and less of a direct correlation with the surface appearance.

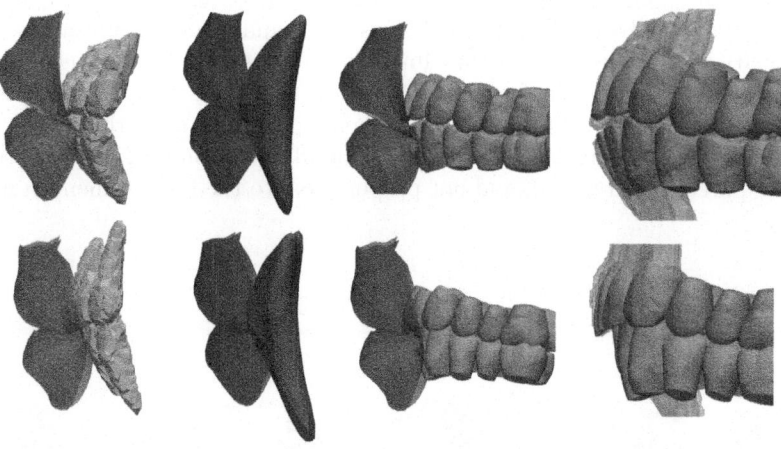

Fig. 5. IO Scan alignment. From left to right, the columns are: the ground truth CBCT data, the model mesh after fitting, the alignment computed by the model, the overlap between aligned IO scan and GT teeth

3.3   Aligning Intraoral Scans

The IO scan alignments calculated with our method can be seen in Fig. 5. The optimisation ran for 32 iterations, and the average time to align each scan was 28 ± 3 s.

A qualitative assessment of the alignment reveals that the teeth are consistently placed in a reasonable position within the oral cavity. The most common error appears along the anteroposterior axis. This is to be expected, as this direction corresponds to the tissue thickness variable, which varies amongst individuals, and may be harder to reliably estimate from the surface shape alone.

Automated quantitative evaluation of the alignment is challenging, due to the fact that IO scans do not contain roots, and have a much higher resolution and different topology compared to the extracted teeth. We use a manual approach to measure how much the position of the output IO scans needs to be adjusted to completely overlap with the CBCT ground-truth. Using a GUI, we rigidly transform the IO scans and measure the norm of the applied translation vector. Thus measured, the mean distance between the aligned IO scan and segmented teeth was 3.3 ± 1.5 mm. For the anteroposterior, transverse, and longitudinal axes, the errors were 2.7 ± 1.8 mm, 0.5 ± 0.5 mm, and 1.2 ± 0.6 mm respectively. The error in alignment is higher than the error in arch-ball reconstruction accuracy, which is explained by the compounding error - an error of arch-ball estimation, followed by an error in correspondence between arch-ball and the IO scan. The linear model M_j achieves a mean distance of 3.4 ± 1.7 mm. In contrast to the previous experiment, the multi-linear model performs marginally better than the linear model. We hypothesise that identifying quality correspondences between the arch-ball and the IO scan is one of the major bottlenecks, which affects both approaches equally. Another limitation of the method is its initialisation sensitivity. The IO scan must first be roughly rotated into the correct orientation which aligns with the model space, thus making the method only semi-automated. A sensitivity analysis reveals that if the IO scans are rotated by $5°$, the reconstructed surfaces are deformed by 0.2 ± 0.5 mm. Landmark-based initialisation or automated landmark detection based on learning approaches could potentially alleviate these issues.

Overall, while improvements can be made, the level of accuracy is sufficient for many orthodontic applications, such as clinical-visualisation or simulation, where small misalignments may be overlooked, or ameliorated by soft-tissue deformations [11].

4   Conclusion

Shape models are a versatile foundation for solving a wide variety of problems in 3D modelling, imaging, and geometry processing. In this work, we propose a multi-linear model of dental and orofacial shape, which captures the correlation between soft tissue and dental structure. To build this model, we introduce a practical and empirically effective representation of the dental arch, and improve the tissue thickness modelling via a ray-casting approach which is well suited to the domain at hand.

We apply this model to the alignment of intraoral (IO) scans, a significant problem in the field. Existing methods are often manual or rely on multiple face scans, making them susceptible to scan noise or variability in new data. Our model performs well on just a single face scan and can be seamlessly integrated as a prior into more specialized approaches.

Our proposed shape model has several opportunities for refinement – for instance, we do not disentangle expression from identity, which impacts the accuracy of the facial components. By including expression and appearance spaces, the model could readily tackle problems such as 3D reconstruction from images, or avatar motion generation. Additionally, integrating physical constraints into the model could help prevent the generation of implausible shapes, which can occur due to its linear assumptions. Finally, scaling the model to include additional anatomy, such as the jaw, gingiva, or individual teeth, would also be a valuable direction for future research.

Overall, a specialized dento-facial model can greatly benefit digital dentistry. Our work addresses some of the unique challenges in this domain, and paves the way for further innovation.

References

1. Achenbach, J., et al.: A multilinear model for bidirectional craniofacial reconstruction. In: Puig, A.P., Schultz, T., Vilanova, A., Hotz, I., Kozlikova, B., Vázquez, P.-P. (eds.) Eurographics Workshop on Visual Computing for Biology and Medicine. The Eurographics Association (2018)
2. Amberg, B., Romdhani, S., Vetter, T.: Optimal step nonrigid ICP algorithms for surface registration. In: 2007 IEEE Conference on Computer Vision and Pattern Recognition (2007)
3. Blanz, V., Vetter, T.: A morphable model for the synthesis of 3D faces, pp. 187–194 (1999)
4. Bravo, L.A., Canut, J.A., Pascual, A., Bravo, B.: Comparison of the changes in facial profile after orthodontic treatment, with and without extractions. Br. J. Orthod. **24**(1), 25–34 (1997)
5. Campobasso, A., Battista, G., Muzio, E.L., Muzio, L.L.: The virtual patient in daily orthodontics: matching intraoral and facial scans without cone beam computed tomography. Appl. Sci. **12**(19), 9870 (2022)
6. Dorda, D., et al.: Evaluating a differentiable facial fem model with in-vivo simulated data for orthodontic treatment outcome prediction. Comput. Biomech. Med. (2024, forthcoming)
7. Egger, B., et al.: 3D morphable face models–past, present, and future. ACM Trans. Graph. **39**(5) (2020)
8. Garrido, P., et al.: Corrective 3D reconstruction of lips from monocular video. ACM Trans. Graph. **35**(6) (2016)
9. Goparaju, A., et al.: On the evaluation and validation of off-the-shelf statistical shape modeling tools: a clinical application. CoRR, abs/1810.03987 (2018)
10. Li, T., Bolkart, T., Black, M.J., Li, H., Romero, J.: Learning a model of facial shape and expression from 4D scans. ACM Trans. Graph. **36**(6), 1–17 (2017)
11. Milojevic, A., et al.: Autoskull: learning-based skull estimation for automated pipelines. LNCS, vol. 15007 (2024)
12. Nauwelaers, N., et al.: Exploring palatal and dental shape variation with 3D shape analysis and geometric deep learning. Orthod. Craniofac. Res. **24**(S2), 134–143 (2021)
13. Podobnik, G., Vrtovec, T.: Metrics revolutions: groundbreaking insights into the implementation of metrics for biomedical image segmentation (2024)
14. Qiu, Z., et al.: Sculptor: skeleton-consistent face creation using a learned parametric generator. ACM Trans. Graph. **41**(6) (2022)
15. Rader, J., Lyons, T., Kidger, P.: Optimistix: modular optimisation in JAX and equinox (2024)

16. Schneider, D.C., Eisert, P.: Fitting a morphable model to pose and shape of a point cloud. In: Magnor, M.A., Rosenhahn, B., Theisel, H. (eds.) 14th International Workshop on Vision, Modeling, and Visualization, VMV 2009, 16–18 November 2009, Braunschweig, Germany, pp. 93–100. DNB (2009)
17. Semper-Hogg, W., et al.: Virtual reconstruction of midface defects using statistical shape models. J. Craniomaxillofac. Surg. **45**(4), 461–466 (2017)
18. Vlasic, D., Brand, M., Pfister, H., Popović, J.: Face transfer with multilinear models. ACM Trans. Graph. **24**(3), 426–433 (2005)
19. Wu, C., et al.: Model-based teeth reconstruction. ACM Trans. Graph. **35**(6) (2016)
20. Najafi, H.Z., Sabouri, S., Ebrahimi, E., Torkan, S.: Esthetic evaluation of lip position in silhouette with respect to profile divergence. Am. J. Orthod. Dentofacial Orthop. **149**(6), 863–870 (2016)

Out-of-Distribution Detection in Gastrointestinal Vision by Estimating Nearest Centroid Distance Deficit

Sandesh Pokhrel[1], Sanjay Bhandari[1], Sharib Ali[6], Tryphon Lambrou[3], Anh Nguyen[5], Yash Raj Shrestha[2], Angus Watson[3], Danail Stoyanov[7], Prashnna Gyawali[4], and Binod Bhattarai[1,3,7(✉)]

[1] Nepal Applied Mathematics and Informatics Institute for Research (NAAMII), Lalitpur, Nepal
{sandesh.pokhrel,sanjay.bhandari}@naamii.org.np
[2] University of Lausanne, Lausanne, Switzerland
[3] University of Aberdeen, Aberdeen, UK
binod.bhattarai@abdn.ac.uk
[4] West Virginia University, Morgantown, USA
[5] University of Liverpool, Liverpool, UK
[6] University of Leeds, Leeds, UK
[7] University College London, London, UK

Abstract. The integration of deep learning tools in gastrointestinal vision holds the potential for significant advancements in diagnosis, treatment, and overall patient care. A major challenge, however, is overconfident predictions, even when encountering unseen or newly emerging disease patterns, which undermines the reliability of such tools. We address this critical issue of reliability in gastrointestinal vision through the lens of out-of-distribution (OOD) detection, which handles previously unseen or emerging diseases as OOD samples.

To this end, we hypothesize that the features of an in-distribution example will cluster closer to the centroids of their ground truth class, resulting in a shorter distance between the example and the nearest centroid. In contrast, OOD examples maintain more or less an equal distance from all class centroids. Based on this hypothesis, we propose a novel Nearest-Centroid Distance Deficit (NCDD) score in the feature space for gastrointestinal OOD detection. Evaluations across Resnet, ViT, DeiT and MLPmixer and two publicly available benchmarks, Kvasir2 and Gastrovision, demonstrate the effectiveness of our approach compared to several state-of-the-art methods. The code is available at: bhattarailab/NCDD.

Keywords: Feature Centroid · Gastrointestinal Disease · Nearest Centroid · OOD Detection

---

S. Pokhrel and S. Bhandari—These authors contributed equally to this work.

S. Ali et al. (Eds.): MIUA 2025, LNCS 15917, pp. 190–200, 2026.
https://doi.org/10.1007/978-3-031-98691-8_14

1   Introduction

Gastrointestinal diseases are among the most prevalent globally, with over seven billion cases and 2.8 million deaths reported in 2019 [35]. In the same year, 38.4% of prevalent diseases had digestive origins [34], with mortality rates increasing significantly from 2000 to 2019. Endoscopy is a common diagnostic tool, and deep learning, particularly CNNs, has shown promise in recognizing anatomical landmarks and detecting abnormalities such as gastric cancer [13], polyps, ulcerative colitis, and esophagitis [8,26,29]. The rise of capsule endoscopy has further increased the need for automated diagnosis [16]. However, while classification models effectively identify normal anatomical landmarks, they struggle with abnormalities, especially rare and novel ones ,due to limited training data, leading to overconfident predictions and reduced reliability [36]. Additionally, treating abnormalities as distinct classes in classification models makes them error-prone when encountering unseen cases [4,22,27]. In medical deep learning, out-of-distribution (OOD) detection has attracted much attention recently in detecting abnormality as OOD [1,21] rather than arbitrarily classifying an in-distribution class. COOpD [1] formulated abnormalities as OOD to separate homogeneous healthy regions from heterogeneous pathological images of chest x-rays while Mehta et al. [20] proposed a mixup strategy to correct the long tail data problem in realistic settings of a skin lesion for OOD detection. The MOOD [38] challenge highlights the importance of flagging OODs as they support experts in detecting incidental findings.

Deep latent space representations and clustering-based methods have been widely used for OOD detection both in medical imaging as well as natural images. Dinari et al. [6] improved class separation using a conditional variational model and used class-dependent log-likelihood values of a deep feature ensemble of the test points for OOD detection, while Sundar et al. [31] utilized sensitive latent variables of β-VAEs to detect OOD samples. Sinhamahapatra et al. [28] explored clustering of learned embeddings to classify OOD samples. However, these latent representation-based methods lack adaptability across different model architectures. For better adaptability, logits-based [10,12,19], probability-based [3], gradient-based [17], and other feature space-based [18,30] methods have proven effective. The non-parametric KNN-OOD method [30] uses the distance between a sample image in feature space and the k-th nearest neighbour from the training set to determine ID and OOD samples. Looking deeper inside the overall network rather than representations, BLOOD [14] looks into the gradient information within separate layers of the network to separate OOD from ID data. From a geometric perspective, Neco [2] utilized properties of neural collapse for OOD detection. Although these methods have been validated in real-word settings, their effectiveness in medical applications, particularly in GI remains largely unexplored. GI endoscopy presents unique challenges, such as low intra class variability and subtle visual differences in healthy and abnormal findings, making reliable OOD detection more complex.

In this paper, we tackle the challenge of developing reliable abnormality detection algorithms for gastrointestinal vision by introducing a novel OOD detection framework. We frame healthy anatomical landmarks as ID, and OOD examples correspond to any abnormalities in these landmarks. To detect OOD cases, we propose Nearest Centroid Distance Deficit (NCDD), which introduces a distance deficit score by leveraging both nearest and non-nearest centroid distances, allowing for better differentiation of near-OOD cases. Minimizing the cross-entropy loss during landmark classification in ID examples naturally minimizes intra-class distances and maximizes inter-class separation, making ID representations more compact. However, OOD examples remain more dispersed in feature space as they are unseen. By using both an image's proximity to its nearest ID centroid and its distance from non-nearest centroids, NCDD improves OOD detection.

Our specific contributions can be summarized as follows:

- We formulate abnormality detection as an OOD detection problem for models trained to classify anatomical landmarks, allowing us to detect the presence of pathologies in endoscopic images without the need for retraining the model explicitly on abnormal samples.
- We introduce a novel distance-based OOD detection method, NCDD, that exploits the information from the class clusters to distinguish ID from OOD.
- Our method is a post-hoc approach, making it straightforward to implement across various model architectures.

Our method is evaluated on two different gastrointestinal datasets and four separate classifier backbones, ResNet-18 [9], ViT [7], DEiT [33] and MLP-Mixer [33], demonstrating its superior performance compared to existing methods.

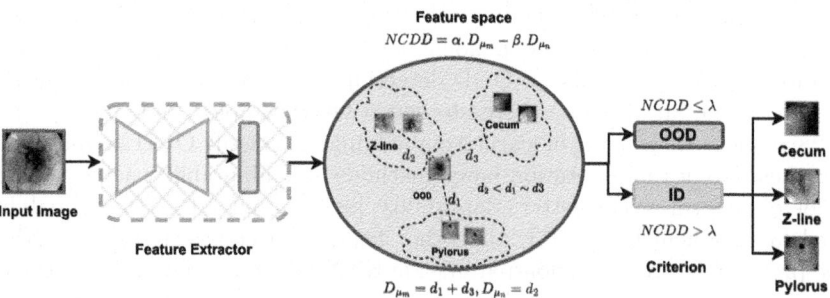

Fig. 1. Overview of NCDD OOD detection method, utilizing a feature extractor trained on classifying ID classes. The Nearest Centroid Distance Deficit (NCDD) score quantifies the sample's uncertainty and is compared against a threshold to determine whether it is out-of-distribution (OOD) or not.

2   Method

Preliminaries: We consider supervised multi-class classification, where X is the input space, $Y = \{1, 2, \ldots, C\}$ is the label space and P_{XY} is the distribution over $X \times Y$. Let P_{in} be the marginal distribution of X which is comprised of the healthy person data (In-Distribution). For supervised learning, a neural network $f : X \rightarrow \mathbb{R}^{|Y|}$, is trained on i.i.d samples extracted from $P_{X,Y}$, to minimize the loss function L over the input dataset. Here, $f : X \rightarrow \mathbb{R}^{|Y|}$ is the classification predicted for input X by the model f. The model f consists of an encoder φ and a fully connected layer FC. Feature vector z: $\varphi(x)$ is produced from the encoder φ. At test time, the trained network can be presented input from a distribution P_{out}, quite different from P_{in}. The main objective of the out-of-distribution detection is to differentiate whether the sample belongs to P_{in} or P_{out}. With a threshold λ chosen to have a true positive rate of 95% over the ID validation data, OOD detection reformulates abnormality detection as binary classification problem where a decision function $g(x)$ is defined by the scores produced by the scoring function $SC(x)$ and a threshold λ, as given by:

$$g(x) = \begin{cases} OOD, & \text{if score} \leq \lambda \\ ID, & \text{otherwise} \end{cases} \tag{1}$$

Since our OOD detection method depends upon a supervised classification model, we use the cross-entropy loss function to optimize model parameters: $L = -\sum_{i=1}^{C} y_i \log(\hat{y}_i)$ where, C is the number of classes, y_i is the true probability of class i (usually 0 or 1 for hard labels) and $\hat{y}_i$ is class i's predicted probability.

Since we train a landmark classification model on ID examples our approach uses cross-entropy loss but the proposed OOD score (NCDD) can be adapted to other objective functions suitable for close-set classification problems. Cross-entropy loss shapes the feature space by increasing confidence in correct classifications ($\hat{y}_i$ close to 1) and separating class clusters while tightening intra-class distances [5]. This clustering behavior, as depicted in the embedding space in Fig. 2(b), forms the foundation of our out-of-distribution (OOD) detection method. Specifically, we utilize the structured distribution of in-distribution (ID) samples around their respective class centroids to distinguish them from OOD samples.

Building on this observation, we hypothesize that OOD data will exhibit distinct positioning relative to class centroids in feature space. Unlike ID samples, which cluster tightly around their nearest centroid due to intra-class attraction, OOD samples tend to be more dispersed and exhibit similar distances to their nearest ($D_{o\mu n}$) and non-nearest centroids (D_{o1}, D_{o2}), i.e., $D_{o\mu n} \sim D_{o1} \sim D_{o2}$, as they lack strong alignment with any specific ID class. In contrast, ID samples are significantly closer to their nearest centroid ($D_{i\mu n} < D_{i1} \sim D_{i2}$) while also maintaining larger distances from non-nearest centroids due to inter-class repulsion. Thus, OOD samples are more dispersed, leading to smaller summed distances to non-nearest centroids ($D_{o1} + D_{o2} < D_{i1} + D_{i2}$). This difference in spatial distribution enables Nearest Centroid Distance Deficit (NCDD) to effectively quantify how dispersed an OOD sample is across multiple class centroids, an aspect that prior OOD detection methods have largely overlooked. As demonstrated in Fig. 2(b) and validated in Table 3 (left), this approach provides a more robust measure for distinguishing OOD samples from ID data.

2.1   Nearest Centroid Distance Deficit

Centroid Estimation: To compute class-specific centroids, we average the feature representations of examples belonging to a class, as defined by the equation, $\mu_c = \frac{1}{N_c} \sum_{i=1}^{N_c}$ where, N_c is the total number of samples belonging to class c, and z_i^c represents the feature representation of the i-th sample in class c within the training dataset.

Computing NCDD: Given a test image x, we obtain its feature representation as z. Then, the Euclidean distance to each class centroid is calculated as $D_c = \|\mu_c - z\|_2$. We then define the distance of a test sample to its nearest cluster centroid as the nearest centroid distance $D_{\mu_n} = argmin_c\, D_c$ and the sum of its distances to all other centroids as non-nearest distance $D_{\mu_m} = \sum_{c \neq argmin_c D_c} D_c$.

Finally, our proposed OOD score for a test image is computed as the sum of its distances to non-nearest centroids, minus the distance to the nearest neighbour,

$$\text{NCDD} = \alpha \cdot D_{\mu_m} - \beta \cdot D_{\mu_n}, \tag{2}$$

where, $\alpha = \log\left(\frac{\|\mathbf{z}\|_1}{10^{\alpha_1}}\right)$ and $\beta = \log\left(\frac{\|\mathbf{z}\|_1}{10^{\alpha_2}}\right)$ represent the weight for each distance measure and α_1 and α_2 serve as hyperparameters, tuned during test time and based on the unique attributes of the datasets. Motivated by the work of Zihan Zhang et al. [37], which demonstrated that log of L1-norm of the penultimate layer feature, *i.e.,* $\|\mathbf{z}\|_1 = \sum_{i=1}^n |z_i|$, captures the notion of OOD detection, we incorporate this into the weight terms α and β further to enhance the effectiveness of our proposed OOD score. By incorporating the logarithm, the weights α and β become more sensitive to changes in the magnitude of the feature vector of individual OOD data, further scaling the importance of D_{μ_m} and D_{μ_n} accordingly. The decision for whether a test image is an OOD or not can be determined following the decision function 1. If the score for a data-point is smaller than the threshold, estimated by cross-validation, it is marked as OOD. Figure 1 demonstrates the overall pipeline of our method and how distances in feature spaces are taken into consideration to compute our OOD score.

3   Experiments

To test our method in real-world settings, we employed two multi-class endoscopy datasets designed for Gastrointestinal Disease Detection: Kvasir [23] and Gastrovision [15]. These datasets include images from normal and anatomical findings and the most common abnormalities occurring in various upper and lower GI tract regions. We preprocessed this dataset into an OOD setting [24,25] and designated the classes related to normal findings and anatomical landmarks as in-distribution (ID) classes while segregating the abnormal categories as out-of-distribution (OOD) classes.

Datasets: The **Kvasirv2** [23] dataset comprises 8 categories depicting anatomical landmarks, pathological findings, or endoscopic procedures within the gastrointestinal (GI) tract with 1000 images for each class. The anatomical landmarks in the Kvasirv2 dataset encompass the z-line, pylorus, and cecum. At the same time, pathological findings include esophagitis (ESO), polyps (POL), and ulcerative colitis (UC) and images related to polyp removal, namely the "dyed and lifted polyp" (DLP) class and the "dyed resection margins" (DRM). We designated the classes derived from healthy anatomical landmarks in the Kvasirv2 dataset as ID classes, treating the remaining classes as OOD representing unhealthy cases. We randomly selected 2400 in-distribution images for model training and employed 600 ID images, combined with 5000 OOD images, to assess the final model's performance in OOD detection. The **Gastro-vision** [15] dataset comprises a total of twenty-seven categories, featuring 8,010 images obtained from examinations of both the upper and lower gastrointestinal (GI) tracts. The dataset is categorized into normal findings, anatomical landmarks(11 classes) and pathological findings, and therapeutic interventions(16 classes). To facilitate model training, we randomly selected 3804 in-distribution images(normal findings and anatomical landmarks), utilizing a combination of 955 ID images and 3241 OOD images to comprehensively evaluate the final model's performance in OOD detection.

Table 1. Quantitative Comparison with other methods in terms of AUC↑ and FPR95↓ for different architectures on the Kvasirv2 dataset. Bold characters denote the best performance and underlined characters denote the second-best performance for a metric.

Method	ResNet-18		ViT-Small		DeiT		MLP-Mixer	
	AUC ↑	FPR95↓	AUC ↑	FPR95↓	AUC ↑	FPR95↓	AUC ↑	FPR95↓
MSP	**87.57**	33.06	85.93	39.74	74.57	52.26	78.66	48.54
ODIN	86.95	40.48	83.84	42.10	74.15	52.18	78.19	47.28
Energy	86.00	43.28	83.52	43.12	72.92	53.82	70.70	54.86
Entropy	87.55	33.02	85.87	39.6	74.56	52.38	78.66	48.14
MaxLogit	86.04	43.04	83.53	43.12	72.92	53.82	70.70	54.86
KNN	86.59	36.02	90.74	38.44	82.9	52.9	88.77	31.80
BLOOD	52.1	93.56	51.61	93.10	52.65	93.92	50.66	94.58
Neco	86.29	41.88	87.87	27.8	68.45	66.88	73.81	52.1
FDBD	84.77	36.88	88.31	29.0	71.01	53.84	75.39	49.96
NCDD (Ours)	85.68	**30.86**	**91.61**	**22.94**	**87.09**	**37.9**	**92.44**	**21.92**

Implementation Details: We experimented on different architectures, including ResNet-18 [9], ViT-Small [7], DeiT-base [33], and MLP-Mixer-small [32], on both datasets. The models were trained using PyTorch v2.1.0 on an NVIDIA A100 GPU for 20 epochs with a batch size of 32 using the Adam optimizer with an initial learning rate 1×10^{-4}. All models were initialized with ImageNet pre-trained weights with cross-entropy as the objective function. The input images were resized to 224×224 pixels. To tune the hyperparameters α_1 and α_2, we synthesized OOD validation data by modifying ID images with random rectangular masks and speckle noise following Hendrycks et al. [11] shown in Table 3 (Right).

4 Results

We assessed the efficacy of our method's OOD detection in gastrointestinal settings against established state-of-the-art OOD detection methods from existing literature, logit-based methods MSP [10], ODIN [17], Energy [19], Entropy [3], MaxLogit [12], and feature-based methods KNN [30], FDBD [18], NECO [2]. The model's performance for OOD evaluation was optimal for the respective downstream task with following accuracies in the test set: ResNet-18 98.57%, ViT 99.10%, DeiT 99.16%, MLPmixer 99.5% indicating the models' capability for landmark classification.

Table 2. Quantitative comparison with other methods in terms of AUC↑ and FPR95↓ for different architectures on the Gastrovision dataset. Bold characters denote the best performance and underlined characters denote second-best performance for a metric.

Method	ResNet-18		ViT-Small		DeiT		MLP-Mixer	
	AUC ↑	FPR95↓	AUC ↑	FPR95↓	AUC ↑	FPR95↓	AUC ↑	FPR95↓
MSP	69.82	87.2	75.08	84.36	69.53	86.05	72.35	88.12
ODIN	74.12	79.54	79.36	68.40	77.48	72.69	78.17	70.26
Energy	73.11	85.25	78.62	73.62	75.91	75.56	77.31	72.66
Entropy	70.53	85.81	75.50	81.06	72.49	79.39	74.31	81.06
MaxLogit	72.95	84.91	78.45	75.53	75.0	79.17	76.44	77.29
KNN	71.37	83.62	78.43	80.87	**85.69**	54.71	78.71	74.27
BLOOD	53.11	92.88	52.02	93.37	53.16	93.09	53.36	93.40
Neco	73.31	84.57	80.16	75.53	78.67	72.45	78.45	73.31
FDBD	72.63	80.93	75.75	75.81	76.01	74.45	73.89	77.14
NCDD (Ours)	**79.1**	**72.6**	**83.95**	**55.63**	85.37	**52.48**	**80.93**	**60.5**

Quantitative Results: AUC and **FPR95** assess the OOD detection method's performance. AUC measures the area under the ROC curve, with higher values indicating better performance. FPR95 represents the false positive rate when the true positive rate is 95%, with smaller values indicating better performance. We report both values in percentages. Results in Table 1 and 2 compare our method with existing SOTA methods. The generalizability and model-agnostic nature of our method is supported by the fact that NCDD consistently outperforms established OOD methods in both AUC and FPR95 scores across various model architectures like ResNet-18, ViT, MLP-Mixer, and DEiT. Since low FPR95 is essential in the OOD detection task as it reduces the false positive rate, ultimately enhancing the trustworthiness of the model, NCDD consistently achieves lower FPR95 in comparison to other SOTA methods and thus enhancing the trustworthiness of an AI-assisted procedure in gastrointestinal diagnosis.

Qualitative Results: The qualitative performance comparison of our proposed method with popular OOD methods as presented in Fig. 2, clearly demonstrates the superior robustness of NCDD against multiple OOD methods across different cases of abnormalities.

For instance, in the case of severe OOD examples like Polyps (POL), which pose significant classification challenges, NCDD exhibits remarkable accuracy. While methods like KNN-OOD and Neco often misclassify these complex cases as in-distribution, our method successfully identifies these samples as OOD. Since, esophagitis has complete feature overlap with z-line, all OOD methods fail in correctly classifying esophagitis as an OOD class.

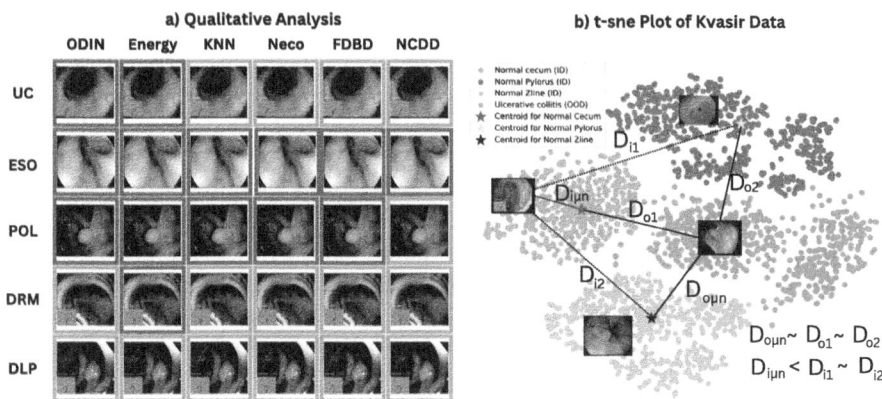

Fig. 2. a) Qualitative and comparison of NCDD with other state-of-the-art OOD methods using the Kvasirv2 dataset on small ViT model. Red frames highlight OOD examples that were incorrectly predicted as ID by OOD detection methods, while green frames indicate correctly detected OOD cases. **b)** t-SNE visualization of the feature space. In-distribution classes–z-line (pink), cecum (brown), and pylorus (magenta)– are clustered around their respective centroids, while the OOD class ulcerative colitis (orange) appears distant from all ID centroids.

Ablation Study: Ablation experiments were performed to assess the impact of different distance terms on out-of-distribution (OOD) score performance. As shown in Table 3 (left), incorporating both nearest and non-nearest centroid distances improves performance over using only the nearest centroid distance. However, optimal results are achieved by appropriately scaling both terms.

Table 3. *LEFT*: Significance of D_{μ_m} and D_{μ_n} for OOD scoring for Resnet-18 on Kvasirv2 dataset. *RIGHT*: Hyperparameter study for NCDD on Resnet-18 with synthetic validation OOD obtained from Kvasirv2 dataset following Hendrycks et al.

Distance Scores				Hyperparameter Study	
Distance	**Mean ID**	**Mean OOD**	**FPR↓**	**Value (α_1, α_2)**	**FPR↓**
				$-1, 1$	29.67
D_{μ_m}	5.82	5.36	33.60	$-1, 0$	**28.83**
$-D_{\mu_n}$	-0.16	-0.64	33.50	$1, 1$	29.00
$D_{\mu_m} - D_{\mu_n}$	5.66	4.72	32.42	$0, 0$	29.17
$\alpha \cdot D_{\mu_m} - \beta \cdot D_{\mu_n}$	47.95	40.01	**30.86**	$-2, 0$	29.67

5   Conclusion

Reformulating abnormality detection in gastrointestinal images as an OOD problem enables improved recognition of abnormalities in the GI tract through a model trained only on abundant normal anatomical landmark. We introduced a novel distance-based OOD detection method, Nearest Centroid Distant Deficit (NCDD), which utilizes the feature space distance of ID data in multi-class gastrointestinal image datasets and its relative positioning in feature space to discern them from OOD samples. NCDD outperforms the previous state-of-the-art OOD detection methods, evaluated through AUC and FPR95. Overall, we demonstrate the potential for supervised models on OOD detection as a general-purpose tool for flagging abnormalities in endoscopy images from gastrointestinal settings.

References

1. Almeida, S.D., et al.: cOOpD: reformulating COPD classification on chest CT scans as anomaly detection using contrastive representations. In: Medical Image Computing and Computer Assisted Intervention – MICCAI 2023 (2023)
2. Ammar, M.B., et al.: NECO: NEural collapse based out-of-distribution detection. In: The Twelfth International Conference on Learning Representations (2024)
3. Chan, R., et al.: Entropy maximization and meta classification for out-of-distribution detection in semantic segmentation. In: Proceedings of the IEEE/CVF International Conference on Computer Vision, pp. 5128–5137 (2021)
4. Chheda, T., et al.: Gastrointestinal tract anomaly detection from endoscopic videos using object detection approach. In: Advances in Visual Computing. Springer (2020)
5. Das, R., et al.: On the separability of classes with the cross-entropy loss function. arXiv preprint arXiv:1909.06930 (2019)
6. Dinari, O., et al.: Variational-and metric-based deep latent space for out-of-distribution detection. In: The 38th Conference on Uncertainty in Artificial Intelligence (2022)
7. Dosovitskiy, A., et al.: An image is worth 16×16 words: transformers for image recognition at scale. arXiv preprint arXiv:2010.11929 (2020)

8. Haile, M.B., et al.: Detection and classification of gastrointestinal disease using convolutional neural network and SVM. Cogent Eng. (2022)

9. He, K., et al.: Deep residual learning for image recognition. In: Proceedings of the IEEE Conference on Computer Vision and Pattern Recognition (2016)

10. Hendrycks, D., et al.: A baseline for detecting misclassified and out-of-distribution examples in neural networks. In: International Conference on Learning Representations (2017)

11. Hendrycks, D., et al.: Deep anomaly detection with outlier exposure. In: International Conference on Learning Representations (2019)

12. Hendrycks, D., et al.: Scaling out-of-distribution detection for real-world settings. arXiv preprint arXiv:1911.11132 (2019)

13. Hirasawa, T., et al.: Application of artificial intelligence using a convolutional neural network for detecting gastric cancer in endoscopic images. Gastric Cancer **21**(4), 653–660 (2018). https://doi.org/10.1007/s10120-018-0793-2

14. Jelenić, F., et al.: Out-of-Distribution detection by leveraging between-layer transformation smoothness. In: The Twelfth International Conference on Learning Representations (2024)

15. Jha, D., et al.: GastroVision: a multi-class endoscopy image dataset for computer aided gastrointestinal disease detection. In: Workshop on Machine Learning for Multimodal Healthcare Data, pp. 125–140. Springer (2023)

16. Koulaouzidis, A., et al.: How should we do colon capsule endoscopy reading: a practical guide. Therap. Adv. Gastrointest. Endosc. (2021)

17. Liang, S., et al.: Enhancing the reliability of out-of-distribution image detection in neural networks. In: International Conference on Learning Representations (2018)

18. Liu, L., et al.: Fast decision boundary based out-of-distribution detector. In: Forty-first International Conference on Machine Learning (2024)

19. Liu, W., et al.: Energy-based out-of-distribution detection. In: Advances in Neural Information Processing Systems, vol. 33, pp. 21464–21475 (2020)

20. Mehta, D., et al.: Out-of-distribution detection for long-tailed and fine-grained skin lesion images. In: Wang, L., Dou, Q., Fletcher, P.T., Speidel, S., Li, S. (eds.) Medical Image Computing and Computer Assisted Intervention – MICCAI 2022. Springer (2022)

21. Mishra, D., et al.: Dual conditioned diffusion models for out-of-distribution detection: application to fetal ultrasound videos. In: Greenspan, H., Madabhushi, A., Mousavi, P., Salcudean, S., Duncan, J., Syeda-Mahmood, T., Taylor, R. (eds.) Medical Image Computing and Computer Assisted Intervention – MICCAI 2023. Springer (2023)

22. Oukdach, Y., et al.: Gastrointestinal diseases classification based on deep learning and transfer learning mechanism. In: 2022 9th International Conference on Wireless Networks and Mobile Communications (WINCOM) (2022)

23. Pogorelov, K., et al.: KVASIR: a multi-class image dataset for computer aided gastrointestinal disease detection. In: Proceedings of the 8th ACM on Multimedia Systems Conference, pp. 164–169 (2017)

24. Pokhrel, S., et al.: TTA-OOD: test-time augmentation for improving out-of-distribution detection in gastrointestinal vision. In: MICCAI Workshop on Data Engineering in Medical Imaging. Springer (2024)

25. Quindós, A., et al.: Self-supervised out-of-distribution detection in wireless capsule endoscopy images. Artif. Intell. Med. **143**, 102606 (2023)

26. Sharma, A., et al.: Deep learning-based prediction model for diagnosing gastrointestinal diseases using endoscopy images. Int. J. Med. Inform. (2023)

27. Sharmila, V., et al.: Detection and classification of GI-tract anomalies from endo-scopic images using deep learning. In: 2022 IEEE 19th India Council International Conference (INDICON) (2022)

28. Sinhamahapatra, P., et al.: Is it all a cluster game?–exploring out-of-distribution detection based on clustering in the embedding space. arXiv preprint arXiv:2203.08549 (2022)

29. Sivari, E., et al.: A new approach for gastrointestinal tract findings detection and classification: deep learning-based hybrid stacking ensemble models. Diagnostics (2023)

30. Sun, Y., et al.: Out-of-distribution detection with deep nearest neighbors. In: Chaudhuri, K., Jegelka, S., Song, L., Szepesvari, C., Niu, G., Sabato, S. (eds.) Proceedings of the 39th International Conference on Machine Learning. Proceedings of Machine Learning Research. PMLR (2022)

31. Sundar, V.K., et al.: Out-of-distribution detection in multi-label datasets using latent space of β-VAE. In: 2020 IEEE Security and Privacy Workshops (SPW). IEEE (2020)

32. Tolstikhin, I.O., et al.: MLP-mixer: an all-MLP architecture for vision. In: Advances in Neural Information Processing Systems (2021)

33. Touvron, H., et al.: Training data-efficient image transformers & distillation through attention. In: International Conference on Machine Learning. PMLR (2021)

34. Wang, R., et al.: Global, regional, and national burden of 10 digestive diseases in 204 countries and territories from 1990 to 2019. Front. Public Health (2023)

35. Wang, Y., et al.: Global burden of digestive diseases: a systematic analysis of the global burden of diseases study, 1990 to 2019. Gastroenterology (2023)

36. Zadorozhny, K., Thoral, P., Elbers, P., Cinà, G.: Out-of-distribution detection for medical applications: guidelines for practical evaluation. In: Multimodal AI in Healthcare: A Paradigm Shift in Health Intelligence, pp. 137–153. Springer (2022)

37. Zhang, Z., et al.: Decoupling MaxLogit for out-of-distribution detection. In: Proceedings of the IEEE/CVF Conference on Computer Vision and Pattern Recognition (2023)

38. Zimmerer, D., et al.: MOOD 2020: a public benchmark for out-of-distribution detection and localization on medical images. IEEE Trans. Med. Imaging (2022)

Deep Learning-Driven Pipeline for Automated Wound Measurement of Chronic Wounds

Ana Filipa Sampaio, Rafaela Carvalho,
and Maria João M. Vasconcelos[✉]

Fraunhofer Portugal AICOS, Porto, Portugal
maria.vasconcelos@fraunhofer.pt

Abstract. Accurate wound size measurement is essential for effective chronic wound management, guiding clinical decisions and predicting treatment efficacy, yet it remains a challenge due to the high time required by the manual measurement process and its subpar reproducibility. This study presents an automated detection, segmentation and measurement pipeline for chronic wounds using computer vision and deep learning. The impact of dataset composition on deep learning-based open wound detection and segmentation is investigated, along with the comparison of three object detection architectures (RetinaNet with MobileNetV2 backbone, and CenterNet with ResNetV1 or MobileNetV2) and two segmentation networks (DeepLabV3+ with ResNet50 backbone, and UPerNet with Swin Transformer). For wound measurement, traditional computer vision methods were employed to estimate the wound's real-world width, height and area. Separate studies evaluated each task, followed by a complete pipeline assessment that couples the developed wound and reference marker detection model with the segmentation and measurement tasks. For wound and marker detection, the RetinaNet-MobileNetV2 achieved the best performance with mAP@.75IoU of 64.67% and 95.44%, respectively. The DeepLabV3-ResNet50 trained with all datasets achieved the best results in wound segmentation, with a Dice score of 89.83% following the complete pipeline, and a mean relative error of 16.09% for area estimation, surpassing the literature results. With the integration of the proposed pipeline in a smartphone application, this research aims to deliver a reliable wound measurement tool, empowering clinicians with accurate and objective data for improved treatment planning and enhanced patient outcomes in chronic wound care.

Keywords: Chronic wounds · Wound measurement · Object detection · Image segmentation · Deep Learning · Telemedicine

1 Introduction

Chronic wounds have a major impact on the patients' life quality. The increasingly ageing population, along with the high prevalence of lifestyle-related comorbidities, make chronic wounds a growing issue, associated with considerable costs

© The Author(s), under exclusive license to Springer Nature Switzerland AG 2026
S. Ali et al. (Eds.): MIUA 2025, LNCS 15917, pp. 201–215, 2026.
https://doi.org/10.1007/978-3-031-98691-8_15

for healthcare systems worldwide [12]. Rigorous monitoring is essential to track wound healing evolution and ensure the efficacy of the applied treatment options [14]. Wound monitoring involves the assessment of wound properties, including the wound bed composition, the wound dimensions and the presence of complications. In particular, the measurement of wound dimensions provides key information to track its evolution [8], as wounds healing properly are expected to show a reduction of size over time. However, the manually registered measurements present low reproducibility and are prone to over-estimation [1].

Digital health solutions for wound monitoring automation have emerged in the past years as a way to address these issues. Smartphone applications based on RGB imaging have great potential to streamline the wound assessment process [9], combining increased accuracy with affordability and ease of use [13]. These solutions rely on image analysis and artificial intelligence algorithms to automate the extraction of wound measurements from images, by combining open wound identification with a metric calibration to obtain wound dimensions in real-world units [8]. To first obtain a identification of the wound, most studies apply deep learning object detection models, ranging from heavier architectures, such as Faster R-CNN, to more lightweight models, as YOLO, EfficientDet and RetinaNet [2,4,24]. Nonetheless, optimal wound detection architecture varies with dataset and evaluation metrics.

For refined wound contour delineation, deep learning segmentation models have dominated most research lines [21] in the past years, replacing traditional computer vision techniques [7]. Multiple Convolutional Neural Network (CNN) models are compared in [27], with a MobileNetV2 network achieving the best results. Some of the most recent works explored the application of transformer-based architectures, like HardNet [15] or SegFormer [3]. Despite the promising wound segmentation performances reported, many of the published studies are hard to compare due to the usage of private datasets [3], and even the ones that resort to public datasets may lack generalisability given their focus on a single wound type or reliance on images from a single centre [15,27].

From all the works addressing wound segmentation, only a limited number use the obtained outline to extract relevant wound measurements (length, width and area) [8]. The framework from [5] uses a multi-coloured ruler as a metric reference and reports a mean relative error (MRE) of 24.5% when evaluating the proposed method's effectiveness in calculating open wound area, using a semi-automatic method. The work of [17] reports 26.2% MRE for wound area measurement using automatically predicted masks when compared with the traditional manual method. In [9], a clinical study evaluated the performance of a commercial solution, Tissue Analytics, in real-world settings, reporting inter-rater reliability values between the estimated and the nurses' measurements in the 79.9–91.9% range for the length, width and area of venous leg ulcers.

Despite the potential for the automation of wound measurement demonstrated by these approaches, the limitations of most studies, i.e., the restricted wound etiologies included and reliance on single-centre data, do not take into account the variability of wound properties (size, shape, edge type, skin phototype, among others) encountered in clinical environments [21]. To address these shortcomings, the present work builds upon our framework from [3] and leverages data from new private datasets from several clinical institutions to introduce diversity into the development and evaluation data. Besides using these datasets to develop the two models that compose the wound measurement pipeline's main steps - object detection and semantic segmentation - the usage of different architectures and hyperparameters for the models was also studied. The complete pipeline was integrated into a smartphone application and its measurement performance was analysed not only overall, but also for different wound sizes, to characterise its robustness under different conditions and highlight its main limitations.

2   Methodology

The automated wound assessment pipeline designed to tackle the inherent challenges and variability of clinical chronic wound monitoring is represented in Fig. 1. It comprises three primary tasks: (i) wound and reference marker detection, (ii) wound segmentation, and (iii) wound measurement.

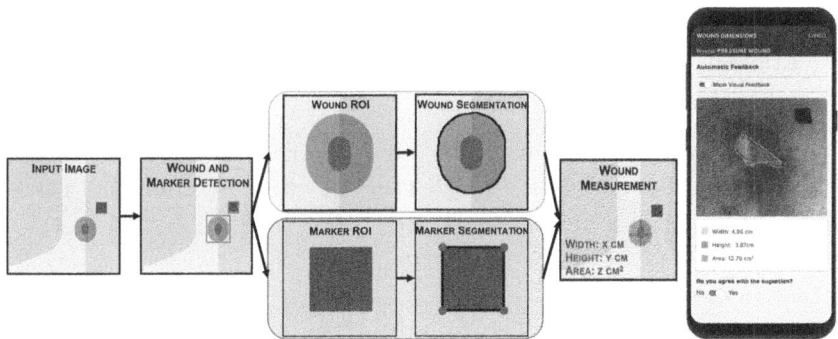

Fig. 1. Overview of the proposed wound assessment pipeline and an example of a screen of the mobile application.

The first stage detects both the wound and a reference marker to define distinct regions of interest (ROIs). The obtained ROIs are then used as input to obtain a fine-grained delineation of the open wound and marker regions, resorting to a deep learning segmentation model and a thresholding-based approach, respectively. The resulting segmentation masks are used to determine wound dimensions (height, width, area), with the marker providing metric calibration.

The presented methodology focused on the development of robust detection and segmentation models, to achieve superior measurement results, and on the integration of the measurement pipeline in a mobile framework to support healthcare professionals. The final smartphone application (Fig. 1) streamlines different steps of the wound monitoring process, leveraging the developed models to guide the image acquisition process (detection) through the usage of the detected ROIs to ensure image adequacy, and to automate the measurement of the wound's dimensions.

3 Experiments

The establishment of the proposed framework involved the development and optimisation of the algorithms that integrate its different modules. This section provides details on the experiments conducted to optimise each algorithm, which were executed on a workstation with four NVIDIA Tesla A100 and V100 GPUs.

3.1 Datasets

In this work, three datasets (Wounds, Wounds Pilot and External), with distinct characteristics, were used for training and testing the different tasks (Table 1).

Table 1. Distribution of the Wound (W), Wounds Pilot (WP) and External (E) datasets per etiology (left) and phototype (right). E has no phototype data.

Etiology	Train Set			Test Set			Total	Type	Train Set		Test Set		Total
	W	WP	E	W	WP	E			W	WP	W	WP	
Pressure	125	87	68	38	25	17	360	I	5	19	4	7	35
Leg Venous	57	28	112	10	4	28	239	II	110	69	39	16	234
Leg Arterial	0	2	2	9	3	1	17	III	94	29	19	12	154
Leg Mixed	5	6	23	2	4	4	44	IV	10	22	5	5	42
Leg Unknown	15	4	-	3	2	-	24	V	5	3	4	5	17
Diabetic Foot	11	4	5	7	4	1	32	VI	-	8	6	2	16
Arterial	9	4	-	2	0	-	15	NA	4	-	1	-	4
Others	6	15	-	7	5	-	33						
Total	228	150	210	78	47	51	764	**Total**	228	150	78	47	503

The first dataset, Wounds (W), previously used for open wound detection [22] and segmentation [3] tasks, consists of 306 images from 103 wounds. The images were collected from nine institutions (from Rehabilitation and Care Units, Primary Health Care, Hospital and Home Care consultations), to ensure a comprehensive representation of wound characteristics encountered in clinical practice. The second dataset, Wounds Pilot (WP), was collected through a clinical pilot study with the aim of validating the previously developed detection and segmentation models. This dataset comprises 197 wound images obtained from ten institutions of the same typologies. An external third-party private dataset (E)

[26], with 261 images acquired in Primary Care Units and Home Care consultations, was also incorporated into this study, to augment and enhance variability in clinical wound representations in venous, arterial and mixed leg ulcers.

The datasets encompass a diverse range of wound types (see Table 1), including pressure ulcers (categories 1–4), diabetic foot ulcers, arterial ulcers, leg ulcers (arterial, venous, mixed or of unknown etiology) and others (e.g., surgical wounds). Pressure ulcers constitute nearly half of the images across all datasets, and venous leg ulcers account for over 30%, primarily due to their important representation in the E dataset. Conversely, arterial ulcers are under-represented. Across all datasets, all skin phototypes are present, with lower phototypes (I, II and III) predominating, constituting 84% of images with known prototypes; however, phototypes V and VI constitute only 7%. Dataset W exhibits a lower representation of phototypes IV, V and VI (around 10% of images) compared to dataset WP, which shows a more balanced distribution with approximately 23%. Phototype and measurement descriptions are absent from the E dataset. In terms of dimensions, wound areas in the W dataset range from 0.01 to 114.68 cm^2, with a mean of 10.05 ± 16.23 cm^2. The WP dataset exhibits a smaller range (0.03–98.14 cm^2), but with a slightly higher mean area (11.94 ± 18.82 cm^2). Wound widths (W: 2.88 ± 2.19 cm, WP: 2.99 ± 2.57 cm) and heights (W: 3.29 ± 2.87 cm, WP: 3.72 ± 3.38 cm) are comparable across datasets.

For the acquisition of the previous datasets, study protocols were submitted and approved by the Health Ethical Committees for data acquisition, and informed consent was obtained from both healthcare professionals and patients. All experiments were performed in accordance with relevant guidelines and regulations. Both the Wounds and Wounds Pilot datasets include wound images with $4\,cm^2$ reference markers of different colours (blue, green, yellow and white). The resulting images were annotated in terms of open wound and marker boundaries by three specialists in wound care (nurses with different years of experience), each responsible for a distinct subset of wound images.

3.2   Wound and Marker Detection

The detection module takes advantage of a CNN-based object detection model that identifies the bounding box location of the wound and marker regions.

Implementation Details. The development of the detection model resorted to a hyperparameter optimisation process based on a random search strategy and within a stratified 3-fold cross-validation scheme. Three model architectures of varying complexity levels from the Tensorflow Object Detection API [11] (TensorFlow 2) were selected: RetinaNet + MobileNetV2 [16,23]; CenterNet + ResNetV1; and CenterNet + MobileNetV2 [6,10]. This selection was based not only on their detection performance but also on the easy conversion to mobile-compatible formats and efficient execution in resource-constrained scenarios, given the need for real-time inference on mobile devices. In the hyperparameter tuning step, five combinations of batch sizes (8 or 16) and learning rates (sampled from the logarithmic range 10^{-6} to 10^{-2}) were tested; the input image size was fixed at 512×512 pixels. The two best models were then re-trained on the whole training set and converted to TensorFlow Lite (TFLite) for mobile deployment. The Wounds and Wounds Pilot datasets were used for training and validation, as they were the only ones containing the necessary reference markers. For testing, both W+WP and W+WP+E datasets were employed to evaluate model performance under conditions similar to the final deployment environment and to analyse generalization across diverse acquisition settings.

Post-processing. The final models' predictions were submitted to an adjusted non-maximum suppression (NMS) step, considering fixed values for the minimum IoU threshold (0.50) and maximum number of detections per class (1), and adjusting the maximum number of detections per image and the minimum score threshold based on the results (see Sect. 4).

Evaluation Metrics. The wound and marker detection model was evaluated using mean Average Precision (mAP) and Average Recall (AR). Specifically, mAP was calculated at Intersection over Union (IoU) thresholds of 0.50 and 0.75, while AR was computed with a maximum of 10 detections. Emphasis was placed on mAP@.75IoU, as this higher IoU threshold better reflects the model's accuracy in delineating precise regions of interest. The final model comparison was also based on the False Positives (FP) and False Negatives (FN), as well as the inference time of the models, in milliseconds (ms).

3.3 Open Wound Segmentation

Pre-processing. For standardization of the input images for the segmentation module, a cropping procedure to isolate the wound ROI was implemented. For the development of the open wound segmentation model, the wound ROI was first extracted using bounding boxes derived from ground-truth (GT) segmentation masks. During the execution of the proposed pipeline, ROI identification is achieved through the wound and marker detection model presented in Sect. 3.2. After finding the wound ROI, a padding margin was applied to preserve the periwound area. For images containing a reference marker (Wounds and Wounds Pilot datasets), the margin was set to 25% of the marker's longest side; on the other hand, for images without a marker (External dataset), a 15% padding margin relative to the wound's bounding box size was used. The resulting padded region defined the final ROI, which was subsequently cropped and resized to a uniform square dimension of 320×320 pixels.

Implementation Details. Segmentation model training employed a stratified 3-fold cross-validation framework with random hyperparameter search. Two segmentation architectures, UPerNet with a Swin Transformer backbone (UPerNet-Swin) and DeepLabV3+ with a ResNet50 backbone (DeepLabV3-R50) pretrained on ImageNet, were evaluated at input resolutions of 320×320 and

384×384 pixels. The search space encompassed learning rates (LR) sampled logarithmically from 10^{-5} to 10^{-3}, Adam and AdamW optimizers, and batch sizes of 8 and 16, with five random hyperparameter combinations tested. For loss functions, DeepLabV3-R50 was trained using a 1:1 weighted sum of Dice loss and cross-entropy, while UPerNet-Swin was optimized using cross-entropy loss. Training was performed for a maximum of 200 epochs, with early stopping triggered after 10 consecutive runs without Dice improvement. The implementation used the MMSegmentation v1.2.1 [19] framework (PyTorch v1.13.1+cu116).

Post-processing. To refine the model-generated outputs and enhance segmentation accuracy, hole filling and small region removal were applied to the predicted masks. Finally, the largest connected component was selected, ensuring only a single wound was considered per detection.

Ablation Study. To assess the influence of dataset composition on wound segmentation performance, different dataset combinations were evaluated: Wounds + Wounds Pilot (W+WP), Wounds + Wounds Pilot + External (W+ WP+E), and a two-stage training paradigm involving pre-training on the External dataset followed by fine-tuning on Wounds + Wounds Pilot (E → W+WP).

Evaluation Metrics. Accuracy (Acc), IoU and Dice coefficient were computed for evaluation of the segmentation performance, with Dice as the principal metric due to its balanced measure of precision and recall.

3.4   Wound Measurement

Implementation Details. Wound dimensions (height, width, area), derived from open wound segmentation masks, were converted to real-world units using a pixel-to-centimetre conversion factor determined from a reference marker of known dimensions. Marker segmentation utilised the HSV colour space for green, yellow and blue markers, with greyscale employed for white markers. Threshold values, empirically determined through histogram analysis, were applied to each colour channel. Marker vertices were then identified by approximating the segmented region's contour to a convex polygon. Only images yielding four detected vertices advanced for wound measurement. To correct for potential marker distortion, the average marker edge length (pixels) was utilised for width and height conversion. Wound area conversion was achieved by calculating the ratio of the marker's segmented area (pixels) to its known area ($4 \, cm^2$).

Evaluation Metrics. For evaluation of the estimated measurements, we employed Mean Relative Error (MRE), Mean Absolute Error (MAE) and the Shrout and Fleiss intraclass correlation coefficient (ICC) [25]. The Bland-Altman plot for the area was also generated to evaluate the agreement of GT and model measurements and analyse possible bias.

4   Results and Discussion

4.1   Wound and Marker Detection

Hyperparameter tuning determined optimal batch size and learning rate combinations for each detection model, yielding average cross-validation metrics. The mAP@.75IoU/AR@10 (%) for the open wound class were of $59.75 \pm 1.73/57.83 \pm 1.19$ for RetinaNet + MobileNetV2 (Ret-M2), $61.67 \pm 4.17/61.36 \pm 2.20$ for CenterNet + ResNetV1 (CentN-R1) and $56.03 \pm 0.55/56.16 \pm 0.81$ for CenterNet + MobileNetV2 (CentN-M2). A higher emphasis was attributed to the open wound metrics because overall the trained models exhibited good mAP@.75IoU/AR@10 values for the marker class, with cross-validation averages above 96.00/86.00%. Given their superior detection sensitivity (AR@10) and accuracy (mAP@.75IoU), Ret-M2 and CentN-R1 models were re-trained on the whole training set with optimal hyperparameters (batch size of 8 and LR of $2.00e^{-4}$ for Ret-M2, and 16 and $4.00e^{-4}$ for CentN-R1). Their post-retraining, TFLite-converted, and post-processed results are presented in Table 2.

To minimise the models' number of FPs and FNs, the minimum score threshold and the maximum number of total detections used in the NMS step were adjusted to the final values of 0.1 and 20, correspondingly. As expected, both models exhibited a lower performance for the W+WP+E test set, due to the inclusion of images from less standardised acquisition conditions, with a high number of images with missed wounds (FNs) in comparison with the one reported in the W+WP test set. The majority of marker FPs originated from the E dataset, which does not include square markers but contains unannotated reference rulers which were mistaken for markers. Nevertheless, both models exhibited satisfactory and robust detection performance on the extended W+WP+E test set, attesting to their robustness under varying conditions.

Table 2. Test results of the analysed models after conversion to TFLite and application of NMS post-processing, for the wound (W) and marker (M) classes. The results were extracted on a server with two AMD EPYC^{tm} 7713P Processors.

Test set	Model	mAP@.75IoU		AR@10		Img FP		Img FN		Inf. Time	
		W	M	W	M	W	M	W	M	Max	Avg
W+WP	CentN-R1	61.03	95.67	**62.90**	91.00	1	1	7	4	1.56	1.46
	Ret-M2	**64.67**	95.44	60.65	92.25	0	1	**5**	1	**0.20**	**0.12**
W+WP+E	CentN-R1	55.96	95.23	**58.63**	91.00	2	8	22	4	1.71	1.46
	Ret-M2	**59.01**	95.44	57.26	92.25	1	25	**12**	1	**0.22**	**0.12**

Comparing the performance of the two models for the open wound class, an identical tendency can be observed for the two test sets, with the Ret-M2 model outperforming the CentN-R1 in terms of mAP@.75IoU, FPs and FNs. Although the CentN-R1 model achieved slightly higher AR@10 values, which could indicate a higher sensitivity to wound regions, the analysis of the FNs shows that it missed the detection of more wound regions than Ret-M2. This undesirable behaviour, in combination with the much higher inference times exhibited by CentN-R1, motivated the selection of Ret-M2 as the final model to be included in the smartphone application. The final Ret-M2 was integrated into a smartphone application and its mobile inference times were evaluated in two smartphones - Pixel 8a and Samsung A25. It achieved average/maximum ROI detection times of 167/ 287 and 175/214 ms, respectively, demonstrating its ability to perform wound and marker detection in real time while maintaining a responsive application.

Comparison with Literature. Even though the present study resorts to the mAP@.75IoU metric, most of the literature studies report wound detection performance for mAP@.50IoU. In terms of this metric, the proposed Ret-M2 model achieved values of 81.30% and 78.64% for the W+WP and W+WP+E test sets. Notwithstanding the difficulty in comparing directly these results with the other approaches reported in the literature, due to the usage of different datasets, it is possible to verify that it surpasses the detection performance reported for the same model architecture on a smaller dataset of similar composition (66.58%) [22], as well as the benchmark reported for diabetic foot ulcer images on the DFUC 2020 dataset using a Faster R-CNN model (65.96%) [4] and more recently achieved on that dataset by an identical architecture RetinaNet with a MobileNet backbone (76.20%) [24]. Still, it could not attain the mAP@.50IoU of 93.90 presented by a YOLO-v3 model on the AZH Wound Localisation database [2], composed by diabetic foot, pressure and venous ulcers.

4.2   Open Wound Segmentation

Hyperparameter Tuning. For each dataset combination, the optimal architecture, input size and hyperparameters were determined based on average cross-validation Dice performance. Table 3 details the optimal hyperparameters and corresponding cross-validation Dice for each dataset combination and for the two architectures evaluated: DeepLabV3-R50 and UPerNet-Swin. As UPerNet-Swin consistently underperformed DeepLabV3-R50 across all combinations, we excluded this architecture from further training on the full dataset.

Ablation Study. A comparative analysis of segmentation results for different dataset combinations, trained with optimal configurations detailed in Table 3, is presented in Table 4. This analysis investigates the influence of dataset composition (refer to Sect. 3.3) on segmentation performance across two test sets.

Across all test sets, the model trained on the combined dataset (W+WP+E) outperformed the other configurations, being consistent with cross-validation results. This superior performance is likely due to the increased dataset size and diversity, enhancing the model's generalization across varied wound characteristics and imaging conditions. Furthermore, the inclusion of the External

Table 3. Optimal hyperparameters and cross-validation performance for each dataset combination.

Dataset Combination	Model	Input	Batch	LR	Optimizer	Dice
		Hyperparameters				Metrics
W+WP	DeepLabV3-R50	320	16	1.31e-04	Adam	90.04 ± 0.54
	UPerNet-Swin	384	8	1.57e-04	AdamW	86.36 ± 1.45
W+WP+E	DeepLabV3-R50	320	16	3.03e-04	Adam	90.41 ± 0.15
	UPerNet-Swin	320	8	4.19e-05	Adam	86.75 ± 0.23
E → W+WP	DeepLabV3-R50	384	16	2.18e-04	AdamW	89.90 ± 0.60

Table 4. GT open wound segmentation results on W+WP and W+WP+E test sets, pre-processed with GT wound/marker ROIs and post-processed.

Model Architecture	Dataset Combination	W+WP			W+WP+E		
		Acc	IoU	Dice	Acc	IoU	Dice
	W+WP	91.38	83.50	91.01	90.01	80.77	89.36
DeepLabV3-R50	W+WP+E	92.01	**84.15**	**91.39**	91.19	**82.46**	**90.39**
	E → W+WP	**92.97**	83.11	90.78	**92.17**	80.82	89.39

dataset, which primarily features venous leg ulcers, pressure ulcers, and diabetic foot ulcers, introduces valuable clinical variability, enhancing the model's ability to handle a broader spectrum of real-world scenarios. Dice scores consistently exceeded 90% in open wound segmentation, demonstrating high contour delineation accuracy which is crucial for reliable measurement and monitoring.

Comparison with Literature. Although test sets vary across studies, our best method (DeepLabV3-R50 trained on W+WP+E) achieves comparable (Dice score around 90% [5,27]) or superior (Dice score of 85% [17]) segmentation results to those reported in the literature [17,18], outperforming all but Ramachandram et al. [20], who achieved a mIoU of 86.44% using the Swift app.

4.3 Wound Assessment Pipeline

From the 125 images in the W+WP test set, 119 were used for segmentation evaluation (Table 5) after removing images with no detected wounds. For measurement analysis (Table 6), 97 images were used, excluding those with undetected markers, incomplete marker contours (less than four vertices), and outliers (9 images) with unreliable area errors. The E dataset was not included in this evaluation due to the absence of reference markers needed for measurement.

Regarding wound segmentation (Table 5), the model trained on W+WP+E dataset also achieved the highest performance. The proposed pipeline demonstrated notable robustness, with only minor reductions in segmentation performance (below 1.6% in Dice) compared to the results outlined in Table 4.

Table 5. Pipeline open wound segmentation results on W+WP and W+WP+E test sets, pre-processed with detected wound/marker ROIs and post-processed.

Model Architecture	Dataset Combination	W+WP			W+WP+E		
		Acc	IoU	Dice	Acc	IoU	Dice
	W+WP	90.19	80.98	89.49	90.28	78.86	88.18
DeepLabV3-R50	W+WP+E	90.70	**81.54**	**89.83**	90.0	**80.54**	**89.22**
	E → W+WP	**91.72**	81.36	89.72	**91.20**	79.57	88.62

Table 6. Wound measurement results using the proposed pipeline on the test set of the W+WP dataset with predicted masks of DeepLabV3-R50 trained on W+WP+E dataset.

	Width	Height	Area
MRE (%)	9.75 ± 11.74	9.61 ± 10.55	16.09 ± 17.99
MAE (cm)	0.27 ± 0.42	0.38 ± 0.61	1.71 ± 3.62
ICC	0.983	0.973	0.980

For wound measurement (Table 6), the final model yielded mean relative errors of 10% for width and height, and 16% for area, and mean absolute errors of 0.3–0.4 cm for width and height, and $1.71\,cm^2$ for the predicted wound area. The agreement between annotations and model predictions, as measured by ICC, is excellent, exceeding 0.97 for all dimensions.

Figure 2 presents the Bland-Altman plot for area agreement between GT and the final pipeline predictions, indicating that errors are low and stable independently of the wound size. A detailed analysis of the area errors by wound size (Table 7) shows mean relative errors between 10% and 15% for wounds larger than $1\,cm^2$, with higher relative errors for wounds smaller than $1\,cm^2$. The increased error for smaller wounds may possibly be attributed to the inherent challenges of segmenting small objects with limited pixel representation. Furthermore, Fig. 3 highlights examples of the outliers not considered for the measurement results (first row), along with correct and incorrect examples of wound estimations (second and third rows, respectively). Some examples of outliers include cases where the marker is wrongly identified due to incorrect placement (first example), and samples where the wound borders appear to be healed, leading to the model overestimating areas (second and last examples). The second row details accurate predictions across wounds of varying sizes, etiologies, and phototypes, demonstrating the robustness of the proposed pipeline. Finally, we also portray incorrect wound estimations, attributed to marker segmentation errors (first, second and last cases) and incorrect open wound segmentation (first, third and last cases). Notably, incorrect marker estimations only occurred in 17 out of the 97 analysed images.

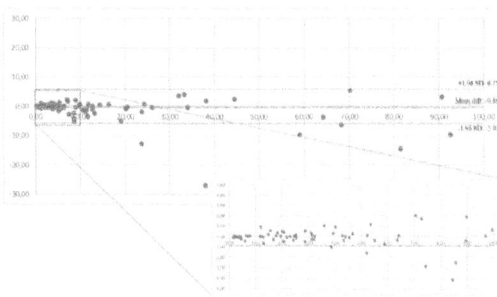

Table 7. Wound area measurement results distributed per wound size using the pipeline for the W+WP test set.

Size	N	MRE	MAE
<0.5	9	21.59 ± 19.51	0.06 ± 0.03
0.5 to 1	6	43.03 ± 40.61	0.31 ± 0.30
1 to 3	21	14.24 ± 12.52	0.26 ± 0.20
3 to 5	15	11.73 ± 10.35	0.44 ± 0.39
5 to 10	14	14.84 ± 12.10	1.10 ± 0.93
10 to 20	12	15.46 ± 13.91	1.86 ± 1.55
20 to 40	11	10.38 ± 11.92	2.88 ± 3.47
> 40	9	13.93 ± 14.19	9.08 ± 7.30

Fig. 2. Bland-Altman plot of area agreement between GT and final model prediction (x axis is the mean area and y axis the difference between the predicted and actual GT wound area).

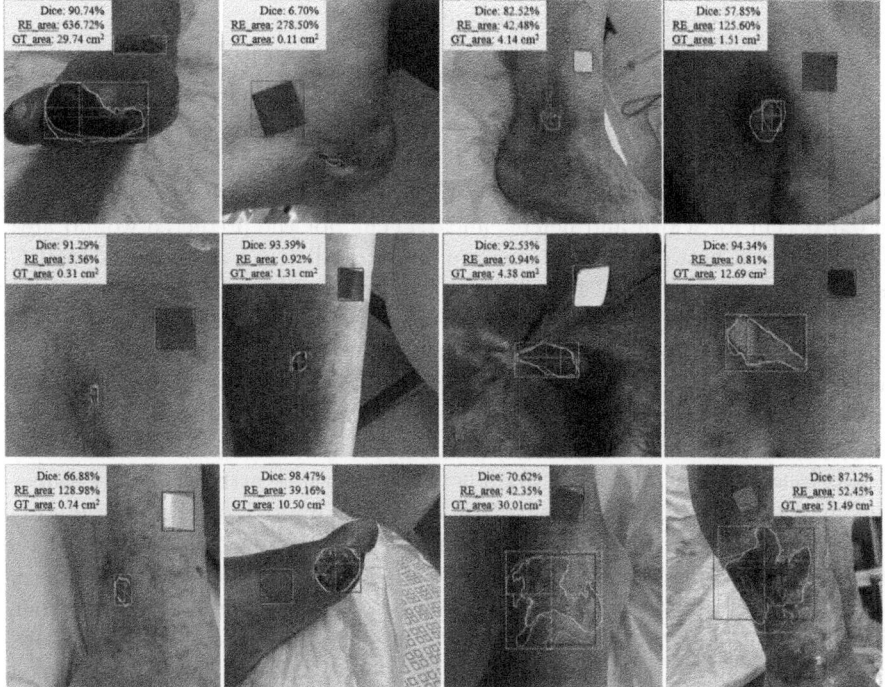

Fig. 3. Examples of outliers removed from the dimension estimation results, correct and incorrect wound estimations (first, second and third rows). Detection BBs of the wound and marker: GT and predicted (cyan/blue); Mask contours: GT and predicted (green/yellow); Dimensions: GT and predicted (orange/red); and predicted marker corners (red). (Color figure online)

Comparison with Literature. Despite comparisons being made across different datasets, our method outperforms the methods presented in [5] using a semi-automatic approach and [17], where MRE of 24.5% and 26.2% were reported, demonstrating the effectiveness of our fully automated approach in assessing the dimensions of wounds. It also surpasses the results of our previous work [3], achieving better mean relative and absolute error values for width, height, and area and also lower standard deviation values for these metrics. The ICC obtained for width, height and area between wound experts and our pipeline was excellent (above 0.97), higher than the Tissue Analytics [9] results, although not directly comparable due to different comparison methods of ground truth. Despite using far more test cases (around 350 wounds), the referred study focuses only on venous leg ulcers, while ours includes wounds from different etiologies.

5   Conclusions and Future Work

This study developed a deep learning-driven pipeline for automated wound measurement, incorporating wound and reference marker detection, wound segmentation, and precise dimension extraction. By experimenting with different state-of-the-art architectures and dataset combinations from three private datasets, the feasibility of robust wound measurement is attested. The best-performing wound and marker detection model was the RetinaNet with MobileNetV2 backbone, which achieved mAP@.75IoU values of 64.67% for the wound and 95.44% for the marker on the W+WP test set. The DeepLabV3+ with ResNet50 backbone yielded the highest segmentation accuracy, with Dice of 89.83%, within the complete pipeline. Dimension estimation using predicted wound masks and segmented markers achieved MRE below 10% and MAE below 0.40cm for width and height, and 16.09% and 1.71 cm^2 for area. Notably, smaller wounds presented higher relative errors in area measurement, however decreasing to a MRE of 13.51% when considering only wounds bigger than 1 cm^2. Moreover, the reliability of these predictions is excellent, as shown by the ICC values above 0.970.

The developed pipeline, in particular its integration into a mobile application, has the potential to streamline wound assessment processes and improve clinical decision-making. By providing clinicians with accurate and objective wound measurements, enabling more effective healing monitoring. Future work will focus on reproducibility studies and pilot testing in real-world settings to validate the pipeline's clinical utility. To further improve the pipeline's measurement capability, marker segmentation will be a primary focus in future developments.

Acknowledgments. This work is under the scope of HfPT, funded by IAPMEI with reference 41, co-financed by Component 5 - Capitalization and Business Innovation, integrated in the Resilience Dimension of the Recovery and Resilience Plan in the scope of the Recovery and Resilience Mechanism (MRR) of the European Union (EU), framed in the Next Generation EU, for the period 2021–2026. The authors thank Paula Teixeira from Unidade Local de Saúde de Matosinhos for sharing the External dataset. The authors thank Raquel Marques from Universidade Católica Portuguesa, Paula Teixeira and Paulo Ramos for their collaboration in the data annotation process.

Disclosure of Interests. The authors have no competing interests to declare that are relevant to the content of this article.

References

1. Alonso, M.C., Mohammed, H.T., Fraser, R.D., JL, R.G.L., Mannion, D.: Comparison of wound surface area measurements obtained using clinically validated artificial intelligence-based technology versus manual methods and the effect of measurement method on debridement code reimbursement cost. Wounds: Compendium Clin. Res. Pract. **35**(10), E330–E338 (2023)
2. Anisuzzaman, D., Patel, Y., Niezgoda, J.A., Gopalakrishnan, S., Yu, Z.: A mobile app for wound localization using deep learning. IEEE Access **10**, 61398–61409 (2022)
3. Carvalho, R., Morgado, A.C., Sampaio, A.F., Vasconcelos, M.J.: Exploring CNN and transformer-based architectures to improve image segmentation for chronic wound measurement. In: International Workshop on Applications of Medical AI, pp. 1–10. Springer (2024)
4. Cassidy, B., et al.: The DFUC 2020 dataset: analysis towards diabetic foot ulcer detection. touchREVIEWS Endocrinol. **17**(1), 5 (2021)
5. Chino, D.Y., Scabora, L.C., Cazzolato, M.T., Jorge, A.E., Traina-Jr, C., Traina, A.J.: Segmenting skin ulcers and measuring the wound area using deep convolutional networks. Comput. Methods Program. Biomed. **191**, 105376 (2020)
6. Duan, K., Bai, S., Xie, L., Qi, H., Huang, Q., Tian, Q.: CenterNet: keypoint triplets for object detection. In: Proceedings of the IEEE/CVF International Conference on Computer Vision, pp. 6569–6578 (2019)
7. Fauzi, M., Khansa, I., Catignani, K., Gordillo, G., Sen, C.K., Gurcan, M.N.: Segmentation and management of chronic wound images: a computer-based approach. In: Chronic Wounds, Wound Dressings and Wound Healing, pp. 115–134 (2021)
8. Foltynski, P., Ciechanowska, A., Ladyzynski, P.: Wound surface area measurement methods. Biocybern. Biomed. Eng. **41**(4), 1454–1465 (2021)
9. Fong, K.Y., et al.: Clinical validation of a smartphone application for automated wound measurement in patients with venous leg ulcers. Int. Wound J. **20**(3), 751–760 (2023)
10. He, K., Zhang, X., Ren, S., Sun, J.: Deep residual learning for image recognition. In: Proceedings of the IEEE Conference on Computer Vision and Pattern Recognition, pp. 770–778 (2016)
11. Huang, J., et al.: Speed/accuracy trade-offs for modern convolutional object detectors. In: Proceedings of the IEEE Conference on Computer Vision and Pattern Recognition, pp. 7310–7311 (2017)
12. Järbrink, K., et al.: The humanistic and economic burden of chronic wounds: a protocol for a systematic review. Syst. Rev. **6**, 1–7 (2017)
13. Kivity, S., et al.: Optimising wound monitoring: can digital tools improve healing outcomes and clinic efficiency. J. Clin. Nurs. **33**(10), 4014–4023 (2024)
14. Le, D.T., Pham, T.D.: Unveiling the role of artificial intelligence for wound assessment and wound healing prediction. Explor. Med. **4**(4), 589–611 (2023)
15. Liao, T.Y., Yang, C.H., Lo, Y.W., Lai, K.Y., Shen, P.H., Lin, Y.L.: HarDNet-DFUS: enhancing backbone and decoder of HarDNet-MSEG for diabetic foot ulcer image segmentation. In: Diabetic Foot Ulcers Grand Challenge, pp. 21–30. Springer (2022)
16. Lin, T.Y., Goyal, P., Girshick, R., He, K., Dollár, P.: Focal loss for dense object detection. In: Proceedings of the IEEE International Conference on Computer Vision, pp. 2980–2988 (2017)

17. Liu, T.J., Wang, H., Christian, M., Chang, C.W., Lai, F., Tai, H.C.: Automatic segmentation and measurement of pressure injuries using deep learning models and a lidar camera. Sci. Rep. **13**(1), 680 (2023). https://doi.org/10.1038/s41598-022-26812-9

18. Mahbod, A., Schaefer, G., Ecker, R., Ellinger, I.: Automatic foot ulcer segmentation using an ensemble of convolutional neural networks. In: 2022 26th International Conference on Pattern Recognition (ICPR), pp. 4358–4364 (2022). https://doi.org/10.1109/ICPR56361.2022.9956253

19. MMSegmentation Contributors: OpenMMLab Semantic Segmentation Toolbox and Benchmark (2020). https://github.com/open-mmlab/mmsegmentation

20. Ramachandram, D., Ramirez-GarciaLuna, J.L., Fraser, R., Martínez-Jiménez, M.A., Arriaga-Caballero, J.E., Allport, J.: Fully automated wound tissue segmentation using deep learning on mobile devices: Cohort study. JMIR Mhealth Uhealth **10**(4), e36977 (2022). https://doi.org/10.2196/36977

21. Reifs Jiménez, D., Casanova-Lozano, L., Grau-Carrión, S., Reig-Bolaño, R.: Artificial intelligence methods for diagnostic and decision-making assistance in chronic wounds: a systematic review. J. Med. Syst. **49**(1), 1–39 (2025)

22. Sampaio, A.F., et al.: Leveraging deep neural networks for automatic and standardised wound image acquisition. In: 9th International Conference on Information and Communication Technologies for Ageing Well and e-Health, pp. 253–261 (2023)

23. Sandler, M., Howard, A., Zhu, M., Zhmoginov, A., Chen, L.C.: MobileNetv2: inverted residuals and linear bottlenecks. In: Proceedings of the IEEE Conference on Computer Vision and Pattern Recognition, pp. 4510–4520 (2018)

24. Scebba, G., et al.: Detect-and-segment: a deep learning approach to automate wound image segmentation. Inform. Med. Unlock. **29**, 100884 (2022)

25. Shrout, P.E., Fleiss, J.L.: Intraclass correlations: uses in assessing rater reliability. Psychol. Bull. **86**(2), 420 (1979)

26. Teixeira, P.: Conjuntos de Imagens para Sistemas de Avaliação de Feridas Crónicas/Image sets for chronic wound assessment systems. Master's thesis, Master's in Medical Informatics, Faculty of Medicine of the University of Porto (2000)

27. Wang, C., et al.: Fully automatic wound segmentation with deep convolutional neural networks. Sci. Rep. **10**(1), 21897 (2020)

Midline-Constrained Loss in the Anatomical Landmark Segmentation of 3D Liver Models

Abdul Karim Abbas⬤, Aodhan Gallagher⬤, Theodora Vraimakis⬤,
James Borgars⬤, Ahmad Najmi Mohamad Shahir⬤, Jibran Raja⬤,
Abhinav Ramakrishnan⬤, and Sharib Ali$^{(\boxtimes)}$⬤

School of Computer Science, University of Leeds, Leeds, UK
s.s.ali@leeds.ac.uk

Abstract. Anatomical landmark segmentation involves identifying specific points or regions within an anatomical structure and is integral to diagnostic processes and surgical guidance. This paper focuses on the segmentation of landmarks in 3D liver models in order to highlight key structures such as the falciform ligament and the liver ridge. The study is motivated by the need to support intraoperative laparoscopic registration tasks, aiming to enhance preoperative-to-intraoperative image fusion and thereby improving the localisation of tumours and vessels within the liver. As current practices typically rely on manual annotation, a process that is time-consuming and prone to human error when performed by less experienced operators, there is a clear need for a more efficient and reliable solution. Some recent works on landmark prediction in 3D liver models either over-predict or under-predict these landmarks. To overcome these challenges, we introduce a novel loss function that enforces geometric constraints by aligning segmentation predictions with a computed central anatomical midline. This strategy not only improves overall anatomical alignment but also ensures that the predictions remain thin and precise, reducing the occurrence of overly broad or misaligned outputs. This approach is utilised in conjunction with the PointNet++ architecture, trained on an extensive combined dataset composed of three smaller datasets, alongside the P2ILF challenge dataset, amounting to 300 unique 3D liver models in total. Our results indicate that our proposed solution forms a robust and precise approach, laying a solid foundation for future advances and feasibility in 3D-2D liver registration for intraoperative use. To improve reproducibility of this work, we have shared our code at: https://github.com/ARMADILLO-VISION/midline-loss.

Keywords: Deep Learning · Midline Loss · 3D Landmark Segmentation · Laparoscopic Liver Surgery · PointNet++

1 Introduction

Anatomical 3D landmark segmentation is an essential task in medical image analysis, as it enables the precise localisation of anatomical structures within

S. Ali et al. (Eds.): MIUA 2025, LNCS 15917, pp. 216–229, 2026.
https://doi.org/10.1007/978-3-031-98691-8_16

3D models [16,17]. The importance of using 3D models via preoperative 3D rendering compared to conventional 2D scans for planning surgical strategies can improve understanding of liver anatomy and help in tissue-preserving surgery [15]. 3D landmark segmentation is particularly important in the context of preoperative-to-intraoperative image fusion [3,6,12]. For this reason, the accurate alignment of 3D models extracted from 3D CT/MRI scans acquired prior to surgery with the intraoperative 2D liver images allows for the understanding and location of important anatomical structures relative to the patient's anatomy during surgery [2,6,10–12].

To achieve a high degree of accuracy in such 3D-2D registration, it is essential to have an automated method for 3D liver landmark segmentation that can accurately predict the positions of key anatomical landmarks on unlabelled liver models [10,12]. The current practice of manual annotation of preoperative 3D liver models is time-consuming and prone to error [22], which motivates the development of a method that can automatically segment the key anatomical landmarks in liver models [12,20]. These landmarks can then be used for the registration process, as they provide reference points for aligning the 3D liver models with the 2D intraoperative images, which can also be done using segmentation of similar anatomical landmarks. In this way, 3D registration is performed automatically, however, less desirable manual and semi-automatic methods still exist for this task.

At present, a study conducted by Acidi et al. [1] shows that the most common reported method of registration is manual registration, with 11 studies proposing this approach as of 2023. This is followed by 9 studies conducted into semi-automatic approaches of registration [1]. There is a clear lack of studies into automatic methods of registration, with 3 studies reporting entirely automated approaches [14,23,26]. A large factor behind this is the lack of publicly available datasets with annotated 3D liver models [4,10], with many datasets containing a limited number of samples [1]. As a result, there is a need for a larger amount of data to be used in deep learning tasks in automated registration, which forms the main approach to our presented solution. Other literature suggests data synthesis as an alternative means to this problem [12].

The recent P2ILF challenge competition [3] curated and released the first comprehensive dataset in this domain with 11 patients, comprised of 9 patients for training and 2 for testing. The authors also performed an objective comparison of methods for 2D landmark segmentation, 3D landmark segmentation and preoperative-to-intraoperative fusion. A number of deep learning methods used by six participating teams were evaluated. For the 3D anatomical landmark segmentation, teams used MeshCNN [7], Graph Convolutional Network (GCN) [9], and PointNet-based architectures [18]. The results of these methods have shown promise, however, they display a high degree of variability with dependency on the quality of the training data. Issues such as under-predicting or over-predicting false positive regions were observed, indicating the need for further improvements in this area of research.

In this work, we propose an approach for anatomical 3D landmark segmentation that addresses these limitations. Our methodology enhances segmentation precision by training the PointNet++ architecture [19] on a large combined dataset of liver models, resulting in an improvement of the generalisation capabilities and robustness of the network across diverse patient livers. In addition, we introduce a novel midline loss function that addresses issues with oversegmenting, generating aligned and thin segmentation outputs resembling the ground truth data. To achieve this, the specialised loss function penalises deviations from a calculated central anatomical midline, promoting consistent and accurate landmark delineation while also discouraging overly large predictions, enforcing thin and anatomically plausible structures. Our approach demonstrates generalisability on unseen scenarios, surpassing baseline with conventional losses and the top-performing P2ILF challenge teams.

2   Methodology

The proposed method uses the PointNet++ neural network in conjunction with an innovative loss formula and is trained on a larger combined dataset, allowing for more accurate segmentation in unseen and unlabelled liver models, thus addressing current challenges in landmark prediction. It is this sourcing of increased data samples along with the implemented midline loss that forms the novelty of this approach. The basis of the loss function is detailed in the following methodology.

2.1   Midline Loss

To achieve precise and thin segmentation of anatomical structures, we propose a midline loss function ($\mathcal{L}_{\mathrm{midline}}$) that explicitly incorporates geometric considerations. This loss is designed to align the segmentation predictions with a computed central anatomical midline derived from ground-truth labels, as well as penalising large deviations that result in overly broad or misaligned outputs.

Let $\mathcal{X}$ be the set of predicted 3D segmentation points for any given class. To estimate the central anatomical axis, we perform a weighted Principal Component Analysis on $\mathcal{X}$, using the segmentation probabilities as weights. This yields a principal direction vector v, which draws the best fit axis through the subset of predicted points $\mathcal{X}$ and naturally emphasises high confidence points while down weighting noisy outliers. We then sample along v to generate the set of candidate midline points $\mathcal{C}$.

Each candidate point $c_k \in \mathcal{C}$ is refined via a differentiable soft-snapping process. This process serves as a smooth projection mechanism, producing a refined point c_k^* using a softmax-weighted combination of all segmentation points:

$$c_k^* = \sum_{i=1}^{N} \alpha_i\, x_i, \quad \text{where} \quad \alpha_i = \frac{\exp\left(-\lambda\,\|x_i - c_k\|\right)}{\sum_{j=1}^{N} \exp\left(-\lambda\,\|x_j - c_k\|\right)}. \tag{1}$$

The set of refined points $\mathcal{S}_p$ defines the predicted midline.

To measure alignment between the predicted segmentation and the midline, each point $x_i \in \mathcal{X}$ is softly projected onto $\mathcal{S}_p$, producing a set of projected points $\hat{\mathcal{X}}$. These projections are subsequently used in the loss calculation to penalise deviations from the midline in a differentiable manner.

The midline loss consists of two complementary components: a deviation loss ($\mathcal{L}_{\mathrm{dev}}$) and an alignment loss ($\mathcal{L}_{\mathrm{align}}$). The deviation loss acts as a thickness controller by penalising the distance between each segmentation point and its nearest soft projection onto the computed midline. In doing so, it encourages the segmentation to remain narrow and closely bound to the midline, thereby reducing the overall thickness of the predicted structure. To control outliers, distances are clamped as needed. A visualisation of this process is shown in Fig. 1. Formally, the deviation loss is defined as:

$$\mathcal{L}_{\mathrm{dev}} = \frac{\sum_{i=1}^{N} w_i \left(e^{\alpha \|x_i - \hat{x}_i\|} - 1 \right)}{\sum_{i=1}^{N} w_i + \epsilon}, \tag{2}$$

where x_i are the segmented points, $\hat{x}_i$ denote their differentiable projections onto the midline, w_i are the segmentation probabilities, and ϵ is a small constant to prevent division by zero.

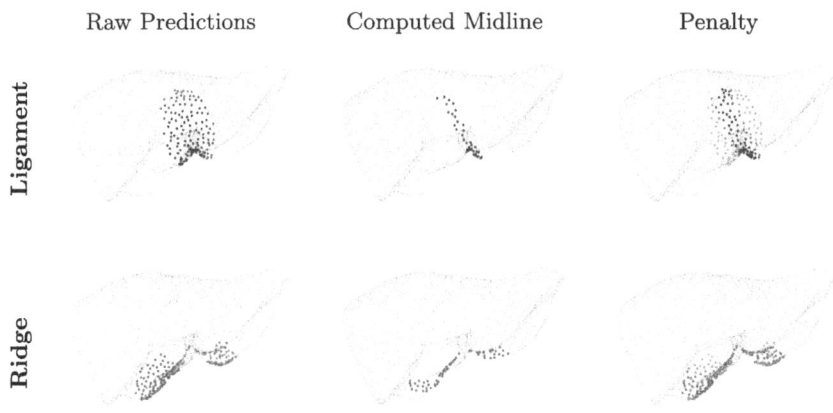

Fig. 1. Visualisation of the penalty computation pipeline for ligament and ridge regions. From left to right: raw segmentation predictions, computed midlines, and resulting deviation-based penalty maps. For ligament, penalty values range from low (blue) to high (green); for ridge, low penalties are shown in red, increasing to yellow for higher deviations from the midline. (Color figure online)

In parallel, the alignment loss ($\mathcal{L}_{\mathrm{align}}$) ensures that the predicted midline (S_p) aligns closely with the ground truth midline (S_{GT}). The predicted midline is derived using wPCA and soft-snapping, while the ground truth midline is obtained by uniformly resampling the ground-truth annotated points. A soft-assigned Chamfer distance measures the spatial discrepancy between these midlines:

$$\mathcal{L}_{\text{align}} = \frac{1}{2} \left(\frac{1}{|S_p|} \sum_{s_p \in S_p} d_{\text{CD}}(s_p, S_{\text{GT}}) + \frac{1}{|S_{\text{GT}}|} \sum_{s_{\text{GT}} \in S_{\text{GT}}} d_{\text{CD}}(s_{\text{GT}}, S_p) \right), \qquad (3)$$

where $d_{\text{CD}}(\cdot, \cdot)$ denotes the Chamfer point-to-midline distance.

The overall midline loss is then defined as:

$$\mathcal{L}_{\text{midline}} = (1 - \lambda_m) \mathcal{L}_{\text{dev}} + \lambda_m \mathcal{L}_{\text{align}}, \qquad (4)$$

with the hyper-parameter λ_m balancing the contributions of the deviation and alignment losses.

To balance the geometry-based midline loss with the weighted cross-entropy loss ($\mathcal{L}_{wCE}$), whose magnitudes may differ significantly during training, we introduce a dynamic scaling factor. This scaling factor ensures that both the geometric constraints and region-based accuracy are optimised simultaneously. The scale is computed as:

$$\beta = \frac{\mathcal{L}_{wCE}}{\frac{1}{2} \left(\mathcal{L}_{\text{midline}}^{\text{ridge}} + \mathcal{L}_{\text{midline}}^{\text{lig}} \right) + \epsilon}, \qquad (5)$$

where $\mathcal{L}_{\text{midline}}^{\text{ridge}}$ and $\mathcal{L}_{\text{midline}}^{\text{lig}}$ each correspond to the same midline formulation ($\mathcal{L}_{\text{midline}}$) computed for the ridge and ligament structures separately. Finally, the combined total loss, incorporating weighted cross-entropy, is expressed as:

$$\mathcal{L}_{\text{total}} = \alpha \mathcal{L}_{wCE} + \beta \left(\lambda_{\text{ridge}} \mathcal{L}_{\text{midline}}^{\text{ridge}} + \lambda_{\text{lig}} \mathcal{L}_{\text{midline}}^{\text{lig}} \right). \qquad (6)$$

2.2 PointNet++

The PointNet++ architecture used in our approach is designed to process and segment 3D point clouds directly, making the conversion of 3D data into point cloud representations a necessary step in our method. The implementation used is adapted from the repository by Yan [25] and is based on the work demonstrated by Qi et al. [19]. The PointNet++ network was trained on the datasets using different loss functions, including the novel midline loss. The optimal hyperparameters and loss functions were selected through an ablation study, detailed in Subsect. 3.2. The standard PointNet architecture was also tested [18].

3 Experimental Setup

3.1 Dataset and Data Preparation

To ensure the robustness and generalisation of our proposed method, we used two publicly available datasets of 3D liver models, including a large dataset obtained from Zhang et al. [27] that combines three public datasets (3Dircadb

[21], LiTS [5], and Amos [8]). The other smaller dataset, consisting of 9 training and 2 test patients, was sourced from the P2ILF challenge [4]. Data for each patient includes a 3D liver model, saved as a wavefront object, and an XML file containing the anatomical annotations. These files are parsed to extract detailed contour information of the type of anatomical structure (ridge or ligament) and the corresponding indices of mesh vertices that define these contours. These extracted annotations were then used to create numerical labels for the 3D mesh vertices. Initially, all vertices are assigned a background label, which is subsequently updated to reflect the presence of specific anatomical features based on the parsed contour data.

To prepare the data for compatibility with the PointNet++ model, the 3D meshes were converted into point cloud arrays. These point clouds typically contain between 4000 and 15000 points, with each point inheriting the label corresponding to the anatomical structures previously identified in the mesh. Our conversion process ensures that each point cloud is standardised by either furthest point sampling or padding the vertices to achieve a fixed number of 4096 points.

Considering the P2ILF dataset contains only 11 patients in total, two patients are pre-emptively reserved for the test set. From the remaining 9, we adopt a 72 split for training and validation. This maintains a reasonable balance between training capacity and validation reliability, given the limited data, while preserving subject independence across all subsets. A similar ratio is used for consistency when applying the split to the combined dataset.

The data is normalised, ensuring all datasets share the same normalisation parameters. Class weights are computed using the inverse square root class frequency weighting method, assigning higher weights to classes with lower frequencies. This is necessary due to heavy class imbalance, with very low frequency in the ligament class compared to the liver class.

We apply augmentation techniques to increase the diversity of the training data and improve the model's generalisation capabilities, as well as its performance on unseen samples. Three different augmentations were performed, including upscaling, downscaling and rotations on the z-axis. Point clouds are randomly scaled in the range of 65%–145% of their original size, and then randomly rotated in the range of $-180°$–$180°$ on the z-axis.

3.2 Ablation Study and Hyper-parameter Selection

To systematically evaluate the impact of the learning rate and loss function components (Eq. 6) on segmentation performance, a structured grid search was performed. Each configuration is trained independently, and the resulting segmentation quality is evaluated using 3D Chamfer distance [24]. Learning rate selection is performed separately through a separate ablation. The evaluated learning rates ranged from 0.00025 to 0.01, examining their effects on convergence stability and final segmentation accuracy. All experiments were conducted on an NVIDIA RTX 4070. A batch size of 32 was set and an AdamW optimiser with default parameters was utilised for training [13]. A learning rate scheduler was implemented to reduce the learning rate once the validation loss plateaued and early stopping was applied if the validation loss remained stagnant.

In our experiments, negative log-likelihood (NLL) loss was adopted as the baseline due to its use as the standard loss in PointNet [18] and PointNet++ [19]. We also evaluated the weighted cross-entropy (wCE) loss, which incorporates the softmax operation internally. Although both losses yield similar outcomes when properly configured, the slight differences in their implementation can influence convergence behaviour and final accuracy, making the inclusion of wCE a valuable alternative for comparison.

The optimal hyper-parameters were selected based on performance on the validation dataset. For the combined dataset [27], the best-performing configuration used a weighted cross-entropy weight of $\alpha_{wce} = 0.25$, with geometry-based ridge and ligament losses set at $\lambda_{\text{ridge}} = 0.5$ and $\lambda_{\text{lig}} = 0.25$. A learning rate of 0.0075 was chosen, as it yields the lowest Chamfer distances. For the P2ILF dataset, the best configuration selected used $\alpha_{ce} = 0.25$, $\lambda_{\text{ridge}} = 0.75$, and $\lambda_{\text{lig}} = 0$, with an optimal learning rate of 0.0005.

4 Results

4.1 Evaluation Metrics

We assess the performance of our segmentation framework using 3D Chamfer distance, which quantifies the point-to-point average distance between the segmented landmarks and the ground truth [24]. It functions by averaging the minimum distance between points in two point clouds. For two point sets X and Y, it is defined as:

$$d_{\text{CD}}(X, Y) = \frac{1}{|X|} \sum_{x \in X} \min_{y \in Y} \|x - y\|_p + \frac{1}{|Y|} \sum_{y \in Y} \min_{x \in X} \|y - x\|_p, \tag{7}$$

where $\| \cdot \|_p$ denotes the p-norm distance of the points.

4.2 Quantitative Results

The quantitative results recorded during the series of ablations are presented in Table 1 and Table 2. Table 1 presents our findings when our models are tested on the P2ILF challenge dataset [4] and Table 2 shows our findings tested on the combined dataset [27]. Furthermore, we include the results of the top two performing teams from the P2ILF challenge paper as a means of comparison against other literature [4]. The two teams included from the P2ILF challenge are: UCL, which achieved the best results on the liver ligament, and NCT, which achieved the best results on the liver ridge. Each model is tested on the hold-out set of the dataset it was trained on, as well as the other dataset to verify generalisation capabilities.

Table 1. Evaluation on the P2ILF challenge test set [4]. LR: learning rate. ch_r, ch_l: Chamfer distances (in mm) for ridge and ligament. ‡: trained on combined dataset [27]. * indicates evaluation on the unseen test set. Highlighted cells represent a metric result that outperforms all P2ILF challenge teams. The best results are in bold.

Model	Loss	LR	Train	ch_r	ch_l	Mean
PointNet++	Midline,wCE	0.01	‡*	**19.70**	**13.46**	**16.58**
PointNet++	NLL	0.0005	P2ILF	22.23	55.77	39.00
PointNet++	wCE	0.01	‡*	23.72	60.26	41.99
PointNet++	wCE	0.0005	P2ILF	38.43	69.62	54.03
PointNet++	Midline,wCE	0.00075	P2ILF	36.11	116.10	76.11
PointNet	NLL	0.01	P2ILF	95.85	73.46	84.65
PointNet++	NLL	0.005	‡*	F	115.54	115.54
PointNet	NLL	0.00075	‡*	199.94	F	199.94
Teams [3]						
UCL	PointNet++	NLL,HFD	0.001	P2ILF	27.97	24.47	26.22
NCT	2×MeshCNN	wCE	NA	P2ILF	27.19	36.38	31.79

Table 2. Evaluation on the combined test set [27]. LR: learning rate. ch_r, ch_l: Chamfer distances (in mm) for ridge and ligament. ‡: trained on combined dataset. *: evaluated on unseen test set. The best results are in bold.

Model	Loss	LR	Train	ch_r	ch_l	Mean
PointNet	NLL	0.00075	‡	7.92	**16.62**	**12.27**
PointNet++	wCE	0.01	‡	**7.13**	18.30	12.71
PointNet++	Midline,wCE	0.01	‡	11.62	21.57	16.60
PointNet++	Midline,wCE	0.00075	P2ILF*	19.50	23.21	21.35
PointNet++	NLL	0.0005	P2ILF*	28.79	17.95	23.37
PointNet	NLL	0.01	P2ILF*	27.39	29.10	28.25
PointNet++	wCE	0.0005	P2ILF*	33.49	23.48	28.49
PointNet++	NLL	0.005	‡	32.21	30.39	31.30

Table 2 indicates that when testing on the combined dataset, the two best performing configurations of PointNet++ with weighted cross-entropy loss and PointNet with negative loss likelihood loss achieve the lowest mean Chamfer distance and ultimately outperform the best performing configurations from the P2ILF challenge [4]. However, it should be noted that despite the high performance on the combined dataset, these configurations generalise poorly to the P2ILF dataset, which can be observed in Table 1. For instance, the PointNet++ configuration using weighted cross-entropy loss records a mean Chamfer distance of 12.71 mm on the combined dataset but deteriorates sharply to 41.99 mm when generalising to the P2ILF dataset. Similarly, the PointNet model with NLL loss (LR = 0.00075) achieves a competitive 12.27 mm on the combined dataset, yet it fails to generalise, reaching 199.94 mm on the P2ILF dataset.

Furthermore, Table 1 highlights that PointNet++ with combined midline and weighted cross-entropy loss functions along with a learning rate of 0.01, when trained on the combined dataset and tested on the P2ILF dataset, outperforms all teams from the P2ILF challenge and achieves the best results out of all our models tested on the P2ILF data. Although the Chamfer distances reported by this model are lower than those presented in Table 2, they nonetheless demonstrate that our proposed method generalises effectively to unseen data, as evidenced by its performance on the hold-out set. For example, this method, using the midline loss at LR = 0.01, reduces the mean Chamfer distance to 16.58 mm – a reduction exceeding 36% compared to the UCL team's method.

4.3   Qualitative Results

Figure 2 provides a comparative visual analysis of segmentation outputs from models trained on the combined dataset for four patients. Two from the P2ILF test set (patient 4 and patient 11) [4] and two from the combined dataset (LiTS-65 and Amos-119) [27]. Figure 3 is also included as a comparison between the top performing teams in the P2ILF challenge and our best model.

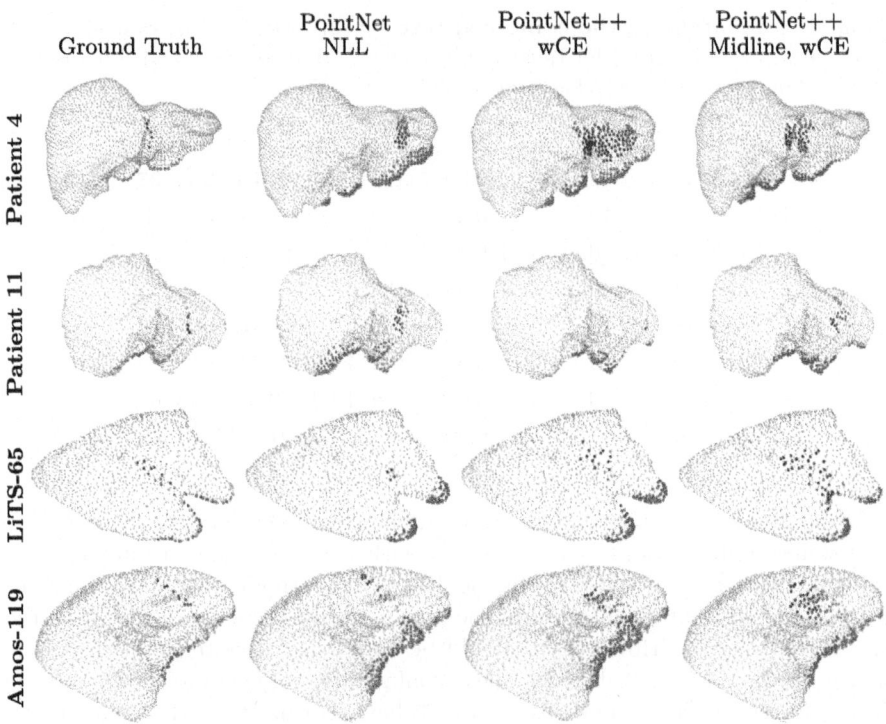

Fig. 2. Qualitative comparison of segmentation results between our proposed method on baselines from P2ILF [4] (patients 4 and 11) and the combined dataset [27] (LiTS-65 [5] and Amos-119 [8]). Ligament points are coloured blue; Ridge points are coloured red. (Color figure online)

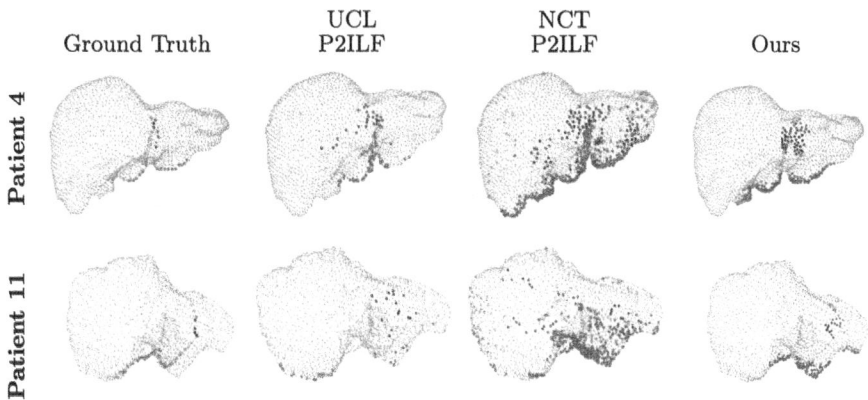

Fig. 3. Qualitative comparison of segmentation results between the two best teams from the P2ILF challenge [4] and our best model. Test patients 4 and 11 are used. Ligament points are coloured blue; Ridge points are coloured red. Points on the backside of the liver are displayed with a lower alpha value. (Color figure online)

The results indicate that the segmentation produced with the midline loss is more closely bound to the ground truth. Notably, for both patient 4 and patient 11 in Fig. 2, the ridge structure is more accurately delineated as the predicted midline closely curves around the ridge, which contrasts the broader, region-like segmentations observed with the weighted cross-entropy model. Although the overall segmentation size remains relatively large for the ligament, the localisation is notably improved with the midline loss, showing a more generalised and anatomically consistent alignment.

These improved results are also evident in the comparisons made in Fig. 3. Segmentations produced by our model demonstrate improvements over the two highest scoring P2ILF teams. In particular, the predicted ridge and ligament regions are more accurately aligned with the ground truth in contrast to the top two P2ILF team's predictions, which are erratic and have incorrectly placed some points behind the liver.

By incorporating a geometric aspect, the midline loss improves localisation by effectively carving the ridge around the liver while ensuring thin segmentation. Similar improvements in localisation and accuracy are also observed on the combined dataset patients (LiTS-65 and Amos-119), particularly for ridge segmentations.

5   Discussion

Our experimental results provide compelling quantitative evidence for the efficacy of our proposed method in 3D liver landmark segmentation. By leveraging a significantly larger combined dataset of 300 unique 3D liver models [27] and incorporating our geometry-constrained midline loss, our PointNet++ model achieves mean Chamfer distances of 16.60 mm on the combined dataset and 16.58 mm on the P2ILF dataset. These outcomes contrast markedly with previously seen approaches, underscoring the limitations faced by earlier methods, particularly those from the P2ILF challenge teams which were constrained by limited training data and consequently struggled to generalise. In contrast, our approach benefits from both a larger, more diverse dataset and a novel loss function that explicitly enforces geometric consistency by penalising deviations from a computed central anatomical midline. This strategy promotes thin and greater-aligned segmentations that more accurately reflect true anatomical structures. Moreover, the enhanced performance is attributed to the incorporation of geometric constraints, which provides stronger regularisation and enables the model to capture complex anatomical variations more robustly. The best results observed on the combined dataset [27], even when using a P2ILF-trained model, highlight the substantial improvements in generalisation achieved by our approach. In particular, the incorporation of the midline loss has proven critical for enabling robust predictions across diverse liver datasets. As shown in Table 2, even when the PointNet++ model with midline and weighted cross-entropy loss was trained solely on the smaller P2ILF dataset (with a learning rate of 0.00075), it still performed relatively well on the combined dataset, achieving a mean Chamfer distance of 21.35 mm compared to 16.60 mm for the model trained on the larger combined dataset (with a learning rate of 0.01).

Furthermore, visual comparisons reveal that the segmentation outputs using the midline loss exhibit a distinct, precise curvature of the ridge that is more tightly bound to the ground truth. In contrast, predictions from models using solely wCE tend to be broader and less defined, resembling a region-like segmentation. The improved localisation achieved by effectively demarcating the ridge around the liver not only confirms the enhanced geometric fidelity of our method but also demonstrates its ability to generalise well to unseen data from different datasets. However, in the particularly challenging LITS 65 case, the ridge is deformed enough that it differs significantly from its typical anatomy and all models detect the two segments separately rather than one continuous prediction. These mispredictions underscore that even other loss functions struggle with extreme anatomical outliers, highlighting the need for strategies specifically designed to handle such extreme cases. Regardless, there is improvement in cross-dataset performance and this is particularly evident when comparing the performance on the combined dataset to that of the P2ILF dataset, where our method substantially reduces mean Chamfer distances and outperforms previous configurations. Overall, the combination of a robust, extensive training dataset with a geometry-aware loss function leads to improvements in both quantitative metrics and qualitative visual assessments, establishing a strong foundation for future advancements in 3D liver segmentation.

Importantly, the enhanced landmark segmentation accuracy carries direct benefits for the laparoscopic 3D2D registration pipeline, especially when considering typical clinical workflows, whereby preoperative 3D liver models must be aligned with intraoperative laparoscopic images to guide instrument navigation and tumour resection [6,10,12]. More precise 3D landmark localisation reduces the spatial uncertainty in the initial alignment step, leading to lower registration error and more stable convergence of feature-based registration algorithms [3,12]. In practice, this can translate to faster registration times and improved spatial overlay.

Despite these advances, a significant limitation remains in the relatively small number of annotated ligament landmarks. The lack of ground-truth labels makes it inherently challenging for the model to learn precise geometry. This scarcity likely contributes to the broad localisation predictions observed in our qualitative results, although the midline loss does mitigate this issue by enforcing geometric consistency to an extent. In practice, the lack of fine-grained detail in the training labels limits the model's ability to capture subtle variations in ligament morphology, regardless of the loss function used. Addressing this will require more extensive high-resolution annotations or targeted data augmentation strategies.

6   Conclusion

In this work, we presented a novel approach for 3D liver segmentation that enhances anatomical accuracy by integrating a geometry-aware midline loss function using a larger, combined dataset. Our method yields notably more precise and robust segmentations than those produced by traditional loss functions, effectively addressing common issues such as overly thick or misaligned predictions observed in previous works. By explicitly constraining the segmentation with geometric information, our approach achieves improved alignment with true anatomical structures and demonstrates superior generalisation across diverse datasets. A major limitation remains in the quality and quantity of existing data. As such, future research should focus on expanding training datasets to encompass greater anatomical diversity, integrating a geometrically constrained loss function that is more tolerant to outliers and the investigation of geometric recognition features within model architectures.

Acknowledgments. This project is part of the National Institute for Health and Care Research (NIHR) Leeds Biomedical Research Centre (BRC) (NIHR203331) pump-priming funding "ARMADILLO" project. The views expressed are those of the authors and not necessarily those of the NIHR or the Department of Health and Social Care.

Disclosure of Interests. The authors have no competing interests to declare that are relevant to the content of this article.

References

1. Acidi, B., Ghallab, M., Cotin, S., Vibert, E., Golse, N.: Augmented reality in liver surgery. J. Visc. Surg. **160**(2), 118–126 (2023). https://doi.org/10.1016/j.jviscsurg.2023.01.008

2. Adagolodjo, Y., Trivisonne, R., Haouchine, N., Cotin, S., Courtecuisse, H.: Silhouette-based pose estimation for deformable organs: application to surgical augmented reality. In: Proceedings of the IEEE/RSJ IROS, pp. 539–544. IEEE (2017). https://doi.org/10.1109/IROS.2017.8202205

3. Ali, S., et al.: An objective comparison of methods for augmented reality in laparoscopic liver resection by preoperative-to-intraoperative image fusion. CoRR abs/2401.15753 (2024). arXiv:2401.15753

4. Ali, S., Jin, Y., Lopez, Y.E., Bartoli, A.: Preoperative to intra-operative laparoscopic fusion challenge (P2ilf) (2022). https://p2ilf.grand-challenge.org, https://doi.org/10.5281/zenodo.6362161. Accessed 24 May 2025

5. Bilic, P., et al.: The liver tumour segmentation benchmark (LiTS). Med. Image Anal. **84**, 102680 (2023). https://doi.org/10.1016/j.media.2022.102680

6. Espinel, Y., Calvet, L., Botros, K., Buc, E., Tilmant, C., Bartoli, A.: Using multiple images and contours for deformable 3D–2D registration of a pre-operative CT in laparoscopic liver surgery. Int. J. Comput. Assist. Radiol. Surg. **17**(12), 2211–2219 (2022). https://doi.org/10.1007/s11548-022-02774-1

7. Hanocka, R., Hertz, A., Fish, N., Giryes, R., Fleishman, S., Cohen-Or, D.: MeshCNN: a network with an edge. CoRR abs/1809.05910 (2018). arXiv:1809.05910

8. Ji, Y., Bai, H., Ge, C., Yang, J., et al.: AMOS: a large-scale abdominal multi-organ benchmark for versatile medical image segmentation. In: Advances in Neural Information Processing Systems, vol. 35, pp. 36722–36732 (2022)

9. Kipf, T.N., Welling, M.: Semi-supervised classification with graph convolutional networks. CoRR abs/1609.02907 (2016). arXiv:1609.02907

10. Koo, B., Robu, M.R., Allam, M., Pfeiffer, M., Thompson, S., et al.: Automatic, global registration in laparoscopic liver surgery. Int. J. Comput. Assist. Radiol. Surg. **17**(1), 167–176 (2022). https://doi.org/10.1007/s11548-021-02518-7

11. Koo, B., Özgür, E., Le Roy, B., Buc, E., Bartoli, A.: Deformable registration of a preoperative 3D liver volume to a laparoscopy image using contour and shading cues. In: Descoteaux, M., Maier-Hein, L., Franz, A., Jannin, P., Collins, D.L., Duchesne, S. (eds.) MICCAI 2017. LNCS, vol. 10433, pp. 326–334. Springer, Cham (2017). https://doi.org/10.1007/978-3-319-66182-7_38

12. Labrunie, M., et al.: Automatic preoperative 3D model registration in laparoscopic liver resection. Int. J. Comput. Assist. Radiol. Surg. **17**(8), 1429–1436 (2022). https://doi.org/10.1007/s11548-022-02641-z

13. Loshchilov, I., Hutter, F.: Decoupled weight decay regularisation. In: Proceedings of the International Conference on Learning Representations (2019)

14. Luo, H., Yin, D., Zhang, S., Xiao, D., et al.: Augmented reality navigation for liver resection with a stereoscopic laparoscope. Comput. Methods Program. Biomed. **187**, 105099 (2020). https://doi.org/10.1016/j.cmpb.2019.105099

15. Montalti, R., et al.: Role of preoperative 3D rendering for minimally invasive parenchyma-sparing liver resections. HPB **25**(8), 915–923 (2023). https://doi.org/10.1016/j.hpb.2023.04.008

16. Oh, N., Kim, J.H., Rhu, J., Jeong, W.K., Choi, G.S., Kim, J.M., Joh, J.W.: Automated 3D liver segmentation from hepatobiliary phase mri for enhanced preoperative planning. Sci. Rep. **13**, 17605 (2023). https://doi.org/10.1038/s41598-023-44736-w
17. Pei, J., Cui, R., Li, Y., Si, W., Qin, J., Heng, P.A.: Depth-driven geometric prompt learning for laparoscopic liver landmark detection. CoRR abs/2406.17858 (2024). arXiv:2406.17858
18. Qi, C.R., Su, H., Mo, K., Guibas, L.J.: PointNet: deep learning on point sets for 3D classification and segmentation. CoRR abs/1612.00593 (2017). arXiv:1612.00593
19. Qi, C.R., Yi, L., Su, H., Guibas, L.J.: PointNet++: deep hierarchical feature learning on point sets in a metric space. CoRR abs/1706.02413 (2017). arXiv:1706.02413
20. Schneider, C., Thompson, S., Totz, J., Song, Y., Sodergren, M.H., et al.: Comparison of manual and semi-automatic registration in augmented-reality image-guided liver surgery: a clinical feasibility study. Surg. Endosc. **34**(10), 4702–4711 (2020). https://doi.org/10.1007/s00464-020-07807-x
21. Soler, L., Hostettler, A., Agnus, V., Charnoz, A., et al.: 3D image reconstruction for comparison of algorithm database: a patient-specific anatomical and medical image database. Technical report, IRCAD, Strasbourg, France (2010). https://www.ircad.fr/research/data-sets/liver-segmentation-3d-ircadb-01/
22. Teatini, A., Pelanis, E., Aghayan, D., et al.: The effect of intraoperative imaging on surgical navigation for laparoscopic liver resection surgery. Sci. Rep. **9**, 18687 (2019). https://doi.org/10.1038/s41598-019-54915-3
23. Thompson, S., Schneider, C., Bosi, M., Gurusamy, K., et al.: In vivo estimation of target registration errors during augmented-reality laparoscopic surgery. Int. J. Comput. Assist. Radiol. Surg. **13**(6), 865–874 (2018). https://doi.org/10.1007/s11548-018-1761-3
24. Wu, T., Pan, L., Zhang, J., Wang, T., Liu, Z., Lin, D.: Balanced chamfer distance as a comprehensive metric for point cloud completion. In: Advances in Neural Information Processing Systems, vol. 34, pp. 29088–29100 (2021)
25. Yan, X.: PointNet/PointNet++ in pytorch (2019). https://github.com/yanx27/Pointnet_Pointnet2_pytorch. Github repository, Accessed 24 May 2025
26. Zhang, P., Luo, H., Zhu, W., Yang, J., et al.: Real-time navigation for laparoscopic hepatectomy using image fusion of pre-operative 3D surgical plan and intraoperative indocyanine green fluorescence imaging. Surg. Endosc. **34**(8), 3449–3459 (2020). https://doi.org/10.1007/s00464-019-07121-1
27. Zhang, X., Ali, S., Han, M., Kang, Y., Wang, X., Zhang, L.: Two-stream meshcnn for key anatomical segmentation on the liver surface. Int. J. Comput. Assist. Radiol. Surg. (2025). In press

DepthClassNet: A Multitask Framework for Monocular Depth Estimation and Texture Classification in Endoscopic Imaging

Bashayer Abdallah[✉][iD] and Shan E Ahmed Raza[iD]

Tissue Image Analytics (TIA) Centre, Department of Computer Science, University of Warwick, Coventry, UK
Bashayer.Abdallah@warwick.ac.uk

Abstract. Monocular depth estimation can play a critical role in medical imaging, providing spatial information that enhances diagnostic accuracy and supports precise surgical interventions. The texture classification in the endoscopic images significantly contributes to the differentiation of tissue types and the identification of pathological changes. Building on this knowledge, we introduce DepthClassNet, an innovative multitask framework designed to simultaneously perform monocular depth estimation and texture classification in endoscopic imaging. Our approach employs a tri-encoder model to integrate RGB images, edge maps, and textual descriptions. The architecture comprises a SWIN transformer as an image encoder, a convolutional neural network (CNN) as an edge encoder, and a modified CLIP text encoder for embedding class textual descriptions. Features from the image and edge encoders are effectively combined via a Feature Fusion Module (FFM), and high-resolution depth outputs are reconstructed through a decoder and depth projection block. We introduce an image embedding block that converts visual data from the SWIN encoder into embeddings that align with CLIP text embeddings. The classification head then computes similarity scores, scales them by a learnable temperature t, and converts them into probabilities. By designing a loss function that combines depth, edge and classification losses with specific weights, our multitask architecture achieves state-of-the-art results on the Colonoscopy Depth - UCL dataset for depth estimation and texture classification.

Keywords: Monocular depth estimation · Medical imaging · Multitask model · Text-based classification

1 Introduction

The prediction of depth maps given a single 2D image, known as monocular depth estimation (MDE), facilitates the reconstruction of three-dimensional spatial information, enabling improved diagnostics [19], understanding the surgical outcomes [17], real-time intervention in medicine [32], and robotic-assisted

© The Author(s), under exclusive license to Springer Nature Switzerland AG 2026
S. Ali et al. (Eds.): MIUA 2025, LNCS 15917, pp. 230–246, 2026.
https://doi.org/10.1007/978-3-031-98691-8_17

surgery [14]. The ability to infer depth from monocular images significantly reduces the dependence on expensive stereoscopic equipment, making advanced imaging more accessible and cost-effective in clinical settings [9, 23]. In endoscopy, MDE enhances depth perception, aiding precise tissue and organ localisation during minimally invasive procedures [7, 12]. However, low texture and inconsistent lighting in endoscopic images demand robust solutions. In addition, patient-specific texture, shape and colour make it challenging to obtain generalisable results without a large number of ground truth maps [20]. These issues are addressed either by synthetically generated data or by simultaneous depth and pose estimation, where the output of the pose network supervises the depth network instead of human expert annotations [26, 31]. For example, the Colonoscopy Depth - UCL dataset [26] includes various subsets classified based on texture and lighting conditions. The categories within the UCL dataset provide a unique opportunity to explore the integration of monocular depth estimation with texture classification, enabling a multitask approach to understanding and analysing endoscopic images. Multitask Learning - MTL approaches have demonstrated significant potential in improving the performance of MDE, where auxiliary tasks such as semantic segmentation, surface normal estimation, and object detection are commonly integrated [28, 30]. This integration reduces computational overhead, making multitask models particularly well-suited for resource-constrained clinical environments [35] and allows the network to better understand scene geometry and motion, overcoming the limitations of single-task approaches.

Accurately inferring a scene's structure, including its intrinsic geometric features, remains a significant challenge that has been insufficiently explored in MDE research within medical imaging [12]. In particular, texture classification plays a crucial role, as accurate characterisation and discrimination of textures significantly enhance the precision and reliability of diagnostic methods such as disease detection and classification [2]. By integrating texture classification with MDE, we can further enhance the precision and reliability of surgical navigation and diagnostic techniques, particularly in addressing the challenges of varying textures and lighting conditions on the endoscopic imaging [35]. For example, in the UCL dataset [26], the texture is classified by material classes, defined by a specific combination of colour, reflectiveness, smoothness, and lighting conditions subclasses are determined by parameters such as spot angle, range, colour, and intensity. This classified dataset motivated us to address the existing gap between depth prediction and texture classification. To achieve this, we propose DepthClassNet, a novel multitask framework designed to simultaneously perform monocular depth estimation and texture classification. The architecture incorporates RGB images, edge maps, and textual prompts, effectively bridging the two tasks within a unified model, as illustrated in Fig. 1, to classify the predicted depth maps based on their texture characterises. For example, for an image with a texture classified by material 1 under lighting condition 2, our model generates a depth map highlighting the texture structure and a classification label with the following text-based description: *The predicted depth map corresponds to Texture 1 under the Lighting Condition 2.*

The key contributions of our DepthClassNet framework are **1)** tri-encoder model to integrate RGB images, edge maps, and textual descriptions. The architecture comprises a SWIN transformer-based image encoder, a convolutional neural network (CNN) edge encoder, and a CLIP text encoder for embedding textual class descriptions. **2)** Image Embedding Block (IEB) processes features extracted from RGB images, enabling effective alignment and comparison with textual embeddings for enhanced classification accuracy, and **3)** a loss function that combines depth, edge, and classification losses. By carefully balancing these terms, we optimise the network to learn representations that capture precise structural cues and high-level semantic information. Our DepthClassNet model does not require post-processing or multi-stage training, as it is trained in an end-to-end manner.

2   Related Work

2.1   Monocular Depth Estimation and Medical Imaging

Monocular depth estimation in medical imaging has emerged as a critical technology due to its potential to improve navigational accuracy [14]. In a colonoscopy, autonomous endorobots equipped with MDE capabilities enable systematic and complete mucosal inspections, increasing the reliability of early disease detection [19]. In addition, many MDE studies considered the depth estimation as a part of a broader multitask learning - MTL problem, where it is integrated within multitasking learning frameworks to simultaneously estimate depth alongside surface normals, segmentation, optical flow, and camera motion, enhancing overall performance through shared feature representations [23, 25, 28, 30]. Despite its potential, applying MDE in clinical settings faces significant challenges, including the lack of ground truth depth maps and annotated datasets in endoscopic videos [12]. Additionally, obstacles such as low texture resolution, inconsistent illumination, and patient-specific variations in tissue appearance complicate the generalisation of the MDE models [20]. Although advances in MDE have enabled real-time depth mapping in surgical settings, significantly enhancing intraoperative navigation and tissue localisation [7,16], the depth estimated is relative, not absolute. This has led researchers to rely on synthetic data or anatomical mesh renderings for model training. For instance, the UCL dataset [26] provides a valuable benchmark with absolute depth and diverse textures under different lighting conditions that mimic real-world variability. Motivated by these insights, we incorporate MDE with texture classification to predict accurate depth maps with corresponding texture feature labels.

2.2   Monocular Depth Estimation and NLP Text-Based Classification

Accurate depth estimation enhances the understanding of object relationships, scene layout, and spatial awareness, which is critical for applications such as medical imaging, robotics, and augmented reality [15,38]. Recent advancements in MDE have explored leveraging NLP techniques to the traditional CV methods. For instance, DepthCLIP [6] utilises pre-trained CLIP models for zero-shot ordinal classification of image patches into depth bins. It frames depth estimation as a classification task by associating image features with textual prompts, such as 'This object is near/far.' However, this method suffers from inherent limitations, including human bias in prompt selection and the discrete nature of language, which restricts the granularity of depth bins. However, recent advancements in MDE within the CLIP framework [3] have introduced learnable prompt tokens to address the limitations of DepthCLIP. These learnable tokens enable the model to adapt depth ranges and contexts, reducing dependence on fixed textual prompts and improving prediction accuracy. Despite these improvements, a significant gap remains in developing an approach that effectively integrates NLP-driven prompt learning, such as text-based classification using natural language inputs, with monocular depth estimation.

To the best of our knowledge, our proposed work is the first to bridge this gap by combining the interpretability of NLP text-driven prompt classification with the precision of monocular depth estimation. The proposed multitasking model incorporates text-based classification and depth estimation in an interconnected, end-to-end process, enabling both tasks to enhance each other and improve overall performance. By leveraging CLIP text-based classification, the approach strengthens semantic understanding and spatial awareness while reducing dependence on fixed textual prompts and enhancing prediction accuracy.

3   Materials and Methods

3.1   Dataset

UCL Dataset [26]: Public colonoscopy dataset for depth prediction in endoscopy. The dataset consists of 16,016 RGB images with corresponding ground truth depth. The images were resized to 256×256 pixels. The depth is scaled between $[0, 1]$, representing a range of $[0, 20]$ cm. The data is organised into groups, each corresponding to one of three lighting conditions and one of three texture settings. The lighting conditions (L1, L2, L3) vary in spot angle, range, colour, and intensity, while the texture settings (T1, T2, T3) differ in colour, reflectiveness, and smoothness. This diversity introduces realistic variations in illumination and surface properties, allowing for robust assessment of depth estimation under a wide range of conditions. As there is no official split for the UCL dataset, we followed Mathew et al. [19] in using split ratios of $8 : 1 : 1$ for training, validation, and testing.

C3VD Dataset [5]: This dataset ontains real images recorded in a phantom with ground-truth depth. In total, 22 short video sequences were registered to generate $10,015$ total frames with paired ground truth depth. The depth is clipped between $[0-100]$ mm. The dataset also includes screening videos acquired by a gastroenterologist with paired ground truth poses and 3D surface models. A real Olympus endoscope has captured the images in a phantom silicone model of a human colon. The data is annotated with ground-truth depth by applying 2D-3D registration of the 3D phantom models. The C3VD dataset is divided according to the colon's four main sections: Cecum, Transverse, Descending, and Sigmoid. Each section is further subdivided based on varying textures to support domain randomisation, resulting in a total of 21 classes. As there is no official split for the C3VD dataset, we followed Rodríguez-Puigvert et al. [27] training and testing splits.

3.2   DepthClassNet Framework

We propose a triple-encoder network to predict high-quality depth maps and their text-based classification by incorporating an NLP text-based classification: Contrastive Language-Image Pre-training (CLIP) [22]. Our approach uses parallel encoding branches to process features from RGB images, edge maps derived using the Scharr filter, and text prompts, as shown in Fig. 1. We introduce the Image Embedding Block (IEB) to process the features extracted from RGB images to facilitate their alignment with textual features effectively. Additionally, we use a combined loss function comprised of depth, edge and classification loss to evaluate the precision of depth prediction and texture description outputs. By balancing these terms, we encourage the network to learn representations that capture precise structural cues and high-level semantic information. To assess the performance of our approach, we conducted experiments on the Colonoscopy Depth - UCL dataset [26] and C3VD dataset [5]. Our DepthClassNet model does not require post-processing or multi-stage training, as it is trained end-to-end.

For the monocular depth estimation (MDE) task, we adapted the MDE-ED model [1] within our framework. MDE-ED employs a dual-encoder structure that integrates edge information to enhance depth estimation accuracy. Since MDE-ED was initially designed for sparse images from LiDAR and Kinetics, and our dataset is fully dense, we empirically found that simplifying the decoder and removing the depth refinement diffusion module from the original MDE-ED architecture provided comparable performance with reduced computational demands. To create DepthClassNet, we modified the MDE-ED decoder architecture to start with the smallest feature maps from the FFM module. Each subsequent decoder block upsamples and refines these feature maps via a transposed convolution layer followed by a ReLU activation function. Skip connections from the FFM are concatenated to each decoder block's output, effectively merging encoder features to enhance the recovery of fine details. This iterative upsampling process progressively reconstructs spatial details and refines the depth map until it reaches half of the final output resolution. Finally, the depth projection block performs the final upsampling to the desired output size. It compresses the decoder output into a single-channel representation through a 1×1 convolution layer, followed by a sigmoid activation to normalise the predicted depth values within the range 0 and 1.

During inference, DepthClassNet demonstrates improved memory efficiency, requiring approximately 1.3 GB of VRAM on a single NVIDIA A5000 GPU

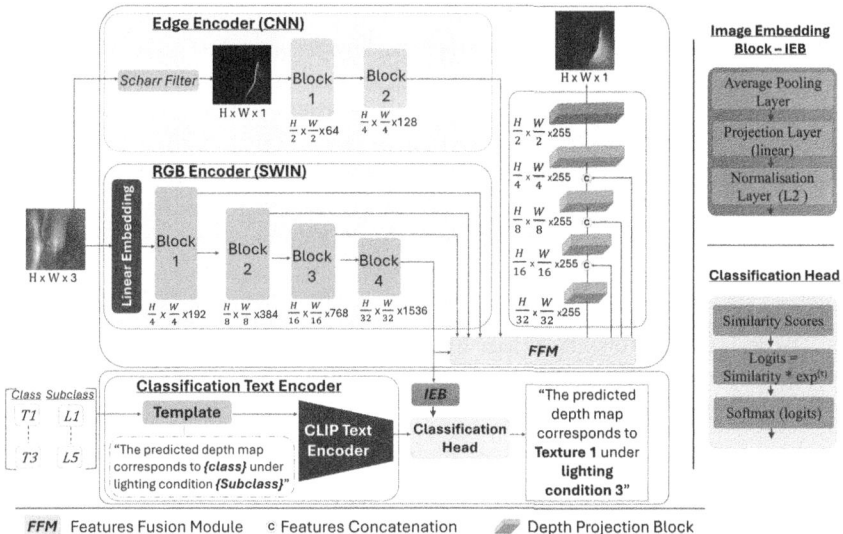

Fig. 1. The proposed DepthClassNet model consists of two main components: MDE and Text-based Classification. The MDE includes an RGB encoder (SWIN) fine-tuned on RGB images and an edge encoder trained on edge maps derived using the Scharr filter. The FFM module takes four inputs from the SWIN and one input of latent features from the Edge Encoder. The fused features from the FFM module are then processed through a multiscale decoder with a final depth projection block to predict the depth map. For the classification task, we generate text prompts that incorporate both the texture class and light condition subclasses. These generated prompts are then input to the CLIP text encoder for fine-tuning. The IEB projects high-dimensional image features extracted from the SWIN encoder into an embedding space that aligns with the dimensionality of the text embeddings. Finally, the classification head calculates the predicted class corresponding to the highest probability. The final outputs of our framework are the depth map and the corresponding text description, including the class name and its associated subclass. During training, edge maps are derived directly from the available ground truth data, enabling the model to learn to predict more accurate edges, while in inference, it is extracted directly from the RGB images.

with a batch size of 1 and input resolution of 256×256. In contrast, the MDE-ED model [1] requires around 1.6 GB of VRAM for a lower-resolution input 228×320. This reduction in memory usage highlights the optimisation of Depth-ClassNet, making it particularly suitable for resource-constrained applications.

3.3   Image Embedding Block - IEB

To adapt CLIP to our framework, where the image encoder is replaced with SWIN as the RGB image encoder, we introduce an Image Embedding Block (IEB) to align the extracted RGB features with the textual embeddings. The high-dimensional image features obtained from the SWIN encoder, denoted as

$X \in \mathbb{R}^{B \times C \times H \times W}$, are initially aggregated using global average pooling over spatial dimensions, yielding the aggregated feature vector $X_{\text{avg}} \in \mathbb{R}^{B \times C}$. Subsequently, the aggregated feature vector X_{avg} is transformed by a linear projection layer to match the dimensionality of the textual embeddings. The projected image embeddings X_{proj} are then normalised using L2 normalisation to ensure unit norm. This normalisation ensures that the cosine similarity between image and text embeddings effectively captures their semantic similarities, independent of embedding magnitude, consequently making these embeddings suitable for downstream text-based classification tasks.

3.4   Text-Based Classification Module

We modified CLIP [22] by utilising feature maps from the SWIN encoder as image embeddings instead of relying on its default image encoder, enhancing the model's ability to capture more discriminative and informative visual representations. In addition, instead of fixed text prompts, we create a custom ontology from dataset-specific descriptive labels, ensuring textual representations align with the data classes. This adaptation shifts CLIP's focus from generic image-text alignment to a specialised framework for texture-based classification, where depth map reconstruction and semantic association are critical for medical imaging. Following CLIP [22], the classification head computes the cosine similarity between the normalised image and text features. Let the image features be $\mathbf{F}_{\text{img}} \in \mathbb{R}^{B \times 512}$ and the normalised text features be $\mathbf{F}_{\text{text}} \in \mathbb{R}^{B \times 512}$. The cosine similarity is computed as $\mathbf{S} = \mathbf{F}_{\text{img}} \cdot \mathbf{F}_{\text{text}}^{\top} \in \mathbb{R}^{B \times N}$, where each entry S_{ij} represents the similarity between an image and one of the N classes.

Next, we scale the similarity scores using a learnable temperature parameter τ, such that logits $= \mathbf{S} \cdot \exp(\tau)$, which modulates the sharpness of the similarity distribution. The softmax function is then applied along the class dimension to convert the logits into a probability distribution over the N classes. The predicted class for each image is determined by $\text{pred}_i = \arg\max_j (\mathbf{p}_i)_j$, for $i = 1, \ldots, B$. The final output obtains the predicted depth map textual description.

3.5   Loss Function

The total loss combines two main Losses: depth loss and classification loss functions:

$$\mathcal{L}_{\text{total}}(Y, \widehat{Y}) = \lambda_1 \, \mathcal{L}_{\text{Depth}}(Y, \widehat{Y}) + \lambda_2 \, \mathcal{L}_{\text{Class}}(C, \widehat{C}) \tag{1}$$

where λ_1 and λ_2 are defined as the weight parameters and empirically set to 0.8 and 0.2, for depth and class losses, respectively.

Depth Loss Function: The depth loss combines two losses to predict depth maps accurately. It contains SiLog [8] and edge losses:

$$\mathcal{L}_{\text{total depth}}(Y, \widehat{Y}) = \lambda \, \mathcal{L}_{\text{SiLog}}(Y, \widehat{Y}) + \mathcal{L}_{\text{Edge}}(Y, \widehat{Y}) \tag{2}$$

where λ is defined as the weight parameters and empirically set to 0.7 and 0.3, for SiLog and Edge losses, respectively. We use the SiLog loss function [8] to enhance scale-invariant depth estimation by minimising logarithmic differences between predicted and ground-truth depths.

To prioritise edge precision over general visual similarity, we modify the Mean Squared Error (MSE) to focus on disparities between edge representations rather than pixel-wise differences:

$$\mathcal{L}_{Edge} = \frac{1}{n} \sum_{i=1}^{H} \sum_{j=1}^{W} \left(E(y)_{ij} - E(\hat{y})_{ij} \right)^2 \tag{3}$$

where $E(y)$ and $E(\hat{y})$ are the edge maps of the true and predicted images, respectively, and $E(y)_{ij}$ and $E(\hat{y})_{ij}$ are the intensity values of the edges at pixel location (i, j), derived using the Scharr filter. n is the total number of samples. This involves computing the gradient magnitudes for each pixel.

By assigning weights to each component of the loss function, we empirically balance the contributions of numerical accuracy, perceptual quality, and structural details.

Classification Loss Function: Given that the model computes cosine similarities between the image and text embeddings, we consider the resulting logits as a probability distribution over the target classes after applying the softmax function. Thus, we employ the cross-entropy loss to quantify the discrepancy between the predicted distribution and the true class labels:

$$\mathcal{L}_{\text{Class}} = - \sum_{i=1}^{n} c_i \log(\hat{c}_i) \tag{4}$$

where c is the true label for class i, and $\hat{c}_i$ denotes the predicted probability for class i. This loss function drives the optimisation process, improving the alignment between image embeddings and corresponding text labels.

4   Results

4.1   Model Implementation

We conduct a series of experiments to train and evaluate the effectiveness of our proposed DepthClassNet model. For training the model, we used a batch size of 8 for 30 epochs on a single node with 2x Nvidia A5000 (24 GB) GPUs. We choose AdamW optimiser with $(\beta_1, \beta_2, w) = (0.9, 0.999, 0.01)$, where w is the weight decay. For data augmentation, we applied a series of random transformations such as resizing, random cropping, horizontal flipping, and random rotations. During inference on a single 256×256 image, the Swin encoder takes 16.76 ms. When combined with the edge encoder, this increases to 17.50 ms. With the addition of the FFM, the inference time rises to 18.89 ms. Overall, the complete DepthClassNet model takes 19.49 ms and requires approximately 1.3 GB of VRAM on a single NVIDIA A5000 GPU with a batch size of 1 and input resolution of 256×256.

4.2   Evaluation Results

Our proposed DepthClassNet model is evaluated on two tasks: monocular depth estimation (MDE) and texture-based classification. For MDE task, we report standard quantitative metrics commonly used in MDE including Absolute Relative Error (**Abs Rel**), Root Mean Squared Error (**RMSE**), and Root Mean Squared Log Error (**RMSE log**), which quantify depth estimation errors, where lower values indicate better depth prediction accuracy. The threshold metrics (δ_1 < 1.25, δ_2 < 1.25^2, δ_3 < 1.25^3) quantify the proportion of predictions within specific error bounds relative to ground truth, with higher percentages reflecting improved performance. For the classification task, to the best of our knowledge, we are the first to address classification on depth datasets. Evaluation is performed using standard metrics: Precision (**P**), Recall (**R**), F1-score (**F1**), Average, and overall Accuracy, providing a comprehensive assessment of the model's ability to distinguish between texture categories accurately.

Evaluation on the UCL Dataset: DepthClassNet achieves state-of-the-art performance with cleaner and smoother depth estimations while preserving sharp object edges. While MDE-ED [1] achieves the lowest errors in Abs Rel and RMSE, together with the highest δ_1 score, indicating strong baseline performance in capturing coarse depth structures, DepthClassNet achieves the best RMSE log (0.116) and the highest δ_2 and δ_3 values, as shown in Table 1. The qualitative results presented in Fig. 2 further illustrate the robustness and precision of our framework.

For the text-based classification, we employed both a traditional CNN-based classification model (ResNet50) and a vision-language model based on Contrastive Language-Image Pre-training (CLIP), to provide a baseline and demonstrate the effectiveness of our approach, as illustrated in Table 3, which presents the classification performance of our DepthClassNet model compared to ResNet and CLIP on the UCL dataset. In Table 3, (T1 L3) corresponds to "The predicted depth map has Texture T1 under the lighting condition L3", (T2 L2) to "The predicted depth map has Texture T2 under the lighting condition L2", and (T3 L2) to "The predicted depth map has Texture T3 under the lighting condition L2". Among the baseline models, ResNet outperforms CLIP, achieving an accuracy of 0.97 compared to 0.95 for CLIP. However, the results indicate that DepthClassNet with fine-tuned CLIP weights achieves perfect classification performance across all categories, with an F1-score and accuracy of 1.00. It demonstrates the significant benefit of our modification by integrating SWIN as an image encoder instead of the original CLIP image encoder, the developed IEB to align the image embeddings, and the fine-tuning of CLIP on domain-specific depth data. Even without fine-tuning, DepthClassNet with frozen CLIP weights outperforms both ResNet and CLIP, achieving an accuracy of 0.98, further validating the architecture. However, when CLIP is fine-tuned on the UCL dataset, despite the strong performance of DepthClassNet, it is important to note that the relatively small dataset size (1456 images) may have contributed to the high classification scores, particularly for the fine-tuned model.

Table 1. Evaluation metrics on the UCL test set for depth estimation. Methods 1–7 were originally trained and evaluated on the UCL dataset by Mathew et al. [19]. Methods [4,36] and [30] were retrained by us for direct comparison, as the UCL dataset was not used in their original works. The best results are highlighted in bold. *LT: Learning Type (USL: Unsupervised Learning, SSL: Self-Supervised Learning, and SL: Supervised Learning).

Method	LT*	Abs Rel $\downarrow$	RMSE $\downarrow$	RMSE log $\downarrow$	$\delta_1 \uparrow$	$\delta_2 \uparrow$	$\delta_3 \uparrow$
SfMLearner [37]	USL	0.451	1.768	0.537	0.366	0.618	0.785
Monodepth1 [10]	USL	0.444	1.755	0.531	0.371	0.625	0.790
DDVO [33]	USL	0.452	1.768	0.538	0.366	0.618	0.785
Monodepth2 [11]	SSL	0.446	1.757	0.532	0.360	0.624	0.789
HR Depth [18]	SSL	0.448	1.762	0.534	0.369	0.621	0.788
AF-SfML2 [29]	SSL	0.352	1.581	0.448	0.445	0.712	0.852
SoftEnNet [19]	SSL	0.145	0.650	0.184	0.823	0.954	0.983
Adabins [4]	SL	0.255	0.048	0.207	0.743	0.832	0.941
NewCRFs [36]	SL	0.152	0.0188	0.187	0.871	0.941	0.970
NDDepth [30]	SL	0.160	0.0189	0.197	0.854	0.933	0.966
MDE-ED [1]	SL	**0.085**	**0.0181**	0.118	**0.962**	0.985	0.991
DepthClassNet	SL	0.142	0.0187	**0.116**	0.954	**0.989**	**0.993**

Evaluation on the C3VD Dataset: DepthClassNet delivers the best overall performance, as demonstrated in Table 2. Our model has the lowest RMSE (2.01) and Abs Rel (0.074) and the highest δ_1, δ_2 and δ_3 accuracies, showing that its depth estimates are both globally precise and locally consistent. Although PPSNet reports the best RMSE log (0.049) and the self-supervised DPT-Hybrid yields the lowest Abs Rel (0.0699), DepthClassNet ranks second (0.075) while simultaneously delivering the smallest Abs Rel. The combination of the lowest linear error (RMSE) and lowest relative error (Abs Rel) shows that DepthClassNet minimises absolute and proportional disparities. Compared with MDE-ED, DepthClassNet reduces RMSE, RMSE log, and Abs Rel, whereas it increases δ_1, δ_2, and δ_3 which emphasises the benefit of our redesigned decoder, edge integration, and joint depth-classification training. The qualitative results demonstrated in Fig. 3 further show the robustness and precision of DepthClass-Net.

Table 3 reports the output of the classification head, where DepthClassNet (frozen CLIP) already surpasses both baselines, reaching 0.93 F1 and 0.93 accuracy, while DepthClassNet (fine-tuned CLIP) delivers the best results, increasing the average F1 and accuracy to 0.95. To ensure a fair comparison with the UCL text-based classification, we used the same evaluation protocol, hyperparameters and metric definitions, when training and testing on the C3VD dataset. These findings mirror the trend observed on the UCL dataset i.e., fine-tuning CLIP within DepthClassNet, coupled with the proposed SWIN encoder and image-

Table 2. Quantitative comparison on the C3VD testset. We utilised the dataset splits as LightDepth [27]. Methods [27,30] were retrained by us for direct comparison, as the UCL dataset was not used in their original works. *LT: Learning Type (USL: Unsupervised Learning, SSL: Self-Supervised Learning, and SL: Supervised Learning). Lower is better for RMSE, AbsRel, and SqRel. Higher is better for δ, and the best results are highlighted in bold.

Method	LT*	RMSE ↓	RMSElog ↓	AbsRel ↓	δ_1 ↑	δ_2 ↑	δ_3 ↑
UNet [27]	SL	5.52	0.113	0.0902	0.9172	0.9943	0.9994
DPT-Hybrid [24]	SSL	4.10	0.086	**0.0699**	0.9640	0.9865	0.9913
MonoDepth2 [11]	SSL	9.11	0.129	–	0.4355	–	–
Wang et al. [34]	SL	7.51	0.155	–	0.4887	–	–
NDDepth [30]	SL	10.89	0.442	0.4851	0.4528	0.7093	0.8731
LightDepth [27]	SSL	5.27	0.107	0.0780	0.9525	0.9961	0.9992
PPSNet [21]	SL	2.06	**0.049**	–	0.8932	–	–
MDE-ED [1]	SL	2.14	0.175	0.0891	0.8874	0.9963	0.9983
DepthClassNet	SL	**2.01**	0.075	0.0743	**0.994**	**0.9986**	**0.9996**

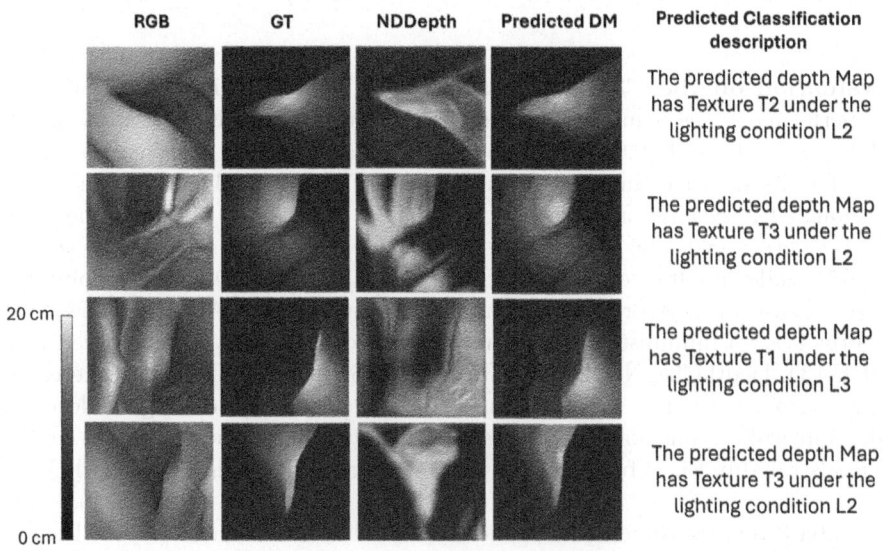

Fig. 2. Our model's predictions on the UCL dataset; the first column displays the RGB images, the second column shows the ground truth, the third column presents results using NDDepth [30], and the fourth column presents the predicted depth maps from our DepthClassNet Model. Our model successfully estimates the depth of the different colon textures. The last column shows the textural description of the results predicted by DepthClassNet.

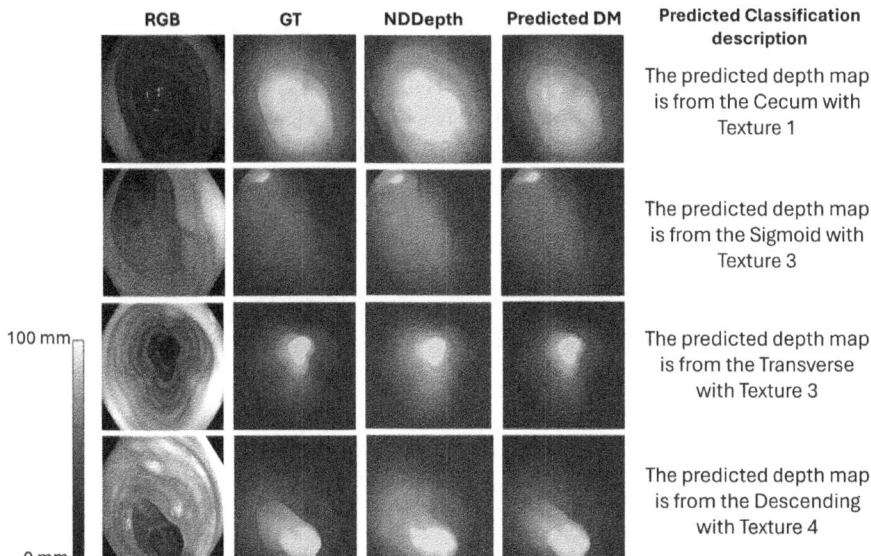

| RGB | GT | NDDepth | Predicted DM | Predicted Classification description |

Fig. 3. Our model's predictions on the C3VD dataset; the first column displays the RGB images, the second column shows the ground truth, the third column presents results using NDDepth [30], and the fourth column presents the predicted depth maps from our DepthClassNet Model. The last column shows the textural description of the results predicted by DepthClassNet.

embedding block yields consistent improvement across all colon sections and texture variants, confirming the model's robustness and its capacity to generalise to a larger more diversified 21-class setting. In Table 3, the labels correspond to the following text descriptions of the depth map classes: Cecum T1/T2/T3: "The predicted depth map is from the Cecum with Textures 1, 2, or 3". Sigmoid T3: "The predicted depth map is from the Sigmoid with Texture 3". Transverse T2/T3/T4: "The predicted depth map is from the Transverse with Textures 2, 3, or 4". Descending T4: "The predicted depth map is from the Descending colon with Texture 4".

Limitations of the Prposed Approach. Despite strong quantitative performance, the proposed method remained sensitive to small intensity variations on almost all the texture-less mucosal surfaces in C3VD dataset. The predicted depth map shows spurious bumps and holes, completely missing the smooth bowl-like gradient seen in the ground truth, as shown in Fig. 4. This indicates higher dependence of the model on local edge cues, when the scene contains little or no texture, or when glare in the upper-left corner obscures gradients. The model generates depth discontinuities instead of recognising that the colon wall is largely planar. The problem likely arises from (i) a weak smoothness term, (ii) a limited receptive field that fails to capture large-scale structure, and (iii) insufficient data augmentation for low-contrast or glare-affected frames. Stronger

Table 3. Per-class, average and overall accuracy on the UCL and C3VD datasets. *DepthClassNet refers to training with frozen CLIP weights, while **DepthClassNet is our model with CLIP fine-tuned on the UCL Dataset.

(a) UCL dataset

Model	Class	P	R	F1
	(T1 L3)	0.92	1.00	0.96
	(T2 L2)	0.94	1.00	0.97
ResNet [13]	(T1 L3)	1.00	0.97	0.99
	Average	0.95	0.99	0.97
	Accuracy			**0.97**
	(T1 L3)	0.90	1.00	0.95
	(T2 L2)	0.99	0.89	0.94
CLIP [3]	(T1 L3)	1.00	0.99	0.98
	Average	0.96	0.96	0.95
	Accuracy			**0.95**
	(T1 L3)	0.99	1.00	0.97
	(T2 L2)	0.96	0.92	0.99
*DepthClassNet	(T1 L3)	1.00	1.00	0.98
	Average	0.98	0.97	0.98
	Accuracy			**0.98**
	(T1 L3)	1.00	1.00	1.00
	(T2 L2)	1.00	1.00	1.00
**DepthClassNet	(T3 L2)	1.00	1.00	1.00
	Average	1.00	1.00	1.00
	Accuracy			**1.00**

(b) C3VD dataset

Class	P	R	F1
Cecum T1	0.90	0.92	0.91
Cecum T2	0.95	0.93	0.94
Cecum T3	0.88	0.90	0.89
Sigmoid T3	0.93	0.96	0.95
Transverse T2	0.89	0.91	0.90
Transverse T3	0.91	0.91	0.92
Transverse T4	0.91	0.91	0.93
Descendin T4	0.91	0.92	0.92
Average	0.91	0.92	0.92
Accuracy			**0.92**
Cecum T1	0.85	0.85	0.85
Cecum T2	0.90	0.90	0.90
Cecum T3	0.92	0.92	0.92
Sigmoid T3	0.94	0.94	0.94
Transverse T2	0.92	0.92	0.92
Transverse T3	0.89	0.89	0.89
Transverse T4	0.89	0.89	0.89
Descendin T4	0.89	0.89	0.89
Average	0.90	0.90	0.90
Accuracy			**0.90**
Cecum T1	0.92	0.90	0.91
Cecum T2	0.94	0.95	0.94
Cecum T3	0.95	0.93	0.94
Sigmoid T3	0.96	0.94	0.95
Transverse T2	0.93	0.92	0.92
Transverse T3	0.94	0.92	0.93
Transverse T4	0.93	0.94	0.93
Descendin T4	0.92	0.93	0.93
Average	0.94	0.93	0.93
Accuracy			**0.93**
Cecum T1	0.92	0.93	0.93
Cecum T2	0.95	0.96	0.96
Cecum T3	0.93	0.94	0.93
Sigmoid T3	0.95	0.98	0.97
Transverse T3	0.94	0.96	0.95
Transverse T3	0.95	0.94	0.95
Transverse T4	0.94	0.94	0.96
Descendin T4	0.94	0.95	0.95
Average	0.94	0.95	0.95
Accuracy			**0.95**

RGB   GT   Predicted DM

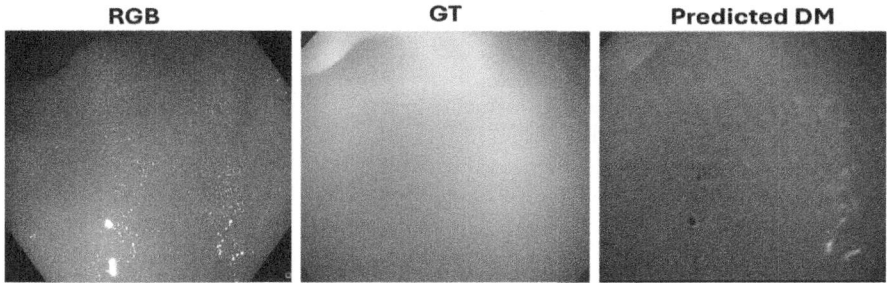

Fig. 4. While making predictions on low texture regions, the proposed model fails to generate good quality depth maps, instead, it generates spurious output as shown in the figure above. The left image is the input to the model, the second image shows the ground truth (GT), and the right image shows the predicted depth map from the proposed model.

smoothness constraints, larger-scale feature aggregation, e.g., using self-attention or multi-scale pooling, might help to suppress these high-frequency artefacts and allow the network to recover the true varying depth profile.

5   Conclusion

In this work, we introduced DepthClassNet, a novel multitask framework that performs monocular depth estimation and texture classification for medical imaging. By leveraging a tri-encoder architecture, incorporating an RGB encoder, an edge encoder, and a modified CLIP text encoder, our model effectively integrates multimodal information to enhance depth prediction and classification accuracy. It demonstrates the significant benefit of our modification by integrating SWIN as an image encoder instead of the original CLIP image encoder and the fine-tuning of CLIP on domain-specific depth data. The Image Embedding Block (IEB) ensures strong alignment between visual and textual representations for classification. Our designed loss function, incorporating depth, edge, and classification components, optimally balances the multitasking learning objectives. Evaluated on the Coloscopy Depth - UCL and the C3VD datasets, DepthClassNet achieves state-of-the-art performance, demonstrating its robustness and effectiveness in medical imaging applications. The results highlight the potential of combining depth estimation and texture classification to improve diagnostic accuracy and surgical planning. Future work will explore generalisation to more extensive and diverse datasets with low-contrast and glare-contaminated frames, and the model's adaptability to other medical imaging modalities, further advancing its applicability in clinical practice.

References

1. Abdallah, B., Raza, S., Sanchez, V.: Edge-guided monocular absolute depth estimation with diffusion-based refinement. In: 2025 IEEE International Conference on Image Processing (ICIP). IEEE (2025)
2. An, G., et al.: Hierarchical deep learning models using transfer learning for disease detection and classification based on small number of medical images. Sci. Rep. **11**(1), 4250 (2021)
3. Auty, D., Mikolajczyk, K.: Learning to prompt clip for monocular depth estimation: exploring the limits of human language. In: 2023 IEEE/CVF International Conference on Computer Vision Workshops (ICCVW), pp. 2031–2049 (2023)
4. Bhat, S.F., Alhashim, I., Wonka, P.: AdaBins: depth estimation using adaptive bins. In: Proceedings of the IEEE/CVF Conference on Computer Vision and Pattern Recognition, pp. 4009–4018 (2021)
5. Bobrow, T.L., et al.: Colonoscopy 3D video dataset with paired depth from 2D–3D registration. Med. Image Anal. **90**, 102956 (2023)
6. Chen, F., Lu, Y.: Can language really understand depth? In: Neural Information Processing, pp. 377–389. Springer, Singapore (2024)
7. Chen, R.J., , et al.: SLAM endoscopy enhanced by adversarial depth prediction. arXiv preprint arXiv:1907.00283 (2019)
8. Eigen, D., Puhrsch, C., Fergus, R.: Depth map prediction from a single image using a multi-scale deep network. In: Advances in Neural Information Processing Systems, pp. 2366–2374 (2014)
9. Gelman, R., Abràmoff, M.D.: A pilot study of deep learning-based monocular depth estimation from fundus photographs. Medinformatics (2024)
10. Godard, C., Mac Aodha, O., Brostow, G.J.: Unsupervised monocular depth estimation with left-right consistency. In: Proceedings of the IEEE Conference on Computer Vision and Pattern Recognition, pp. 270–279 (2017)
11. Godard, C., et al.: Digging into self-supervised monocular depth estimation. In: Proceedings of the IEEE/CVF International Conference on Computer Vision, pp. 3828–3838 (2019)
12. Han, J.J., , et al.: Depth anything in medical images: a comparative study. arXiv preprint arXiv:2401.16600 (2024)
13. He, K., Zhang, X., Ren, S., Sun, J.: Deep residual learning for image recognition. In: Proceedings of the IEEE Conference on Computer Vision and Pattern Recognition, pp. 770–778 (2016)
14. He, Q., et al.: MonoLoT: self-supervised monocular depth estimation in low-texture scenes for automatic robotic endoscopy. IEEE J. Biomed. Health Inform. **28**(10), 6078–6091 (2024). https://doi.org/10.1109/JBHI.2024.3423791
15. Lee, W., Park, N., Woo, W.: Depth-assisted real-time 3D object detection for augmented reality. In: ICAT, pp. 126–132 (2011)
16. Liu, X., et al.: Dense depth estimation in monocular endoscopy with self-supervised learning methods. IEEE Trans. Med. Imaging **39**(5), 1438–1447 (2020). https://doi.org/10.1109/TMI.2019.2950936
17. Liu, X., et al.: Reconstructing sinus anatomy from endoscopic video–towards a radiation-free approach for quantitative longitudinal assessment. In: Medical Image Computing and Computer Assisted Intervention–MICCAI 2020: 23rd International Conference, Lima, Peru, 4–8 October 2020, Proceedings, Part III 23, pp. 3–13. Springer (2020)

18. Lyu, X., et al.: HR-depth: high resolution self-supervised monocular depth estimation. In: Proceedings of the AAAI Conference on Artificial Intelligence, vol. 35, pp. 2294–2301 (2021)

19. Mathew, A., , et al.: SoftEnNet: symbiotic monocular depth estimation and lumen segmentation for colonoscopy endorobots. arXiv preprint arXiv:2301.08157 (2023)

20. Ozyoruk, K.B., et al.: EndoSLAM dataset and an unsupervised monocular visual odometry and depth estimation approach for endoscopic videos. Med. Image Anal. **71**, 102058 (2021)

21. Paruchuri, A., et al.: Leveraging near-field lighting for monocular depth estimation from endoscopy videos. In: European Conference on Computer Vision, pp. 473–491. Springer (2024)

22. Radford, A., et al.: Learning transferable visual models from natural language supervision. In: International Conference on Machine Learning, pp. 8748–8763. PMLR (2021)

23. Rajapaksha, U., et al.: Deep learning-based depth estimation methods from monocular image and videos: a comprehensive survey. ACM Comput. Surv. **56**(12), 1–51 (2024)

24. Ranftl, R., Bochkovskiy, A., Koltun, V.: Vision transformers for dense prediction. In: Proceedings of the IEEE/CVF International Conference on Computer Vision, pp. 12179–12188 (2021)

25. Ranjan, A., et al.: Competitive collaboration: joint unsupervised learning of depth, camera motion, optical flow and motion segmentation. In: Proceedings of the IEEE/CVF Conference on Computer Vision and Pattern Recognition, pp. 12240–12249 (2019)

26. Rau, A., et al.: Implicit domain adaptation with conditional generative adversarial networks for depth prediction in endoscopy. Int. J. Comput. Assist. Radiol. Surg. 1–10 (2019)

27. Rodríguez-Puigvert, J., et al.: LightDepth: single-view depth self-supervision from illumination decline. In: Proceedings of the IEEE/CVF International Conference on Computer Vision, pp. 21273–21283 (2023)

28. Saxena, S., et al.: The surprising effectiveness of diffusion models for optical flow and monocular depth estimation. In: Advances in Neural Information Processing Systems, vol. 36 (2024)

29. Shao, S., et al.: Self-supervised monocular depth and ego-motion estimation in endoscopy: appearance flow to the rescue. Med. Image Anal. **77**, 102338 (2022)

30. Shao, S., et al.: NDDepth: normal-distance assisted monocular depth estimation and completion. IEEE Trans. Pattern Anal. Mach. Intell. (2024)

31. Turan, M., , et al.: Unsupervised odometry and depth learning for endoscopic capsule robots. In: 2018 IEEE/RSJ International Conference on Intelligent Robots and Systems (IROS), pp. 1801–1807. IEEE (2018)

32. Visentini-Scarzanella, M., et al.: Deep monocular 3D reconstruction for assisted navigation in bronchoscopy. Int. J. Comput. Assist. Radiol. Surg. **12**, 1089–1099 (2017)

33. Wang, C., et al.: Learning depth from monocular videos using direct methods. In: Proceedings of the IEEE Conference on Computer Vision and Pattern Recognition, pp. 2022–2030 (2018)

34. Wang, S., et al.: A surface-normal based neural framework for colonoscopy reconstruction. In: International Conference on Information Processing in Medical Imaging, pp. 797–809. Springer (2023)

35. Yang, Y., et al.: A geometry-aware deep network for depth estimation in monocular endoscopy. Eng. Appl. Artif. Intell. **122** (2023). https://doi.org/10.1016/j.engappai.2023.105989

36. Yuan, W., Gu, X., Dai, Z., Zhu, S., Tan, P.: Neural window fully-connected CRFs for monocular depth estimation. In: Proceedings of the IEEE/CVF Conference on Computer Vision and Pattern Recognition, pp. 3916–3925 (2022)

37. Zhou, T., Brown, M., Snavely, N., Lowe, D.G.: Unsupervised learning of depth and ego-motion from video. In: Proceedings of the IEEE Conference on Computer Vision and Pattern Recognition, pp. 1851–1858 (2017)

38. Zia, S., et al.: RGB-D object recognition using deep convolutional neural networks. In: Proceedings of the IEEE International Conference on Computer Vision Workshops, pp. 896–903 (2017)

Assessing the Generalization Performance of SAM for Ureteroscopy Scene Understanding

Martin Villagrana[1], Francisco Lopez-Tiro[1,2], Clement Larose[3],
Gilberto Ochoa-Ruiz[1(✉)], and Christian Daul[2(✉)]

[1] School of Engineering and Sciences, Tecnologico de Monterrey,
Monterrey, Mexico
gilberto.ochoa@tec.mx
[2] CRAN UMR 7039, Université de Lorraine and CNRS, Nancy, France
christian.daul@univ-lorraine.fr
[3] CHRU de Nancy-Brabois, Service d'urologie, Vandœuvre-les-Nancy, France

Abstract. The segmentation of kidney stones is regarded as a critical preliminary step to enable the identification of urinary stone types through machine- or deep-learning-based approaches. In urology, manual segmentation is considered tedious and impractical due to the typically large scale of image databases and the continuous generation of new data. In this study, the potential of the Segment Anything Model (SAM)—a state-of-the-art deep learning framework—is investigated for the automation of kidney stone segmentation. The performance of SAM is evaluated in comparison to traditional models, including U-Net, Residual U-Net, and Attention U-Net, which, despite their efficiency, frequently exhibit limitations in generalizing to unseen datasets. The findings highlight SAM's superior adaptability and efficiency. While SAM achieves comparable performance to U-Net on in-distribution data (Accuracy: 97.68 ± 3.04; Dice: 97.78 ± 2.47; IoU: 95.76 ± 4.18), it demonstrates significantly enhanced generalization capabilities on out-of-distribution data, surpassing all U-Net variants by margins of up to 23%.

Keywords: Segmentation · Deep Learning · Endoscopy

1 Introduction

Kidney stone formation is recognized as a prevalent condition affecting millions of individuals globally. In the United States, lifetime prevalence rates have been reported to range from 7.2% to 10.1%, while higher rates—such as 21.1%—have been observed in specific populations [1]. Early detection and accurate diagnosis of kidney stone formation are essential to ensure the prescription of effective treatments and to mitigate complications, including renal damage, infections,

---

M. Villagrana and F. Lopez-Tiro—Equal contribution.

© The Author(s), under exclusive license to Springer Nature Switzerland AG 2026
S. Ali et al. (Eds.): MIUA 2025, LNCS 15917, pp. 247–260, 2026.
https://doi.org/10.1007/978-3-031-98691-8_18

and recurrent stone formation [2]. Through timely intervention, patient outcomes can be significantly improved, and healthcare costs may be reduced. Due to its high incidence and association with severe pain, the detection of kidney stones is considered a critical component of medical practice, particularly for patients with recurrent episodes or those at elevated risk [3].

The current diagnosis of kidney stones is primarily based on Morpho-Constitutional Analysis (MCA), a process that depends extensively on visual inspection and biochemical analysis performed by clinicians [4]. Consequently, numerous attempts have been made to support this diagnostic process through computer vision-based approaches. Recent advances in deep learning (DL) have demonstrated promising potential for improving kidney stone classification [5–7]. These methods could accelerate diagnosis by automating the traditionally operator-dependent MCA when conducted during endoscopic stone recognition (ESR) procedures [8], a critical advancement for patients requiring immediate intervention. Accurate segmentation of detected kidney stones is regarded as an essential preliminary step prior to classification, as it allows the stone to be isolated from surrounding tissues, thereby enhancing diagnostic accuracy [9]. Deep learning techniques, particularly convolutional neural networks (CNNs) and transformer-based models, have exhibited notable efficacy in segmentation tasks, as relevant features within complex medical images can be automatically identified, improving the reliability of image-based diagnosis [10,11].

Traditional segmentation models, including U-Net and its variants (Attention U-Net and Residual U-Net), have demonstrated strong performance in image segmentation tasks. The U-Net architecture, while recognized for its limited data efficiency, has been shown to effectively preserve spatial information through its encoder-decoder structure, though challenges remain when processing complex or noisy images [12]. Residual U-Net, which incorporates residual connections, has been designed to mitigate issues such as vanishing gradients, thereby enhancing performance in deeper network architectures; however, its increased depth can result in longer training times [13]. Attention U-Net enhances traditional U-Net through the integration of attention mechanisms, enabling the model to concentrate on diagnostically relevant regions, though this improvement comes at the cost of higher computational requirements [14]. More recently, transformer-based models like the Segment Anything Model (SAM) [15] have been developed, offering notable adaptability across diverse image types without necessitating extensive task-specific modifications. Despite SAM's promising generalization capabilities, its implementation remains constrained by computational complexity and significant resource demands.

The segmentation of kidney stone images obtained from ureteroscopy videos has traditionally been conducted manually by clinical experts (Fig. 1a). While this approach has proven effective for limited datasets, its application to large-scale databases has been recognized as impractical due to the time-consuming nature of the process and its inherent dependence on operator skill [8]. These limitations could potentially be addressed through advanced deep learning models like SAM, which have been shown to enable accurate and efficient automated

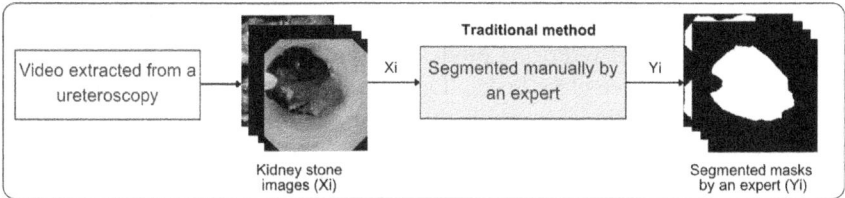

(a) Traditional kidney stone segmenting method.

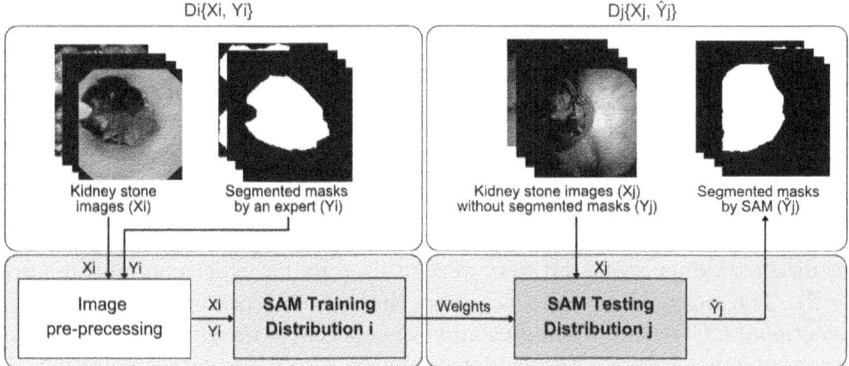

(b) Automatic kidney stone segmentation and generalization method.

Fig. 1. Comparison framework for kidney stone segmentation methods. In traditional approaches (top), frames are extracted from ureteroscopy videos to create Dataset D_i (distribution i), followed by manual expert labeling. The Segment Anything Model pipeline (bottom) is trained on i and its labels, then performs inference on a distinct unlabeled Dataset j (distribution j). Critical note: D_i and D_i represent different data distributions.

segmentation of extensive video collections [15]. SAM's demonstrated capability to generalize across heterogeneous datasets represents a substantial technological advancement, positioning it as a viable alternative to conventional manual segmentation methods for large-scale applications (Fig. 1b).

The principal contributions of this work are summarized as follows:

(i) Demonstrated Superior Generalization of SAM. The Segment Anything Model is shown to exhibit exceptional generalization capabilities for kidney stone segmentation tasks, systematically outperforming traditional architectures (U-Net, Residual U-Net, Attention U-Net). While conventional models exhibit significant performance degradation when applied to unseen data, SAM maintains robust accuracy across both known and unknown distributions when trained on identical datasets. This advancement highlights SAM's potential as a reliable tool for renal image analysis under real-world clinical variability.

(ii) Validated Multi-Class Adaptability Without Retraining. A novel three-class SAM variant ("kidney stone", "laser fiber", and "surrounding tissue") is validated, achieving high performance across both known and unknown distributions—a first in renal segmentation literature. Crucially, this adaptability is accomplished without requiring model retraining, as precision is preserved for both two-class and three-class tasks. This flexibility addresses a critical clinical challenge, where segmentation needs often vary across procedures and patient-specific anatomical presentations.

This work is organized as follows: Sect. 2 details the experimental dataset and methodological framework, with particular emphasis on comparative analysis between conventional deep learning-based segmentation approaches and the SAM. Section 3 presents and analyzes the experimental findings, highlighting key performance comparisons. The study concludes with future research directions and final remarks in Sect. 4.

2   Materials and Methods

2.1   Clinical Image Datasets

Four distinct kidney stone datasets were utilized in our experimental framework (Fig. 2). The image data were acquired through two primary modalities: (1) conventional CCD camera systems and (2) endoscopic imaging captured during ureteroscopic procedures. The key characteristics of these datasets are detailed as follows:

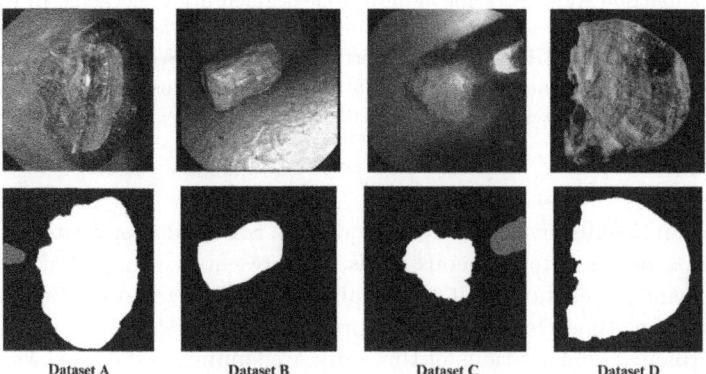

Fig. 2. The four datasets (distributions) of kidney stone images are displayed alongside their corresponding segmentation masks, which include the stone and laser fiber. From right to left: Dataset A (in vivo endoscopic), Dataset B (ex vivo endoscopic), Dataset C (in vivo endoscopic), and Dataset D (ex vivo CCD camera). All datasets enable two-class segmentation (kidney stone and tissue), while only Datasets A and C include a third class (laser).

Database A (D_A): In-vivo Endoscopic Images. This dataset comprises 156 in-vivo endoscopic images capturing three distinct classes: (1) surrounding tissue,

(2) kidney stone, and (3) laser fiber. While designed for either two-class (kidney stone and tissue) or three-class segmentation tasks, only 44 images include complete three-class annotations (with the additional "laser" class). All images feature variable dimensions, typically approximating 1008×1042 pixels [6].

Database (D_B). Ex-vivo Endoscopic Images. This dataset contains 409 ex-vivo images acquired through a simulated renal environment using a kidney cavity phantom. The images feature two annotated classes: kidney stone and surrounding tissue. All images maintain a consistent resolution of 1920×1080 pixels [16].

Database C (D_C). In-vivo Endoscopic Images. This dataset comprises 138 clinical in-vivo images extracted from procedural videos, capturing three distinct classes: (1) living tissue, (2) kidney stones, and (3) surgical instruments (including laser fibers for stone fragmentation). The images are available in two resolutions: 400×400 and 720×720 pixels. This dataset can be used to evaluate the performance of segmentation mode for either two or three classes. Dataset C remains under active clinical acquisition; consequently, all analyses were performed on the most contemporaneous available data stream.

Database (D_D). Ex-vivo CCD-Camera. This dataset consists of 356 ex-vivo images acquired using a charge-coupled device (CCD) imaging system, containing precisely two annotated classes: (1) kidney stone and (2) surrounding environment. The images exhibit variable dimensions, typically approximating 4288×2848 pixels [17].

Data Partitioning and Preprocessing: The datasets were systematically partitioned with an 80%–20% training–testing split for Databases A, B, and D. Database C (153 images) employed a specialized division: 117 training images with two distinct test partitions (21 and 15 images), where test images were extracted from independent video sequences to ensure evaluation robustness.

All images were standardized to square dimensions of 512×512 pixels. Each database includes corresponding ground-truth segmentation masks, which were meticulously annotated by clinical specialists using the original high-resolution images for accurate performance evaluation.

2.2   Kidney Stone Segmentation

This work employs the Segment Anything Model for kidney stone segmentation in ureteroscopic images. The approach requires paired kidney stone images (X_i) and their corresponding ground-truth masks (Y_i) from a source distribution i, formally denoted as $D_i\{X_i, Y_i\}$. The segmentation masks are acquired through conventional manual annotation protocols, where kidney stone boundaries are meticulously delineated by clinical specialists (Fig. 1a).

Automated segmentation is subsequently performed using the SAM, through which new segmentation masks are generated across both the original training distribution (D_i) and previously unseen data distributions (D_j) (Fig. 1b).

2.3   Traditional Method for Segmenting Kidney Stones

The segmentation masks (Y_i) are generated through a standardized protocol where multiple frames exhibiting kidney stones and adjacent tissue are first extracted from ureteroscopic video recordings. These frames are then meticulously annotated at the pixel level by urologists to delineate kidney stone, tissue, and instruments like basket or fiber laser.

Finally, the annotated masks are systematically paired with their corresponding original images (X_i) to form the complete dataset distribution $D_i\{X_i, Y_i\}$ for subsequent analysis.

2.4   Automatic Kidney Stone Segmentation and Generalization

As previously established in Sect. 1, kidney stone segmentation has been demonstrated to be effective for limited datasets but becomes impractical when applied to large-scale collections. To address this limitation, the Segment Anything Model is evaluated using expert-derived annotations from the conventional manual segmentation protocol (Fig. 1a). Following training, the model is employed to automatically produce segmentation masks $(\hat{Y}_i)$, with performance being assessed under two operational conditions: (1) application to the original training distribution $(D_i \rightarrow D_i)$ and (2) generalization to previously unseen data distributions $(D_i \rightarrow D_j)$ (Fig. 1b).

The Segment Anything Model implementation comprises two distinct phases: SAM-training and SAM-testing. During the training phase, an initial preprocessing stage is conducted where input images are normalized and resized to standardized dimensions of 512×512 pixels, ensuring uniform data presentation across all model architectures.

In the SAM-training process, each input image is processed through a transformer-based feature extraction block, where it is condensed into a compact feature matrix. These extracted features are subsequently passed to a decoder head along with relevant model prompts, including potential segmentation masks. Following training completion, the optimized embeddings are utilized during SAM-testing to perform segmentation on either the original data distribution $(D_i \rightarrow D_i)$ or alternative distributions $(D_i \rightarrow D_j)$.

Experimental Setup. This study systematically evaluates the Segment Anything Model's performance in automated mask generation across two distinct class configurations: (1) a two-class paradigm (kidney stone and surrounding tissue) and (2) a three-class paradigm (kidney stone, laser fiber, and tissue). For each configuration, comprehensive evaluations are conducted through both in-distribution and out-distribution experimental designs. The experimental framework is structured to assess model performance under the following conditions:

1. Two-classes configuration. The first configuration focused on binary segmentation (kidney stone vs. tissue) applied to different kidney stone image domains (in-vivo and ex-vivo endoscopic, and ex-vivo CCD-camera).

- *In-distribution:* A single model was trained using SAM-training on dataset A (in-vivo endoscopic images) as the training domain. Once the model was trained with SAM, SAM-testing was performed on the test partition from the same distribution (in-distribution).
- *Out-of-Distribution:* Subsequently, to evaluate the performance of the SAM-trained model on distribution A, inference was performed on the test partition from B, C, and D datasets. Notably, the model trained on A was neither modified nor adapted for these tests, making the evaluations on B, C, and D pure out-distribution cases.

Three U-Net variants—the standard model, Residual U-Net, and Attention-U-Net—were trained to benchmark SAM's performance against classical architectures. All models were trained exclusively on Dataset A and were subsequently evaluated on the test partition of A, B, C, and D datasets. This experimental design was implemented to specifically assess each architecture's out-of-distribution generalization capabilities.

The quantitative evaluation is based on standard metrics: Accuracy, Dice Coefficient, and Intersection over Union (IoU). These metrics can be used for an objective segmentation quality assessment. In the metrics "Accuracy", "Dice", and "IoU", an upward arrow symbol ($\uparrow$) is used to denote that higher values correspond to better performance. Conversely, in the "Error Rate" metric, a downward arrow symbol ($\downarrow$) is employed to indicate that optimal results are those closest to zero.

Testing across four datasets (with distinct distributions) demonstrated the models' generalization capability and robustness for kidney stone segmentation across diverse clinical scenarios. A comparative analysis between SAM and U-Net-based models, including both in-distribution and out-of-distribution evaluations for the selected metrics, is presented in Table 1.

2. Three-classes configuration. The second configuration addresses three-class segmentation (kidney stone, laser, and tissue), utilizing exclusively Datasets A and C as these were the only datasets containing the 'laser' class annotation.

   Due to the limited amount of segmented data available in Dataset A for three classes (44 images), Dataset C (153 images) was selected for SAM initialization. Consequently, Dataset A was reserved exclusively for testing, while the model trained on C was employed for both training and evaluation purposes. Although both datasets A and C were acquired in vivo using an endoscope, they are considered distinct domains. Each dataset was collected at different times with different instruments, resulting in varying image resolutions and quality.

   A dual-model SAM training strategy was implemented: the first model was designed to segment kidney stone and tissue (replicating Experiment 1's approach), while the second model was specialized for laser and tissue segmentation. The predictions from both models were subsequently integrated through fusion to generate final three-class masks, enabling evaluation of SAM's performance on this more complex multiclass task.

- *In-distribution:* For this training phase, the dataset C (comprising 117 training images) was used to initialize SAM-training. The SAM testing procedure was conducted using two separate test partitions. The first test partition consisted of 21 images, while the second included 15 images, both derived from two different ureteroscopy videos.
- *Out-of-Distribution:* The performance of SAM, trained on distribution C and tested with the test partition of dataset A (44 images), was evaluated. It should be noted that the model trained on C was neither modified nor adapted for the test dataset.

The training of the models was performed on a 16 GB Nvidia DGX GPU, using the AdamW Optimizer with a dynamic learning rate adjustment and a warmup phase. A combination of Dice Loss and CE Loss was used to minimize discrepancies between predicted segmentation and ground truth masks. U-Net, Residual U-Net, and Attention U-Net were trained for 80 epochs, while SAM was trained for 200 epochs.

3   Results and Discussion

The segmentation models (SAM and U-Net-based), described in Sect. 2.4, were evaluated using the datasets from Sect. 2.1. Results were obtained for both two-class and three-class segmentation, including quantitative comparisons (Tables 1 and 2) and qualitative evaluations (Figs. 3 and 4). Quantitative analysis was performed using the Intersection over Union (IoU) metric, whose numerical values are reported in this section as performance indicators.

3.1   Segmentation of Kidney Stone and Surrounding Tissue

In Distribution. The SAM model was trained on Dataset A for kidney stone and surrounding tissue segmentation, achieving 95.76 IoU (±4.18) on test data with consistent performance: 97.68% accuracy (±3.04), 97.78% Dice (±2.47), and 4.24% error rate.

Similar results were observed for Distribution A ($D_A \rightarrow D_A$) in Table 1. High performance was demonstrated by SAM (95.76 IoU ±4.18), with comparable results being achieved by both U-Net and Attention U-Net. Although peak performance was not attained by SAM in same-distribution testing (Dataset A), competitive performance was maintained relative to Residual U-Net (97.97 IoU ±1.01).

Figure 3 (first row) presents a qualitative comparison between SAM and U-Net-based segmentation methods. The visualization demonstrates that all models trained on Dataset A achieve near-perfect predictions within their training distribution: both oversegmented (red) and undersegmented (green) pixels are minimal compared to the true positive segmentation mask (blue).

Table 1. Comparison of the performance of four segmentation models (U-Net, Residual U-Net, Attention U-Net, and SAM) across four datasets (A to D). Segmentation is performed for two classes (surrounding tissue or background, and kidney stone). The presented results were measured using segmentation metrics (Accuracy, Dice Score, Intersection over Union, and Error Rate). The best results for each metric are highlighted in bold.

Dataset	Model	Accuracy ↑	Dice ↑	IoU ↑	Error rate ↓
$D_A \rightarrow D_A$	SAM Model	97.68 ± 03.04	97.78 ± 02.47	95.76 ± 04.18	4.24%
	U-Net	97.68 ± 01.38	97.72 ± 01.28	95.77 ± 02.37	4.23%
	ResU-Net	$\mathbf{97.92 \pm 00.96}$	$\mathbf{97.93 \pm 01.01}$	$\mathbf{95.97 \pm 01.91}$	**4.03%**
	AttnU-Net	96.37 ± 02.71	96.24 ± 03.77	92.98 ± 06.02	7.02%
$D_A \rightarrow D_B$	**SAM Model**	$\mathbf{98.71 \pm 02.87}$	$96.39 \pm \ \pm \ \pm 07.70$	$\mathbf{93.74 \pm 09.55}$	**6.26%**
	U-Net	88.8 ± 07.83	73.05 ± 18.58	60.75 ± 22.20	39.25%
	ResU-Net	87.9 ± 07.03	70.85 ± 18.49	57.95 ± 21.82	42.05%
	AttnU-Net	83.83 ± 07.75	65.47 ± 19.37	51.77 ± 21.76	48.23%
$D_A \rightarrow D_C$	**SAM Model**	$\mathbf{95.33 \pm 04.70}$	$\mathbf{92.42 \pm 07.19}$	$\mathbf{86.64 \pm 10.90}$	**13.36%**
	U-Net	86.45 ± 11.38	74.31 ± 22.89	63.37 ± 23.70	36.63%
	ResU-Net	86.09 ± 11.64	71.69 ± 25.58	60.83 ± 25.27	39.17%
	AttnU-Net	85.16 ± 09.95	71.67 ± 20.30	59.08 ± 20.69	40.92%
$D_A \rightarrow D_B$	**SAM Model**	$\mathbf{96.48 \pm 07.91}$	$\mathbf{96.50 \pm 06.20}$	$\mathbf{93.81 \pm 09.47}$	**6.19%**
	U-Net	87.59 ± 12.96	78.73 ± 25.35	70.58 ± 27.59	29.42%
	ResU-Net	89.51 ± 11.02	84.13 ± 18.92	76.19 ± 22.41	23.81%
	AttnU-Net	89.31 ± 11.78	82.85 ± 21.42	75.11 ± 24.42	24.89%

Across all models, the error rates for in-distribution evaluation (Dataset A) remain relatively low: approximately 4% for SAM, U-Net, and Residual U-Net, while Attention U-Net shows a slightly higher error rate of 7%. However, out-of-distribution experiments demonstrate a significant increase in error rates due to the distribution shift.

Out-of-Distribution. The SAM model, trained on Dataset A and evaluated across Datasets B, C and D, was demonstrated to achieve consistently superior performance compared to U-Net-based architectures in all evaluations.

Specifically for Dataset B (ex vivo endoscopic images), an IoU of 93.74 (±9.55) was recorded, significantly exceeding the results obtained by: the standard U-Net 60.75 (±22.20), Residual U-Net 57.95 (±21.82), and Attention U-Net 51.77 (±21.76). While standard U-Net maintained the second-highest performance at 60.75 (±22.20), it remained 32% inferior to SAM in terms of the IoU metrics. Figure 3 (second row) qualitatively compares segmentation performance on out-of-distribution data: while U-Net-based models (trained on Dataset A) missegment kidney stones as surrounding tissue in Dataset B due to challenging illumination and phantom conditions, SAM maintains accurate segmentation, correctly distinguishing both classes.

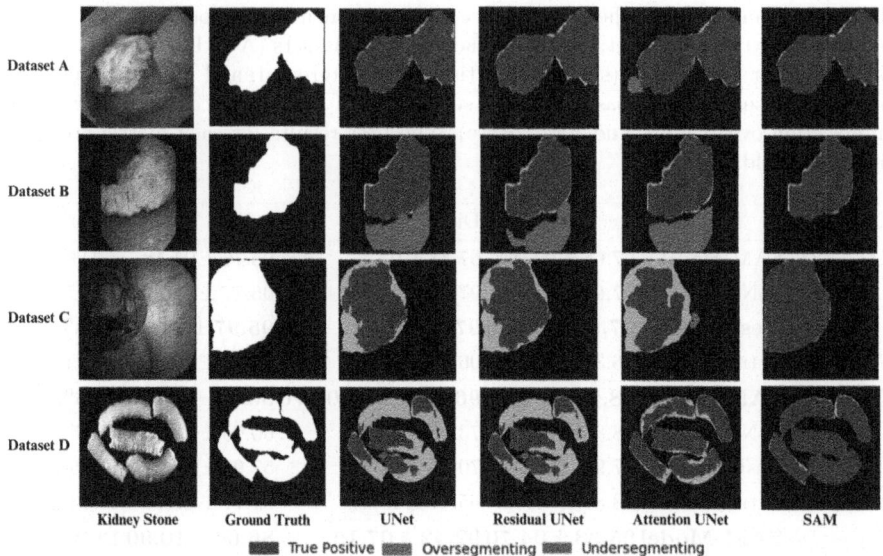

Fig. 3. A qualitative comparison is presented across rows (Datasets A-D) and columns (kidney stone image, ground truth mask, U-Net, Residual U-Net, Attention U-Net, and SAM), where results are color-coded as: blue (true positives/correct segmentation), red (oversegmentation/false positives), and green (undersegmentation/false negatives). (Color figure online)

In the evaluation of Model A on Dataset C (in vivo endoscopic images, different distribution), SAM achieved an IoU of 86.64 ($\pm$10.90), outperforming all U-Net-based models. The highest performance among U-Net variants was observed with standard U-Net at 63.37 IoU ($\pm$23.70), while Residual U-Net and Attention U-Net were found to have comparable results of 60.83 ($\pm$25.27) and 59.08 ($\pm$20.69) respectively. Regarding the qualitative results in Fig. 3 (third row), the U-Net-based methods now correctly identify the target region. However, challenges like non-uniform illumination (similar to Dataset A) cause kidney stone undersegmentation (green pixels), particularly for edge pixels near the scene boundaries.

The final evaluation was performed on Model A trained using Dataset D (ex vivo CCD-camera images), which is characterized by fragmented kidney stones (post-extraction) in contrast to the intact stones typically found in Datasets A-C. Superior performance was demonstrated by SAM with an IoU of 93.81 ($\pm$9.47), followed by Residual U-Net [76.19 ($\pm$22.41)] and Attention U-Net [75.11 ($\pm$24.42)], whose results were found to be closely matched. The lowest performance was observed with standard U-Net at 70.58 ($\pm$27.59) IoU, representing a 23.23% decrease relative to SAM.

As shown in Table 1, SAM trained on Distribution A and tested on in-distribution data maintains an error rate of 4.03%, outperforming all U-Net-

Table 2. Quantitative results of the SAM model trained on Dataset C (in vivo endoscopic dataset) for three-class segmentation (kidney stone, laser fiber, and surrounding tissue) are reported. Evaluation was performed on two distinct test partitions from Dataset C (corresponding to different video sequences) and additionally on Dataset A.

Dataset	Class	Accuracy ↑	Dice ↑	IoU ↑	Error Rate ↓	Support
$D_C \to D_C$	**Laser**	91.00 ± 06.56	94.22 ± 05.63	**89.56 ± 09.23**	**10.44%**	
	Stone	91.00 ± 06.56	87.84 ± 06.65	78.93 ± 10.30	21.07%	21
	Mean	91.00 ± 06.56	91.03 ± 06.14	84.24 ± 09.77	15.76%	
$D_C \to D_C$	Laser	84.03 ± 10.81	83.60 ± 11.81	73.58 ± 17.37	26.42%	
	Stone	99.21 ± 00.58	87.24 ± 07.85	**78.13 ± 11.16**	**21.87%**	15
	Mean	91.62 ± 05.70	85.42 ± 09.83	75.85 ± 14.27	24.15%	
$D_C \to D_A$	Laser	99.70 ± 00.21	87.87 ± 16.98	81.11 ± 18.49	18.89%	
	Stone	94.55 ± 04.44	95.21 ± 04.18	**91.13 ± 06.79**	**8.87%**	44
	Mean	97.12 ± 02.33	91.54 ± 10.58	86.12 ± 12.64	13.88%	

based models. Furthermore, SAM demonstrates robust out-of-distribution generalization across Datasets B, C, and D, consistently achieving both the highest performance in term of IoU and lowest error rates in all test scenarios.

3.2 Segmentation of Kidney Stone, Laser Fiber and Surrounding Tissue

Section 3.1 evaluated the performance of various segmentation models (SAM and U-Net-based architectures) for binary classification of kidney stones and surrounding tissue under both in-distribution and out-of-distribution conditions. A comprehensive analysis was conducted across all datasets described in Sect. 3.2, as these datasets were fully annotated for binary segmentation tasks.

Section 3.2 now focuses exclusively on SAM's performance for in-distribution (Dataset C) and out-of-distribution (Dataset A) scenarios involving three-class segmentation (kidney stone, surrounding tissue, and laser). All results are reported using Intersection over Union (IoU) metrics to maintain consistency with prior analyses.

The quantitative results of this section are presented in Table 2, showing SAM's performance when trained on 117 images from Dataset C and evaluated across three test sets: (1) the first in-distribution partition (21 support images), (2) a second in-distribution partition (15 support images from a different video sequence), and (3) an out-of-distribution evaluation using 44 laser-containing images from Dataset A's 138-image collection. The results are presented for the "kidney stone" and "laser" classes, with the mean value being calculated as the average of these two classes.

In-Distribution The following performance metrics were observed for the SAM model trained on Dataset C and evaluated on the first test partition (21 support

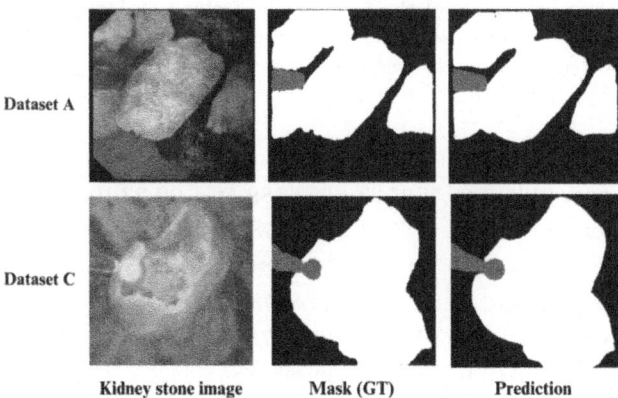

Dataset A

Dataset C

Kidney stone image   Mask (GT)   Prediction

Fig. 4. Qualitative comparison of segmentation results for three classes (kidney stone, laser, and surrounding tissue). From left to right: Kidney stone image, segmentation mask (ground truth), and the prediction generated by the SAM model trained on Dataset C. The first row corresponds to in-distribution results, while the second represents out-of-distribution performance.

images): an IoU of 89.56 (±9.23) with a 10.44% error rate was achieved for the laser class, while a slightly lower IoU of 78.93 (±10.30) and 21.07% error rate were recorded for the kidney stone class.

Superior performance was demonstrated by the model for the "kidney stone" class compared to the "laser" class when evaluated on the second test partition C (15 support images). An IoU of 78.13 (±11.16) was achieved for kidney stone segmentation, while a slightly lower IoU of 73.58 (±17.37) was recorded for laser detection. Similar error rates of approximately 20% were observed for both classes.

Out-of-Distribution To determine the performance of the SAM model trained on Dataset C, the same model used in the in-distribution experiments was evaluated on a different distribution, Dataset A (support: 44 images). It showed superior performance for the "Kidney stone" class, with a 91.13±6.79 IoU and an 8.87% error rate, compared to the "laser" class, which achieved an 81.11±18.49 IoU and an 18.89% error rate. Despite being tested on Dataset A and trained on Dataset C, it achieved even better performance than the in-distribution predictions on Dataset C.

Figure 4 qualitatively compares the segmentation predictions of the SAM model (trained on Dataset C) when evaluated on both in-distribution and out-of-distribution data. Strong performance is observed for both the "kidney stone" and "laser" classes across distributions.

Finally, the SAM model (trained on the in-vivo endoscopic dataset C) for three classes (kidney stone, laser fiber, and surrounding tissue) was used to evaluate the full sets A, B, C, and D for two classes (kidney stone and tissue), aimed at determining its performance when segmenting two-class images. Encouraging results were obtained: for dataset A (in-vivo endoscopic, out-of-distribution), an IoU of 91.60±8.49 and an error rate of 8.40% were achieved. For dataset B (ex-vivo endoscopic, out-of-distribution), an IoU of 90.60±14.62 and an error rate of 9.40% were recorded. The best performance in both metrics was observed in dataset C (in-distribution), with an IoU of 93.71±1.15 and an error rate of 6.29%. Finally, for dataset D (Ex-vivo CCD-Camera, out-of-distribution), an IoU of 91.97±13.07 and an error rate of 8.03% were attained.

4   Conclusions

This study demonstrates that the two-class SAM model outperforms traditional segmentation models (e.g., U-Net, Residual U-Net, Attention U-Net) in kidney stone segmentation. While traditional models performed well on their training dataset, their accuracy significantly declined on unseen datasets. In contrast, SAM, trained on the same data, achieved robust performance on the original dataset and generalized effectively across diverse datasets, maintaining high segmentation precision.

For the three-class SAM model ("kidney stone, laser fiber, and surrounding tissue"), strong performance was observed both in-distribution and out-of-distribution. Notably, the model retained its accuracy when classifying both two and three classes without retraining.

SAM's ability to generate precise, artifact-free segmentations—combined with superior cross-dataset generalization—establishes it as the most reliable model for kidney stone segmentation. These findings underscore the importance of adaptable models for clinical applications with inherent data variability.

Acknowledgements. The authors acknowledge the support of the "Secretaría de Ciencia, Humanidades, Tecnología e Innovación" (SECIHTI), the French Embassy in Mexico, and Campus France through postgraduate scholarships, as well as the Data Science Hub at Tecnológico de Monterrey. This work was also funded by Azure Sponsorship credits from Microsoft's AI for Good Research Lab under the AI for Health program and the French-Mexican ANUIES-CONAHCYT Ecos Nord grant (MX 322537). This work is also partially supported by the Worldwide Universities Network (WUN) project Optimize: "Novel robust computer vision methods and synthetic datasets for minimally invasive surgery".

References

1. Moftakhar, L., Jafari, F., Johari, M.G., Rezaeianzadeh, R., Hosseini, S.V., Rezaianzadeh, A.: Prevalence and risk factors of kidney stone disease in population aged 40–70 years old in Kharameh cohort study: a cross-sectional population-based study in Southern Iran. BMC Urol. **22**(1), 205 (2022)
2. Chew, B.H., Miller, L.E., Eisner, B., Bhattacharyya, S., Bhojani, N.: Prevalence, incidence, and determinants of kidney stones in a nationally representative sample of us adults. JU Open Plus **2**(1), e00006 (2024)

3. Daudon, M., Jungers, P., Bazin, D., Williams, J.C.: Recurrence rates of urinary calculi according to stone composition and morphology. Urolithiasis **46**(5), 459–470 (2018). https://doi.org/10.1007/s00240-018-1043-0

4. Daudon, M., Jungers, P.: Clinical value of crystalluria and quantitative morpho-constitutional analysis of urinary calculi. Nephron Physiol. **98**(2), 31–36 (2004)

5. Lopez-Tiro, F., et al.: On the in vivo recognition of kidney stones using machine learning. IEEE Access **12**, 10736–10759 (2024)

6. Estrade, V., et al.: Deep morphological recognition of kidney stones using intra-operative endoscopic digital videos. Phys. Med. Biol. **67**(16), 165006 (2022)

7. Mendez-Ruiz, M., et al.: On the generalization capabilities of FSL methods through domain adaptation: a case study in endoscopic kidney stone image classification. In: Pichardo Lagunas, O., Martínez-Miranda, J., Martínez Seis, B. (eds.) MICAI 2022. LNCS, vol. 13612, pp. 249–263. Springer, Cham (2022). https://doi.org/10.1007/978-3-031-19493-1_21

8. Estrade, V.: Towards automatic recognition of pure and mixed stones using intra-operative endoscopic digital images. BJU Int. **129**(2), 234–242 (2022)

9. Ghosh, T., Li, L., Chakareski, J.: Effective deep learning for semantic segmentation based bleeding zone detection in capsule endoscopy images. In: 2018 25th IEEE International Conference on Image Processing (ICIP), pp. 3034–3038. IEEE (2018)

10. Lopez, F., et al.: Assessing deep learning methods for the identification of kidney stones in endoscopic images. In: 2021 43rd Annual International Conference of the IEEE Engineering in Medicine & Biology Society (EMBC), pp. 2778–2781. IEEE (2021)

11. Gupta, S., Ali, S., Goldsmith, L., Turney, B., Rittscher, J.: Multi-class motion-based semantic segmentation for ureteroscopy and laser lithotripsy. Comput. Med. Imaging Graph. **101**, 102112 (2022)

12. Ronneberger, O., Fischer, P., Brox, T.: U-net: convolutional networks for biomedical image segmentation. In: Navab, N., Hornegger, J., Wells, W.M., Frangi, A.F. (eds.) MICCAI 2015. LNCS, vol. 9351, pp. 234–241. Springer, Cham (2015). https://doi.org/10.1007/978-3-319-24574-4_28

13. Alom, Md.Z., Yakopcic, C., Hasan, M., Taha, T.M., Asari, V.K.: Recurrent residual u-net for medical image segmentation. J. Med. Imaging **6**(1), 014006 (2019)

14. Li, Z., Zhang, H., Li, Z., Ren, Z.: Residual-attention UNet++: a nested residual-attention u-net for medical image segmentation. Appl. Sci. **12**(14), 7149 (2022)

15. Kirillov, A., et al.: Segment anything. In: Proceedings of the IEEE/CVF International Conference on Computer Vision, pp. 4015–4026 (2023)

16. El Beze, J., et al.: Evaluation and understanding of automated urinary stone recognition methods. BJU Int. **130**(6), 786–798 (2022)

17. Corrales, M., Doizi, S., Barghouthy, Y., Traxer, O., Daudon, M.: Classification of stones according to Michel Daudon: a narrative review. Eur. Urol. Focus **7**(1), 13–21 (2021)

Modelling Uncertainty in Graph Convolutional Networks for Edge Detection in Mammograms

Fredrik A. Dahl[1]([⊠]) , Amund Vedal[1] , Line Eikvil[1] , Solveig Thrun[2] ,
Michael Kampffmeyer[1,2] , and Solveig Hofvind[3]

[1] The Norwegian Computing Center (NR), Oslo, Norway
fadahl@nr.no
[2] UiT The Arctic University of Norway, Tromsø, Norway
[3] Cancer Registry of Norway, Norwegian Institute of Public Health, Oslo, Norway

Abstract. Delineation of structures and estimation of landmarks in mammograms is a critical step in the evaluation of image quality in breast cancer screening, but requires the estimation of the uncertainty of the predicted landmarks to refer uncertain cases to clinicians. Of particular importance – and the focus of this work – is on the pectoral muscle, where the variability in muscle visibility across images introduces significant uncertainty. While graph convolutional networks (GCN) have been demonstrated to accurately predict landmarks by explicitly leveraging structural relationships between landmarks, they typically lack the ability to provide accurate uncertainty estimates for the landmarks. To address this shortcoming, in this work we propose a novel GCN-based approach that not only locates key points along the muscle boundary but also provides accurate uncertainty estimates, capturing both the aleatoric and epistemic uncertainties. Our method was evaluated on in-house annotated mammograms demonstrating comparable accuracy to human annotators, while at the same time providing highly accurate uncertainty estimates, confirming its potential for identifying cases that require human review. We further validate our proposed approach on the publicly available CSAW-S and INBreast datasets, demonstrating its robustness to domain shift, as well as its potential to detect incorrect or untypical annotations.

Keywords: Uncertainty · Graph convolutional neural networks · Mammography

1 Introduction

Breast cancer is the most common form of cancer among women worldwide, and mammographic screening is an effective way of detecting cancers at an early stage. However, to ensure reliable identification of potential breast cancer indicators and ensure the best possible visualization of breast tissue, mammography

S. Ali et al. (Eds.): MIUA 2025, LNCS 15917, pp. 261–275, 2026.
https://doi.org/10.1007/978-3-031-98691-8_19

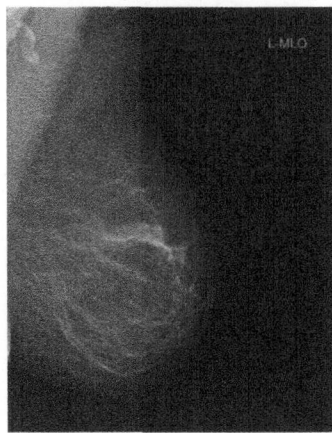

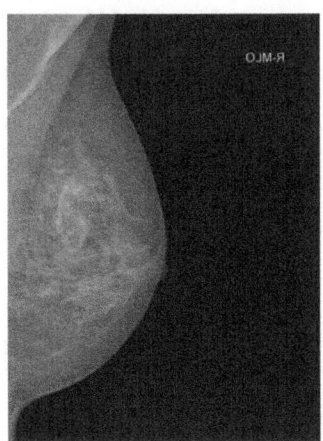

Fig. 1. Sharp muscle edge.   **Fig. 2.** Blurry muscle edge.

image quality must be consistently high. This includes both technical quality in the form of image sharpness and contrast as well as the proper positioning, which ensures that the relevant parts of the breast are depicted. The quality of the images significantly impacts the rates of patient recall and the detection of cancer through screening, thus affecting the accuracy and reliability of the screening process. Therefore, mammograms routinely undergo quality assessment by radiographers, which would benefit from automatic analysis.

An important part of the quality assessment concerns the depiction of the pectoral muscle in the mediolateral oblique (MLO) view, relating to its size, its shape, and its orientation [11]. The muscle should be located in the top left (right) corner of a standard X-ray mammogram in MLO-view. The complexity of the task varies considerably, as shown in Figs. 1 and 2, where the edge of the muscle is clearly visible in the former and more blurry in the latter.

While not specifically focusing on edge detection of the pectoral muscle, several approaches have been previously proposed to segmenting the muscle, using various proprietary versions of convolutional neural nets (CNNs). [7] apply a method similar to a U-Net and concludes it works better than traditional imaging techniques. [1] use a CNN model heatmaps generated by a GradCam method. PeMNet [14] uses a InceptionResNetv2 backbone and a complex up-sampling scheme to generate pixel masks. [3] use a U-Net to segment the muscle. [13] uses deep learning in the way of a modified U-Net model to segment pectoral muscle volume from computed tomography images. However, these approaches lack mechanisms to quantify uncertainty (explicit probability distributions or confidence intervals) of the muscle edge location, which is critical in an image quality control setting, where evaluations should be referred to humans in critical cases where the predicted locations are likely to be substantially off target. Moreover, given the segmentation focus, small segmentation errors can cause significant edge distortions, particularly for the localization of the lower boundary point, which is important since the length of the depicted muscle is a quality criterion.

In this work, we instead approach the problem from a landmark detection perspective, leveraging Graph convolutional neural nets (GCNs) to detect landmarks on the muscle edge and capture relationships between them, thereby improving the relative positioning of the landmarks. This approach has the added advantage that landmark based modelling naturally extends to locating of additional singular key points that are used for quality assessment of mammogram, such as the nipple and the inframammary fold. While these are not included in the present study, this is a natural extension of this work, which can also benefit from learning the geometric relations among the points.

In order to detect the muscle edge, we adopt a modification of the "Deep Adaptive Graph" (DAG) framework, which has previously been used for identifying key points in faces [6]. Our contribution in this work is an extension of the DAG framework that provides an explicit probabilistic model for the location of the key points. We train the model to output estimates of the aleatoric (truly random) uncertainties together with the key point coordinates, capturing the variability in ground truth due to annotator differences. In addition we estimate the epistemic (model related) uncertainties through the variations within a model ensemble, and combine the aleatoric and epistemic uncertainties to create accurate confidence intervals. To our knowledge, this is the first approach to explicitly model both the aleatoric and epistemic uncertainty in GCNs for landmark detection.

We demonstrate the effectiveness of the proposed approach to provide accurate uncertainty estimates on both an in-house dataset and the public CSAW-S dataset, while further demonstrating that these uncertainty estimates can also been leveraged to detect incorrect or atypical annotations on the public CSAW-S and INBreast datasets.

2 Methods

We include only an informal description of the "Deep Adaptive Graph" (DAG) framework [6], which we build on, and refer to this source for technical details. The model's basic task is to locate a vector of points $v \in \mathbb{R}^{n \times 2}$ in an image as close as possible to the ground truth of correct locations v^*. It uses a high-resolution convolutional net (HRNet) to generate a feature map for the given image. These features are fed into a GCN together with the geometry of a current location estimate v and give a vector Δv as output. The process starts with an initial point vector v_0, which is updated iteratively: $v_{i+1} = v_i + \Delta v_i$, which is intended to move toward v^*. The algorithm described by [6] also included a so-called global step prior to the Δv updates, but this was not included in the present application. We let T be the number of local steps and for convenience define $\mu = v_T$. In the following, we present how this approach is extended to capture both the aleatoric and epistemic uncertainty.

2.1 Aleatoric Uncertainty Estimation

By aleatoric uncertainty we mean uncertainty about the ground truth that is "truly random" in the sense that it cannot be eliminated by any amount of training data or any kind of model [4]. It represents the randomness among different annotators - or even the same annotator at different times - in how they place the markings. In the image of Fig. 2, e.g. the delineation of the lower part of the muscle is likely to vary substantially in this way.

Earlier research on aleatoric uncertainty in GCN models focus on labelling problems, where the task is to assign properties to the nodes in a graph [10]. A recent overview of uncertainty in GCN models is given in [12], which gives a taxonomy of types and sources for uncertainties, and ways to estimate them. Our work is different in the way that we develop an architecture that allows the model to estimate 2-dimensional locations in parallel with uncertainty estimates for the same locations[1]. We accomplish this by extending the method of Li et al. [6] with the inclusion of a separate GCN module that estimates aleatoric uncertainties through parametrized random distributions. It is structurally equivalent to the GCN module that computes Δv and is applied after the last iteration T. It takes as input the HR-net features evaluated at the locations μ together with the geometric features of μ. The output is denoted by $\log(b) \in \mathbb{R}^{n \times 2}$, where b_x^i and b_y^i represent the uncertainties for μ_x^i and μ_y^i, respectively.

Rather than the traditional deep learning approach of defining a loss function which measures the distance from the desired outcome, we view the entire model as a parameterized statistical model of the training data. For each point in v^{*i}, we assume that v_x^{*i} has the Laplace (double exponential) distribution with median μ_x^i and scale parameter b_x^i, which we denote as $v_x^{*i} \sim \mathcal{L}(\mu_x^i, b_x^i)$ and similarly $v_y^{*i} \sim \mathcal{L}(\mu_y^i, b_y^i)$. We assumed all components to be independent, which gives the following likelihood:

$$
L = \prod_k^M \prod_i^n \prod_{j \in \{x,y\}} \frac{1}{2b_j^{k,i}} \exp\left(-\frac{|v_j^{*k,i} - \mu_j^{k,i}|}{b_j^{k,i}} \right)
$$

Here, k runs over the M training images, i runs over the n key points and j runs over the x and y dimension.

Our approach is to optimize the model parameters with respect to this likelihood function, but as usual in statistical modelling, we minimize $-\log(L)$ instead, which has the same optimum and more favourable numerical properties:

$$
-\log L = \sum_k^M \sum_i^n \sum_{j \in \{x,y\}} \log(2b_j^{k,i}) + \frac{1}{b_j^{k,i}} |v_j^{*k,i} - \mu_j^{k,i}|
$$

Minimizing this expression amounts to training the model end-to-end to estimate locations μ_x^i, μ_y^i and uncertainties b_x^i, b_y^i for a given input image. To our

---

[1] Note, while such an approach has been investigated in the broader computer vision context [5], to our knowledge, it has not been explored in a GCN setting.

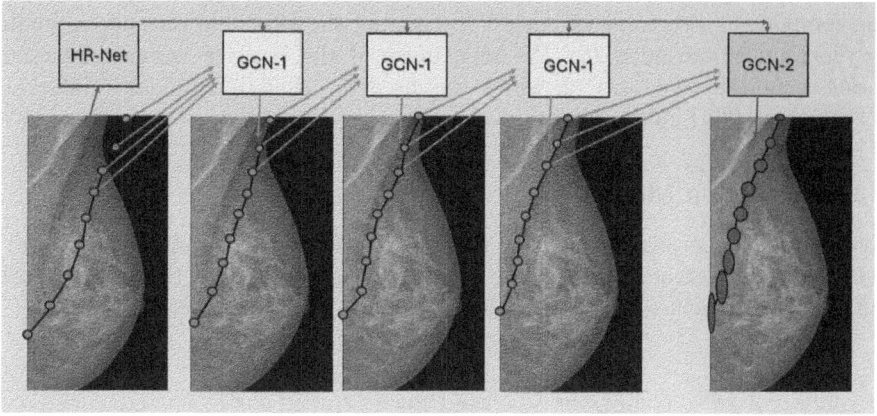

Fig. 3. Computational pipeline. (Color figure online)

knowledge, this approach to estimating aleatoric uncertainties for GCN models is novel.

We also considered using normal distributions instead of Laplace, but chose the latter because it is the natural generalization of the L1-error that was used by [6]. It has the property that it penalizes deviations linearly rather than quadratically, which makes it more robust. Normal distributions might place too much emphasize on the cases where the model has trouble reproducing the ground truth.

Model Pipeline. The model pipeline is shown in Fig. 3. The HR-Net (blue color) computes localized features, which are fed into the GCN models. GCN-1 (yellow) reads the HR-Net features at the initial points, combined with their geometry, and moves the points (hopefully) toward the correct locations. This process is repeated T times. Then GCN-2 (red) takes the HR-Net features of these final locations as input, together with their geometry, and outputs the estimated x- and y- uncertainties, illustrated with red ellipses. The entire model is trained end-to-end to optimize the Laplace log-likelihood of the ground truth data.

2.2 Epistemic and Combined Uncertainty Estimation

Our approach for estimating epistemic (model related) uncertainty [4] is more standard and straight forward. We train a set of models with cross-validation, and use them as an ensemble when evaluating the test sets [2]. For each x- and y-value of each output point for a given image we estimate the standard deviation among the ensemble model outputs, and treat this as the epistemic uncertainty.

For the aleatoric uncertainty, we computed the average $\log(b)$ tensors over the ensemble and used the exponential of this average as our b-values. We computed the component-wise total variance V by adding the ensemble variance estimate to the Laplace variance $2b^2$. We then inverted the Laplace variance function to get a modified $\hat{b} = \sqrt{V/2}$, which was used to calculate confidence intervals according to the Laplace distribution.

2.3 Evaluation Methodology

The predictive performance of the model was assessed by computing the average absolute difference between the predicted coordinates and the ground truth annotations. Specifically, we used the following L1-error metric:

$$\frac{1}{2nM^{\text{test}}} \sum_{k=1}^{M^{\text{test}}} \sum_{i=1}^{n} \sum_{j \in \{x,y\}} |v_j^{*k,i} - \mu_j^{k,i}|$$

where M^{test} is the number of images in the test set, n is the number of key points, v^* denotes the ground truth locations, and μ the predicted locations. The location values v^* and μ were scaled to the range $[0, 1]$, so the error estimates can be interpreted as fractions of the image height and width.

In addition to the predictive performance, we evaluated the calibration of the model's uncertainty estimates. To assess whether the predicted uncertainties correctly reflect the empirical errors, we computed *standardized errors* by dividing the absolute prediction errors by the predicted standard deviations. Under the model assumptions, these standardized errors should approximately follow a standard Laplace distribution.

We quantify the discrepancy between the predicted and empirical distributions by the maximum absolute difference between the cumulative distribution function (CDF) of the standard Laplace distribution, denoted by $F(x)$, and the empirical CDF of the standardized errors, denoted by $\hat{F}(x)$. Specifically, we compute the Kolmogorov–Smirnov (KS) statistic:

$$KS = \sup_x |F(x) - \hat{F}(x)|.$$

It has an intuitive interpretation as the maximum difference between the predicted cumulative probability and the observed fraction of standardized errors above or below any threshold. Hence, its unit of measurement is probability, and it provides an upper bound on the calibration error of the model's uncertainty predictions.

It would be possible to perform hypothesis tests with the KS statistic to formally compare F and $\hat{F}$. However, such testing is less relevant in our context. First, the sample size is large enough that even small and practically unimportant deviations would likely yield statistically significant results. Second, the data points are strongly correlated within each image, which violates the independence assumption of the KS test. Instead, we report its magnitude and evaluate calibration visually through various plots. The results of these evaluations are presented in Sect. 5 and visualized through scatter plots of empirical errors versus predicted uncertainties.

3   Data Sets

3.1   Norwegian Breast Screening Data

From the Norwegian breast screening program, we included a random sample of 639 MLO-view mammograms, which we in the following refer to as the 'NBSP' dataset. Of these, a random sub-sample of 545 images was used for training and 94 for testing.

The training set was annotated by the first author, who has no formal background in radiology or radiography, but has extensive experience in analyzing mammograms. The test set was annotated independently by two radiographers.

The annotations consisted of sequences of points placed along the perceived edge of the pectoral muscle, from the top downward. The number of points per image varied, and the annotators adjusted the spacing so that the points were placed more densely in regions with higher curvature, ensuring that linear interpolation would accurately capture the border.

3.2   INBreast

To evaluate the generalizability of our models, we also tested them on the external INBreast dataset [9], which contains 200 annotated MLO-view mammograms. The annotations in this dataset were made in a similar manner to those in NBSP, but with shorter intervals between points also in regions with low curvature, resulting in a larger total number of key points per image.

3.3   CSAW-S

We further evaluated the model's performance on the publicly available CSAW-S dataset [8], which includes annotations of the pectoral muscle. The dataset is divided into a training/validation set with 156 images and a test set containing 16 images. While medical experts provided the annotations of the pectoral muscle in the test set, the annotations for the training/validation set were made by non-experts without medical training, resulting in more inconsistent annotations.

4   Experimental Setup

4.1   Annotation Standardization

As described in Sect. 3, the datasets included in this study differed in the number and placement of annotated points along the pectoral muscle border. In particular, the NBSP and INBreast datasets contained sequences of manually placed key points, with varying density and number of points per image, while the CSAW-S dataset provided segmentation masks.

To facilitate a uniform evaluation across datasets, we standardized the annotations by extracting $n = 10$ equidistant key points along the annotated pectoral muscle border in each image. For datasets with point annotations (NBSP and

INBreast), this was done by re-sampling the original sequences. For CSAW-S, we extracted the muscle contour from the segmentation mask and similarly sampled $n = 10$ equidistant points. In all cases, the first point was located on the upper edge and the last point on the vertical edge of the image.

4.2   Hyperparameters and Training Procedure

The HR-net was set up with a depth of 32, while the GCN modules that compute the Δv and b tensors had 6 layers and 256 filters. The number of coordinate iterations T was set to 3. In line with [6], we used the average of the ground truth locations v^* over the training set as starting values v_0.

The models were trained using the ADAM optimizer with a learning rate of 0.0001 and a batch size of 4 over 200 epochs. The cross-validation used 5 folds, where each model was trained on 4 folds and validated on the remaining one. The parameters achieving the highest log-likelihood on the validation fold were saved. This procedure inflates performance on the validation fold but was used solely to create a model ensemble for evaluation on the test sets, not to cross-validate the models' performance on the training data.

When the model ensemble was tested on the CSAW-S and INBreast datasets, no re-training, fine-tuning or domain adaptation was applied.

4.3   Image Preprocessing

Only minimal image preprocessing was performed. Right-side images were flipped so that all images had the breast on the left side, with the pectoral muscle in the top left corner, if present. All images were resized to 512×512 pixels, and pixel values were re-scaled to the range $[0, 1]$. No data augmentation was applied.

5   Results

5.1   NBSP

The model ensemble trained on the NBSP training set achieved high predictive accuracy on the NBSP test set. The average L1-error was 0.0054, which is comparable to the average disagreement between the two radiographers (0.0057), and lower than the individual model-to-radiographer differences (0.0061 and 0.0062). This suggests that the model's point predictions are essentially on par with expert-level performance.

The uncertainty estimates were also well-calibrated. Figure 4 shows the histogram of the standardized errors plotted against the standard Laplace distribution, while Fig. 5 shows the comparison of the same cumulative distributions. The KS for the standardized error distribution was 0.0345, so the standardized probability estimates were off by less than 3.5% compared to the cumulative Laplace.

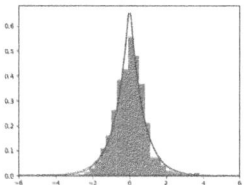

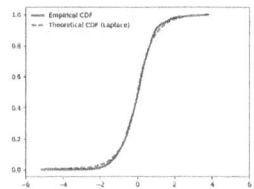

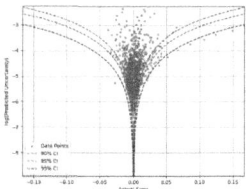

Fig. 4. Histogram of standardized error distribution, NBSP test set.

Fig. 5. Comparison of the empirical and theoretical cumulative distribution, NBSP test set.

Fig. 6. Prediction errors by predicted error size with CI curves, NBSP test set.

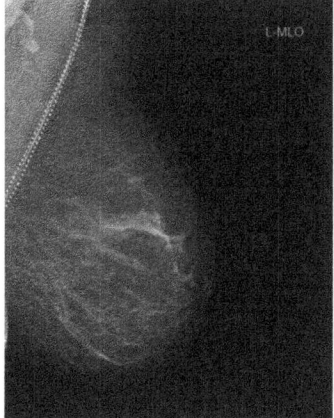

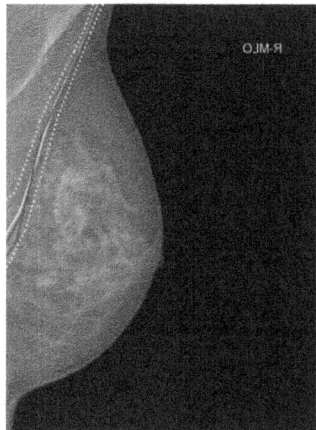

Fig. 7. Sharp muscle edge. (Color figure online)

Fig. 8. Blurry muscle edge. (Color figure online)

Figures 4 and 5 show the fit of the model's uncertainty estimates aggregated over all the data by first standardizing the errors by dividing each point estimate with its estimated uncertainty. We are also concerned with how well the predicted uncertainty fits the actual errors for different levels of the former. The model might have a heteroskedasticity problem if the size of the errors were systematically underestimated for low uncertainties and overestimated for higher, or vice versa, which would "wash out" in Figs. 4 and 5.

To investigate this, we have designed the "fountain plot" in Fig. 6. It shows a scatter plot with observed errors on the x-axis and predicted uncertainty on a log-scale on the y-axis. For each level of the predicted uncertainty we have plotted the upper and lower confidence interval limits for 90%, 95% and 99% confidence levels, which are the curved lines in the figure. The figure shows that the scatterplot follows the confidence interval curves nicely, showing little sign of heteroskedasticity.

In Figs. 7 and 8 we revisit the mammograms from Figs. 1 and 2, with annotations and model output. The two red curves show the radiographers' annotations.

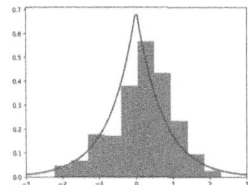

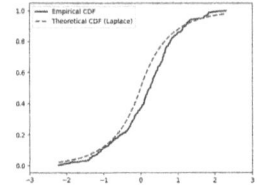

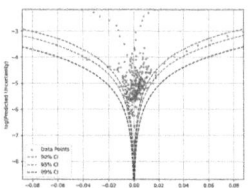

Fig. 9. Histogram, CSAW-S test set.

Fig. 10. Cumulative distribution, CSAW-S test set.

Fig. 11. Fountain plot, CSAW-S test set.

The solid yellow curve shows the model prediction and the dotted yellow curves show the 99% confidence band, interpolated from the key point locations and corresponding confidence intervals. In Fig. 7 the muscle edge is clearly visible, the curves are almost indistinguishable, and the confidence band is narrow. In Fig. 8, the muscle edge is more blurry, particularly near the bottom, which is nicely captured by the widening confidence bands. There we also see a slight divergence between the radiographers' annotations.

5.2   CSAW-S

The CSAW-S test set gave an L1-error of 0.0059, which is similar to the NBSP results and compatible with this being a high-quality data set. The KS statistic was 0.166, which is much higher than for NBSP. However, this statistic is less meaningful for a dataset with only 16 images, and the same applies to the Figs. 9 and 10. The fountain plot in Fig. 11 would also require more data, but for what it is worth, it indicates a reasonable spread within the confidence curves with no outliers, which confirms the claim that these annotations were made by professionals.

The CSAW-S training and validation set had an L1-error as high as 0.0141, which indicates severe discrepancies in the point predictions. The KS statistic of 0.106 was also high, despite a high number of images (156). The poor uncertainty calibration is confirmed by the plots in Figs. 12, 13 and 14. The histogram and cdf plot shows that the standardized errors have a wider distribution than the Laplace, and the fountain plot shows many observations far outside the 99% confidence curves.

Figures 15, 16, 17 and 18 show the two images with the largest standardized errors with and without annotations. The solid yellow curves are the model's estimated muscle boundaries and the dotted curves show the 99% confidence bands, while the red curves give the human annotations. The annotation in Fig. 16 is clearly incorrect, as the top part undoubtedly represents a skin fold rather than the pectoral muscle. The same appears to be the case in Fig. 18, although it is less obvious.

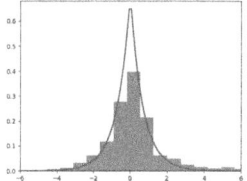 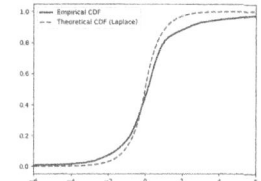 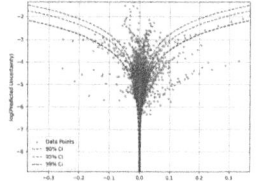

Fig. 12. Histogram, CSAW-S training set.

Fig. 13. Cumulative distribution, CSAW-S training set.

Fig. 14. Fountain plot, CSAW-S training set.

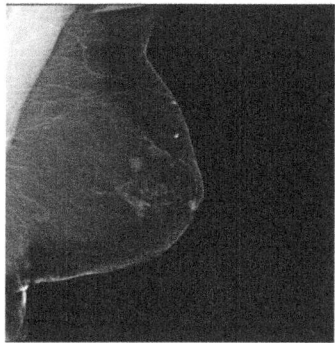 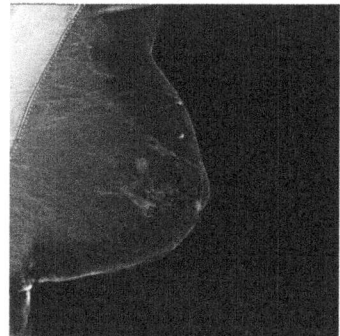

Fig. 15. CSAW-S image 1.

Fig. 16. CSAW-S image 1 with annotation (red) and model output (yellow). (Color figure online)

5.3 INBreast

Figures 19, 20 and 21 show that there are also inconsistencies for the INBreast data set, with L1-error = 0.0120 and the KS = 0.125. The figures all show a shift toward the left, which means that the model's x- and y- point estimates tend to be lower than the annotation coordinates.

The Figs. 22, 23, 24 and 25 show the two images that account for the largest discrepancies. Our conclusion is not as clear cut as in the CSAW-S case, but we would tend to agree with the model's markings, as we are unable to see the lower part of the annotated muscle. At the very least we can conclude that the INBreast annotators have annotated larger areas as pectoral muscle than us in uncertain cases. This explains the left shift in Figs. 19, 20 and 21.

5.4 Summary of Results Across Datasets

Overall, these results clearly illustrate the model's strong predictive capability and reliable uncertainty estimation when annotations are consistent and accurate, and conversely highlight its sensitivity to annotation quality.

Table 1 summarizes the predictive accuracy and uncertainty calibration across all datasets. The model demonstrated high accuracy on the NBSP and

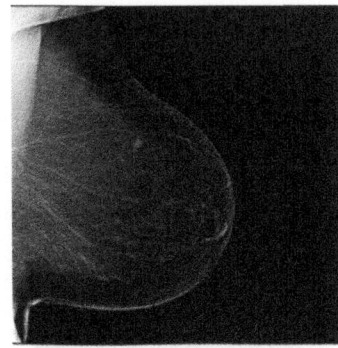

Fig. 17. CSAW-S image 2.

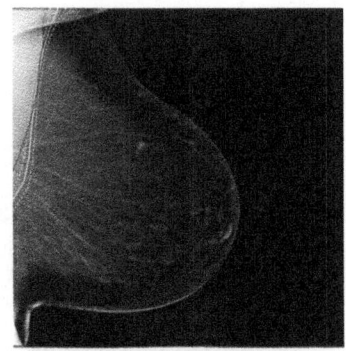

Fig. 18. CSAW-S image 2 with annotation (red) and model output (yellow). (Color figure online)

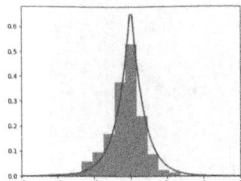

Fig. 19. Histogram, INBreast.

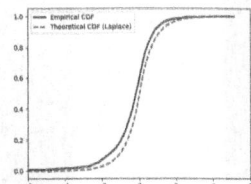

Fig. 20. Cumulative distribution, INBreast.

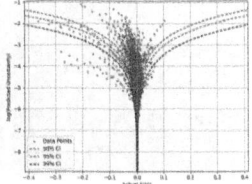

Fig. 21. Fountain plot, INBReast.

CSAW-S test sets, with L1-errors comparable to expert-level disagreement. The uncertainty estimates were well-calibrated on NBSP, with a low KS statistic (0.032), and reasonably calibrated on CSAW-S test images, despite a higher KS value (0.166), which is likely inflated due to the small sample size.

In contrast, performance on the CSAW-S training/validation set was weaker, with a higher L1-error KS statistic of 0.106, attributed to inaccurate annotations by non-experts, in some cases incorrectly including skin folds.

For INBreast, the L1-error was lower than for CSAW-S training/validation, but more than twice as high as with NBSP and CSAW-S test. Also the KS statistic was high despite a larger set of 200 images. Image inspection showed that this was likely due to an annotation practice that included far more possible muscle tissue in uncertain cases, compared to the NBSP annotations.

5.5   Expected Domain Shift

A drop in accuracy is expected when a model is evaluated on images that come from a different scanner, population, or labelling protocol. Here we purposely kept the original NBSP weights—no re-training, fine-tuning, or domain-

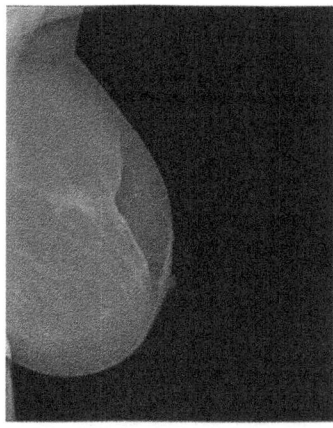

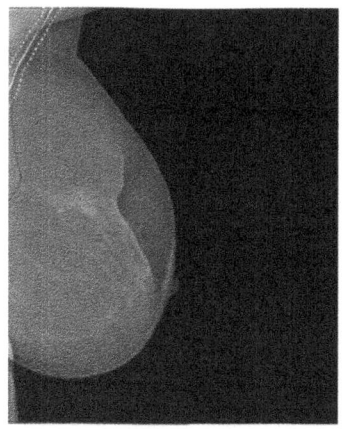

Fig. 22. INBreast image 1.

Fig. 23. INBreast image 1 with annotation (red) and model output (yellow). (Color figure online)

Table 1. Summary of predictive accuracy (L1-error) and uncertainty calibration (KS statistic) across datasets.

Dataset	L1-error (mean absolute error)	KS statistic (calibration)
NBSP	0.0054	0.032
CSAW-S (test)	0.0059	0.166
CSAW-S (train/val)	0.0141	0.106
INBreast	0.0120	0.125

adaptation—so the lower scores on CSAW-S and INBreast may partly reflect the well-known effect of domain shift rather than a flaw in the approach; standard adaptation techniques could be layered on later if desired.

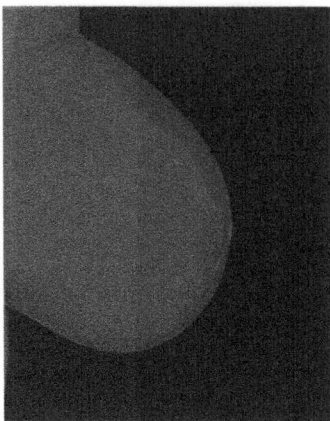

Fig. 24. INBreast image 2.

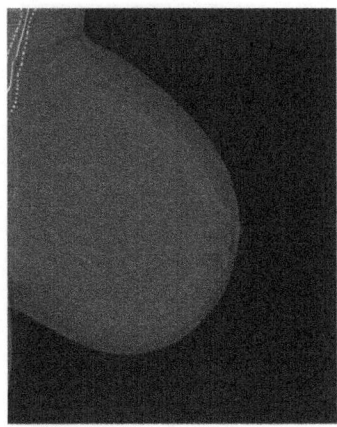

Fig. 25. INBreast image 2 with annotation (red) and model output (yellow). (Color figure online)

6   Conclusion

In this work, we introduced a GCN model for keypoint localization that simultaneously estimates landmark coordinates and aleatoric uncertainty through optimization of the model's log-likelihood. This approach, standard in classical statistics but rarely applied in machine learning, proved essential for accurate uncertainty calibration.

We have applied this method successfully to the problem of localizing keypoints on the border of the pectoral muscle in mammograms. For the NBSP test set, the model achieved a localization accuracy on par with the two radiographers, and also achieved a very accurate uncertainty calibration.

The model performed less well on two external data sets, but inspection of specific problem images indicated that the issue was with incorrect annotations (or at least different annotation practices) rather than the model. The combination of the model's localization and uncertainty outputs enabled us to identify these images where the annotations were clearly incompatible with the model.

The proposed uncertainty-aware framework has potential applications in any clinical workflow where keypoint localization is a relevant task. The primary use of the model's uncertainty estimates will likely be to flag cases that should be inspected by a human expert. However, the present application shows that the method can also be used to find inconsistencies in human annotations.

References

1. Brahim, M., Westerkamp, K., Hempel, L., Lehmann, R., Hempel, D., Philipp, P.: Automated assessment of breast positioning quality in screening mammography. Cancers **14**(19), 4704 (2022). https://doi.org/10.3390/cancers14194704. https://www.mdpi.com/2072-6694/14/19/4704

2. Dutschmann, T.M., Kinzel, L., ter Laak, A., Baumann, K.: Large-scale evaluation of k-fold cross-validation ensembles for uncertainty estimation. J. Cheminform. **15**(1), 49 (2023). https://doi.org/10.1186/s13321-023-00709-9

3. Guo, Y., Zhao, W., Li, S., Zhang, Y., Lu, Y.: Automatic segmentation of the pectoral muscle based on boundary identification and shape prediction. Phys. Med. Biol. **65**(4), 045016 (2020). https://doi.org/10.1088/1361-6560/ab652b

4. Hüllermeier, E., Waegeman, W.: Aleatoric and epistemic uncertainty in machine learning: an introduction to concepts and methods. Mach. Learn. **110**(3), 457–506 (2021). https://doi.org/10.1007/s10994-021-05946-3

5. Kendall, A., Gal, Y.: What Uncertainties Do We Need in Bayesian Deep Learning for Computer Vision? (2017). https://doi.org/10.48550/arXiv.1703.04977

6. Li, W., et al.: Structured landmark detection via topology-adapting deep graph learning. In: Vedaldi, A., Bischof, H., Brox, T., Frahm, J.-M. (eds.) ECCV 2020. LNCS, vol. 12354, pp. 266–283. Springer, Cham (2020). https://doi.org/10.1007/978-3-030-58545-7_16

7. Ma, X., et al.: Automated pectoral muscle identification on MLO-view mammograms: comparison of deep neural network to conventional computer vision. Med. Phys. **46**(5), 2103–2114 (2019). https://doi.org/10.1002/mp.13451

8. Matsoukas, C., et al.: Adding seemingly uninformative labels helps in low data regimes. In: Proceedings of the 37th International Conference on Machine Learning, pp. 6775–6784. PMLR (2020). https://proceedings.mlr.press/v119/matsoukas20a.html. ISSN 2640-3498

9. Moreira, I.C., Amaral, I., Domingues, I., Cardoso, A., Cardoso, M.J., Cardoso, J.S.: INbreast: toward a full-field digital mammographic database. Acad. Radiol. **19**(2), 236–248 (2012). https://doi.org/10.1016/j.acra.2011.09.014

10. Vashishth, S., Yadav, P., Bhandari, M., Talukdar, P.: Confidence-Based Graph Convolutional Networks for Semi-supervised Learning (2019). https://arxiv.org/abs/1901.08255v2

11. Waade, G., et al.: Assessment of breast positioning criteria in mammographic screening: agreement between artificial intelligence software and radiographers. J. Med. Screening **28**, 096914132199871 (2021). https://doi.org/10.1177/0969141321998718

12. Wang, F., Liu, Y., Liu, K., Wang, Y., Medya, S., Yu, P.S.: Uncertainty in Graph Neural Networks: A Survey (2024). https://doi.org/10.48550/arXiv.2403.07185

13. Yang, Z., Choi, I., Choi, J., Jung, J., Ryu, M., Yong, H.S.: Deep learning-based pectoralis muscle volume segmentation method from chest computed tomography image using sagittal range detection and axial slice-based segmentation. PLOS ONE **18**(9), e0290950 (2023). https://doi.org/10.1371/journal.pone.0290950. https://journals.plos.org/plosone/article?id=10.1371/journal.pone.0290950

14. Yu, X., Wang, S.H., Górriz, J.M., Jiang, X.W., Guttery, D.S., Zhang, Y.D.: PeMNet for pectoral muscle segmentation. Biology **11**(1), 134 (2022). https://doi.org/10.3390/biology11010134

Classification of Gastroscopy Images Under Extreme Class Imbalance: A Deep Learning Pipeline

Adrian Krenzer$^{(\boxtimes)}$, Tobias Friedetzki, Max Dietsch, and Frank Puppe

Julius-Maximilians University of Würzburg, Sanderring 2, 97070 Würzburg, Germany
adrian.krenzer@uni-wuerzburg.de

Abstract. Class imbalance is a critical challenge in medical image classification, particularly in gastroscopy, where accurately detecting underrepresented pathological conditions is essential for clinical decision-making. This paper investigates algorithm-level techniques' effectiveness in addressing severe class imbalance in gastroscopy image classification. A curated data set comprising four clinically relevant categories was constructed: normal, esophagitis, Barrett's esophagus, and gastric polyps by consolidating and reclassifying samples from two open-access sources: the HyperKvasir and GastroVision datasets. The resulting dataset exhibits a pronounced imbalance ratio of approximately $\rho \approx 73$, closely reflecting real-world diagnostic scenarios. To mitigate the adverse effects of imbalance, we evaluate the performance of two algorithm-level methods: Focal Loss and a cost-sensitive learning strategy (CoSen). These methods were integrated into deep learning pipelines based on a convolutional neural network and transformer architectures. Experimental results demonstrate that both approaches substantially improve the F1-score, particularly for the minority polyp class. The best model achieved a 40.4% increase in F1 score for one class compared to the baseline, underscoring the value of algorithmic imbalance mitigation strategies for gastrocopy image classification.

Keywords: Machine learning · Deep learning · Endoscopy · Gastroenterology · Automation · Classification · Computer vision

1 Introduction

Image classification has become an increasingly vital tool in medical diagnostics, particularly in gastroenterology, where procedures such as gastroscopy generate large volumes of visual data. Gastroscopy is a minimally invasive endoscopic technique that enables direct visualization of the mucosal lining of the esophagus, stomach, and proximal duodenum. This procedure is critical for detecting and monitoring conditions such as ulcers, esophagitis, Barrett's esophagus, polyps, and early-stage gastrointestinal (GI) cancers. With the growing availability of endoscopic image data, machine learning and deep learning models have emerged

© The Author(s), under exclusive license to Springer Nature Switzerland AG 2026
S. Ali et al. (Eds.): MIUA 2025, LNCS 15917, pp. 276–292, 2026.
https://doi.org/10.1007/978-3-031-98691-8_20

as promising tools to support clinical decision-making by automatically detecting and classifying pathological findings [1, 8–10]

However, a persistent and fundamental challenge in applying machine learning to medical imaging is the problem of class imbalance. In most real-world clinical datasets, pathological findings are rare relative to normal or benign conditions. This results in a disproportionate distribution of class samples, where majority classes dominate the training data and minority classes often representing the most clinically significant cases are severely underrepresented. In gastroscopy, for example, images depicting common findings such as normal mucosa or mild gastritis are far more prevalent than those showing rare but critical conditions like gastrointestinal stromal tumors or Barrett's esophagus. This imbalance can severely impair the performance of classification models, leading to biased predictions, high false-negative rates for rare conditions, and ultimately, reduced clinical utility.

Addressing class imbalance is thus not merely a technical consideration but a necessity for building reliable and equitable diagnostic systems. If left unmitigated, class imbalance can compromise a model's ability to detect high-risk pathologies, undermining the promise of AI in supporting early diagnosis. Traditional strategies to tackle imbalance include data-level techniques such as oversampling, undersampling, and synthetic data generation. However, these methods often fall short in medical applications, where data diversity is limited and class boundaries are subtle. As a result, there is growing interest in algorithm-level solutions, such as cost-sensitive learning and specialized loss functions, that adapt model training to focus more effectively on underrepresented classes.

In this work, we investigate the effectiveness of algorithm-level methods for addressing severe class imbalance in the classification of gastroscopy images. We construct a curated dataset by consolidating and reclassifying samples from two publicly available sources, HyperKvasir [2] and GastroVision [7], into four clinically meaningful categories: normal, esophagitis, Barrett's esophagus, and gastric polyps. The resulting dataset reflects a realistic clinical distribution with a pronounced imbalance ratio of approximately $\rho \approx 73$. We calculate the imbalance ratio ρ as following:

$$\rho = \frac{max_i|C_i|}{min_i|C_i|} \tag{1}$$

C_i represents the samples of class i. The functions $max_i|Ci|$ and $min_i|Ci|$ determine the maximum and minimum class sizes among all classes, respectively. We apply and evaluate two established algorithmic approaches Focal Loss and a cost-sensitive learning strategy (CoSen) on state-of-the-art deep learning architectures, namely EfficientNet-B4 [21] and Swin Transformer [14].

By systematically analyzing the impact of these methods on classification performance, particularly for minority classes, this study contributes to the development of more robust and clinically applicable AI systems in gastroenterology. Our findings underscore the critical role of algorithm-level techniques in mitigating the limitations imposed by imbalanced datasets and improving diagnostic performance for rare but medically significant conditions.

The main contributions of this paper are as follows:

1) *We construct a class-imbalanced gastroscopy dataset based on publicly available sources and reorganize it into four clinically relevant categories.*
2) *We introduce a pipeline for gastroscopy image classification and evaluate its effectiveness in improving classification performance under severe class imbalance. The code is open source*[1]
3) *We demonstrate that these techniques significantly enhance performance for underrepresented classes, particularly gastric polyps, thereby improving the clinical utility of the models.*

2   Related Work

Beginning in 2016, Deeba et al. [6] conducted a comprehensive analysis of the performance of various classifiers across different class distributions within training datasets. The authors utilized multiple datasets exhibiting varying degrees of class imbalance, specifically focusing on capsule endoscopy images categorized as either bleeding or non-bleeding. A key finding of their study was that ensemble methods demonstrated greater robustness to class imbalance compared to other approaches. During the year 2017, Li et al. [12] investigated the impact of combining transfer learning with data augmentation and resampling techniques. The objective of the study was to classify endoscopic images into bleeding and non-bleeding categories, with the dataset exhibiting an imbalance ratio of approximately $\rho \approx 14.6$. For the pretraining task, the researchers employed the ImageNet dataset. Training an Inception-v3 model without transfer learning resulted in an accuracy of 95.5%, whereas utilizing transfer learning achieved an accuracy of 98.6%. It is important to note that the results of the work of Li et al. should not be directly compared to this study due to the relative simplicity of the dataset used by Li et al., as evidenced by the high performance of the CNN trained without transfer learning.

In 2022, Mahmood et al. [15] proposed a custom CNN architecture to detect GI tract abnormalities at low computational costs. In their work, they used parts of the Kvasir-Capsule dataset [19] having an initial imbalance ratio of $\rho \approx 60$ and comprising over 18,827 images across 14 classes. They employed a synthetic oversampling technique known as BL-SMOTE to achieve a uniform distribution of samples across all classes. Without the BL-SMOTE technique, their approach achieved a micro-averaged F1-score of 88.2%, while using the BL-SMOTE technique achieved a micro-averaged F1-score of 98.1%, leading to a performance improvement of around 11.2%. Throughout the year 2023, Yue et al. [23] proposed a new loss function called CI loss. This CI loss takes into account both the class frequency and prediction probability of the ground-truth class to determine the weight of each sample. It allows the minority classes to have a greater impact on gradient descent during the training process compared to the majority classes. In their research, they used the whole HyperKvasir dataset [2]

---

[1] https://github.com/Adrian398/Gastroscopy-classifcation-pipeline.

containing 10,662 images across 23 classes and an imbalance ratio of $\rho \approx 191$. The CI loss, in conjunction with a self-developed CNN, was able to increase the macro-averaged F1-score from 60.9% observed when using normal cross-entropy loss to 62.5%, even outperforming the Focal Loss [13] with 62.0%.

In 2024, Li et al. [11] introduced an uncertainty-aware network leveraging handcrafted features and employing representation and classifier decoupling alongside metric learning to tackle class imbalance. They compiled a dataset of 3,492 images encompassing 3 classes: a normal class and two classes differentiating between severe and non-severe esophagitis. The dataset exhibited an imbalance ratio of approximately $\rho \approx 2.3$. By utilizing their proposed method, Li et al. attained a macro-averaged F1-score of 90.1%, representing a performance improvement of roughly 7.0% compared to using only a ResNext50 [22] architecture, which achieved a macro-averaged F1-score of 84.0%.

Similarly in 2024, Sun et al. [20] addressed the issue of class imbalance in lesion samples within endoscopic images. The study utilized a private dataset consisting of three classes - adenoma cases, polyp cases, and cancer cases - with an imbalance ratio of approximately $\rho \approx 3.7$. Sun et al. introduced a novel loss function, termed LSDA loss, which leverages Bayesian principles to prioritize specific sample categories, thereby achieving balanced classification accuracy across all categories. The application of LSDA-Loss resulted in a micro-averaged F1-score of 91.0%. However, the performance of the Focal Loss was not significantly inferior to that of LSDA loss. The most important papers discussed in this section are concisely summarized and encapsulated within Table 1.

Table 1. An overview of data imbalance approaches for endoscopy image evaluation

Source	Method	Task/Dataset	Performance
Li et al. [12] 2017	augmentations, resampling, and transfer learning	classifying bleeding and non-bleeding images	Acc.: 98.6%
Yue et al. [23] 2023	custom CNN + CI loss	classifying HyperKvasir dataset	F1-score: 62.5% (macro-averaged)
Li et al. [11] 2024	uncertainty-aware networks	classifying normal and esophagitis images	F1-score: 90.1% (macro-averaged)
Sun et al. [20] 2024	LSDA loss	detecting adenoma, polyp, and cancer images	F1-score: 91.0% (micro-averaged)

The dataset used in this research contains fewer classes, and the distribution of samples per class differs significantly from those in related works. As a result, it is not directly comparable to the datasets used in the studies previously discussed.

3   Data

This study exclusively employed data obtained from gastroscopy procedures. Due to the relative scarcity of publicly available gastroscopy datasets compared to the most prevalent colonoscopy datasets. Identifying suitable resources posed a notable challenge. The first dataset utilized in this study is the HyperKvasir dataset [2]. This comprehensive dataset comprises both images and videos spanning the entire gastrointestinal (GI) tract, including data acquired through gastroscopy. In total, the dataset contains 10,662 images and 374 videos, representing a wide range of anatomical landmarks and pathological findings. For the purposes of gastroscopy-specific research, the relevant subset of the Hyper-Kvasir dataset includes the following categories: Z-line (932 samples), pylorus (999 samples), retroflex-stomach (764 samples), Barrett's esophagus (41 samples), Barrett's short segment (53 samples), esophagitis grade A (403 samples), and esophagitis grades BD (260 samples).

The second dataset, GastroVision, introduced by Jha et al. [7], also spans both lower and upper GI tract imaging. As an open-access resource, GastroVision includes 8,000 images across 27 distinct labeled classes. The majority of these images were captured using white-light imaging technology, with a select few obtained through narrow-band imaging. For the purposes of this study, relevant classes from the GastroVision dataset include pylorus (393 samples), Barrett's esophagus (95 samples), gastroesophageal junction (330 samples), gastric polyps (65 samples), esophagitis (107 samples), normal esophagus (140 images), normal stomach (969 images), and duodenal bulb (205 images). In the course of this study, data from the HyperKvasir and GastroVision datasets were systematically consolidated and reclassified to form a new, streamlined dataset comprising four distinct classes.

The newly constituted "normal" class includes a variety of images that depict typical, non-pathological features of the upper GI tract. It includes the Z-line, pylorus, and retroflex-stomach classes from the Hyperkvasir dataset, as well as the pylorus and gastroesophageal junction classes from the GastroVision dataset. In total, this class features 4,732 images, offering a comprehensive view of the standard anatomical landscapes within the upper GI tract. As an additional note, it should be mentioned that more images of normal stomach and normal esophagus could be included in this class, particularly those from the GastroVision dataset. However, we chose not to use them to avoid further exacerbating the existing data imbalance.

The "esophagitis" class is tailored to encapsulate varying degrees of esophageal inflammation, bringing together esophagitis grade A and esophagitis grade B-D from the Hyperkvasir dataset alongside the esophagitis class from GastroVision. This integration yields a total of 770 images.

We establish a "Barrett's" class. This class combines Barrett's and Barrett's short segment from Hyperkvasir with Barrett's esophagus from GastroVision, culminating in a set of 189 images. This collection is pivotal for examining the nuances of this precancerous condition.

Lastly, the "polyp" class is singularly sourced from the gastric polyp category of the GastroVision dataset. This class, focused exclusively on images of gastric polyps, underscores the importance of these growths within the stomach lining for gastroenterological examination. Although this class is relatively small in size, its inclusion in the dataset is imperative due to its extraordinary significance in contemporary healthcare.

This reclassification into 4 main categories serves not only to streamline the dataset but also to enhance the clarity and focus of the research, enabling a more targeted investigation into these critical areas of gastroscopy. For a visualization of the class distribution within the dataset, Fig. 1 presents a detailed diagram illustrating this aspect. A notable feature of the used dataset is its significant imbalance ratio, quantified at approximately $\rho \approx 73$. Beyond the pronounced disparity, a critical concern is the sparse representation of images in the minority classes, particularly those pertaining to the polyp and Barrett's categories.

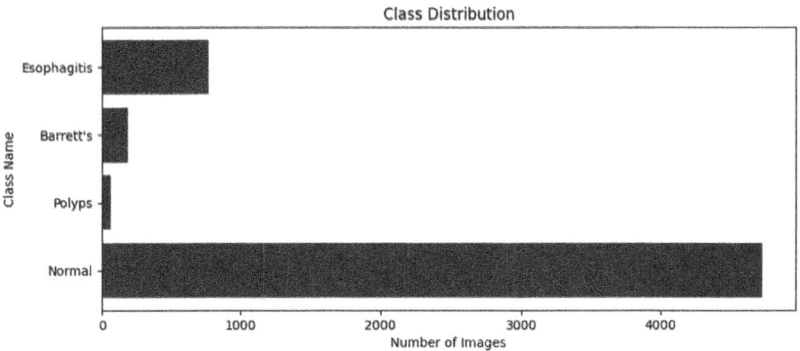

Fig. 1. Class distribution of the dataset

4   Methods

To address the severe class imbalance present in our dataset, we designed a comprehensive multi-stage pipeline, illustrated in Fig. 2. This pipeline integrates both data-level and algorithm-level strategies in a structured manner, enabling systematic performance improvements for underrepresented classes. The process begins with class-specific data augmentation, which is applied selectively to the minority classes (Barrett's esophagus, esophagitis, and gastric polyps) in order to artificially increase their sample diversity and size. Specifically, we employ geometric transformations (e.g., rotations of 90°, 180°, and 270°), photometric adjustments (e.g., contrast and brightness alterations), and elastic and perspective transformations. These augmentations are intentionally targeted to avoid further inflating the already dominant normal class, while providing meaningful variability to the underrepresented pathological classes.

Following augmentation, we apply random oversampling (ROS). This step ensures that the minority class samples are adequately represented during training by duplicating augmented instances until the class distributions are approximately balanced. In the final training dataset, this strategy reduced the original imbalance ratio from approximately $\rho \approx 73$ to a more manageable ratio of $\rho \approx 7.4$, significantly mitigating the skewness without discarding any valuable data.

To further enhance model robustness, particularly in recognizing gastrointestinal patterns, we incorporate transfer learning via pretraining on a colonoscopy image dataset. This pretraining leverages domain-related knowledge, as images from colonoscopy share anatomical and textural similarities with gastroscopy data, albeit originating from different regions of the gastrointestinal tract. The pretrained weights are then fine-tuned on our rebalanced gastroscopy dataset to adapt the models to the specific classification task.

Finally, we use two algorithm-level techniques to explicitly address residual imbalance effects during model optimization:

Focal Loss (FL): a loss function that down-weights the loss assigned to well-classified examples, thereby focusing the model's attention on harder-to-classify, typically minority, samples.

CoSen (Cost-Sensitive Learning): A cost-adjustment strategy that dynamically penalizes misclassifications based on class frequency and inter-class similarity, encouraging the model to allocate greater learning capacity to underrepresented or easily confused classes.

By integrating these stages into a unified training procedure, we construct a highly adaptable and imbalance-aware classification pipeline.

To choose the best models for our setting, we systematically evaluated five prominent neural network architectures. The architectures considered in this study are ResNet-50, DenseNet-121, EfficientNet-B4 [21], the Vision Transformer (ViT), and the Swin Transformer [14]. We included ResNet-50 and DenseNet-121 for the widespread use in computer vision tasks [3]. We selected EfficientNet-B4 for its exceptional trade-off between computational efficiency and accuracy [21]. EfficientNet-B4 leverages a compound scaling technique to simultaneously optimize network depth, width, and resolution.

To assess the potential of Transformer-based models, we also incorporated the Vision Transformer (ViT) and the Swin Transformer into our experiments. The ViT treats input images as sequences of patches and applies self-attention to capture long-range dependencies. We further included the Swin Transformer, following the Swin-S configuration as proposed by Liu et al. [14]. This model employs a hierarchical structure with shifted window attention, which enhances the model's capacity to capture local and global visual features more efficiently than traditional ViTs. Given these strengths, Swin Transformer offered a compelling architecture for our classification task.

We divide the dataset in training, validation, and test subsets, adhering to a distribution ratio of 70%, 10%, and 20%, respectively. It is important to note that this division results in a significant imbalance within the training dataset: only

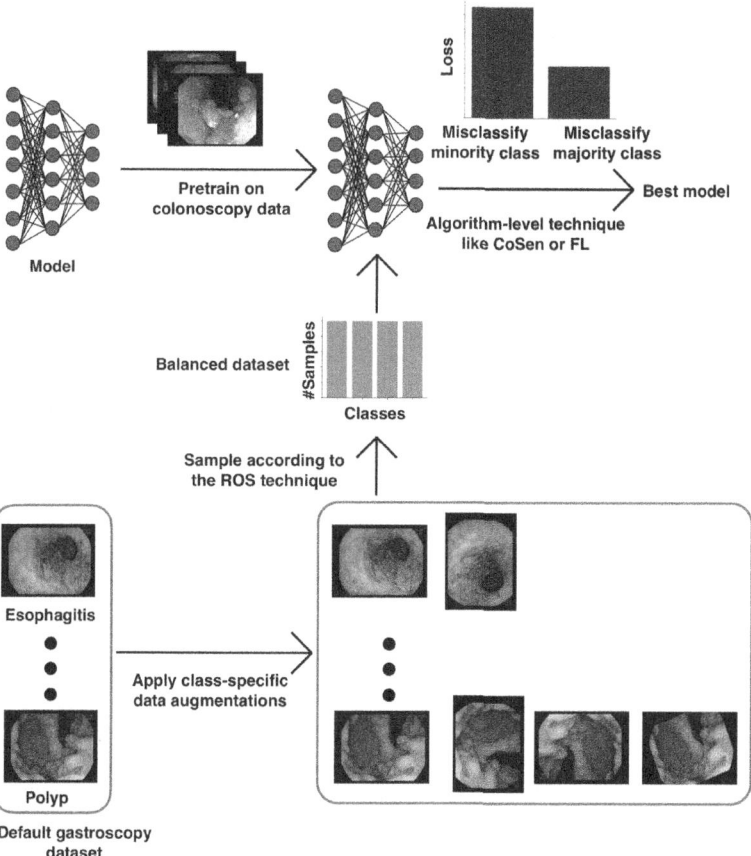

Fig. 2. Overview of the deep learning pipeline to address extreme class imbalance. The approach includes random oversampling (ROS), cost-sensitive learning (CoSen), and focal loss (FL) to improve performance on minority classes.

45 polyp images and 132 Barrett's images are available for training, compared to 3,312 images of normal conditions. This disparity highlights the pronounced imbalance and scarcity of certain classes in the default dataset. In the training phase, all images will be uniformly resized to a resolution of 640×640 pixels. This decision is based on the observations of Tan et al. [21], who stated that larger images indeed lead to better classification performance, and Richter et al. [17], who noted that decreasing the input resolution too much can result in significantly lower classification performance. Additionally, it is crucial to balance the input size, as excessively large inputs can drastically increase the computational and memory overhead. To explore the impact of various learning configurations, each model will be trialed with learning rates set at 0.01 and 0.001, in addition to a learning rate schedule that begins at 0.01 and reduces by a factor of 0.5 every 30 epochs. All experiments will span a total of 100 epochs for every model

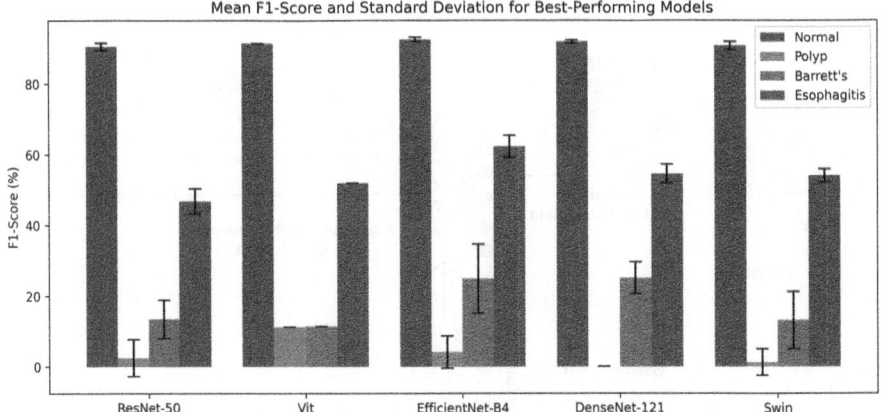

Fig. 3. Mean F1-score and standard deviation for each class of the models trained without data imbalance methods

and learning rate strategy. Given the relatively small size of the validation set, which could lead to significant fluctuations in validation outcomes, selecting an optimal epoch based on these results is impractical. Instead, a robust evaluation approach will be employed for the test dataset, wherein the performances of the last 10 epochs (from epoch 91 to epoch 100) are averaged to determine various metrics for each model and its corresponding learning rate schedule. All experiments detailed in this study were conducted using the Python-based frameworks MMpretrain [5] and MMengine [4], both of which are sophisticatedly constructed on top of PyTorch [16]. These frameworks were chosen for their robustness and versatility in handling complex deep learning tasks. We use a NVIDIA GeForce™ RTX 3090 GPU, equipped with an impressive 24 GB of available memory. Each model underwent training with the maximum batch size permissible by the GPU's capacity.

5   Results

In the evaluation of the default models the EfficientNet-B4 architecture stands out with an accuracy of 85.8%. In Fig. 3, the mean F1-score and its standard deviation are visually represented for each model and class. While the determination of a clear leader in terms of precision, recall, and F1-score is less straightforward, all models exhibit challenges with the polyp class. Despite these challenges, EfficientNet-B4, alongside the ViT, shows promise, balancing accuracy and F1-score for polyps adequate. The performance of both EfficientNet-B4 and Swin Transformer models is noteworthy when identifying esophagitis, showcasing strong recall and precision. As anticipated, the detection of the normal class is a task at which all models excel, reflecting their adeptness at recognizing common presentations. Therefore, we chose EfficientNet-B4 (CNN) and Swin Transformer (Transformer) for our further analysis.

Table 2. Performance summary of EfficientNet-B4 and Swin Transformer across stages: Default training, +Aug (Augmentation), +FL (Focal Loss), and +CoSen (Class Oversampling with Semantic Enhancement). Acc = Accuracy, F1-Polyps = F1-score for polyp class, F1-Avg = Average F1-score over all classes.

Stage	EfficientNet-B4			Swin Transformer		
	Acc (%)	F1-Polyps (%)	F1-Avg (%)	Acc (%)	F1-Polyps (%)	F1-Avg (%)
Default	50.1	4.1	45.5	52.9	1.2	39.7
+ Aug	80.6	10.2	50.3	78.8	18.1	42.9
+ FL	83.1	35.1	53.9	81.2	20.8	43.8
+ CoSen	**87.1**	**44.5**	**56.8**	84.2	24.7	48.8

After selecting these two models, we further integrated them with our pipeline, as shown above. The different steps and changes in the application of our pipeline are shown in Table 2. Additionally, the table shows details of the best experiments conducted with FL. The Swin Transformer demonstrates a significant performance improvement in the F1-score of the polyp class.

Table 3. Per-class performance for EfficientNet-B4 and Swin Transformer using our full pipeline. N = Normal, P = Polyp, B = Barrett's, E = Esophagitis.

Metric	EfficientNet-B4				Swin Transformer			
	N	P	B	E	N	P	B	E
Recall (%)	95.6	37.1	24.4	55.1	92.2	17.9	21.3	57.4
Precision (%)	91.4	10.0	22.1	56.2	91.5	47.5	21.8	57.5
F1-score (%)	93.4	44.5	28.4	60.7	91.8	24.7	21.4	57.3
Loss (CoSen)	–							
Schedule	lr_decr				lr_decr			
Accuracy (%)	87.1				84.2			

Table 3 shows a more detailed view of our final pipeline showing results for all different classes. Furthermore, the confusion matrices for the two best-performing models are displayed in Fig. 4. The confusion matrix of the Swin Transformer indicates a significant increase in the performance of the polyp class, while the performance of the Barrett's class decreased. The performance of the normal and esophagitis classes remained nearly constant. The Barrett's class is often misclassified as esophagitis class.

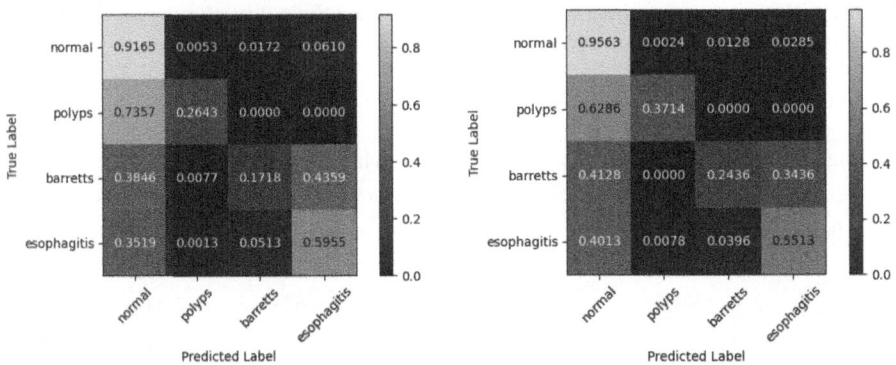

Fig. 4. Averaged and normalized confusion matrices of the best Swin Transformer and EfficientNet-B4 models

A similar pattern is observed with the trained EfficientNet-B4 model. The polyp class shows a significant performance boost, whereas the performance of the Barrett's class decreases, and the esophagitis class remains constant, also misclassifying Barrett's images as esophagitis images. Additionally, the EfficientNet-B4 model was able to improve its performance for the normal class.

The best model trained using a combination of data-level and algorithm-level techniques to address the imbalance in the dataset achieved a macro-averaged F1-score of 56.8% for EfficientNet-B4, representing a 11.3% performance increase over its baseline. For the Swin Transformer, the model attained a macro-averaged F1-score of 48.8%. For the polyp class the increase in F1 was even higher with 44.4 % compared to the baseline.

6   Discussion

We further compare our pipeline against the literature of gastrocopy image classification. Jha et al. [7] conducted a benchmark evaluation using the GastroVision dataset, which was also utilized in this research to construct the default dataset. Their best-performing model which belongs to the DenseNet family was trained for 150 epochs. The training process utilized sophisticated learning schedules and the Adam optimizer. Furthermore, they implemented transfer learning and applied various data augmentation techniques to improve the model's robustness and generalization capabilities. In their study, their baseline model achieved an F1-score of 31.0% for the esophagitis class and 33.0% for the polyp class. These F1-scores are lower than those obtained by the best-performing models in this work, which reached an F1-score of 60.7% for the esophagitis class and 44.5% for the polyp class.

However, this comparison is not straightforward due to differences in the number of classes considered. Jha et al.'s research involved a greater number of classes, including those concerning the lower GI tract, making the classification task more complex due to the increased number of predictions required.

Conversely, this complexity is slightly mitigated by a more balanced class distribution in their dataset compared to the default dataset used in this study. The imbalance in the default dataset was a primary source of misclassifications, as evidenced by the confusion matrices.

An additional study by Sarsengeldin et al. [18] utilized CNNs and Capsule Networks to perform classification on the HyperKvasir dataset. They achieved performance comparable to this research, reaching a macro-averaged F1-score of 55.0% and an accuracy of 85.0%. However, their results cannot be directly compared to those of this work for several reasons. Their dataset included a significantly higher number of classes, incorporating those from the lower GI tract. This inclusion leads to some classes being more easily distinguishable, as lower GI tract images and upper GI tract images can be effectively separated due to different color distributions. Furthermore, it has to be mentioned that the HyperKvasir dataset contained classes that are already relatively balanced in comparison to the majority class. This means the imbalance is often attributed to a small subset of classes that contain extremely few images, meaning the majority of classes in this dataset do not have a significant imbalance. Moreover, certain classes, such as accessory tools, are relatively straightforward for neural networks to predict. The differences between the HyperKvasir dataset and the default dataset used in this study are further elaborated in the following paragraph. These distinctions suggest that comparisons between the results of Sarsengeldin et al. and those obtained in this work should be approached with caution. Nevertheless, the achieved F1-score and accuracy are comparable, as they exhibit nearly identical values. Similar observations can be made when comparing this work to the research about the intersection of medical imaging and data imbalance presented in Sect. 2. While Yue et al. [23] also used the HyperKvasir dataset and the CI loss, achieving an F1-score of 62.5%, their dataset contains a smaller proportion of classes with high imbalance ratios compared to the default dataset used in this study. In contrast, a significant portion of the classes in the generated dataset used throughout this research exhibit high imbalance ratios. This marks a fundamental difference between the dataset used in their research and the default dataset used in this study. The usage of the HyperKvasir dataset led to more classes exhibiting high F1-scores overall, resulting in a higher F1-score in the work of Yue et al. compared to the one obtained in this work. In contrast, this study uses a dataset consisting of 4 classes, 3 of which are significantly imbalanced. Notably, the Barrett's and polyp classes exhibit a very high imbalance compared to the majority class. As these two classes contribute as much to the macro-averaged F1-score as the esophagitis and normal classes combined, the F1-score observed in this work is significantly lower. In their study, Yue et al. utilized not only the proposed CI loss but also the FL loss. Using the FL loss, they achieved an F1-score of 62.0%, which is slightly lower than the score obtained with the CI loss. Given the small difference in performance between the FL and CI losses and the fact that the FL loss was already incorporated into the experiments of this study, the author considers the results obtained by Yue et al. to be comparable to those achieved in this study.

Moreover, this study corroborates the findings of Li et al. [12], demonstrating that transfer learning is indeed an effective approach for addressing dataset imbalance. The high accuracy values reported by Li et al. can be largely attributed to the relatively low imbalance ratio and the simplicity of the dataset they employed, in contrast to the dataset used in this work. The dataset used by Li et al. is considered less challenging, as evidenced by the fact that the CNN without transfer learning already achieved an accuracy of 95.5%.

When comparing this study with the work by Li et al. [11], it becomes clear that the datasets used are not directly comparable. The primary reason is that Li et al. employed an imbalance ratio of approximately $\rho \approx 2.3$, which is significantly lower than that used in this study, thereby making their classification task easier. This is evidenced by the fact that standard CNNs, such as ResNeXt50, achieved an impressive F1-score of 84.0% on their dataset. While Li et al.'s method demonstrated a 7.0% improvement over the ResNeXt50 architecture, this enhancement is not substantial enough to conclusively establish their approach as a superior solution for addressing data imbalance. To provide further insight into the performance of the networks activation maps for the best models are generated for the same test set images. This analysis involves the EfficientNet-B4 and the Swin Transformer.

Figure 5 illustrates the models activation maps for different polyp images. The EfficientNet-B4 demonstrates robust performance, focusing its attention predominantly on the polyp formations and successfully classifying all three polyp images correctly. This targeted detection marks a significant improvement

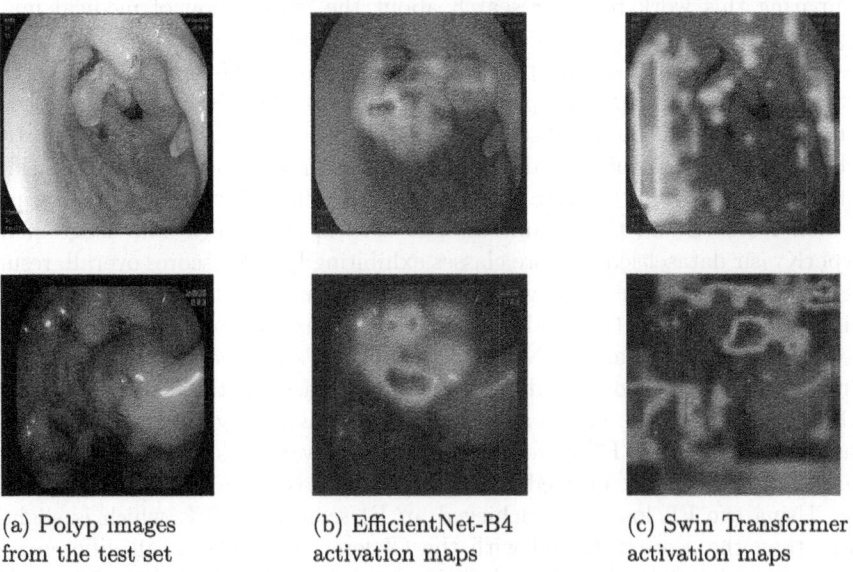

(a) Polyp images   (b) EfficientNet-B4   (c) Swin Transformer
from the test set   activation maps   activation maps

Fig. 5. Activation maps for polyp images of the best EfficientNet-B4 and Swin Transformer models

over its baseline activation maps, reflecting its enhanced performance for this class. In contrast, the Swin Transformer directs its attention to many small, fragmented areas, although it still manages to correctly classify the image in the third row as polyp. Like its baseline activation maps, the Swin Transformer tends to focus on the edges of images, which might contribute to its generally weaker performance relative to the EfficientNet-B4. Nonetheless, notable improvements are visible in the Swin Transformer's activation maps, indicating strides in model optimization. Similar observations can be made when examining the activation maps for esophagitis images Fig. 6. The EfficientNet-B4 model demonstrates a dedicated approach by focusing on a few distinct areas, effectively recognizing and accurately classifying all displayed images of esophagitis. In contrast, the Swin Transformer disperses its attention over numerous small, fragmented regions. Despite this less concentrated focus, the Swin Transformer is able to correctly identify the second and third images as esophagitis, showcasing its capability to discern relevant features among broader scanning patterns. Both models exhibit a tendency to concentrate on transitions from light red to dark red areas within the mucosa, a characteristic feature of esophagitis. Compared to their baseline performances, both models show enhanced detection capabilities in these updated maps, underscoring the substantial performance improvements achieved through the techniques employed to address data imbalance. Further underscoring these improvements, enhanced activation maps for both models illustrated the critical role of the combination of data-level and algorithm-level interventions in tackling dataset imbalances. Both models have begun to concen-

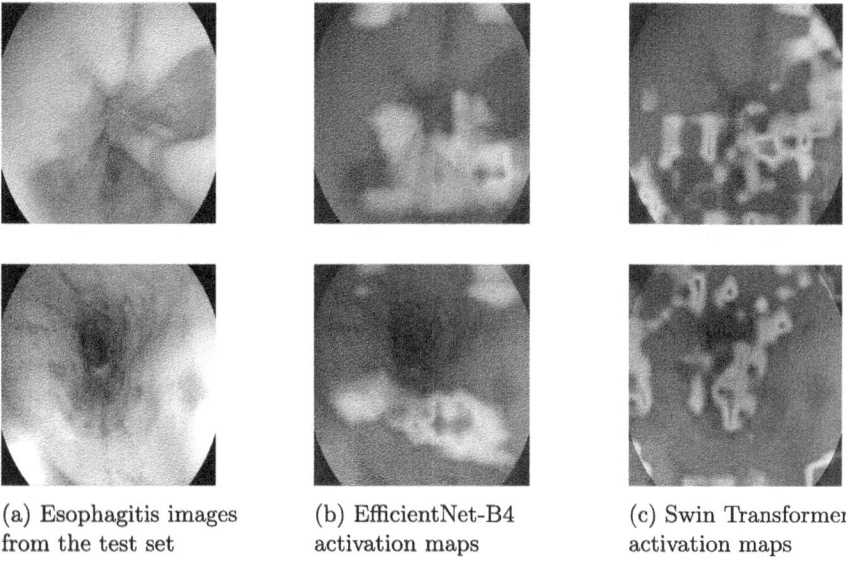

(a) Esophagitis images
from the test set

(b) EfficientNet-B4
activation maps

(c) Swin Transformer
activation maps

Fig. 6. Activation maps for barret images of the best EfficientNet-B4 and Swin Transformer models

trate on disease-specific features for the polyp and esophagitis classes. Moreover, it is notable that the improvement in model performance is primarily observed in the polyp class, which benefits the most from the techniques used to address dataset imbalance. One reason for this is that the applied techniques specifically target dataset imbalance, which was the primary cause of misclassifying polyp images, as evidenced by the confusion matrices. However, the misclassification of Barrett's images was not solely due to the overwhelming number of normal images and the resulting dataset imbalance. Instead, it also stemmed from the similar visual characteristics of Barrett's and esophagitis images, making it inherently more challenging for the network to distinguish between these conditions. This issue is not directly addressed by the techniques employed.

7   Conclusion

This study addressed the pressing issue of class imbalance in gastroscopy image classification by proposing a deep learning pipeline that integrates data-level and algorithm-level strategies. By consolidating images from the HyperKvasir and GastroVision datasets into a clinically relevant four-class dataset, we created a challenging benchmark with a high imbalance ratio ($\rho \approx 73$), closely mirroring real-world diagnostic conditions. Through systematic experimentation, we demonstrated that the combination of targeted data augmentation, class-specific oversampling, transfer learning, and algorithmic methods such as Focal Loss and CoSen significantly enhances classification performance, particularly for underrepresented classes. Notably, our best model based on EfficientNet-B4 achieved a macro-averaged F1-score of 56.8%, representing a substantial improvement of 11.3% over the baseline. The F1-score for the critical minority polyp class increased by 40.4%, underscoring the effectiveness of our approach. Activation map analyses further revealed that the models trained with imbalanceaware strategies focused more accurately on disease-relevant regions, contributing to improved interpretability. However, challenges remain in distinguishing visually similar conditions such as Barrett's esophagus and esophagitis, which may require more advanced feature disentanglement or attention mechanisms.

Overall, our findings highlight the importance of tailored imbalance mitigation techniques in medical image analysis pipelines. Future work could explore advanced hybrid losses, semi-supervised learning, or curriculum learning to further improve model robustness and diagnostic reliability in highly imbalanced medical datasets.

Acknowledgement. This research project is funded by the Bavarian Research Institute for Digital Transformation (bidt), an institute of the Bavarian Academy of Sciences and Humanities. Additionally this study was supported by bayerische Hochschulagentur (BTHA) under grant BTHA-JC-2024-52. The author is responsible for the content of this publication.

Disclosure of Interests. The authors have no competing interests.

References

1. Ali, S., et al.: Deep learning for detection and segmentation of artefact and disease instances in gastrointestinal endoscopy. Med. Image Anal. **70**, 102002 (2021)
2. Borgli, H., et al.: Hyperkvasir, a comprehensive multi-class image and video dataset for gastrointestinal endoscopy. Sci. Data **7**(1), 283 (2020)
3. Chenghao, L., Liang, E., Chen, M.: Characterizing resnet's universal approximation capability (2023)
4. Contributors, M.: Openmmlab's foundational deep learning library based on pytorch. https://github.com/openmmlab/mmengine. Accessed 2024
5. Contributors, M.: Openmmlab's pre-training toolbox and benchmark. https://github.com/openmmlab/mmpretrain. Accessed 2024
6. Deeba, F., Mohammed, S.K., Bui, F.M., Wahid, K.A.: Learning from imbalanced data: a comprehensive comparison of classifier performance for bleeding detection in endoscopic video. In: 2016 5th International Conference on Informatics, Electronics and Vision (ICIEV), pp. 1006–1009 (2016). https://doi.org/10.1109/ICIEV.2016.7760150
7. Jha, D., et al.: Gastrovision: a multi-class endoscopy image dataset for computer aided gastrointestinal disease detection. In: Workshop on Machine Learning for Multimodal Healthcare Data, pp. 125–140. Springer, Cham (2023)
8. Krenzer, A., et al.: Automated classification of polyps using deep learning architectures and few-shot learning. BMC Med. Imaging **23**(1), 59 (2023)
9. Krenzer, A., Hekalo, A., Puppe, F.: Endoscopic detection and segmentation of gastroenterological diseases with deep convolutional neural networks. In: EndoCV@ISBI (2020)
10. Krenzer, A., et al.: Fast machine learning annotation in the medical domain: a semi-automated video annotation tool for gastroenterologists (2021)
11. Li, X., Wu, Q., Wang, M., Wu, K.: Uncertainty-aware network for fine-grained and imbalanced reflux esophagitis grading. Comput. Biol. Med. **168**, 107751 (2024)
12. Li, X., Zhang, H., Zhang, X., Liu, H., Xie, G.: Exploring transfer learning for gastrointestinal bleeding detection on small-size imbalanced endoscopy images. In: 2017 39th Annual International Conference of the IEEE Engineering in Medicine and Biology Society (EMBC), pp. 1994–1997. IEEE (2017)
13. Lin, T.Y., Goyal, P., Girshick, R., He, K., Dollár, P.: Focal loss for dense object detection. In: Proceedings of the IEEE International Conference on Computer Vision, pp. 2980–2988 (2017)
14. Liu, Z., et al.: Swin transformer: hierarchical vision transformer using shifted windows. In: Proceedings of the IEEE/CVF International Conference on Computer Vision, pp. 10012–10022 (2021)
15. Mahmood, S., et al.: A robust deep model for classification of peptic ulcer and other digestive tract disorders using endoscopic images. Biomedicines **10**(9), 2195 (2022)
16. Paszke, A., et al.: Pytorch: an imperative style, high-performance deep learning library. In: Advances in Neural Information Processing Systems, vol. 32 (2019)
17. Richter, M.L., Shenk, J., Byttner, W., Arpteg, A., Huss, M.: Feature space saturation during training. arXiv preprint arXiv:2006.08679 (2020)
18. Sarsengeldin, M., et al.: Gastrointestinal disease diagnosis with hybrid model of capsules and CNNs. In: 2023 IEEE International Conference on Electro Information Technology (eIT), pp. 143–146. IEEE (2023)

19. Smedsrud, P.H., et al.: Kvasir-capsule, a video capsule endoscopy dataset. Sci. Data **8**(1), 142 (2021)
20. Sun, W., Zhao, R., Zhang, K., Gao, J., Qu, G.: Distribution-aware loss for lesions detection using white-light endoscopy in colorectal region. IEEE Access (2024)
21. Tan, M., Le, Q.: Efficientnet: rethinking model scaling for convolutional neural networks. In: International Conference on Machine Learning, pp. 6105–6114. PMLR (2019)
22. Xie, S., Girshick, R., Dollár, P., Tu, Z., He, K.: Aggregated residual transformations for deep neural networks. In: Proceedings of the IEEE Conference on Computer Vision and Pattern Recognition, pp. 1492–1500 (2017)
23. Yue, G., Wei, P., Liu, Y., Luo, Y., Du, J., Wang, T.: Automated endoscopic image classification via deep neural network with class imbalance loss. IEEE Trans. Instrum. Meas. **72**, 1–11 (2023)

Temporally Consistent Smoke Removal from Endoscopic Video Images

Silja Janßen$^{(\boxtimes)}$ ⓘ, Mohamed Oumeslakht, and Kevin Köser ⓘ

Department of Computer Science, Kiel University, Christian-Albrechts-Platz 4, 24118 Kiel,
Germany
silja.janssen@cs.uni-kiel.de

Abstract. The use of electrocautery or laser ablation in endoscopic surgeries produces smoke which obscures the view of the surgeon. Smoke removal methods aim to remove smoke from affected images and provide corresponding clear views. However, methods developed so far generally apply to single-image inputs and do not take the temporal consistency of video data into account, which can lead to flickering artefacts. To cope with this effect, we propose to process multiple subsequent video frames at the same time, providing more information to the system. For our first results into this direction, we implemented a 3D U-Net architecture to process sequential video data with time acting as the third dimension. We further created novel video datasets from surgical recordings and synthetic smoke overlays to train the model on, and quantitatively compared its performance to a baseline 2D U-Net that processes each frame separately. Results show that our proposed model is able to recover structures from smoky images and generate a clear output with higher SSIM values compared to the baseline, though PNSR is slightly better for the 2D approach. However, when utilizing optical flow and warping error to compare subsequent output video frames, we can show that the 3D approach significantly increases the temporal consistency.

Keywords: smoke removal · 3D U-Net · neural network · image inpainting · computer vision · endoscopy

1 Introduction

Endoscopic surgery and specifically robotic assisted endoscopic surgery, where tools are inserted into the abdominal cavity through minor incisions, have gained large popularity in the recent decades [2]. However, while the procedure is minimally invasive, the view of the surgeon is at the same time limited through the digital eye of the (stereo-) endoscope. Smoke produced by electrocautery and laser ablation, meant for reducing the bleeding while cutting tissue, may obscure the image. AI-based image enhancement techniques are an option to improve the video image clarity, but care must be taken that they do not introduce artefacts like flickering which might distract the surgeon even more.

In this contribution, we report on our early results on employing a 3D U-Net architecture to remove smoke from endoscopic video images. Our model takes multiple

S. Ali et al. (Eds.): MIUA 2025, LNCS 15917, pp. 293–301, 2026.
https://doi.org/10.1007/978-3-031-98691-8_21

sequential video frames as input and therefore has more information to ensure temporal consistency. We created video evaluation data sets and propose warping error as a metric to analyse the temporal consistency in smoke-reduced videos.

Previous works on endoscopic smoke removal can mostly be divided into three categories: dark channel prior (DCP), Cyclic Generative Adversarial Networks (Cycle-GAN) and U-Net architectures. DCP methods, such as introduced by He et al. [5] and applied to endoscopy by Tchaka [11], focus on removing haze by estimating light transmission and haze thickness from locally dark pixels in single images. However, they assume homogeneous haze and may not be able to deal with the heterogeneous density of smoke. CycleGAN [16] is an image-to-image translation approach which translates an input image into another domain, for example by applying an art style to it. The mapping from one domain to the other is learned on unpaired image data, meaning that images from both domains are available, but there is no direct correlation between them. Examples for the application to medical endoscopy are implemented by Hu [6], Zhou [15] and Zhang [14]. In this instance, smoke-free and smoky endoscopic images can be used for the training process without needing to display the exact same surgical scenes.

In recent years, several datasets for endoscopic smoke removal were created, facilitating approaches based on supervised learning. The U-Net structure [10] proved suitable for the generation of smoke-free images from paired data and was for instance implemented by Chen [4], Lin [8] and Ma [9].

The main limitation of the aforementioned approaches is that they typically process single images, leading to a lack of temporal consistency when it comes to video data. Exceptions to the single-image paradigm include those that apply optical flow. Optical flow can be used to merge information from prior frames in a video sequence and was for example recently implemented by Wu et al. [13]. However, their approach depends on the presence of a pre-smoke reference frame which the smoky image is adjusted to via optical flow. Thus, in cases of large movement during periods of smoke, optical flow methods may not always be applicable.

In contrast, we propose to employ a 3D U-Net architecture where the third dimension lies in the temporal space, with the goal to preserve temporal consistency in video data. We take five sequential images as input and compute output for the middle image, utilising information from the surrounding frames for the detection and removal of smoke. We further created a video dataset composed of smoke-free surgery scenes overlaid with smoke on which the model was trained, and then evaluated it in comparison with a baseline U-Net.

2   Materials and Methods

A video dataset was created from surgical recordings at the University Hospital of Schleswig-Holstein (UKSH), on which the proposed 3D U-Net was trained. We further implemented a baseline U-Net to evaluate the performance of both in comparison.

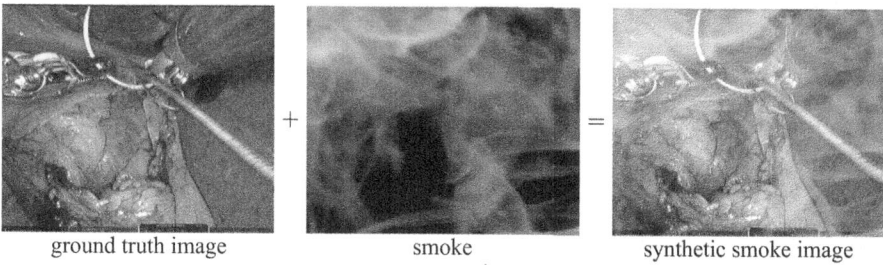

ground truth image   smoke   synthetic smoke image

Fig. 1. Generation of synthetic smoke images

2.1   Video Dataset

To construct the dataset, a robotic assisted partial kidney resection surgery was recorded. From the endoscopic recordings, smoke-free scenes were carefully selected to provide ground truth data without the occurrence of smoke. The video scenes display a variety of tissue types and organs, namely fatty tissue, colon, liver and kidney. Surgical tools move through most images, and the presence of blood varies across the scenes. The two longest extracted video clips have a duration of 6:17 and 4:24 min, producing 11,272 and 7,920 frames respectively at a recording rate of 30 frames per second and a size of 436×350 pixels. Two additional smoke-free scenes of 1:23 min length yielded 2,504 frames each.

We created corresponding synthetic smoke images from video frames of real smoke in front of a black background, which have been created for artistic purposes and provided through a public video platform [1]. Multiple videos were selected and combined to obtain a high variety of smoke in density, shape and general appearance. The video frames were cropped and resized to match the ground truth scenes, and smoke was extracted and superimposed on the ground truth images according to the following equation:

$$I_{img\_smoke} = \alpha \times I_{white} + (1 - \alpha) \times I_{img\_GT}, \tag{1}$$

$$\alpha = \frac{1}{255} \times I_{smoke} \tag{2}$$

with I_{img_GT} being the ground truth image, I_{white} a white image of the same size as I_{img} and α the opacity derived from the greyscale smoke image I_{smoke}. Figure 1 illustrates the process.

The resulting paired video datasets, consisting of one smoke-free and one smoky video each, were split into training and test data. The two longest videos were selected for the training, yielding a dataset of 19,192 sequential synthetic smoke frames, and the two shorter scenes with a total of 5,008 frames were used for testing purposes. Example frames are shown in Fig. 2, and Fig. 3 illustrates a scene of five consecutive frames. All videos display a high variety of anatomical structures and thus serve as suitable datasets for the training of our implemented 3D U-Net model.

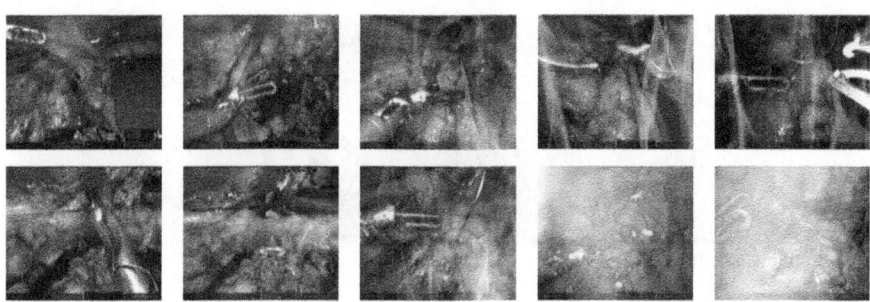

Fig. 2. Example scenes overlaid with synthetic smoke of varying shape and thickness

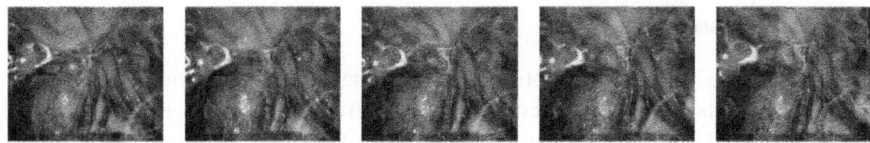

Fig. 3. Consecutive frames of a synthesized smoky scene

2.2   3D U-Net Architecture

We propose a 3D U-Net to process multiple sequential video frames with the aim of achieving high temporal consistency in the output. The basic U-Net architecture [10] was extended to a 3D U-Net following the example of Cicek et al. [3], but in contrast to their work, the third dimension represents time instead of space.

The model takes five sequential video images as input. The encoder path contains five convolutional blocks, each consisting of two 3D convolution layers followed by BatchNorm3D normalisation and ReLU activation functions. After each block, max-pooling is applied in the spatial dimensions to reduce the image resolution but preserve the temporal depth.

The decoder merges the features from the bottom layers, which are upsampled by transposed convolutions, with those preserved through skip connections. Afterwards, 3D convolution, normalisation and activation are applied in each block analogous to the encoder. The final layer applies a 3D convolution with a kernel size of $1 \times 1 \times 1$, which reduces the number of output channels to three to produce a single coloured image.

Our proposed network takes five sequential video frames as input and reduces them to a single output image, which corresponds with the middle frame. The Mean Squared Error (MSE) loss is computed from this image and the respective ground truth and minimised using the Adam optimiser.

2.3   Comparison to Baseline U-Net

A baseline U-Net was implemented to provide a basis for evaluations. It was implemented following the architecture originally proposed by Ronneberger et al. [10]. Its architecture is analogue to the proposed 3D U-Net, but as the input is a single image, it contains 2D convolutions only. It was trained on the same video dataset, where each frame was regarded as a single independent image.

3 Results

We present performance metrics for the baseline 2D U-Net in comparison with the proposed 3D U-Net in Table 1. The testing dataset, containing two smoke-free video scenes overlaid with synthetic smoke, displays various surgical scenes, mostly during either the cutting or suturing phase. All metrics were calculated across the two scenes with 5,008 sequential ground truth and 5,008 corresponding smoky images in total. Since the 3D architecture computes outputs only for the middle frame out of 5 sequential images, we obtain 2,500 testing images for each scene, 5,000 in total.

Structural Similarity Index Measure (SSIM) and Peak Signal-to-Noise Ratio (PSNR) values were calculated to evaluate the reconstruction abilities. While the 3D U-Net yielded a higher SSIM value and was able to recover structures better, the PSNR value was lower in comparison to the baseline.

To evaluate the temporal consistency of both models, we implemented the warping error (WE) [7] between one image I_t and the warped subsequent image $\hat{I}_{t+1}$ following the equation:

$$E_{warp} = \frac{1}{T-1} \sum_{t=1}^{T-1} \frac{1}{255} \frac{1}{H \times W} |I_t - \hat{I}_{t+1}| \qquad (3)$$

Warping error describes the difference between two consecutive video frames where one is warped to match the other frame based on optical flow calculation. Thus, it removes the proportion of difference caused by tissue or object movement, and focuses on the frame difference due to image inference. Since the warping does not yield perfectly identical images, we present the warping error for optical flow-corrected ground truth video sequences in comparison to the warping error for 2D and 3D U-Nets. We computed optical flow for the ground truth images and warped each frame, ground truth, 2D and 3D U-Net output, with the same transformation. The computed WE value now describes the percentual difference between one frame and the warped subsequent frame. Figure 4 illustrates the smoothed warping error for 100 sequential sample images.

In addition, we computed Frames per Second (FPS) from each model's inference time per frame to evaluate the applicability for real-time performance:

$$FPS = \frac{1}{\text{inference time (s)}} \qquad (4)$$

Figure 5 presents exemplary qualitative results for the testing dataset on which all metrics were computed. To evaluate the real-life performance of our model, we applied it to scenes from the recorded surgical video which displayed actual surgical smoke. Qualitative results can be seen in Fig. 6. Since corresponding ground truth does not exist for the real smoke scenes, these figures can not be evaluated quantitatively.

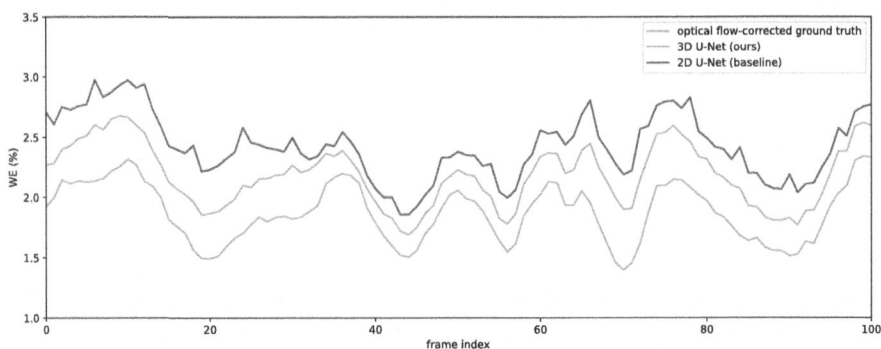

Fig. 4. Warping error (WE) plotted across 100 sequential frames, smoothed over 5 values

Table 1. Evaluation metrics for both models in comparison. The best values are printed in bold, excluding ground truth values.

Model	Mean SSIM	Mean PSNR (dB)	Mean WE (%)	FPS
3D U-Net (Ours)	**0.9392**	27.05	**1.76**	16
2D U-Net (Baseline)	0.9346	**29.13**	1.89	**38**
Ground Truth	–	–	1.50	30

4   Discussion

In this section we discuss the results presented in the previous tables and figures. Quantitative results show that both models, our proposed 3D architecture and the baseline 2D U-Net, were able to remove smoke from surgical scenes to a large degree. This is supported by the high SSIM values of 0.9392 and 0.9346, respectively. While the 3D architecture yielded a slightly higher SSIM value, the PSNR was lower. The qualitative figures indicate that our approach produces cleaner images and recovers structures more clearly, but may induce discolouration in light or naturally hazy areas.

In addition to the classical image metrics, we computed the warping error as an indicator for temporal consistency. Contrary to other video consistency metrics such as the keypoint-based Fréchet Video Distance [12], warping error measures global consistency across the image and is ideal for low-contrast inpainting situations like surgical smoke. The qualitative analysis shows that our proposed architecture yielded a lower WE value, meaning a reduced difference between warped consecutive frames, in comparison to the baseline 2D U-Net. This proves an increased temporal consistency. While most smoke removal networks process only single images and compute the corresponding output for each frame of a video sequence separately, irregularities can be observed when the output is recomposed into a video format, such as uneven smoke removal and flickering between frames. Our proposed 3D U-Net model reduces these irregularities and generates smoother, more stable video output.

Inference times indicate that the 3D architecture increases computation times significantly compared to the baseline U-Net. As such, our model is useful for research

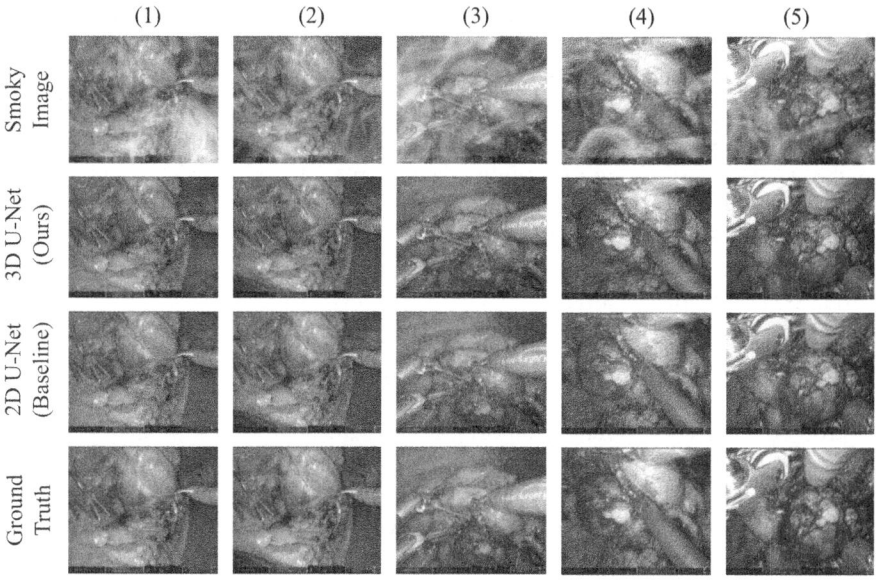

Fig. 5. Five images from synthetic smoke scenes and the outputs in comparison

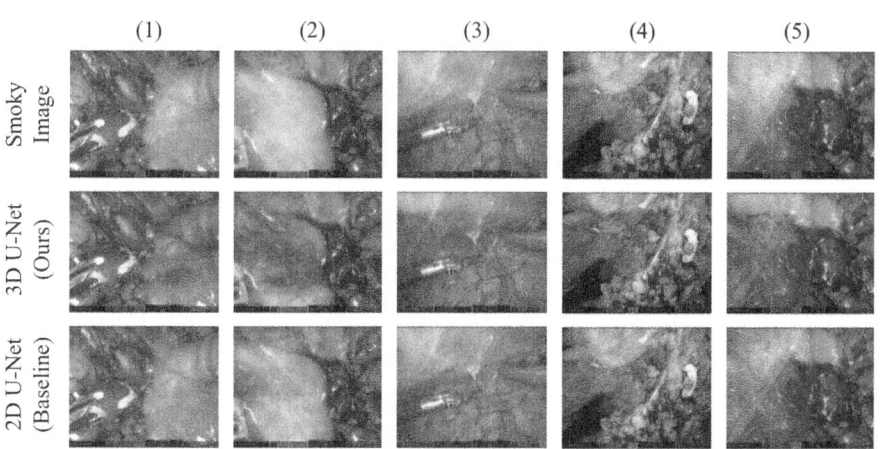

Fig. 6. Five images displaying real surgical smoke and the respective outputs

purposes only and requires some improvements before it becomes applicable for real-time uses. Since we compute output for the middle image out of five sequential frames, processing depends on the availability of images from the future, resulting in a natural delay of two frames in the output computation. To combat this weakness, our architecture can be adapted to process only three frames and exclude the ones expected from the future, potentially decreasing computation times further. This reduction may, however, come at the cost of decreased output quality.

The application to real surgical smoke images shows that while our model is limited by the training on synthetic data, it can handle real images too, as seen in Fig. 6. The baseline U-Net, trained on the same synthetic dataset, displays only small improvements compared to the input data. Our proposed model, however, produces a much cleaner view. The performance can be improved even more through the inclusion of a higher variety of smoke in the training dataset. We selected artistic captures of real smoke with a high variety of shapes to create our synthetic data, and the scale of the smoke can be easily adapted. However, the captures lack the spray mist that often accompanies surgical smoke, an appearance unique to wet environments and hard to reproduce in synthetic situations.

5   Conclusion

We propose a 3D U-Net architecture to process sequential frames of smoky surgical videos and remove the smoke efficiently while ensuring temporal consistency. Our implemented model is based on a U-Net structure, but extended in the temporal dimension to process five sequential images. The five images are considered a 3D volume and undergo 3D convolutions before being reduced to a single output image, corresponding to the middle frame in a temporal arrangement. We compare this architecture to a baseline U-Net. We created a synthetic dataset from surgical recordings overlaid with images of real smoke, and used this datatset for the training of both models.

Results show that our model is able to remove smoke, recover obscured structures and produce clear output images. At the same time, the output is temporally more consistent when viewing video data, which is reflected in the decreased warping error.

Future works aim to increase the performance of our model through a higher variety of smoke. While we included videos displaying various shapes and densities of smoke in the generation of our dataset, it does not cover all appearances of surgical smoke specifically and is still limited by this factor. We also aim to increase the performance of our model and make it applicable in real-time.

Acknowledgments. This work was funded through the project TWIN-WIN (AI Funding of the State of Schleswig-Holstein, Germany) and conducted in cooperation with the Kurt Semm Center for laparoscopic and robotic assisted surgery at the University Hospital of Schleswig-Holstein (UKSH). The authors thank Dr. Thomas Becker, Almut Kalz and Felix Prell from the UKSH for their kind support through the TWIN-WIN project and for their assistance in the recording of the data.

Disclosure of Interests. The authors declare no conflicts of interests.

References

1. ASHI-VFX: Smoke effects stock video footage | royalty free videos | background video effects | - YouTube. Accessed 31 Mar 2025
2. Brunner, M., ElGendy, A., Denz, A., Weber, G., Grützmann, R., Krautz, C.: Robot-assisted visceral surgery in Germany: analysis of the current status and trends of the last 5 years using data from the StuDoQ|Robotics registry. Die Chirurgie **94**(11), 940–947 (2023). https://doi.org/10.1007/s00104-023-01940-8

3. Çiçek, Ö., Abdulkadir, A., Lienkamp, S.S., Brox, T., Ronneberger, O.: 3D U-net: learning dense volumetric segmentation from sparse annotation. In: Ourselin, S., Joskowicz, L., Sabuncu, M.R., Unal, G., Wells, W. (eds.) MICCAI 2016. LNCS, vol. 9901, pp. 424–432. Springer, Cham (2016). https://doi.org/10.1007/978-3-319-46723-8_49

4. Chen, L., Tang, W., John, N.W.: Unsupervised learning of surgical smoke removal from simulation. In: The Hamlyn Symposium on Medical Robotics. HSMR2018, The Hamlyn Centre, Faculty of Engineering, Imperial College London, pp. 75–76 (2018). https://doi.org/10.31256/hsmr2018.38

5. He, K., Sun, J., Tang, X.: Single image haze removal using dark channel prior. In: 2009 IEEE Conference on Computer Vision and Pattern Recognition, pp. 1956–1963. IEEE (2009). https://doi.org/10.1109/cvpr.2009.5206515

6. Hu, Z., Hu, X.: Cycle-consistent adversarial networks for smoke detection and removal in endoscopic images. In: 2021 43rd Annual International Conference of the IEEE Engineering in Medicine & Biology Society (EMBC), pp. 3070–3073. IEEE (2021). https://doi.org/10.1109/embc46164.2021.9629657

7. Lai, W.S., Huang, J.B., Wang, O., Shechtman, E., Yumer, E., Yang, M.H.: Learning blind video temporal consistency. In: European Conference on Computer Vision (ECCV) (2018)

8. Lin, J., et al.: A desmoking algorithm for endoscopic images based on improved u-net model. Concurr. Comput. Pract. Exp. **33**(22) (2021). https://doi.org/10.1002/cpe.6320

9. Ma, L., Song, H., Zhang, X., Liao, H.: A smoke removal method based on combined data and modified u-net for endoscopic images. In: 2021 43rd Annual International Conference of the IEEE Engineering in Medicine & Biology Society (EMBC), pp. 3783–3786. IEEE (2021). https://doi.org/10.1109/embc46164.2021.9630222

10. Ronneberger, O., Fischer, P., Brox, T.: U-net: convolutional networks for biomedical image segmentation. In: Navab, N., Hornegger, J., Wells, W.M., Frangi, A.F. (eds.) MICCAI 2015. LNCS, vol. 9351, pp. 234–241. Springer, Cham (2015). https://doi.org/10.1007/978-3-319-24574-4_28

11. Tchaka, K., Pawar, V.M., Stoyanov, D.: Chromaticity based smoke removal in endoscopic images. In: Styner, M.A., Angelini, E.D. (eds.) Medical Imaging 2017: Image Processing, vol. 10133, p. 101331M. SPIE (2017). https://doi.org/10.1117/12.2254622

12. Unterthiner, T., van Steenkiste, S., Kurach, K., Marinier, R., Michalski, M., Gelly, S.: Towards accurate generative models of video: a new metric & challenges ArXiv (2018)

13. Wu, R., et al.: Self-supervised video desmoking for laparoscopic surgery. In: European Conference on Computer Vision (ECCV) (2024)

14. Zhang, G., Gao, X., Meng, H., Pang, Y., Nie, X.: A self-supervised network-based smoke removal and depth estimation for monocular endoscopic videos. IEEE Trans. Visual Comput. Graph. **30**(9), 6547–6559 (2024). https://doi.org/10.1109/tvcg.2023.3347438

15. Zhou, Y., Hu, Z., Xuan, Z., Wang, Y., Hu, X.: Synchronizing detection and removal of smoke in endoscopic images with cyclic consistency adversarial nets. IEEE/ACM Trans. Comput. Biol. Bioinf. **21**(4), 670–680 (2024). https://doi.org/10.1109/tcbb.2022.3204673

16. Zhu, J.Y., Park, T., Isola, P., Efros, A.A.: Unpaired image-to-image translation using cycle-consistent adversarial networks. In: 2017 IEEE International Conference on Computer Vision (ICCV), pp. 2242–2251. IEEE (2017). https://doi.org/10.1109/iccv.2017.244

Toward Patient-Specific Partial Point Cloud to Surface Completion for Pre to Intra-operative Registration in Image-Guided Liver Interventions

Nakul Poudel[1(✉)], Zixin Yang[1], Kelly Merrell[1], Richard Simon[2], and Cristian A. Linte[1,2]

[1] Center for Imaging Science, Rochester Institute of Technology,
Rochester, NY 14623, USA
np1140@rit.edu
[2] Biomedical Engineering, Rochester Institute of Technology,
Rochester, NY 14623, USA

Abstract. Intra-operative data captured during image-guided surgery lacks sub-surface information, where key regions of interest, such as vessels and tumors, reside. Image-to-physical registration enables the fusion of pre-operative information and intra-operative data, typically represented as a point cloud. However, this registration process struggles due to partial visibility of the intra-operative point cloud. In this research, we propose a patient-specific point cloud completion approach to assist with the registration process. Specifically, we leverage VN-OccNet to generate a complete liver surface from a partial intra-operative point cloud. The network is trained in a patient-specific manner, where simulated deformations from the pre-operative model are used to train the model. First, we conduct an in-depth analysis of VN-OccNet's rotation-equivariant property and its effectiveness in recovering complete surfaces from partial intra-operative surfaces. Next, we integrate the completed intra-operative surface into the Go-ICP registration algorithm to demonstrate its utility in improving initial rigid registration outcomes. Our results highlight the promise of this patient-specific completion approach in mitigating the challenges posed by partial intra-operative visibility. The rotation equivariant and surface generation capabilities of VN-OccNet hold strong promise for developing robust registration frameworks for variations of the intra-operative point cloud.

Keywords: Image-guided liver surgery · point cloud completion · pre-to intra-operative registration

1 Introduction

Registration methods play a vital role during image-guided interventions in assisting surgeons to target the key regions of interest, such as tumors and ves-

S. Ali et al. (Eds.): MIUA 2025, LNCS 15917, pp. 302–316, 2026.
https://doi.org/10.1007/978-3-031-98691-8_22

sels, that lie beneath the organ surface. Image-to-physical registration aligns pre-operative Computed Tomography (CT) or Magnetic Resonance Imaging (MRI) data, represented as a point cloud or mesh, to intra-operative data acquired using surgical tracking devices or cameras, often represented as a point cloud [4,17]. However, the registration [3,17] faces challenges caused by the partial intra-operative visibility that arises due to constrained camera viewpoints and occlusions [3,5,7]. Therefore, it is necessary to address the issue of partial visibility, which prevents registration methods from performing with sufficient accuracy.

The reconstruction of an intra-operative 3D liver surface from a partially visible surface has the potential to mitigate the partial visibility issue faced by registration methods. Toward this effort, Jia *et al.* [5] proposed a non-rigid registration framework that integrates a learning-based point completion network to generate a complete surface from sparse intra-operative data to guide non-rigid registration. However, the proposed method still requires a rigid registration as the initialization. Foti *et al.* [2] adopted a Variational Autoencoder on pre-operative models to generate a full liver surface from a partial point cloud, which undergoes an iterative optimization procedure to generate an intra-operative surface. However, this approach also requires manually identified correspondences between the generated mesh and the intra-operative point cloud, which is non-trivial.

In this work, we propose a patient-specific pipeline to improve image-to-physical registration (and hence pre- to intra-operative registration) by completing partial intra-operative liver surfaces. The pipeline leverages a vector neuron-based occupancy network (VN-OccNet [1]) to recover a complete liver mesh from a partial intra-operative point cloud. VN-OccNet offers two key advantages for the registration: (1) rotation equivariance, which addresses the failure of conventional models under varying orientations of intra-operative data [12], and (2) the ability to generate watertight meshes rather than point clouds, enabling uniform surface sampling—a crucial feature for registration methods requiring consistent point density [15,17]. We adopt a patient-specific training strategy that synthesizes intra-operative liver surfaces by deforming a pre-operative patient-specific liver model, hence allowing the model to focus on patient-specific geometry and deformation patterns. We first evaluate VN-OccNet's ability to generate rotation-equivariant surfaces across diverse rotation settings. We then compare registration outcomes using completed surfaces against those using only partial point clouds. Results show that the reconstructed surfaces significantly reduce registration error, highlighting the benefit of surface completion towards enhancing registration accuracy.

2   Methodology

2.1   Problem Definition

We define the intra-operative partial liver point cloud as the target point cloud $\mathcal{T} = \{t_i\}_{i=1}^{N} \in \mathbb{R}^3$ and the pre-operative liver point cloud as the source point cloud $\mathcal{S} = \{s_i\}_{i=1}^{M} \in \mathbb{R}^3$. Let $f_\theta(x_i, z)$ denote the trained VN-OccNet, where θ

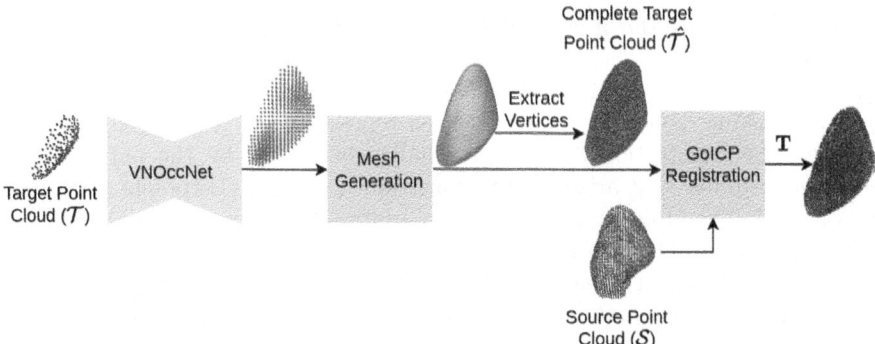

Fig. 1. Overview diagram of proposed pipeline: The target point cloud is input to the trained VN-OccNet to output occupancy points (magenta). An integrated mesh generation reconstructs a mesh from the predicted occupancy. The mesh vertices are extracted to represent the complete target point cloud and registered with a source point cloud. (Color figure online)

represents the learned parameters, x_i represents the ith query point, and z is the latent representation of $\mathcal{T}$. The solution is to utilize $f_\theta(x_i, z)$ to reconstruct a complete estimate of the target point cloud, denoted as $\widehat{\mathcal{T}}$, and subsequently perform registration with $\mathcal{S}$.

2.2   Proposed Pipeline

Our proposed pipeline illustrated in Fig. 1 consists of three key stages: (1) Generation of occupancy points from a target point cloud using VN-OccNet, (2) Mesh construction from the predicted occupancy points, and (3) Registration, where the complete target point cloud (obtained by extracting vertices from the generated mesh) is aligned with the source point cloud using the Go-ICP registration method.

Vector Neuron Occupancy Network (VN-OccNet): To accomplish the rotation-equivariant point cloud completion task, VN-OccNet [1] leverages the original OccNet architecture [10], with a vector-based equivariant encoder. The decoder is invariant, where all the operations are non-vector. The target point cloud $\mathcal{T} = \{t_i\}_{i=1}^{N} \in \mathbb{R}^3$ is input to the encoder network, and outputs equivariant latent vector-list features z. The query set $\mathcal{X} = \{x_i\}_{i=1}^{K} \in \mathbb{R}^3$, set of points that encloses the liver, and latent feature z are input to the decoder network to output the occupancy probabilities between 0 and 1. Points with probability greater than or equal to a threshold c correspond to occupancy points that implicitly represent the liver surface. Since VN-OccNet aims to predict whether or not each point in the query point set corresponds to a liver surface point, binary cross-entropy classification loss is utilized to learn the parameters θ.

Mesh Generation: Meshes are constructed by first identifying the voxels that intersect the liver surface using the Multiresolution Isosurface Extraction (MISE) algorithm [10]. The algorithm starts with a fixed query set with an initial resolution of 32^3, consisting of 31^3 voxels, each containing 8 points. For all 32^3 points in the query set, the occupancy probability is determined using the trained VN-OccNet. The points inside the surface are identified by applying a threshold value of $c = 0.4$. Voxels that are entirely inside or outside the surface are separated from the surface-intersecting voxels by checking if at least two adjacent points of a voxel differ in occupancy (i.e., one point is inside and the other is outside). Each such ambiguous voxel that intersects the surface is further subdivided into 8 subvoxels, generating 19 additional points. The VN-OccNet is queried again to find the occupancy probability for the newly generated query points. This process is repeated until all ambiguous regions have been subdivided down to the finest voxel grid resolution of 128^3. Finally, the surface-intersecting voxels obtained are passed to the Marching Cubes algorithm [8] to generate the surface mesh.

Rigid Registration Using Go-ICP: To evaluate the effectiveness of incorporating the complete intra-operative target surface generated from using the proposed protocol into the registration, we utilize the Go-ICP registration algorithm [15] to compare the registration outcomes between using the initial, incomplete target point clouds and the complete intra-operative surface meshes generated using the proposed method.

For the remainder of the manuscript, we refer to these registrations as registration w/ surface completion (when the complete surface mesh is utilized) and registration w/o surface completion (when only the original partial point cloud is utilized). The registration algorithm yields the transformation ($\mathbf{T}$), which aligns the source point cloud to the target point cloud.

3 Experiments

3.1 Datasets

The experiments utilize the following datasets: an *in silico* phantom dataset is used to train and test VN-OccNet, and an *in vitro* phantom dataset is used to assess the registration performance.

***In Silico* Phantoms:** We used the undeformed No. 1 synthetic phantom constructed based on a patient-specific CT image according to the methods proposed by Yang *et al.* [18] briefly described in further detail in the next sub-section. To simulate deformed models, the deformation simulation pipeline described in [11] is followed, which models the liver as a neo-Hookean hyperelastic material with a Young's modulus of 2–5 kPa and a Poisson's ratio of 0.35. Three forces of magnitude up to 3N and zero boundary conditions, along with the material properties, were input to the finite element solver to output deformed liver models. The complete target point clouds are obtained by extracting the mesh vertices. In total, 4,969 deformed models were generated.

Training an occupancy network requires transforming liver models into a representation comprising a liver point cloud, a set of query points enclosing the liver, and corresponding occupancy values that indicate whether each query point lies inside or outside the liver surface. We followed the pipeline of Stutz *et al.* [12] to generate this data format. The generated data was divided into training, validation, and testing sets with a ratio of 8:1:1.

***In Vitro* Phantoms:** We used the *in vitro* phantom dataset described and released in [18], which includes four pairs of underformed and deformed models. Phantoms were manufactured using synthetic gelatin (Humimic Gelatin # 0, Humimic Medical, Fort Smith, AK, USA) poured into a 3D-printed mold generated [9] from a patient-specific liver model obtained from OpenHELP [6]. They were deformed by placing wedges of different gradients underneath part of the liver phantom. The surfaces and fiducial marker locations are segmented from CT scans. As Go-ICP requires a long time to estimate rigid registration, we utilized No. 1 and No. 3 phantoms within the dataset in this work, as shown in Fig. 2. No. 1 and No. 3 phantoms feature 53 and 176 fiducials, respectively.

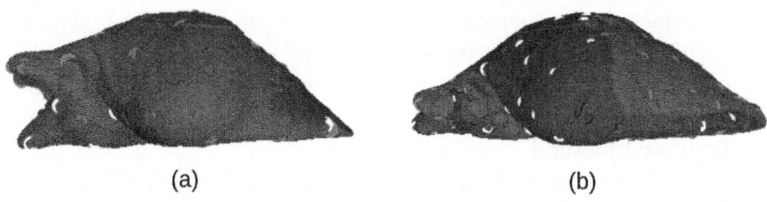

(a)   (b)

Fig. 2. The purple phantoms in (a) and (b) represent the undeformed No. 1 and phantom No. 3, respectively, while the blue phantoms represent their deformed counterparts. (Color figure online)

3.2   VN-OccNet Training and Testing Setup

Target Point Cloud Generation: In training, target point clouds are dynamically generated from the complete point clouds. First, we crop the posterior surfaces of the deformed liver models. The anterior surface points are then downsampled to D points. A viewpoint is randomly selected, and the N nearest surface points relative to this viewpoint are extracted to create the target point cloud. For testing, we follow the approach proposed in [19] to simplify the qualitative analysis, where five distinct viewpoints are selected for each liver model, as illustrated in Fig. 3.

Rotation Setup: VN-OccNet is trained in three different modes based on the rotation imposed on the target point clouds: without any imposed rotations, with rotations restricted to the Z-axis, and with SO(3) rotations. We imposed random rotations within the range $[-\frac{\pi}{2}, \frac{\pi}{2}]$ for Z-axis and SO(3) rotation modes.

In the non-rotation mode, all target point clouds are aligned and share the same pose. The evaluation involves four train/test rotation settings: I/I, where both training and testing are conducted on non-rotated target point clouds; Z/Z, where both training and testing involve rotations of target point clouds along the Z-axis; Z/SO(3), where training is performed with Z-axis rotations, while testing involves SO(3) rotations; and SO(3)/SO(3), where both training and testing involve SO(3) rotations.

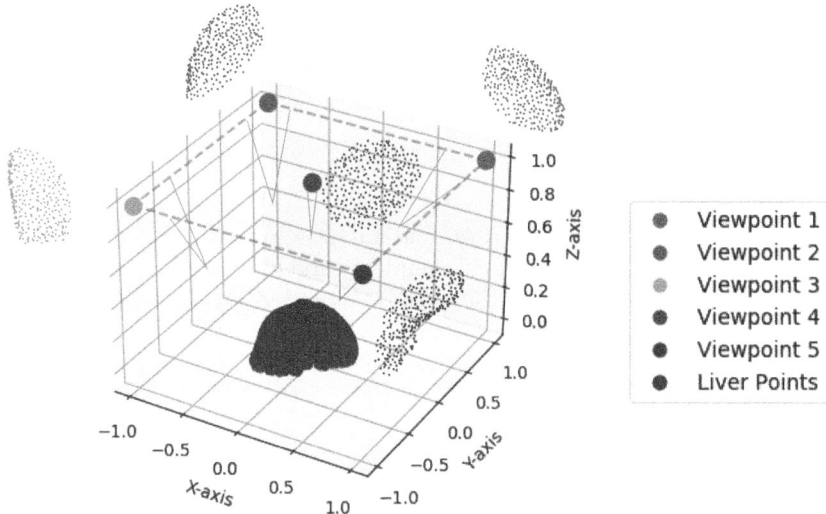

Fig. 3. Visualization of five target point clouds generated for each intra-operative liver model during testing. Each target is captured from a unique viewpoint, with different regions of the liver obscured to mimic varying intra-operative visibility.

3.3 VN-OccNet Implementation

We employed the PyTorch implementation of the VN-OccNet by Deng *et al.* [1]. The anterior liver points were downsampled to $D = 1000$, and $N = 300$ nearest points from the viewpoint were chosen to create the target liver point cloud, yielding a surface visibility of approximately 30%. The network was trained with a batch size of $B = 8$ and a learning rate of 0.0001, using the Adam optimizer. The optimal threshold value c was determined to be 0.4 based on the validation dataset. Training was performed for 604 epochs on a NVIDIA A100 GPU, with all other hyperparameters kept unchanged from the original implementation. To verify the rotation equivariance property, we further compared VN-OccNet with OccNet [10], which does not include rotation equivariance design.

3.4   Registration Evaluation Setup

In a manner similar to the five target point clouds generated for each liver model during testing in the previous Subsect. 3.2, five target point clouds are generated for each *in vitro* phantom (No. 1 and No. 3) to perform registration. A set of 100 random SO(3) rotations within the range $[-\frac{\pi}{2}, \frac{\pi}{2}]$ are applied to the target point clouds, resulting in 500 target point clouds at different orientations for each phantom. Registration w/ surface completion is performed by utilizing the complete target point clouds reconstructed from target point clouds featuring a minimum of 30% visibility. To test the influence of the increment of surface coverage, registration w/o surface completion was performed at three different visibilities of the target point cloud at around 30%, 40%, and 50% by varying the value of D, where $D = 1000, 750$, and 600, respectively.

3.5   Evaluation Metrics

Chamfer Distance (CD-L2), F-Score, and Intersection over Union (IoU) were used to evaluate the performance of complete target surface generation. Moreover, the Target Registration Error (TRE) computed across a set of fiducials was used to assess registration performance.

CD-L2 measures the bidirectional similarity between the complete generated target and ground truth target points:

$$d_{CD}(\hat{\mathcal{T}}, \mathcal{G}) = \frac{1}{|\hat{\mathcal{T}}|} \sum_{\hat{t} \in \hat{\mathcal{T}}} \min_{g \in \mathcal{G}} \|\hat{t} - g\|_2 + \frac{1}{|\mathcal{G}|} \sum_{g \in \mathcal{G}} \min_{\hat{t} \in \mathcal{P}} \|g - \hat{t}\|_2, \tag{1}$$

where $|\hat{\mathcal{T}}|$ and $|\mathcal{G}|$ represent the total number of points in the complete generated target and ground truth target point cloud, respectively, and $d_{CD}(\hat{\mathcal{T}}, \mathcal{G})$ denotes the Chamfer Distance between the point sets $\hat{\mathcal{T}}$ and $\mathcal{G}$.

The F-Score measures the quality of the reconstructed surface by balancing precision $P(d)$ and recall $R(d)$. Precision measures the fraction of complete target points that lie within a threshold $d = 1\,\mathrm{mm}$ of the nearest ground truth target points, and recall measures the fraction of ground truth target points that lie within d of the nearest complete target points:

$$\text{F-Score}(d) = \frac{2P(d)R(d)}{P(d) + R(d)}. \tag{2}$$

IoU measures the ratio of the intersection to the union of the occupancy values of the generated and ground truth targets, as defined in Eq. (3):

$$\text{IoU} = \frac{|\text{occ}_{gt} \cap \text{occ}_{pred}|}{|\text{occ}_{gt} \cup \text{occ}_{pred}|}, \tag{3}$$

where occ_{gt} and occ_{pred} represent the ground truth and predicted occupancy values, respectively, and $|\cdot|$ denotes the number of true occupancy labels.

TRE measures the Euclidean distance between the estimated target fiducial markers $\mathbf{F}_{\mathrm{tgt},i}$ and the transformed source fiducial markers $\mathbf{T}(\mathbf{F}_{\mathrm{src},i})$:

$$\mathrm{TRE} = \frac{1}{F} \sum_{i=1}^{F} \|\mathbf{F}_{\mathrm{tgt},i} - \mathbf{T}(\mathbf{F}_{\mathrm{src},i})\|_2, \tag{4}$$

where F is the total number of fiducial markers.

4 Results

4.1 Mesh Construction Results

Table 1 presents the performance of the intra-operative surface completion for OccNet and VN-OccNet across four different train/test configurations: I/I, Z/Z, Z/SO(3), and SO(3)/SO(3). OccNet achieves the best performance across all metrics in the I/I setting. However, its performance significantly deteriorates when tested with target liver point clouds with rotations along the Z-axis and SO(3).

Table 1. Performance of OccNet and VN-OccNet: I/I represents training and testing without any rotations of target point cloud, Z/Z denotes training and testing with rotations along the Z-axis, Z/SO(3) involves training with Z-axis rotations and testing with SO(3) rotations, and SO(3)/SO(3) refers to both training and testing with SO(3) rotations. CD-L2 and IoU represent the Chamfer Distance (in mm) and Intersection over Union.

	I/I	Z/Z	Z/SO(3)	SO(3)/SO(3)
OccNet				
F-Score	0.57 ± 0.20	0.47 ± 0.17	$\mathbf{0.07 \pm 0.07}$	0.33 ± 0.12
CD-L2	2.75 ± 1.52	3.51 ± 1.88	$\mathbf{29.43 \pm 13.41}$	4.87 ± 2.27
IoU	0.89 ± 0.06	0.86 ± 0.07	$\mathbf{0.35 \pm 0.18}$	0.18 ± 0.07
VN-OccNet				
F-Score	0.52 ± 0.17	0.51 ± 0.18	$\mathbf{0.51 \pm 0.18}$	0.50 ± 0.18
CD-L2	3.30 ± 1.91	3.29 ± 1.89	$\mathbf{3.25 \pm 1.83}$	3.41 ± 2.02
IoU	0.87 ± 0.07	0.87 ± 0.07	$\mathbf{0.87 \pm 0.06}$	0.86 ± 0.07

While data augmentation along SO(3) improves performance to some extent, it remains impractical to encode all possible SO(3) rotations during training, making the model susceptible to failure when encountering unseen liver poses during testing. Although VN-OccNet does not outperform OccNet in the I/I setting, it maintains consistent performance across Z/Z, Z/SO(3), and SO(3)/SO(3), demonstrating robustness to rotations.

Unlike OccNet, VN-OccNet does not show performance improvement due to data augmentation, indicating that its inherent rotation-equivariant properties reduce reliance on augmented training data. The statistical significance

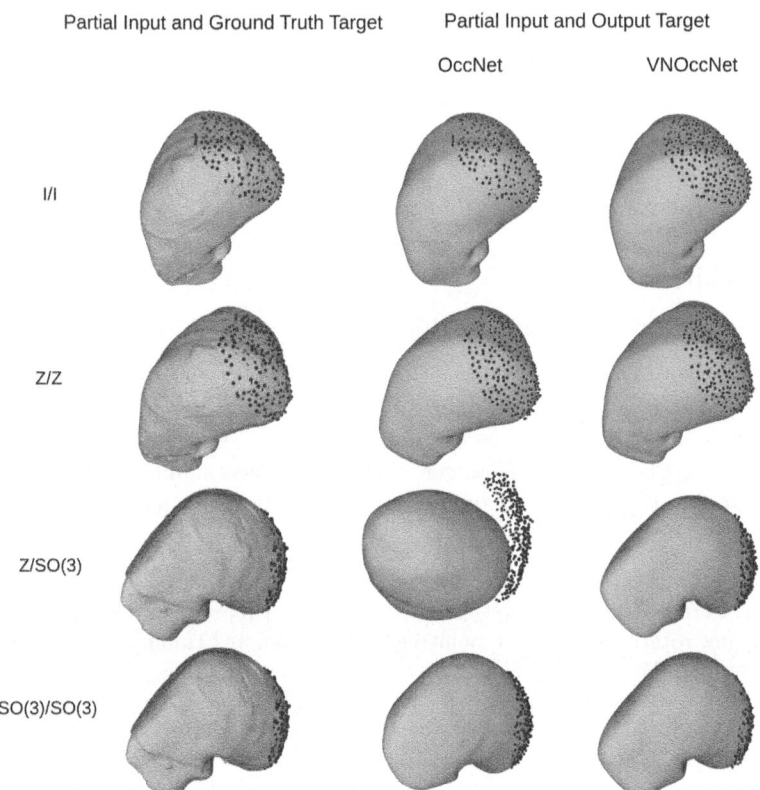

Fig. 4. Visualization of mesh reconstruction results: The first column displays the target input point clouds alongside the ground truth target mesh. The second column presents the complete target liver surfaces generated by OccNet and VN-OccNet. Qualitative results are shown for four train/test configurations: I/I (first row), where both training and testing involve non-rotated target point clouds; Z/Z (second row), where training and testing are restricted to Z-axis rotations; Z/SO(3) (third row), where training uses Z-axis rotations and testing employs SO(3) rotations; and SO(3)/SO(3) (fourth row), where both training and testing involve SO(3) rotations.

of OccNet and VN-OccNet performance was evaluated by comparing all three evaluation metrics using a Wilcoxon Rank Sum test at a significance level of $\alpha = 0.05$. The test yielded p-values less than α ($p < \alpha$), confirming that the performance differences between VN-OccNet and OccNet across various train/test setups are statistically significant.

Figure 4 presents the target point clouds, ground truth target mesh surfaces, and complete target mesh surfaces generated by OccNet and VN-OccNet across four different train/test configurations: I/I, Z/Z, Z/SO(3), and SO(3)/SO(3). The performance gap in surface generation is evident in the Z/SO(3) case, where OccNet struggles to generate a target mesh surface that accurately resembles the ground truth target mesh. In the SO(3)/SO(3) setting, the mesh generated by OccNet lacks the correct geometry, indicating an incorrect reconstruction. In contrast, the mesh generated by VN-OccNet is able to capture correct geometry and better alignment of the target point cloud with the reconstructed mesh.

4.2 Go-ICP Registration Results

Table 2 summarizes the Target Registration Error (in mm) measured between target fiducial markers and source fiducial markers. The measurements are reported for registration w/ and w/o surface completion. The registration w/o surface completion is performed using the target point clouds at three visibility levels (30%, 40%, and 50%), and registration w/ surface is performed using the completed surface meshes generated from the 30% visible target point clouds.

Table 2. Target Registration Error (TRE) (in mm) measured between target fiducial markers and transformed source fiducial markers for phantoms No. 1 and No. 3. For registration w/o surface completion, TRE is evaluated at intra-operative visibility levels of 30%, 40%, and 50%. For registration w/ surface completion, the full surfaces are reconstructed from the target point clouds with 30% visibility.

Phantom	W/O surface completion			W/ surface completion
	30% Visibility	40% Visibility	50% Visibility	
No. 1	33.13 ± 13.89	30.39 ± 12.60	26.04 ± 7.81	**5.19 ± 1.34**
No. 3	39.87 ± 15.07	32.79 ± 14.97	25.87 ± 10.36	**3.35 ± 0.61**

The registration for phantom No. 1 yields the TRE of 33.13 ± 13.89 mm for the 30% visibility of target point clouds. However, when using the complete target point clouds generated from the same 30% visible target, the TRE significantly decreased to 5.19 ± 1.34 mm. This notable improvement demonstrates the effectiveness of VN-OccNet's surface completion in enhancing registration performance. Furthermore, as the visibility of the target point clouds increased, TRE progressively decreased, confirming that a lower visibility ratio leads to higher registration errors.

A Wilcoxon Rank Sum test, conducted at a significance level of $\alpha = 0.05$, showed statistically significant differences ($p < \alpha$) between the three cases of registration w/o surface completion and registration w/ surface completion.

Figure 5 displays the results for registration w/ surface completion and w/o surface completion for *in vitro* phantom No. 1 and No. 3. The registration w/o surface completion struggles to find the correct alignment between the source and target point clouds. The incorrect registration is evident when the complete ground truth target is overlaid onto the registered results. However, registration w/ surface completion is able to correctly align the source and target point clouds.

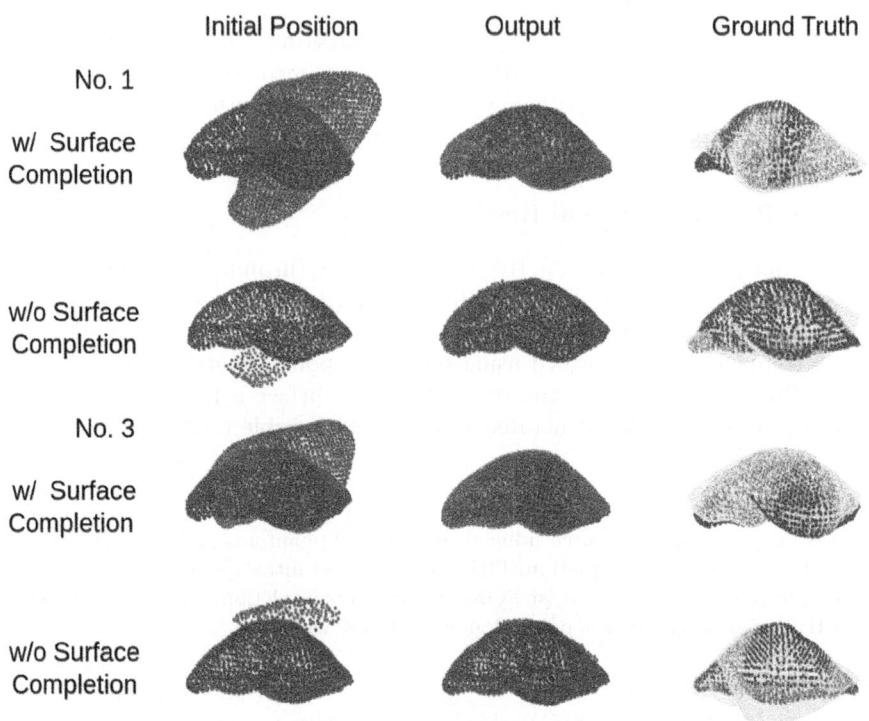

Fig. 5. The registration results are displayed for the source point cloud (purple) and the target point cloud (blue) for phantoms No. 1 and No. 3. For easy visualization, the source point cloud is fixed and the target point clouds are moving. The first column represents the initial position of the source and target point clouds. The second column displays the registered results. To see the correctness of the registration, the third column overlays the ground truth target point cloud (yellow). The registrations are performed using partial surface (30% visibility) and full surface generated from the same partial surface. (Color figure online)

Similarly, Fig. 6 shows the registration between source and target fiducial markers for phantom No. 1 and phantom No. 3. The transformations were determined using a target point cloud with 30% visibility for registration w/o surface completion and a reconstructed completed surface mesh from the same target point cloud for registration w/ surface completion. For the registration w/o surface completion, the registered source fiducial markers are misaligned with respect to the target fiducial markers. In contrast, in registration w/ complete surface, the source and target fiducial markers are closely aligned, demonstrating improved registration.

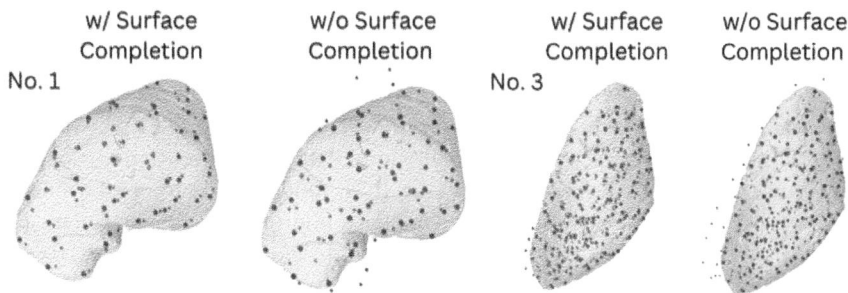

Fig. 6. Visualization of target fiducial markers (purple) and registered source fiducial markers (blue) for *in vitro* phantom No. 1 and No. 3. The target point clouds utilized for registration w/o surface completion have 30% visibility, and the full point clouds are reconstructed from the same targets for registration w/ surface completion. The ground truth target liver surface is overlaid for improved visualization. (Color figure online)

5   Discussion

The partial visibility of intra-operative point clouds poses challenges for both initial rigid and non-rigid registration methods in image-guided liver surgery. To address this issue, we propose a patient-specific, learning-based surface completion approach. In this work, we initially validate the effectiveness of this approach in facilitating the initial rigid registration.

Initial rigid registration has relied on global optimization techniques [15] and the establishment of reliable correspondences using handcrafted [13] or learning-based methods [17]. However, these approaches are often sensitive to partial liver surfaces and inconsistent point cloud densities. In contrast, our method tackles the problem at its root by employing surface completion through learning-based techniques. Unlike previous completion approaches that require rigid initialization [5] or manual interaction [2], our method operates without such dependencies. We utilize a vector-based occupancy network—VN-OccNet—due to its robustness to rotation and its ability to generate watertight meshes in just 0.25 seconds per mesh, making it a strong candidate for this task.

We first verify the rotation-equivariance property of VN-OccNet, which is essential for our application. Recent work [12] evaluated several widely used point completion methods and found them unsuitable for this task. We compared VN-OccNet with the original OccNet, which lacks a rotation-invariant design, under various training and testing conditions, using extensive quantitative and qualitative evaluations. Furthermore, we assessed registration performance by integrating completed surfaces with Go-ICP, a method known for its robustness to partial visibility [16]. Results show that our reconstructed surfaces significantly reduce registration errors, demonstrating the value of surface completion in improving registration accuracy. However, Go-ICP, which takes approximately 16 s per registration, is computationally intensive, suggesting that integrating surface completion directly into learning-based registration methods may offer a more efficient solution.

An additional challenge lies in the variation of liver geometries across different patients, which can hinder surface completion. To overcome this, we adopt a patient-specific training strategy that simulates intra-operative surfaces by deforming a pre-operative patient-specific liver model. This approach enables the network to learn patient-specific geometries and deformation patterns. Our results show that this strategy allows the model to generalize effectively to realistic deformations observed in *in vitro* phantoms. Nonetheless, the requirement to train a new model for each patient may limit its practicality in resource-constrained environments.

It is also important to note that real intra-operative data may exhibit more complex patterns, such as noise, holes, and occlusions, than those seen in our simulations. This discrepancy poses a challenge for learning-based methods, which generally assume the test data distribution is similar to that of the training data. As such, improving generalization to diverse, realistic intra-operative point clouds remains an open challenge.

6   Conclusion and Future Work

This paper presents a pipeline that incorporates VN-OccNet to generate a complete liver surface from partial intra-operative point cloud data, using the reconstructed surface for subsequent registration. We demonstrate the effectiveness of VN-OccNet in producing accurate and complete surface reconstructions, which significantly enhance registration performance. While partial intra-operative data typically hampers the accuracy of most registration methods, our results indicate that the proposed pipeline provides a promising solution to this challenge.

In future work, we plan to investigate the integration of surface completion with non-rigid registration, explore patient-generic surface completion strategies, incorporate completion into end-to-end learning-based registration pipelines, and develop a more robust simulation pipeline capable of generating realistic intra-operative point clouds with noise, holes, and occlusions.

Acknowledgments. We would like to acknowledge the generous support for this work by the National Institutes of Health – National Institute of General Medical Sciences under Award No. R35GM128877 and the National Science Foundation - Division of Chemical, Bioengineering and Transport Systems under Award No. 2245152. We would like to thank the Research Computing team at Rochester Institute of Technology [14] for providing computing resources for this research. We gratefully acknowledge Bidur Khanal for his insightful feedback and encouragement throughout this work.

References

1. Deng, C., Litany, O., Duan, Y., Poulenard, A., Tagliasacchi, A., Guibas, L.J.: Vector neurons: a general framework for so (3)-equivariant networks. In: Proceedings of the IEEE/CVF International Conference on Computer Vision, pp. 12200–12209 (2021)
2. Foti, S., et al.: Intraoperative liver surface completion with graph convolutional VAE. In: Uncertainty for Safe Utilization of Machine Learning in Medical Imaging, and Graphs in Biomedical Image Analysis: Second International Workshop, UNSURE 2020, and Third International Workshop, GRAIL 2020, Held in Conjunction with MICCAI 2020, Lima, Peru, 8 October 2020, Proceedings 2, pp. 198–207. Springer (2020)
3. Heiselman, J.S., et al.: Characterization and correction of intraoperative soft tissue deformation in image-guided laparoscopic liver surgery. J. Med. Imaging **5**(2), 021203 (2018)
4. Heiselman, J.S., Collins, J.A., Ringel, M.J., Peter Kingham, T., Jarnagin, W.R., Miga, M.I.: The image-to-physical liver registration sparse data challenge: comparison of state-of-the-art using a common dataset. J. Med. Imaging **11**(1), 015001 (2024)
5. Jia, M., Kyan, M.: Improving intraoperative liver registration in image-guided surgery with learning-based reconstruction. In: ICASSP 2021-2021 IEEE International Conference on Acoustics, Speech and Signal Processing (ICASSP), pp. 1230–1234. IEEE (2021)
6. Kenngott, H.G., et al.: OpenHELP (Heidelberg laparoscopy phantom): development of an open-source surgical evaluation and training tool. Surg. Endosc. **29**, 3338–3347 (2015)
7. Lin, B., Sun, Y., Qian, X., Goldgof, D., Gitlin, R., You, Y.: Video-based 3D reconstruction, laparoscope localization and deformation recovery for abdominal minimally invasive surgery: a survey. Int. J. Med. Robot. Comput. Assist. Surg. **12**(2), 158–178 (2016)
8. Lorensen, W.E., Cline, H.E.: Marching cubes: a high resolution 3D surface construction algorithm. In: Proceedings of the 14th Annual Conference on Computer Graphics and Interactive Techniques, SIGGRAPH 1987, pp. 163–169. Association for Computing Machinery, New York (1987). https://doi.org/10.1145/37401.37422
9. Merrell, K., Jackson, P., Simon, R., Linte, C.: Developing and evaluating the fidelity of patient specific kidney emulating phantoms for image-guided intervention applications. In: Medical Imaging 2023: Image-Guided Procedures, Robotic Interventions, and Modeling, vol. 12466, pp. 318–323. SPIE (2023)
10. Mescheder, L., Oechsle, M., Niemeyer, M., Nowozin, S., Geiger, A.: Occupancy networks: learning 3D reconstruction in function space. In: Proceedings of the IEEE/CVF Conference on Computer Vision and Pattern Recognition, pp. 4460–4470 (2019)
11. Pfeiffer, M., et al.: Non-rigid volume to surface registration using a data-driven biomechanical model. In: Martel, A.L., et al. (eds.) MICCAI 2020. LNCS, vol. 12264, pp. 724–734. Springer, Cham (2020). https://doi.org/10.1007/978-3-030-59719-1_70
12. Poudel, N., Yang, Z., Merrell, K., Simon, R., Linte, C.A.: Evaluation of intraoperative patient-specific methods for point cloud completion for minimally invasive liver interventions. In: Medical Imaging 2025: Image-Guided Procedures, Robotic Interventions, and Modeling, vol. 13408, pp. 376–384. SPIE (2025)

13. Robu, M.R., et al.: Global rigid registration of CT to video in laparoscopic liver surgery. Int. J. Comput. Assist. Radiol. Surg. **13**, 947–956 (2018)
14. Rochester Institute of Technology: Research computing services (2025). https://doi.org/10.34788/0S3G-QD15, https://www.rit.edu/researchcomputing/
15. Yang, J., Li, H., Campbell, D., Jia, Y.: Go-ICP: a globally optimal solution to 3D ICP point-set registration. IEEE Trans. Pattern Anal. Mach. Intell. **38**(11), 2241–2254 (2015)
16. Yang, Z., et al.: Resolving the ambiguity of complete-to-partial point cloud registration for image-guided liver surgery with patches-to-partial matching. arXiv preprint arXiv:2412.19328 (2024)
17. Yang, Z., Simon, R., Linte, C.A.: Learning feature descriptors for pre-and intra-operative point cloud matching for laparoscopic liver registration. Int. J. Comput. Assist. Radiol. Surg. **18**(6), 1025–1032 (2023)
18. Yang, Z., Simon, R., Merrell, K., Linte, C.A.: Boundary constraint-free biomechanical model-based surface matching for intraoperative liver deformation correction. IEEE Trans. Med. Imaging 1 (2024). https://doi.org/10.1109/TMI.2024.3515632
19. Yu, X., Rao, Y., Wang, Z., Liu, Z., Lu, J., Zhou, J.: PoinTr: diverse point cloud completion with geometry-aware transformers. In: Proceedings of the IEEE/CVF International Conference on Computer Vision, pp. 12498–12507 (2021)

EfficientDet with Knowledge Distillation and Instance Whitening for Real-Time and Generalisable Polyp Detection

Raneem Toman[1]($\boxtimes$) (iD), Venkataraman Subramanian[2,3] (iD), and Sharib Ali[1] (iD)

[1] School of Computer Science, Faculty of Engineering and Physical Sciences,
University of Leeds, LS2 9JT Leeds, UK
`{scrmat,s.s.ali}@leeds.ac.uk`
[2] Leeds Institute of Medical Research at St James's, University of Leeds, Leeds, UK
`v.subramanian@leeds.ac.uk`
[3] Leeds Teaching Hospitals NHS Trust, Leeds, UK

Abstract. Despite numerous techniques developed for polyp detection, the issue of generalisability to new centres and populations while maintaining fast inference persists. To address this, we compile a multicentre train set consisting of 1941 images, and use it to push the generalisability of the real-time EfficientDet for polyp detection by employing a knowledge distillation teacher-student architecture and instance whitening. We train a large EfficientDet teacher on the combined Kvasir-Seg and Polyp-Gen datasets and subsequently use its softened output probabilities to guide a smaller EfficientDet student, aiming to improve generalisability and speed while preserving performance. To further enhance generalisability across different clinical settings and patient populations, we integrate instance whitening into the backbones of both teacher and student networks to mitigate domain-specific variations, especially in patient populations like IBD. We compare our model with the state-of-the-art (SOTA) models DETR, RetinaNet, and Faster R-CNN under detection and inference metrics on the following benchmark datasets: Kvasir-SEG (seen centre and population), PolypGen-C6 (unseen centre), and our in-house IBD dataset (unseen centre and population). Our approach improves AP50:95 over the best performing benchmark -RetinaNet- by 3.97%, 10.67%, and 11.07% on the Kvasir-SEG, PolypGen-C6, and IBD datasets respectively, highlighting the significant role of instance whitening and distillation in boosting the model's ability to generalise to new, unseen data distributions, particularly in the in-house IBD dataset, making our model clinically applicable.

Keywords: Polyp detection · Knowledge distillation · EfficientDet · Instance whitening

1 Introduction

Colorectal cancer (CRC) is the third most common cancer and the second leading cause of cancer-related deaths worldwide. The burden of CRC is projected

© The Author(s), under exclusive license to Springer Nature Switzerland AG 2026
S. Ali et al. (Eds.): MIUA 2025, LNCS 15917, pp. 317–328, 2026.
https://doi.org/10.1007/978-3-031-98691-8_23

to increase from around 1.9 million new CRC cases and 930 thousand deaths in 2020 to nearly 3.2 million new cases and 1.6 million deaths by 2040 [18]. However, the incidence and impact of CRC can be significantly reduced by early detection through screening; colorectal polyps, which are swellings in the mucosal epithelium of the intestine, are a recognized risk factor for CRC, so their early diagnosis and removal are very important for improved patient outcomes. Colonoscopy is a crucial screening technique used for polyp detection and treatment planning; however, there are still variations between clinicians in their ability to accurately detect and diagnose polyps due to their different levels of expertise, specialties, and the high variability in the morphologies of polyps [23, 27]. For example, inflammatory bowel disease (IBD) patients present with polyps that are flatter and blend in with the inflamed tissue, making them more challenging to detect endoscopically [20]. The need to alleviate this operator dependency has made automated polyp detection using deep learning methods an active area of research.

Despite the numerous techniques developed in the field of polyp detection, the issue of generalisability to new acquisition systems, centres, and populations persists. This is because such supervised models are trained on publicly available datasets, which represent either a single centre or a single cohort/population, and since the test set used for evaluation is similar to the data used for training, these models tend to struggle when assessed on new data distributions [3]. Differences in data distribution could arise from the use of different endoscopes, different modalities, or inherent variability between different patients [1]. Thus, it is crucial to overcome the lack of generalisability studies in polyp detection by exploring different algorithms' adaptivity to new data collected in varying settings.

The field of automated polyp detection has been an active area of research for over two decades; earlier handcrafted techniques made use of polyp textures and colours to locate them, but more recently deep learning convolutional neural network (CNN) based methods have been the go-to approach due to their elevated performance and speed [22]. These methods can be grouped into two main categories: single-stage and multi-stage detectors. Multi-stage, also known as region-based detectors, comprise an object region proposal stage before final localisation and classification, these include the different Region Based CNN (RCNN) detectors, Feature Pyramid Networks (FPN), and DetectoRS [26]. On the other hand, single-stage detectors perform object classification and localisation directly from input images without the need for region proposal; these include the you only look once (YOLO) detectors, single-shot multibox detectors (SSD), RetinaNet, and Efficientdet [26]. RCNNs have been known to achieve accurate object detection, but with a cost of inference time. At the same time, models like early YOLO and SSD detectors have shown real-time performance but compromised accuracy [12]. EfficientDet, on the other hand, leverages compound scaling and weighted feature fusion to balance this trade-off between accuracy and computational speed [25]. In addition to CNN-based detectors, there has been increasing interest in using transformers, which use patch-based attention modelling and can be implemented either as a standalone model or integrated with the aforementioned methods, such as detection transformers (DETR) [5]. Still, they have limitations to overcome when it comes to computational complexity and detecting small objects [21]. Most recent work has demonstrated the outstanding advancements in polyp detection: YONA (You Only Need one Adjacent Reference-frame) method achieved accurate and efficient polyp detection on video frames through relying on only the previous frame to detect polyps in the current one instead of multi-frame collaborations [15]. Moreover, a recently developed two-stage transformer outperformed existing state of the art methods (SOTAs) in terms of accuracy [16], but its efficiency was not evaluated. A Yolov4 model also achieved accurate and real-time performance through optimising training parameters, strong augmentation, and customising anchor boxes [6]. While these SOTAs showcase promising performance, they still suffer the speed-accuracy trade-off, and some of them do not report both accuracy and speed metrics.

Knowledge distillation is a well-known technique for model compression and faster polyp detection [9], but recent work has shown it can improve generalisability in object detection and polyp segmentation [7,19]. The primary goal of knowledge distillation is to train a small student to approximate the performance of a larger, more accurate teacher by using its softened output probabilities as they provide more information about the relationships between classes, capture the knowledge of the teacher model, and introduce a regularization effect, thus tackling data limitation and computational expense issues [10]. Additionally, instance whitening has been shown to be successful in separating the domain-invariant content information from the domain-variant style information through applying a linear whitening transformation (WT) that decorrelates the feature maps of individual instances (images), making it more likely to generalise across domains, such as different centres and patient populations.

Motivated by these works, this paper will explore the generalisability of the EfficientDet object detection model with the EfficientNet backbones through leveraging a knowledge distillation teacher-student architecture to achieve real-time inference [24,25]. The proposed approach makes use of the Kvasir-Seg and PolypGen public datasets [13] to train a large EfficientDet teacher model, which is then frozen and used to guide the training of a small EfficientDet student model [2]. Our contributions can be summarized as follows: 1) We propose knowledge distillation between two EfficientDet models to increase detection speed while maintaining performance and improving generalisability 2) We apply instance whitening (IW) to further improve EfficientDet's generalisability and robustness 3) Finally, we assess the generalisability of methods in two contexts: i) on an unseen centre ii) on a different patient population dataset (IBD) compared to the trained model (non-IBD).

2   Method

2.1   Overview

Figure 1 summarizes the student-teacher framework applied in this paper; the teacher is an EfficientDet with EfficientNetb5 backbone (27.7 million parameters), and the student is an EfficientDet with EfficientNetb2 backbone (7.7 million parameters). The teacher is pretrained in a supervised manner on a multicentre dataset, frozen, then used to train the student to approximate its performance by using its softened output probabilities, in addition to the ground truth. In the backbones of both the teacher and student, batch normalization is replaced with instance whitening to remove style information and improve generalisability to new distributions.

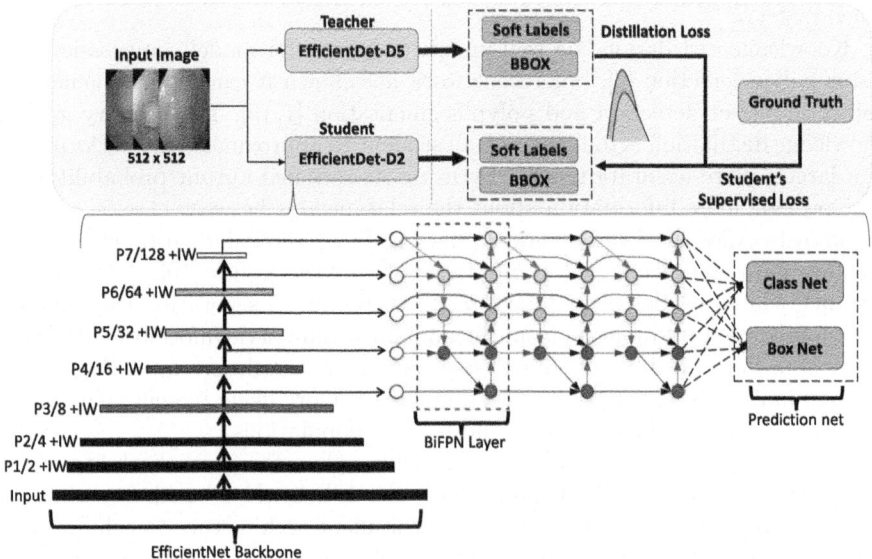

Fig. 1. Architecture of the implemented student-teacher distillation framework with instance whitening applied to the EfficientNet backbones.

2.2   Feature Extraction and Detection Network

EfficientDet was introduced as a solution for balancing accuracy with fast performance compared to conventional detection models [25]. Its architecture can be summarised in three key components: a highly efficient backbone network called EfficientNet, a novel feature pyramid network named BiFPN (Bidirectional Feature Pyramid Network) designed for effective multiscale feature aggregation, and a streamlined detection head. Furthermore, EfficientDet employs compound scaling, which systematically optimizes the depth, width, and resolution of the backbone, BiFPN, and detection head networks simultaneously. By scaling these dimensions in a balanced manner, EfficientDet can achieve improved accuracy without a significant increase in computational cost, making it a highly practical choice for polyp detection [24].

For an input image, the EfficientNet backbone produces feature maps at various output strides. EfficientDet typically takes feature maps from the backbone corresponding to output strides of 8 (P3), 16 (P4), and 32 (P5) as the initial input to the BiFPN, as shown in Fig. 1. The BiFPN then efficiently fuses these multiscale features and can also create additional higher-level features (like P6 and P7 with output strides of 64 and 128) through further downsampling. The detection head then takes these multiscale features and makes the final predictions for object bounding boxes and their corresponding class labels. EfficientDet employs a shared prediction head across all feature levels of the BiFPN.

2.3 Instance Whitening

For polyp detection models to be robust on out-of-distribution data, their domain generalisation capabilities would need to be improved. Inspsired by [8], we apply Instance Whitening (IW) to the EfficientNet backbones in the teacher and student. The core idea of IW is to normalize the feature statistics of each individual instance (image) within a batch. This process aims to remove instance-specific style variations, making the feature representations more focused on the underlying content. The application of IW within the EfficientNet backbone involves inserting an IW layer after one or more of the convolutional blocks. For a given feature map $X \in \mathbb{R}^{C \times H \times W}$ corresponding to a single instance in a batch (where C is the number of channels, H is the height, and W is the width), the Instance Whitening transformation can be summarized as follows:

$$\tilde{X}_{i,j,k} = \frac{X_{i,j,k} - \mu_i}{\sigma_i + \epsilon} \tag{1}$$

where:

- $\tilde{X}$ is the whitened feature map.
- $X_{i,j,k}$ is the value of the i-th channel at spatial location (j, k).
- $\mu_i = \frac{1}{H \times W} \sum_{j=1}^{H} \sum_{k=1}^{W} X_{i,j,k}$ is the mean of the i-th channel across the spatial dimensions for the current instance.
- $\sigma_i = \sqrt{\frac{1}{H \times W} \sum_{j=1}^{H} \sum_{k=1}^{W} (X_{i,j,k} - \mu_i)^2}$ is the standard deviation of the i-th channel across the spatial dimensions for the current instance.
- ϵ is a small constant added for numerical stability (e.g., 10^{-5}).

2.4 Loss Function

The loss function for training the student model incorporates a term that measures the difference between the student's predictions and the frozen teacher's soft labels, as recommended by [11], and the bounding boxes. Moreover, a term to penalise the difference between the student's predictions and the hard ground-truth labels and bounding boxes is added. Equation 2 shows the implementation of the loss function, where the student loss represents the class focal loss and the bounding boxes Huber loss between the student and the ground truth. Distillation loss, on the other hand, represents the class probability distributions' Kullback–Leibler divergence (KLD) loss and bounding boxes SmoothL1 loss between the student and the teacher. Lambda is the weight assigned to the student loss, which was set to be 0.5.

$$\mathcal{L}_{\text{total}} = (1 - \lambda)\,(\mathcal{L}_{\text{Huber}} + \mathcal{L}_{\text{Focal}}) + \lambda\,(\mathcal{L}_{\text{SmoothL1}} + \mathcal{L}_{\text{KLD}}) \qquad (2)$$

3   Experiments and Results

3.1   Datasets

The Kvasir-Seg dataset is a manually segmented polyp dataset annotated with the assistance of medical experts. The dataset comprises 1000 images, masks, and bounding boxes [13]. PolypGen is a six-center dataset comprising 3762 annotated polyp frames from more than 300 patients. The data contains both polyp and non-polyp frames, white light imaging (WLI) and narrow band imaging (NBI) modalities, and different sizes and types of polyps [2]. However, data containing WLI polyp images only was used. Images from the first 5 centres in PolypGen and 900 images from Kvasir-SEG were used for training and validation so as to push the model's generalisability. In total, 1941 images were used for training, and 223 for validation. To test the generalisability of our model, we first test on the seen centre of Kvasir-SEG (100 test images), then on an unseen centre, PolypGen C6, comprising 88 images. Finally, to evaluate the generalisability of our model on an unseen centre and patient population, we employ our in-house dataset consisting of 116 WLI images collected from 45 patients with inflammatory bowel disease (IBD) under the REC ethical approval reference 17/EM/0033. All frames contain visible polyps and are annotated with bounding box labels validated independently by two expert endoscopists, each with over 10 years of clinical experience. This dataset was sourced from retrospective colonoscopy records collected between 2017 and 2020 at Leeds Teaching Hospitals NHS Trust (LTHT), one of the largest IBD centres in the UK, which manages follow-up care for approximately 5,000 IBD patients and performs around 250 surveillance colonoscopies annually. These data were specifically curated to identify patients at elevated risk of dysplasia, a precursor to colorectal cancer.

3.2   Evaluation Metrics

Standard object detection metrics were used for performance assessment [17]. Most importantly, Average Precision (AP) was reported at Intersection over Union (IoU) thresholds of 50 and 50:5:95. These merely represent different levels of overlap between the target bounding boxes and the predicted bounding boxes.

To assess the model's efficiency and real-time applicability, the frames processed per second (FPS) during inference was also reported.

3.3 Implementation Details

The datasets were normalized, and different geometric and photometric augmentations were applied to the training images and bounding boxes. The images had varying sizes across all datasets, so they were resized to 512×512 as EfficienDet takes images of 128×128 size multiplication [25]. All models were trained on an NVIDIA L40S 48 GB GPU using Pytorch. The same pre-processing pipeline was applied in all models, where a batch size of 8 was used, with a learning rate of $1e^{-4}$, and AdamW as the optimiser.

3.4 Results

Quantitative Results. Tables 1, 2, and 3 show object detection results across different settings. Table 1 compares performance on the seen-centre Kvasir-SEG dataset against existing state-of-the-art methods. Table 2 presents generalisation results on unseen-centre data from the PolypGen-C6 dataset. Table 3 further evaluates generalisation to unseen centre and population shifts using our in-house IBD dataset. We compare our method to three types of detectors: multi-stage (Faster R-CNN), single-stage (RetinaNet), and detection transformer (DETR).

Table 1. Detection metrics on the seen data centre (Kvasir-SEG).

Methods	Params	AP50:5:95	AP50	FPS
Faster R-CNN	27M	0.537	0.799	61
DETR	41.3M	0.698	0.860	34
RetinaNet	34M	0.679	0.878	83
Ours (B2 Student +IW)	7.7M	0.706	0.920	223

Table 2. Detection metrics on the unseen data centre (PolypGen-C6).

Methods	Params	AP50:5:95	AP50	FPS
Faster R-CNN	27M	0.454	0.741	35
DETR	41.3M	0.508	0.698	23
RetinaNet	34M	0.525	0.745	70
Ours (B2 Student +IW)	7.7M	0.581	0.805	239

Table 3. Detection metrics on unseen centre and population data (IBD dataset).

Methods	Params	AP50:5:95	AP50	FPS
Faster R-CNN	27M	0.261	0.447	31
DETR	41.3M	0.252	0.426	23
RetinaNet	34M	0.289	0.488	69
Ours (B2 Student +IW)	7.7M	0.321	0.513	239

Table 4. Ablation on unseen centre and population IBD dataset.

Methods	Params	AP50:5:95	AP50	FPS
Teacher B5	27.7M	0.309	0.505	129
Teacher B5+IW	27.7M	0.32	0.511	128
B2 (no distillation)	7.7M	0.251	0.440	227
B2+IW (no distillation)	7.7M	0.270	0.440	237
Student B2 (distillation)	7.7M	0.270	0.440	237
Student B2 (distillation+IW)	7.7M	0.321	0.513	239

Qualitative Results: Figure 2 shows a comparison between the different methods' predictions on the different datasets compared to the ground truth. Challenging cases like small, multiple, and flat polyps are used to compare the different methods. The application of IW is improving the detection accuracy in both the teacher and student, and the distilled student seems to have less false positives compared to the teacher. The predictions are mostly accurate, but the most persistent issues were false positives, where the model confuses structures similar to polyps for polyps, which is common in polyp detection [4]. Another issue is that the models cannot properly distinguish edges in flatter polyps and miss them completely as in the IBD image, as the small polyp follows its surrounding's morphology, which is expected, given the overall flat and blended nature of these polyps.

4 Discussion

The results presented in Tables 1, 2, and 4 demonstrate the effectiveness of our EfficientDet-based framework, which leverages a lightweight EfficientNet-B2 student model trained using knowledge distillation from a stronger EfficientNet-B5 teacher, alongside instance whitening (IW) applied to both models. This combination enhances both performance and generalisation, while maintaining a compact and fast architecture.

4.1 Generalisability to Unseen Data

Our distilled student model with IW achieves the highest AP50 (0.920) and AP50:5:95 (0.706) among all compared models, including DETR and RetinaNet,

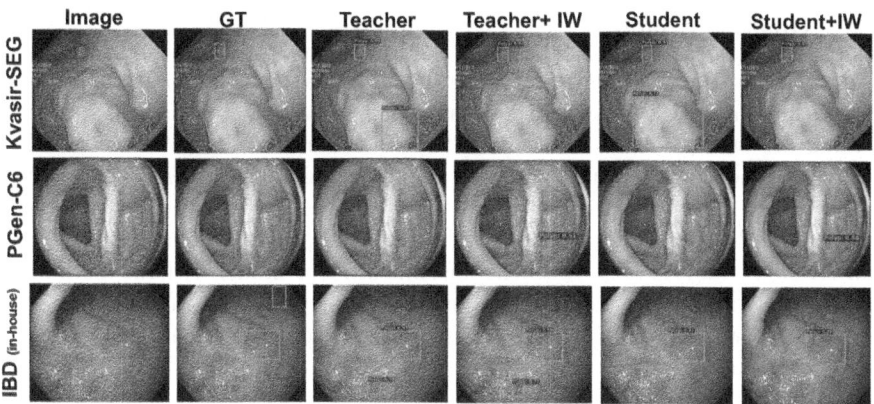

Fig. 2. Qualitative results of different methods on Kvasir-SEG, PolypGen-C6 and in-house IBD datasets

while operating with the fewest parameters (7.7M). Notably, it runs at 223 FPS, outperforming even single-stage detectors like RetinaNet in both speed and accuracy (real-time requirement in HD WLI colonoscopy is around 60 FPS). This demonstrates that combining distillation with IW yields a highly efficient yet accurate detector for in-domain scenarios.

In the unseen-centre PolypGen-C6 dataset (Table 2), where domain shift poses a significant challenge, the proposed student model maintains strong performance with an AP50 of 0.805 and AP50:95 of 0.581. These results are superior to DETR, RetinaNet and Faster R-CNN, achieving gains of 10.67% in AP50:95 and 8.05% in AP50 over RetinaNet and improving robustness to moderate distribution shifts. The IBD dataset, on the other hand, introduces a more severe shift, combining changes in acquisition and patient population with the challenging polyp morphologies mentioned in Sect. 1. This causes a noticeable drop in performance across all methods, but despite this challenge, our student model achieves the best AP50:95 (0.321) and a strong AP50 (0.513), outperforming all baseline detectors and improving on RetinaNet by 11.07% in AP50:95 and 5.12% in AP50. This highlights the strength of distillation and IW in learning generalisable representations from a stronger teacher. Importantly, this is achieved with a low-latency model, reinforcing its suitability for real-world clinical environments where inference speed is critical.

4.2   Efficiency-Accuracy Trade-Off

Across all datasets, our student model offers an excellent balance of performance, model size, and speed. It achieves comparable or superior accuracy to much larger models while being up to 10× faster than DETR. This makes it particularly well-suited for clinical scenarios requiring real-time polyp detection with limited computational resources.

4.3   Ablation Analysis

The ablation study (Table 4) reveals the individual and combined benefits of distillation and IW. Without either, the baseline B2 model performs the worst. Adding IW or distillation in isolation provides marginal gains. However, when both are used together, performance improves significantly (AP50:5:95 from 0.251 to 0.321), surpassing even the teacher B5 model. Overall, the ablation study on the IBD dataset shows that our full method improves AP50:5:95 by 27.89% and AP50 by 16.59% relative to the baseline student model without distillation or IW. This suggests a complementary effect: distillation transfers high-level semantic knowledge, while IW improves feature decorrelation and generalisation across domains.

4.4   Limitations and Future Work

While our model generalises well, performance under severe domain shifts (e.g., IBD) still leaves room for improvement. Future work could explore semi-supervised or self-supervised learning [14, 28], and better domain generalisation techniques. Additionally, evaluating on larger multi-centre datasets and including temporal information from video frames could further enhance performance in clinical deployments.

5   Conclusion

This paper explored the application of a knowledge distillation-based teacher-student framework using the EfficientDet architecture to address the challenges of real-time and generalisable polyp detection, particularly in out-of-domain datasets. Our results have shown that the framework has successfully maintained accuracy with improved speed and generalisability, a crucial factor for practical clinical translation. Furthermore, the integration of instance whitening within the network architecture contributed to enhanced model generalisability, enabling robust performance across diverse datasets. The state-of-the-art performance achieved on these challenging datasets highlights the potential of our proposed framework to overcome limitations associated with domain shift and underscores its practical utility for the development of reliable and efficient automated polyp detection systems in real-world endoscopic procedures.

Acknowledgments. The work was supported in part by UK Research and Innovation (UKRI) [CDT grant number EP/S024336/1], Crohn's & Colitis UK (M2023-5) and the Academy of Medical Sciences (SBF0010\1191). This work was undertaken on the Aire High-Performance Computing (HPC) system at the University of Leeds, UK.

References

1. Ali, S.: Where do we stand in AI for endoscopic image analysis? Deciphering gaps and future directions **5**(1), 1–13. https://doi.org/10.1038/s41746-022-00733-3
2. Ali, S., et al.: A multi-centre polyp detection and segmentation dataset for generalisability assessment **10**(1), 75. https://doi.org/10.1038/s41597-023-01981-y
3. Bar, O., et al.: Impact of data on generalization of AI for surgical intelligence applications **10**(1), 22208. https://doi.org/10.1038/s41598-020-79173-6
4. Bian, H., Jiang, M., Qian, J.: The investigation of constraints in implementing robust AI colorectal polyp detection for sustainable healthcare system **18**(7), e0288376. https://doi.org/10.1371/journal.pone.0288376
5. Carion, N., Massa, F., Synnaeve, G., Usunier, N., Kirillov, A., Zagoruyko, S.: End-to-end object detection with transformers. https://doi.org/10.48550/arXiv.2005.12872. http://arxiv.org/abs/2005.12872
6. Carrinho, P., Falcao, G.: Highly accurate and fast YOLOv4-based polyp detection **232**, 120834. https://doi.org/10.1016/j.eswa.2023.120834
7. Chavarrias-Solanon, P.E., Ali-Teevno, M., Ochoa-Ruiz, G., Ali, S.: Knowledge distillation with a class-aware loss for endoscopic disease detection. https://doi.org/10.48550/arXiv.2207.09530
8. Choi, S., Jung, S., Yun, H., Kim, J., Kim, S., Choo, J.: RobustNet: improving domain generalization in urban-scene segmentation via instance selective whitening. http://arxiv.org/abs/2103.15597
9. Gammulle, H., Chen, Y., Sridharan, S., Klein, T., Fookes, C.: Learning through guidance: knowledge distillation for endoscopic image classification. https://doi.org/10.48550/arXiv.2308.08731
10. Gou, J., Yu, B., Maybank, S.J., Tao, D.: Knowledge distillation: a survey. Int. J. Comput. Vision **129**(6), 1789–1819 (2021). https://doi.org/10.1007/s11263-021-01453-z
11. Hinton, G., Vinyals, O., Dean, J.: Distilling the knowledge in a neural network. https://doi.org/10.48550/arXiv.1503.02531
12. Huang, J., et al.: Speed/accuracy trade-offs for modern convolutional object detectors. https://doi.org/10.48550/arXiv.1611.10012
13. Jha, D., et al.: Kvasir-SEG: a segmented polyp dataset. https://doi.org/10.48550/arXiv.1911.07069
14. Ji, G.P., Zhang, J., Campbell, D., Xiong, H., Barnes, N.: Rethinking polyp segmentation from an out-of-distribution perspective **21**(4), 631–639. https://doi.org/10.1007/s11633-023-1472-2
15. Jiang, Y., Zhang, Z., Zhang, R., Li, G., Cui, S., Li, Z.: YONA: you only need one adjacent reference-frame for accurate and fast video polyp detection. https://doi.org/10.48550/arXiv.2306.03686
16. Lima, A.C.D.M., et al.: A two-stage method for polyp detection in colonoscopy images based on saliency object extraction and transformers **11**, 76108–76119. https://doi.org/10.1109/ACCESS.2023.3297097
17. Lin, T.Y., et al.: Microsoft COCO: common objects in context. https://doi.org/10.48550/arXiv.1405.0312
18. Morgan, E., et al.: Global burden of colorectal cancer in 2020 and 2040: incidence and mortality estimates from GLOBOCAN **72**(2), 338–344. https://doi.org/10.1136/gutjnl-2022-327736
19. Ragu, Raj, A., Rahul, G.S., Chand, S., Preejith, S., Sivaprakasam, M.: XP-NET: An attention segmentation network by dual teacher hierarchical knowledge distillation for polyp generalization

20. Shah, S.C., Itzkowitz, S.H.: Colorectal cancer in inflammatory bowel disease: mechanisms and management **162**(3), 715–730.e3. https://doi.org/10.1053/j.gastro.2021.10.035

21. Shehzadi, T., Hashmi, K.A., Stricker, D., Afzal, M.Z.: Object detection with transformers: a review. https://doi.org/10.48550/arXiv.2306.04670

22. Shin, Y., Balasingham, I.: Comparison of hand-craft feature based SVM and CNN based deep learning framework for automatic polyp classification. In: 2017 39th Annual International Conference of the IEEE Engineering in Medicine and Biology Society (EMBC), pp. 3277–3280. https://doi.org/10.1109/EMBC.2017.8037556. ISSN: 1558-4615

23. Shine, R., Bui, A., Burgess, A.: Quality indicators in colonoscopy: an evolving paradigm **90**(3), 215–221. https://doi.org/10.1111/ans.15775

24. Tan, M., Le, Q.V.: EfficientNet: rethinking model scaling for convolutional neural networks. https://doi.org/10.48550/arXiv.1905.11946

25. Tan, M., Pang, R., Le, Q.V.: EfficientDet: scalable and efficient object detection. In: 2020 IEEE/CVF Conference on Computer Vision and Pattern Recognition (CVPR), pp. 10778–10787. IEEE. https://doi.org/10.1109/CVPR42600.2020.01079

26. Zaidi, S.S.A., Ansari, M.S., Aslam, A., Kanwal, N., Asghar, M., Lee, B.: A survey of modern deep learning based object detection models. https://doi.org/10.48550/arXiv.2104.11892

27. Zhao, S., et al.: Magnitude, risk factors, and factors associated with adenoma miss rate of tandem colonoscopy: a systematic review and meta-analysis **156**(6), 1661–1674.e11. https://doi.org/10.1053/j.gastro.2019.01.260

28. Ali, M., Ochoa-Ruiz, G., Ali, S.: A semi-supervised teacher-student framework for surgical tool detection and localization, **11**(4), 1033–1041 (2023). https://doi.org/10.1080/21681163.2022.2150688

Author Index

S. Ali et al. (Eds.): MIUA 2025, LNCS 15917, pp. 329–332, 2026.
https://doi.org/10.1007/978-3-031-98691-8

The manufacturer's authorised representative in the EU is Springer
Nature Customer Service Centre GmbH, Europaplatz 3, 69115 Heidelberg,
Germany. If you have any concerns regarding our products, please
contact ProductSafety@springernature.com

Printed and bound by CPI Group (UK) Ltd, Croydon, CR0 4YY
28/04/2026
02098521-0004